NEW PLAYWRIGHTS
The Best Plays of 2006

SMITH AND KRAUS PUBLISHERS
Contemporary Playwrights / Full-Length Play Anthologies

Humana Festival: 20 One-Act Plays 1976–1996
Humana Festival 1993: The Complete Plays
Humana Festival 1994: The Complete Plays
Humana Festival 1995: The Complete Plays
Humana Festival 1996: The Complete Plays
Humana Festival 1997: The Complete Plays
Humana Festival 1998: The Complete Plays
Humana Festival 1999: The Complete Plays
Humana Festival 2000: The Complete Plays
Humana Festival 2001: The Complete Plays
Humana Festival 2002: The Complete Plays
Humana Festival 2003: The Complete Plays
Humana Festival 2004: The Complete Plays
Humana Festival 2005: The Complete Plays

New Playwrights: The Best Plays of 1998
New Playwrights: The Best Plays of 1999
New Playwrights: The Best Plays of 2000
New Playwrights: The Best Plays of 2001
New Playwrights: The Best Plays of 2002
New Playwrights: The Best Plays of 2003
New Playwrights: The Best Plays of 2004
New Playwrights: The Best Plays of 2005

Women Playwrights: The Best Plays of 1995
Women Playwrights: The Best Plays of 1996
Women Playwrights: The Best Plays of 1997
Women Playwrights: The Best Plays of 1998
Women Playwrights: The Best Plays of 1999
Women Playwrights: The Best Plays of 2000
Women Playwrights: The Best Plays of 2001
Women Playwrights: The Best Plays of 2002
Women Playwrights: The Best Plays of 2003

If you would like information about forthcoming Smith and Kraus books, you may receive our annual catalogue, free of charge, by sending your name and address to *Smith and Kraus Catalogue, PO Box 127, Lyme, NH 03768.* Or call us at (888) 282-2881, fax (603) 643-1831. www.SmithandKraus.com

NEW PLAYWRIGHTS

The Best Plays
of 2006

CONTEMPORARY PLAYWRIGHTS
SERIES

SK
A Smith and Kraus Book

A Smith and Kraus Book
Published by Smith and Kraus, Inc.
177 Lyme Road, Hanover, NH 03755
www.SmithandKraus.com

© 2007 by Smith and Kraus, Inc.
All rights reserved

Songs in the play *Bulrusher* are copyright by Eisa Davis, except for "For All We Know," written by Fred J. Coots and Samuel M. Lewis. For permission for use in performance, contact ASCAP.

Manufactured in the United States of America
Cover and text design by Julia Gignoux, Freedom Hill Design, Cavendish, Vermont
Kenny Finkle photo by Peter Bellamy. Barbara Dana photo by David Hiller.

First Edition: February 2007
10 9 8 7 6 5 4 3 2 1

Library of Congress Control Number: 2007920055
ISBN 978-1-57525-559-0

CONTENTS

FOREWORD

I go to the theater approximately four or five times a week, and I read two or three hundred plays a year — I'm a drama nut. The plays in this anthology are the best ones I could find by new playwrights, produced during the 2005–2006 theater season. Well, you might ask: What is a "new playwright"?

Many of the plays I either read or see each year are by not-so-new authors, as most professional theater companies have long-standing relationships with certain playwrights — which all too often turns them into private clubs, new members need not apply — as far as new playwrights are concerned. Still, somehow, new playwrights manage to get their work produced. There are literally hundreds of new plays produced by professional and semi-professional theaters each year, God love 'em, and somehow new playwrights are in this number. I define a "new playwright" as a writer who is still at the stage where he or she is struggling for recognition and production. There is an "A-List" of playwrights for whose latest opus theaters often compete: the Albees, the McNallys, the Shanleys, and so forth. The playwrights whose work I have included in this book are not among these big names. Maybe someday they will be, who's to tell? All of them, though, are fresh new voices whose work has thrilled and entertained audiences both nationally and in New York.

Herein, you will find dramas, comedies, realism, non-realism — a cornucopia of contemporary American playwriting talent. The comedies include John Cariani's *Almost, Maine* and Kenny Finkle's *Indoor/Outdoor,* both of which enjoyed modestly successful Off-Broadway runs. *Almost, Maine* is an evening of ten-minute plays about the denizens of a rural Maine town so small it makes Tuna, Texas, look like a thriving metropolis — all played by an intrepid handful of actors. *Indoor/Outdoor* is a charming comedy about a cute young female and her trials and tribulations with the man she lives with. The female is a cat named Samantha, and Finkle tells her story from birth to death in a way that will make you laugh, will charm you, and will move you — even if you hate cats.

Another delightful comedy herein is Michael Golamco's *Cowboy Versus Samurai* — produced Off-Broadway by the National Asian American Theatre Co. (NAATCO) — about the only three Asian-Americans living in a small town in Wyoming. Golamco explores issues of identity amongst Asian Americans in a most humorous way, and even dares to borrow a famous plot device from Cyrano de Bergerac to do so.

Six Years by Sharr White was produced at Actors Theatre of Louisville's famed Humana Festival. It's a drama about what Tom Brokaw has dubbed The Greatest Generation. The play focuses on a marriage as it develops over many years, starting just after the end of World War II and ending during the Vietnam era. I found it wonderfully written and incredibly moving.

War in Paramus also takes place during the Vietnam era, and it tells the story of an American family. It's wonderful production was directed by Austin Pendleton at Abingdon Theatre Co., often a source of the plays I have chosen for the anthologies I have edited for Smith and Kraus. Another such source in the past has been Urban Stages, a New York City Off-Broadway group, which this year provided *Bulrusher* by Eisa Davis, a poignant, often poetic play about a mixed-race orphan girl living in a small town in California.

Finally, last but not least, I have chosen *In the Continuum,* an award-winning drama by Dania Gurira and Nikkole Salter, who performed it both at New York City's Primary Stages and in its Off-Broadway commercial transfer to the Perry Street Theatre. In it, the authors/actresses played a disparate group of American and African black women, dealing with the tragedy of AIDS.

I hope you enjoy these wonderful new plays.

— *D. L. Lepidus*

INTRODUCTION

As a young girl growing up in a small town, Chongju, South Korea, I felt like "a frog in a well" that can see only a limited sky. To escape from my small world, I spent much of my time reading foreign novels translated into Korean, especially by European and American writers. Fascinated and deeply touched by many of their stories, I wished that someday I, too, could write something so beautiful and inspiring that would touch the hearts of many people. If I had such talent, I promised myself, I would use it to bring people together from different worlds. Oh, how I dreamed of leaping out of my well!

My first leap was attending a university in Seoul. At an elite school in that big city, my world expanded with a greater capacity to dream. There, I learned about modern theater for the first time from plays I read. I dreamed of taking another leap, an enormous one: to go to America to study theater arts. But my family had traditional expectations for me and did not approve of my dreams of lone adventure. With no money or family support, it seemed to be an impossible dream. All I could do was pray for a miracle.

My prayer was answered. An American sponsor offered to pay my airfare to Los Angeles. So, I came to America with one suitcase and a pack of sky-high dreams. After much difficulty, I obtained admission to the graduate theater arts program at UCLA. I didn't know exactly what to specialize in: playwriting, screenwriting, directing or acting — I was interested in all. Then I met a playwriting teacher who changed the course of my life. He encouraged me to write plays to introduce Korean people and their culture to Americans, who I had discovered, knew very little about Korea. Eagerly I learned the basic principles of dramatic writing: 1) be certain of the theme; 2) create a particular situation with characters in conflict; 3) show rather than tell.

With no command of the English language, aspiring to become a playwright seemed to be another impossible dream. Fortunately, that teacher taught me to believe that I could be creative with the language itself and find my own way of writing. He also taught me to believe that what mattered most was my passion to tell my stories. I had the passion and the courage but didn't know how to write in English what I wanted to say. So, out of necessity, my own way of writing evolved: Use simple words to let the characters in conflict express their complex emotions. Those "simple words" had to come from my heart, fully understanding the characters I created and what needed to be portrayed through them. That is the way I write best to this day.

As I struggled to survive in Hollywood's artistic community as an immigrant woman writer, my passion to write grew deeper. I explored television/screenwriting and poetry writing for many years. My work, rooted in my bi-cultural experiences, was unique, but not regarded as part of mainstream America. I was always an outsider. Every step toward achievement proved to be a great challenge, but I was determined to persevere. Compounded by my own experiences in America, I was compelled to write about the human struggles and sufferings of those who had no voice. To portray them, playwriting was the most ideal medium. I took an opportunity to participate in the Mentor Playwrights Program at Mark Taper Forum in Los Angeles, followed by a fellowship from the USC Professional Writing Program, where I started to work on a play about the Korean "comfort women."

Writing a play is a rewarding but painfully difficult process for me. To find a theater and have it produced is another matter that is far more challenging. What I envision on the page doesn't always come true onstage, and rewriting is inevitable and seemingly never ending. Yet, theater is the home where I find the most excitement and freedom. In theater, I am allowed to speak truthfully no matter how controversial or idealistic my words may be. And I find it truly exciting to work in collaboration with many talented and dedicated people who create such magic out of the blueprint of my script. When the audience embraces the universal truth I wish to convey, it is the most gratifying reward.

The 2004 production of *Comfort Women* at Urban Stages in New York brought my impossible dream to life. To be included in *New Playwrights: The Best Plays of 2005* was the acceptance for which I had long dreamed, finally to be part of America. I am certain that every playwright in this volume and previous volumes is as deeply grateful as I am to D. L. Lepidus for recognizing the merits of his or her work and to Smith and Kraus for recording it in print for permanent validation.

I salute all who dare to leap!

— *Chungmi Kim*

ALMOST, MAINE

John Cariani

for Northern Maine and the people who live there

ORIGINAL PRODUCTION

Almost, Maine was produced by Jack Thomas/Bulldog Theatrical and Bruce Payne at the Daryl Roth Theatre, New York City, opening on January 12th 2006. The play was directed by Gabriel Barre, scenery by James Youmans, lights by Jeff Croiter, costumes by Pamela Scofield, and incidental music by Julian Fleisher. Production stage manager: Karyn Meek. The cast was as follows:

PETE, STEVE, LENDALL, RANDY, MAN . . . . Todd Cerveris
GINETTE, GLORY, WAITRESS, GAYLE, HOPE . . . . Finnerty Steeves
EAST, JIMMY, CHAD, PHIL, DAVE . . . . Justin Hagan
SANDRINE, MARVALYN, MARCI, RHONDA . . . . Miriam Shor

Almost, Maine received its world premiere production at the Portland Stage Company (Anita Stewart, Artistic Director; Tami Ramaker, Managing Director) in Portland, Maine, on October 29th 2004. The play was directed by Gabriel Barre; the set design was by James Youmans; the lighting design was by Tim Hunter; the costume design was by Pamela Scofield; the incidental music was by Julian Fleisher; and the production stage manager was Myles C. Hatch. The cast was as follows:

PETE, MAN, LENDALL, RANDY, MAN . . . . Larry Nathanson
GINETTE, GLORY, GAYLE, HOPE . . . . Wendy Stetson
EAST, STEVE, CHAD, PHIL, DAVE . . . . Justin Hagan
WOMAN, MARVALYN, MARCI, RHONDA . . . . Ibi Janko

Almost, Maine was developed at the Cape Cod Theatre Project (Andy Polk, Artistic Director) in 2002.

Almost, Maine is a play for as few as four (and as many as nineteen) actors, told in eight episodes, with a Prologue and an Epilogue:

PROLOGUE

ACT I

Episode 1: Her Heart
Episode 2: Sad and Glad
Episode 3: This Hurts
Episode 4: Getting It Back

INTERLOGUE

ACT II

EPILOGUE

NOTES

On place:

Almost, Maine is a mythical composite of three Northern Maine towns: Presque Isle (my hometown, pop. 9,500, and the largest city in Northern Maine; Ashland (pop. 1,474; gateway to the North Maine Woods), and Portage Lake (pop. 390; the town I picture when I think of Almost, Maine). Almost is very far inland (two hundred miles from the ocean) and very far north (four hundred miles north of Boston, Massachusetts). Located in the remote heart of Aroostook (say, "uh-ROO-stick") County — the sparsely populated northernmost county in Maine — Almost, Maine occupies what is (in reality) officially designated as Township Thirteen, Range Seven. If you have a detailed map of Maine, look for the town of Portage Lake. Almost would be just west — and maybe a little north — of Portage Lake.

Winters in Almost, Maine are long (October to May), cold (the area's average temperature in January 2005 was three degrees Fahrenheit and the average annual snowfall is 110 inches), and can be pretty bleak: Almost is in an empty land of wide open space and big sky. Potato farms dominate to the east; the North Maine Woods, to the west. *National Geographic* once printed something to this effect: "They call Montana 'Big Sky Country.' Well . . . 'they' haven't seen Northern Maine."

On the northern lights (the aurora borealis):

The northern lights are brilliant, ribbon-like, other-worldly displays of light. Northern Mainers are fortunate: They live just inside the southernmost tip of a ring defining the area in which the northern lights regularly appear. Growing up, I remember being treated to a northern lights show at least once a year.

The northern lights occur when atoms become "excited." During solar storms, electrons are sent streaming toward the Earth. As these electrons enter the Earth's atmosphere, they strike and excite atoms, ionizing them — charging them by knocking out an electron. When this happens to enough atoms, the brilliant light display that is the aurora borealis hovers and streaks across the sky. When the aurora fades, it's because the affected atoms have returned to their grounded state. *Almost, Maine* is a play about people who are normally very grounded, but who have become very excited by love . . . and other extraordinary occurrences.

On time:
The plot of each episode of *Almost, Maine* climaxes with some sort of "magical moment." I have this notion that the magical moments in all of the episodes are happening at exactly the same time — as the clock strikes nine — and that the northern lights and the magical moments are giving rise to one another. At first, I thought it might be neat to have the northern lights appear as each magical moment occurs. But I didn't want to dilute the climax of each episode or muddle the impact of the "magical moment" of each episode with a fancy northern lights display. So I thought it might be better to revisit the northern lights in the transitions between each episode of the play. These "revisitings" will be denoted as "transitional auroras" in the script and will be suggested throughout. They might help audiences understand that each episode of *Almost, Maine* is taking place at the same time, and that this play is all about one moment in time — what happens to people in a heartbeat.

On punctuation:
Almost, Maine employs a lot of very specific overlapping dialogue. You'll often see this symbol: //. It will appear inside a particular character's line. It simply means that the next character to speak should begin his or her line where the // appears in the speech of the character who is currently speaking. Sometimes this "railroad tracks" method is hard to work out on the written page, so you will also see this symbol: >. It will appear mid-sentence — at the end of a line that is not a complete thought. It simply means that the character speaking should drive through to the end of the thought, which will be continued in his or her character's next line(s).

On the people:
The people of *Almost, Maine* are not "Downeasters." They are not fishermen

or lobstermen. They don't wear galoshes and rain hats. They don't say, "Ayuh." They are like Minnesotans — but without the midwestern accents.

The people of *Almost, Maine* are honest and true. They are not cynical. They are smart. They just wonder about things in a different way than the rest of us do. They speak simply, honestly, truly, and from the heart. They are never precious about what they say or do.

On presenting *Almost, Maine:*
Please keep in mind that "cute" will kill this play. *Almost, Maine* is inherently pretty sweet. There is no need to sentimentalize the material. Just . . . let it be what it is: a play about real people who are really, truly, honestly dealing with the toughest thing there is to deal with in life: love. If you do this play don't forget how much the people of *Almost, Maine* are hurting. Honor the ache, play the pain (keep most of it covered), and don't forget that *Almost, Maine* is a comedy. Sadness is the funniest thing in the world.

CHARACTERS
All characters are 25–35.
Prologue
    PETE and GINETTE, who have been dating for a little while
Her Heart
    EAST, a repairman, and GLORY a hiker
Sad and Glad
    JIMMY, a heating-and-cooling guy; SANDRINE, his ex-girlfriend; a salty WAITRESS
This Hurts
    MARVALYN, a woman who is used to protecting herself, and STEVE, an open, kind fellow whose brother protects him
Getting It Back
    GAYLE and LENDALL, longtime girlfriend and boyfriend
Interlogue
    PETE, from the Prologue
They Fell
    RANDY and CHAD, two "County boys."
Where It Went
    PHIL, a working man, and his hard-working wife, MARCI
Story of Hope
    HOPE, who has traveled the world, and a MAN, who has not

Seeing the Thing
    RHONDA, a tough chick, and DAVE, the not-so-tough guy who loves her
Epilogue
    PETE and GINETTE, from the Prologue

SETTING
Various locales in Almost, Maine, a small, remote, mythical town in Northern Maine.

TIME
The present. Everything takes place at about 9 o'clock on a cold, clear, moonless Friday night in the middle of winter.

Almost, Maine

PROLOGUE

Music. It is a cold Friday night in the middle of winter in a small, mythical town in Northern Maine called Almost, Maine. A field of stars — a clear, cold, moonless, northern night sky — serves as the backdrop for the entire play. Lights up on Pete and Ginette sitting on a bench in Pete's yard, looking at the stars. They are not sitting close to each other at all. Pete is sitting on the stage right end of the bench; Ginette, on the stage left end. Music fades. Long beat of Pete and Ginette looking at the stars. Ginette keeps stealing glances at Pete.

GINETTE: Pete, I — . . . *(She's about to say, "I love you.")*
PETE: What?
GINETTE: *(Can't quite do it.)* I just . . . am having a nice time, Pete.
PETE: I'm glad, Ginette.
GINETTE: I always do with you.
PETE: I'm glad.
　　　(They enjoy this moment together. There's nothing else to say, so . . . back to the sky.)
GINETTE: *(Still can't say what she wants to say.)* And the *stars* are just — . . . I didn't know you knew all that stuff //, after all this time, I didn't know you knew all that!
PETE: Well, it's not — . . . It's just stuff my dad taught me . . .
　　　(Then there's nothing else to say, so . . . back to the stars. Beat. Ginette turns to Pete.)
GINETTE: Pete —
PETE: *(Turning to Ginette.)* Yeah?
GINETTE: I love you.
　　　(Pete just stares at Ginette. Beat. He looks away from her. Beat. And does not respond. Beat. Ginette takes this in; deflates; then looks away from him, trying to figure out what has happened. We now have two people looking a little like deer caught in headlights. Pete is dealing with what Ginette has just said to him; Ginette is dealing with Pete's response — or lack thereof — to what she has just said. Big . . . long . . . pause. Finally, there's nothing else for Pete to say but the truth, which is:)
PETE: I . . . love you, too.

GINETTE: Oh! *(Big relief.)*

(Pete and Ginette feel JOY! Ginette shivers — a happy kind of shiver.)

PETE: Oh, are you cold? // Wanna go inside?

GINETTE: No, no. No. I just wanna sit. Like this. Close. *(Pete and Ginette shouldn't be close to each other at all — but for them, it's close.)* I feel so close to you tonight. It's nice to be close to you, Pete. *(Beat. She gets closer to him.)* It's safe. *(Beat. She gets closer to him again.)* I like being close. Like this. I mean, I can think of other . . . *ways* . . . of being close to you *(i.e., sex, and they enjoy this sweetly, truly — Pete probably can't believe she brought this up, but he's probably very happy that she did!)* but that's not — . . . I like this right now. This kind of close. Right next to you. *(She gets even closer to him; leans right up against him. Beat.)* You know, right now, I think I'm about as close to you as I can possibly be. *(She is very content.)*

PETE: *(Beat. Honestly discovering.)* Well . . . not really.

GINETTE: What?

PETE: *(He is simply and truly figuring this out.)* Not really. I mean, if you think about it in a different way, you're not really close to me at all. You're really actually about as far away from me as you can possibly be. I mean, if you think about it, technically — if you're assuming the world is round, like a ball, *(Gathering snow to make a snowball for use as a visual.)* the farthest away you can be from somebody is if you're sitting right next to them. See, if I'm here *(Points out a place on the snowball that represents him, so the audience can see.)*, and you're here *(Points out a place on the snowball that represents her, and it's right next to him — practically the same place he just pointed to.)*, then . . . *(Pete now demonstrates that if you go around the world the OTHER way — all the way around the world the OTHER way — that he and Ginette are actually as far away from each other as they can possibly be. Little beat.)* . . . that's far . . .

GINETTE: *(Taking this in — what on earth does he mean?)* Yeah. *(Disheartened, Ginette moves all the way to the other end of the bench. She doesn't feel like being "close" anymore.)*

PETE: *(Pete takes this in: His "interesting thought" seems to have moved the evening's proceedings in a direction he didn't intend! Then, trying to save the evening, hopeful:)* But now . . . you're closer. *(Because she actually is closer, the way he just described it.)*

GINETTE: *(Puzzled.)* Yeah. *(Perhaps hurt, she stands up and starts to leave. What else is there to do? After she takes barely a step or two, Pete stops her with:)*

PETE: And closer . . .

(Ginette stops. She turns and looks at Pete, then turns back, and starts to leave, but as she takes another step away from him, Pete again interrupts her step with:)

PETE: And closer . . .

(Ginette stops again. She turns and looks at Pete, then turns back and starts to leave again, but as she does so, Pete stops her with:)

PETE: And closer . . .

(Ginette stops again; looks at Pete again; takes another step . . . and another and another and another and another. With each step she takes, Pete says, ". . . and closer and closer and closer and closer . . ." When she is just about to exit, Ginette stops. She is trying to figure out what's going on, what Pete is saying. She looks at Pete; she looks off left; looks at Pete again; looks off left again; and then leaves, taking step after step. With every single step she takes, Pete calls to her, telling her, with great hope, that she's ". . . closer and closer and closer and closer . . ." until, eventually, Ginette is gone, exiting stage left, with Pete still calling, ". . . and closer," with every single step she takes. Unfortunately, with every step she takes, Ginette is getting farther and farther away from Pete. This is not necessarily what Pete intended, and his "closer's" trail off. Music. Lights fade on a sad, confused, helpless Pete. He looks at his snowball. What has he done? And we begin . . .

ACT I

with Episode One, which is entitled . . .

HER HEART

Music fades. The lights fade up on a woman standing in the front yard of an old farmhouse in Almost, Maine. She is clutching a brown paper grocery bag to her chest. She is looking up at the sky. A porch light comes on. We hear a screen door open and slam as a man enters. He watches her for a while. He is wearing a big warm coat and plaid pajamas.)

MAN: Hello.

WOMAN: *(To him.)* Hello. *(Resumes looking at the stars.)*

MAN: I thought I saw someone . . . I was about to go to bed. I saw you from my window . . . *(Beat.)* Can I — ? . . . Is there something I can do for you?

WOMAN: *(To him.)* Oh, no. I'm just here to see the northern lights. *(Back to sky.)*

MAN: OK. OK. It's just — it's awful late and you're in my yard . . .

WOMAN: Oh, I hope you don't mind! I'll only be here tonight. I'll see them tonight. The northern lights. And then I'll be gone. I hope you don't mind . . .

MAN: *(Looking out.)* Is that your tent?

WOMAN: Yes.

MAN: You've pitched a tent . . . >

WOMAN: So I have a place to sleep, >

MAN: in my yard . . .

WOMAN: after I see them, I hope you don't mind.

MAN: Well, it's not that I —

WOMAN: Do you mind?

MAN: Well, I don't know if —

WOMAN: Oh, no, I think you mind!

MAN: No, it's not that I mind —

WOMAN: No, you do! You do! Oh, I'm so sorry! I didn't think you would! I didn't think — . You see, it says in your brochure >

MAN: My brochure?

WOMAN: that people from Maine wouldn't mind. It says *(Pulling out a brochure about Maine tourism.)* that people from Maine are different, that they live life "the way life *should* be,"* and that, "in the tradition of their brethren in rural northern climes, like Scandinavia," that they'll let people who are complete strangers like cross-country skiers and bikers and hikers camp out in their yard, if they need to, for nothing, they'll just let you. I'm a hiker. Is it true? >

MAN: Well —

WOMAN: that they'll just let you stay in their yards if you need to? 'Cause I need to. Camp out. 'Cause I'm where I need to be. This is the farthest I've ever traveled — I'm from a part of the country that's a little closer to things — never been this far north before, or east, and did you know that Maine is the only state in the country that's attached to only one other state?!?

MAN: Umm —

---

*If you ever go to Maine by car, via Interstate 95, you will be greeted by a sign, erected by the Maine Office of Tourism, that reads, "Maine: The Way Life Should Be."

WOMAN: It is! *(Taking in all the open space.)* Feels like the end of the world, and here I am at the end of the world, and I have nowhere to go, so I was counting on staying here, unless it's not true, I mean, *is* it true? >

MAN: Well —

WOMAN: Would you let a hiker who was where she needed to be just camp out in your yard for free? >

MAN: Well —

WOMAN: I mean, if a person really needed to, >

MAN: Well —

WOMAN: reallyreally needed to?

MAN: Well, if a person really needed to, sure, but —

WOMAN: *(Huge relief.)* Oh, I'm so glad, then!! Thank you!!

(The woman hugs the man. In the hug, the bag gets squished between their bodies. When they part, the man is holding the woman's bag. The exchange of the bag is almost imperceptible to both the man and the woman, and to the audience. Immediately after hugging the man, the woman resumes looking intently for the northern lights. Then, realizing she doesn't have her bag:)

WOMAN: Oh my gosh! I need that!

MAN: Oh. Here. *(He gives it back.)*

WOMAN: Thank you.

MAN: Sure. *(Beat.)*

(The woman resumes looking at the stars.)

MAN: OK — . OK . . . *(Beat.)* So you're just lookin' for a place to see the northern lights from?

WOMAN: Yeah. Just tonight.

MAN: Well, you know, you might not see 'em tonight, 'cause // you never really know if —

WOMAN: Oh, no. I'll see them. Because I'm in a good place: Your latitude is *good.* And this is the right time: Solar activity is at an eleven-year peak. Everything's in order. And, boy, you have good sky for it. *(Taking in the sky.)* There's lots of sky here.

MAN: Used to be a potato farm.

WOMAN: I was gonna say — no trees in the way. And it's *flat!* Makes for a big sky! *(Beat.)* So — you're a farmer? . . .

MAN: No. *Used* to be a farm. I'm a repairman.

WOMAN: Oh.

MAN: Fix things.

WOMAN: Oh. *(Laughs.)*

MAN: What?

WOMAN: You're not a lobsterman.

MAN: No . . .

WOMAN: I guess I thought that everyone from Maine was a lobsterman and talked in that funny . . . way like they do in Maine, and you don't talk that way.

MAN: Yeah, well, I'm from here . . . and this is how we talk up north, pretty much.

WOMAN: Yeah.

MAN: Plus, ocean's a couple hundred miles away. Be an awful long ride to work if I was a lobsterman.

WOMAN: *(Enjoying him.)* Yeah. Well, anyway, thank you. Thank you for letting me stay. *(Not looking at the man — there's some shame, here.)* I've had a bad enough time of things lately not to be given a bad time, here —
(The man, inexplicably drawn to her, kisses the woman. When they break, the bag has exchanged clutches imperceptibly — the man has it. And now we have two stunned people.)

MAN: Oh . . .

WOMAN: *(Trying to figure out what has happened.)* Um . . .

MAN: Oh.

WOMAN: Um . . .

MAN: Oh, boy.

WOMAN: Um . . .

MAN: I'm sorry. I just — . . . I think I love you.

WOMAN: Really.

MAN: *(Perplexed.)* Yeah. I saw you from my window and . . . I love you.

WOMAN: Really.

MAN: Yeah.

WOMAN: Well . . . — that's very nice — . . . but there's something I think you should know: I'm not here for that.

MAN: Oh, no! I didn't think you were!

WOMAN: I'm here to pay my respects. To my *husband*.

MAN: Oh —

WOMAN: Yeah: my *husband*. Wes. I just wanted to say good-bye to him, 'cause he died recently. On Tuesday, actually. And, see, the northern lights — did you know this? — the northern lights are really the torches that the recently departed carry with them so they can find their way to heaven, and, see, it takes three days for a soul to make its way home, to heaven, and this is Friday! This is the third day, so, you see, I *will* see them, the northern lights, because they're *him*: He'll be carrying one of the torches.

And, see, I didn't leave things well with him, so I was just hoping I could come here and say good-bye to him and not be bothered, but what you did there just a second ago, that bothered me, I think, and I'm not here for that, so maybe I should go // and find another yard —

MAN: No! No! I'm sorry if I . . . if I've behaved in a way that I shouldn't have —

WOMAN: *(Leaving.)* No //, I think —

MAN: No! I really don't know what happened, >

WOMAN: Well, I do, I know what happened —

MAN: I'm not the kind of person who does things like that. Please. Don't go. Just do what you need to do. I won't bother you. Maybe just . . . consider what I did a very warm Maine welcome?

WOMAN: *(Stopping; charmed.)* All right. All right. *(Beat.)* I'm — . My name's Glory.

MAN: I'm East. For Easton. It's the name of the town — little ways that way — where I was born. Mess up on the birth certificate . . . "a son, *Easton*, born on this 6th day of January, _____ *(Insert appropriate year.)* in the town of *Matthew*, Maine" . . . instead of the other way around . . .

GLORY: *(Amused.)* Aw, I'm sorry . . . >

EAST: Naw . . .

GLORY: so, *(Referring to the place.)* Easton, >

EAST: Yeah —

GLORY: yeah, I passed through there on my way here, and by the way, *(Scanning the horizon.)* where is "here," where am I? I couldn't find it on my map.

EAST: Um . . . Almost.

GLORY: What?

EAST: You're in unorganized territory. Township thirteen, Range seven.

(Glory checks her map.)

EAST: It's not gonna be on your map, 'cause it's not an actual town, technically.

GLORY: What //do you mean —

EAST: See, to be a town, you gotta get organized. And we never got around to gettin' organized, so . . . we're just Almost.

GLORY: Oh . . .

(They enjoy this. Beat. Glory now deals with the fact that she is missing her bag. She was clutching it to her chest, and now it's gone. This should upset her so much that it seems like it affects her breathing.)

GLORY: Oh!

EAST: What?

GLORY: *(Seeming to be having trouble breathing.)* My heart!

EAST: What? Are you // OK?

GLORY: My heart! *(Pointing to the bag.)*

EAST: What?

GLORY: You have my heart!

EAST: I — ?

GLORY: In that bag, it's in that bag! >

EAST: Oh.

GLORY: Please give it back, // please! It's my heart. I need it. Please!

EAST: OK. OK. OK. *(He gives her the bag.)*

GLORY: Thank you. *(Her breathing normalizes.)*

EAST: You're welcome. *(A long beat while East considers what he has just heard.)* I'm sorry, did you just say that . . . your *heart* is in that bag?, is that what you just said?, that // your heart — . . . ?

GLORY: Yes.

EAST: *(Considers.)* Well — . . . it's heavy.

GLORY: Yes.

EAST: Why is it in that bag?

GLORY: It's how I carry it around.

EAST: Why?

GLORY: It's broken.

EAST: What happened?

GLORY: Wes broke it.

EAST: Your husband?

GLORY: Yeah. He went away.

EAST: Oh.

GLORY: With someone else.

EAST: Oh, I'm sorry.

GLORY: Yeah. And when he did that, I felt like my heart would break. And that's exactly what happened. It broke: hardened up and cracked in two. Hurt so bad, I had to go to the hospital, and when I got there, they told me they were gonna have to take it out. And when they took it out, they dropped it on the floor and it broke into nineteen pieces. Slate. *(Shakes the bag, which should be filled with small pieces of slate. They make a great sound when shaken.)* It turned to slate.

EAST: *(Takes this in. Beat. His only response is:)* Great for roofing. *(Beat. Then, dawning on him:)* Wait a second, how do you breathe? If your heart is in that bag, how are you *alive?*

GLORY: *(Indicating the heart that's now in her chest.)* Artificial . . .

EAST: Really!?

GLORY: Yeah. 'Cause my real one's broken.

EAST: Then — why do you carry it around with you?

GLORY: It's my *heart*.

EAST: But it's broken.

GLORY: Yeah.

EAST: 'Cause your husband left you.

GLORY: Yeah.

EAST: Well, why are you paying your respects to him if he left you?.

GLORY: Because that's what you do when a person dies, you pay them respects —

EAST: But he left you, >

GLORY: Yeah, but —

EAST: and it seems to me that a man who leaves somebody doesn't deserve any respects.

GLORY: *(Deflecting until "Because I killed him.")* Well, I just didn't leave things well with him, >

EAST: *(Pushing her until "Because I killed him.")* What do you mean? —

GLORY: and I need to apologize to him.

EAST: But he *left* you!, >

GLORY: I know, but I —

EAST: why should you apologize?

GLORY: Because!

EAST: Because why?

GLORY: Because I killed him!

EAST: Oh. *(This stops East; he backs off a bit.)*

GLORY: And I'd like to apologize. *(Beat. Then, admission:)* See, he had come to visit me when I was in recovery from when they put my artificial heart in — I was almost better; I was just about to go home, too — and he said he wanted me back. And I said, "Wes, I have a new heart now. I'm sorry . . . It doesn't want you back . . . " And that just killed him.

EAST: *(Relief.)* Oh. But, it didn't kill him, you didn't *kill* him —

GLORY: Yes, I did! Because he got so sad that my new heart didn't want him back, he just tore outta the hospital, and . . . an ambulance that was comin' in from an emergency didn't see him and just . . . took him right out, and if I'd have been able to take him back, >

EAST: Glory —

GLORY: he wouldn't have torn outta there like that, >

EAST: Glory!

GLORY: and been just taken out like that, and so, I just feel that, for closure, the right thing to do is —

(Inexplicably drawn to her, East kisses Glory. When she pulls away, he has her heart again. She takes it back.)

GLORY: Please don't do that anymore.

EAST: I love you!

GLORY: Well, don't.

EAST: Why?

GLORY: Because I won't be able to love you back: I have a heart that can pump my blood and that's all. The one that does the other stuff is broken. It doesn't work anymore. *(Again, inexplicably drawn to her, East deliberately kisses Glory. Glory pulls away. East has her heart again. Glory grabs it from him; East grabs it right back.)*

EAST: Please let me have this.

GLORY: *(Trying to get her heart back.)* No! It's mine!

EAST: *(Keeping her heart.)* I can fix it!

GLORY: I don't know if I want you to!

EAST: Glory! —

GLORY: *(Going after her heart.)* East, please give that back to me!

EAST: *(Keeping her heart.)* But it's broken. >

GLORY: Please — !

EAST: It's no good like this.

GLORY: But it's my heart, East!

EAST: Yes, it is. And I believe *I* have it.

(This stops Glory. Beat.)

EAST: . . . And I can fix it. *(Beat.)* I'm a repairman. I repair things. It's what I do.

(Beat. East crouches, places the bag on the ground, and starts to open it in order to examine its contents. Music. As he opens the bag, music up, and the northern lights appear in front of Glory, above Glory, on the field of stars behind Glory. Glory sees them . . . and they're a thing of wonder.)

GLORY: Oh! Oh, wow! Oh, wow! Oh, they're so beautiful . . . *(Remembering who they are.)* Oh! Oh! — Wes!! Wes!! Good-bye! I'm so sorry! . . . Good-bye, Wes!

(And the northern lights — and Wes — are gone. Glory turns to East, who has taken a piece of her heart out of the bag, and is examining it. Music out. A beat. Then in the clear:)

GLORY: Hello, East.

(Music continues. East looks at Glory, and then begins repairing her

heart . . . as the lights fade. The aurora lingers — first transitional aurora. End of "Her Heart." After the lights have faded, and "Her Heart" is over, we begin Episode Two, which is entitled . . .

SAD AND GLAD

Music fades. Lights up on Jimmy sitting alone at a table in Almost, Maine's local hangout, the Moose Paddy. He is nursing a couple of Buds. Sandrine enters, stage right, coming from the bathroom, cheerily heading back to her friends, who are offstage left. Jimmy sees Sandrine, stops her.)

JIMMY: Sandrine!

SANDRINE: Hmm? *(This is a bit awkward — a little awful. Then, overcompensating:)* Jimmy!

JIMMY: Hey!

SANDRINE: Hey!

JIMMY: Hey!!

SANDRINE: Hey!!

JIMMY/SANDRINE: *(Jimmy hugs Sandrine. Sandrine doesn't really take the hug or hug him back.)* Heyyyy!!!

JIMMY: How you doin'?!?

SANDRINE: Doin' pretty good! How are you doin'?!?

JIMMY: I'm good, I'm good! How are ya?!?

SANDRINE: I'm good, good. Great.

JIMMY: Great.

SANDRINE: Yeah!

JIMMY: That's great!

SANDRINE: Yeah!

JIMMY: That's great!

SANDRINE: Yeah!

JIMMY: That's great!

SANDRINE: Yeah.

JIMMY: You look great.

SANDRINE: Oh . . .

JIMMY: You look great.

SANDRINE: Thanks.

JIMMY: You do. You look so great.

SANDRINE: Thanks, Jimmy.

JIMMY: So pretty. So pretty.

SANDRINE: Thanks. *(Beat.)*

JIMMY: Here, have a seat.

SANDRINE: Oh, Jimmy, I can't —

JIMMY: Oh come on, I haven't seen you in . . . well, *months* . . .

SANDRINE: Yeah.

JIMMY: . . . and months and months and months and months and months and months and *months,* how does that happen? Live in the same town as someone and never see 'em? >

SANDRINE: I don't know . . .

JIMMY: I mean, I haven't seen you since that night before that morning when I woke up and you were just gone.

SANDRINE: Yeah, I —

WAITRESS: *(Entering.)* Look at you two, tucked away in the corner over here. Lucky I found ya! *(Referring to Jimmy's couple of Buds.)* Is the man and his lovely lady ready for another round?

JIMMY/SANDRINE: Well — / No! We're not together.

JIMMY/SANDRINE: We'll — / We're all set, thanks.

JIMMY/SANDRINE: Yeah — /All set!

JIMMY: Yeah.

WAITRESS: OK. Well, holler if you need anything.

SANDRINE: Thanks.

WAITRESS: No really — you gotta holler. It's busy up front!

SANDRINE: OK.

> *(Waitress exits.)*

JIMMY: *(Fishing.)* So . . . You here with anybody, or —

SANDRINE: Yeah, the girls.

JIMMY: Oh.

SANDRINE: We're uh . . . *(Covering.)* girls' night! We're in the front. Actually, I just had to use the ladies' room, so I should get back to // them.

JIMMY: Oh, but I haven't seen you! They'll survive without you for a minute or two! So what's been — what you been up to? >

SANDRINE: *(Giving in, sitting.)* Well —

JIMMY: Did you know that I took over Dad's business?

SANDRINE: Yeah, that's great . . .

JIMMY: I run it now, >

SANDRINE: I heard that.

JIMMY: I'm runnin' it, >

SANDRINE: Heard that.

JIMMY: runnin' the business, >

SANDRINE: Congratula>

JIMMY: runnin' the whole show,>

SANDRINE: tions, good for you, good for you.

JIMMY: the whole shebang, thanks, yeah. We still do heating and cooling,>

SANDRINE: Yeah?

JIMMY: and we've expanded, too, we do rugs now, we shampoo 'em.

SANDRINE: Oh.

JIMMY: It's a lotta work. A lotta work. I'm on call a lot: Weekends, holidays, you name it, 'cause, you know, your heat goes, people die, it's serious.

SANDRINE: Yeah.

JIMMY: Yeah. Like, I do Thanksgivin', Christmas, 'cause I let the guys who work for me, like, East helps with repairs sometimes, I let 'em have the day off so they can be with their families since I'm all alone this year.

SANDRINE: Oh.

JIMMY: Yeah. *(Driving the point home.)* I really don't have anybody anymore, really. My brother and sister got canned, so they left town, and>

SANDRINE: Right —

JIMMY: Mom and Dad retired, headed south.

SANDRINE: Yeah, I heard that.

JIMMY: Vermont.

SANDRINE: Oh.

JIMMY: Yeah, winters there are a lot easier. And then Spot went and died on me . . .

SANDRINE: Oh, Jimmy, I didn't know that . . .

JIMMY: Yeah. He was old, it was his time, so, like I said, I really don't have anybody anymore, really . . . but, so, um, I was wonderin' — would you like to come over? Get a movie or somethin'?

SANDRINE: Oh —

WAITRESS: *(Entering.)* And I forgot to tell ya — don't forget: Friday night special at the Moose Paddy: Drink free if you're sad. So, if you're sad, or if you two little lovebirds are ready for another coupla Buds or somethin', you just let me know, all right?

SANDRINE: No, we're —

JIMMY: OK.

WAITRESS: OK.

SANDRINE: OK.

(Waitress exits.)

JIMMY: So whatta you say? Wanna come on over, for fun —

SANDRINE: No, Jimmy. I can't. I can't. *(Getting up to leave.)* I really gotta get back with the girls.

JIMMY: Naw —

SANDRINE: *(Forceful, but kind.)* Yeah, Jimmy, yeah. I gotta. 'Cause, see . . . oh, gosh, I've been meanin' to tell you this for a while: There's a guy, Jimmy. I've got a guy.

JIMMY: *(Huge blow. But he's tough.)* Oh.

SANDRINE: Yeah.

JIMMY: Well . . . good for you. Gettin' yourself out there again.

SANDRINE: Yeah.

JIMMY: Movin' on . . .

SANDRINE: Yeah, well, actually, Jimmy, it's more than me just gettin' myself out there and movin' on. Um . . . this is my . . . bachelorette party. *(Beat. Then off his blank look:)* I'm gettin' married.

JIMMY: Oh.

SANDRINE: Yeah.

JIMMY: Wow.

SANDRINE: Yeah.

JIMMY: Wow.

SANDRINE: Yeah.

JIMMY: Wow.

SANDRINE: Yeah.

JIMMY: Wow. That's — . . . Thought you said you weren't gonna do that. Get married. Thought it wasn't for you, you told me. *(Beat.)* Guess it just wasn't for you with me. *(Beat.)* So, who's . . . who's the lucky guy?

SANDRINE: Martin Laferriere *(Say, "la-FAIRY-AIR.")*. You know him? The uh —

JIMMY: The ranger guy, over in Ashland.

SANDRINE: Yeah, yeah, yeah!

JIMMY: Wow.

SANDRINE: Yeah.

JIMMY: He's a legend. Legendary. I mean, if you're lost on a mountain in Maine, he's the guy you want lookin' for you.

SANDRINE: Yeah.

JIMMY: I mean, if you're lost out there in this big bad northern world, Martin La*ferriere's* the guy you want to have go out there and find you.

SANDRINE: Yeah.

JIMMY: And he . . . found you.

SANDRINE: Yeah. I'm sorry I never told you — I actually thought you woulda known, I thought you would have heard . . .

JIMMY: How would I have heard?

SANDRINE: Well, you know . . . people talk.

JIMMY: Not about things they know you don't wanna hear, they don't. And I gotta be honest . . . that's not somethin' I woulda wanted to hear . . . *(Beat.)* So . . . when's the big event?

SANDRINE: Um . . . tomorrow!

JIMMY: Really.

SANDRINE: Yup.

JIMMY: Well then . . . *(Jimmy downs his Bud, and then raises his arm, to get the waitress' attention. As he does so, his unbuttoned sleeve slides up his arm a little. He hollers:)* HEY!

SANDRINE: *(Not wanting Jimmy to draw attention to them.)* What are you doin'?

JIMMY: Getting our waitress, she said holler, *(Calling to waitress.)* HEY! *(To Sandrine.)* What's her name?

SANDRINE: I don't know, she's new // here.

JIMMY: *(To waitress.)* HEY!

SANDRINE: What are you doin'?

JIMMY: We gotta celebrate! You got found! And you deserve it. He's quite a guy.

SANDRINE: Oh, Jimmy.

JIMMY: And so are you.

SANDRINE: *(That was the nicest thing a guy like Jimmy could say to a girl.)* Jimmy . . .

JIMMY: *(Arm raised, hollering to waitress.)* HEY!

SANDRINE: *(Noticing a black marking on Jimmy's arm.)* Jimmy — whoah — hey! What's that?

JIMMY: What?

SANDRINE: That. *(Referring to the black marking on his arm.)*

JIMMY: *(Covering it.)* Oh, nothin', tattoo.

SANDRINE: What?

JIMMY: Tattoo. *(Then, to waitress.)* Hey!

SANDRINE: *(Intrigued.)* When did you get that?

JIMMY: After you left.

SANDRINE: *(Intrigued.)* Jimmy! Well — what's it of, what's it say?

JIMMY: Nothin', nothin' —

SANDRINE: *(She grabs his arm and rolls up his sleeve, to reveal, on the inside of his forearm, in big, bold letters:)* "Villian." *(Rhymes with "Jillian.")*

JIMMY: *Villain.*

SANDRINE: Who's Villian?

JIMMY: *Villain.* It's supposed to say, "Villain."

SANDRINE: What?

JIMMY: It's supposed to say, "Villain."

SANDRINE: Well, it doesn't say, "Villain," it says, "Villian."

JIMMY: I know, I spelled it wrong — >

SANDRINE: What?

JIMMY: They spelled it wrong. It says, "Villian" but it's supposed to say, "Villain."

SANDRINE: Well, why is it supposed to say, "Villain"? Why would you want a tattoo that says, "Villain"?

JIMMY: 'Cause . . .

SANDRINE: 'Cause why?

JIMMY: Just 'cause.

SANDRINE: Just 'cause *why?*

JIMMY: Just 'cause . . . when a guy's got a girl like you . . . Well, I just think that losin' a girl like you, drivin' a girl like you away . . . >

SANDRINE: Jimmy, you didn't drive me away —

JIMMY: is just plain criminal. Criminal. It's *villainy!* And it should be punished! So I punished myself. I marked myself a villain. So girls would stay away. So I'd never have to go through . . . what I went through with you. Again. Can I kiss you?

SANDRINE: No. *(Beat. But then she kisses Jimmy on the cheek. Beat. Then, referring to his tattoo:)* You can get that undone, you know.

JIMMY: Yeah. *(Beat.)*

SANDRINE: I gotta head. *(She goes.)*

JIMMY: Yeah. *(Then, stopping Sandrine.)* I'm — . *(Sandrine stops.)* I'm glad you got found.

SANDRINE: Thanks, Jimmy.

(Sandrine goes back to her bachelorette party — and she is welcomed back heartily. We hear this. Jimmy hears this. He is alone, sad, and stuck there. Maybe he gets his coat off his chair. Time to go home. Alone. As usual. Beat.)

WAITRESS: *(Entering.)* Hey! Sorry! You were wavin' me down. I saw you, but it's so busy in the front! There's this bachelorette party: those *girls!* Good thing it's not, "Drink free if you're glad," 'cause those girls are wicked *glad.* Gosh — had to fight my way through to find you, but I did it, I found ya! So: What'd ya need, what can I do ya for? Another Bud?

JIMMY: Um . . . *(He's sad, looking off to where Sandrine went.)*

WAITRESS: *(Looking off to where Sandrine went . . . seeing the empty chair . . . putting the pieces together.)* Oh, pal . . . Um . . . Um . . . Well, remember, like I said, Moose Paddy special: Drinks are free if you're sad. OK? Just tell me you're sad, and you'll drink free. *(Beat.)* Just say the word. Let me know. 'Cause I know from sad, and you're lookin' pretty sad.

(No response from Jimmy. He's just sad.)

WAITRESS: OK. Well, my name's Villian if you need anything. *(Note to actress playing Villian: The next line may be used if you feel you need it for clarity. It's just a back up, in case you feel the first mention of your name isn't heard, or if the audience is slow to catch on. Use it if you need it; don't if you don't — up to you.)* Just ask for Villian. *(She goes.)*

JIMMY: *(Her name registers. He calls to her.)* Villian!?!

VILLIAN: *(She stops.)* Yeah?

JIMMY: Hi.

VILLIAN: Hi . . .

JIMMY: I'm not sad. I just would like another Bud.

VILLIAN: All right. *(Leaving.)*

JIMMY: Villian!!

VILLIAN: *(Stopping.)* Yeah?

JIMMY: I'm glad you found me.

VILLIAN: Aw . . . *(Leaving, to herself.)* "I'm glad you found me," that's adorable . . . *(Music. Looks like Jimmy might stay. Maybe he's a little glad. He sits back down; deals with his tattooed forearm in some way. Lights fade. Transitional aurora. End of "Sad and Glad." After the lights have faded, and "Sad and Glad" is over, we begin Episode Three, which is entitled . . .*

THIS HURTS

Music fades. Lights up on a woman finishing up ironing a man's clothes. She is in the laundry room of Ma Dudley's Boarding House, in Almost, Maine. She starts folding the man's shirt she was ironing, but thinks better of it, and, instead, deliberately crumples it and throws it into her laundry basket. She picks up the iron, wraps the cord around it, preparing to put it away. As she does so, she burns herself on it.)

WOMAN: Ow! Dammit!

(A man, sitting on a bench, takes note of this and writes "iron" in a homemade book labeled THINGS THAT CAN HURT YOU. Meanwhile, the woman has exited to return the iron to its proper place. She returns to deal with the ironing board, which must also be returned to its proper place — the same place she just brought the iron. After folding up the

ironing board, she turns to exit, and accidentally wallops the man in the head with the ironing board, knocking him off the bench he was sitting on.)

WOMAN: Oh, no! I'm sorry! I'm sorry! Oh . . . I didn't see you, are you OK?!?

MAN: Yeah.

WOMAN: No you're not!! I smashed you with the ironing board, I wasn't even looking! Are you hurt?

MAN: No.

WOMAN: Oh, you must be!! I just smashed you! Where did I get you?

MAN: In the head.

WOMAN: In the head!?! Oh, *(Going to him.)* come here, are you OK?

MAN: Is there any blood?

WOMAN: No.

MAN: Any discoloration?

WOMAN: No.

MAN: Then I'm OK.

WOMAN: Well, I'm gonna go get you some ice.

MAN: No. I can't feel things like that.

WOMAN: Like what?

MAN: Like when I get smashed in the head with an ironing board. I don't get hurt.

WOMAN: What?

MAN: I can't feel pain.

WOMAN: Oh, Jeezum Crow *(Say "JEE-zum CROW" — it's a euphemism.),* what the hell have I done to you? >

MAN: Nothin' —

WOMAN: You're talkin' loopy, listen to you, goin' on about not being able to feel pain, that's delusional, I've knocked the sense right outta ya!

MAN: No, I'm OK.

WOMAN: Shh! Listen: I was gonna be a nurse, so I know: You're hurt. You just took a good shot right to the head, and that's serious.

MAN: No, it's not serious. I don't think an ironing board could really hurt your head, 'cause, see, *(Forcing his THINGS THAT CAN HURT YOU book on her.)* ironing boards aren't on my list of things that can hurt you, >

WOMAN: *(Dealing with this book.)* What is this? —

MAN: plus, there's no blood or discoloration from where I got hit, so . . . >

WOMAN: Well, you can be hurt and not be bleeding or bruised —

MAN: And my list is pretty reliable, 'cause my brother Paul is helping me make it, and I can prove it to you: See, I bet if I took this ironing board, like this, and hit you with it, that it wouldn't hurt you *(He smashes her in the head with ironing board.)*, see?, // that didn't hurt.

WOMAN: OW!! *(Scrambling to get away from him.)*

MAN: Oh!

WOMAN: Ow! What the hell was that?! // Why did you do that?

MAN: Oh! I'm sorry. // Did that hurt?

WOMAN: God!

MAN: Ooh . . . it did, didn't it?

WOMAN: Ow!

MAN: I didn't think it would 'cause, see, ironing boards are not on my list of things that can hurt you, but, gosh, maybe they should be on my list, because —

WOMAN: What are you talkin' about?

MAN: I have a list of things that can hurt you, my brother Paul is helping me make it, and ironing boards aren't on it.

WOMAN: Well, that ironing board hurt me.

MAN: Yeah.

WOMAN: So you should add it to your list.

MAN: Yeah. *(He adds "ironing board" to his list of THINGS THAT CAN HURT YOU. He then picks up a book labeled THINGS TO BE AFRAID OF.)* Should I be *afraid* of ironing boards?

WOMAN: Well, if someone swings it at your head and wallops you with it, yes . . .

MAN: Well, it's not — I have a list of things to be afraid of, too — and ironing boards are not on this list either.

WOMAN: Well they shouldn't be, really.

MAN: No?

WOMAN: No, you shouldn't be *afraid* of ironing boards.

MAN: No?

WOMAN: No.

MAN: But they can *hurt* you.

WOMAN: Yeah.

MAN: So I should be *afraid* of them.

WOMAN: No.

MAN: So I *shouldn't* be afraid of them?

WOMAN: Right.

MAN: But they can *hurt* me.

WOMAN: Well, if they're used the way you used it, yeah.

MAN: Oh-oh-oh! So, they're kind of like the opposite of God?

WOMAN: What?

MAN: Well, ironing boards can *hurt* me, but I shouldn't be *afraid* of them, but God, my brother Paul says, God won't *hurt* me, but I should *fear* him.

WOMAN: I guess.

MAN: Boy, this is getting very complicated.

WOMAN: What is?

MAN: This business of learning what hurts, what doesn't hurt, what to be afraid of, what not to be afraid of.

WOMAN: Are you sure you're OK? // you're just goin' on and on about crazy stuff —

MAN: Oh, yeah, see, I have congenital analgesia, he thinks. Some // people —

WOMAN: What? — >

MAN: Congenital // analge —

WOMAN: Who thinks?

MAN: My brother Paul. Some people call it hereditary sensory neuropathy type four, but . . . it just means I can't feel pain. You can hit me if you want to, to see!

WOMAN: No.

MAN: Go ahead. It won't hurt. See? *(He hits his head with the book. Composition books work pretty well, because they make a great sound and don't actually hurt!)*

WOMAN: OW!

MAN: See? *(He hits his head again.)*

WOMAN: OW!

MAN: See? *(Hits his head again.)*

WOMAN: OW!

MAN: Go ahead. *(He offers her the book labeled THINGS THAT CAN HURT YOU so she can hit him with it.)*

WOMAN: No!

MAN: Come on!

WOMAN: No!

MAN: Come on!

WOMAN: NO!

MAN: OK. You don't have to. Most people don't. Hit me. Most people just go away. You can go away, too, if you want to. That's what most people do when I tell them about myself. My brother Paul says I just shouldn't tell people about myself, because I scare them, so I've actually recently put "myself" on my list of things to be afraid of, but —

(Her curiosity getting the better of her, the woman comes up from behind the

*man and wallops him on the back of the head with the book labeled
THINGS THAT CAN HURT YOU.)*

WOMAN: Oh, my gosh!, I'm sorry, //oh my gosh! I just clocked you — >

MAN: You hit me! Most people go away, but you hit me!

WOMAN: I had to *see* [what would happen]! But, are you OK?

MAN: Yeah, I don't feel // pain!

WOMAN: — Don't feel pain, right, of course you're OK! — but — are you sure?

MAN: Well, is there any blood?

WOMAN: No.

MAN: Any discoloration?

WOMAN: No.

MAN: Then I'm OK.

WOMAN: Well, buddy, you can be hurt and not even look like it. >

MAN: But —

WOMAN: Trust me. There are things that hurt you that make you bruised and
bloody and there are things that hurt you that don't make you bruised
and bloody and . . . they all hurt. *(Beat. Then, giving him back the book
labeled THINGS THAT CAN HURT YOU:)* I'm Marvalyn.

MAN: I'm Steve. I live on the third floor. Room eleven.

MARVALYN: *(Deflecting.)* I live with my boyfriend, Eric. I love him very much.

STEVE: Yeah. We saw you move in.

MARVALYN: Yeah. Our roof collapsed from all the snow in December. We're
just here until we can get our feet back on the ground.

STEVE: Oh. Well, that's good, 'cause that's what Ma Dudley says her boarding
house is. A place where people can live until they get their feet back on
the ground. My brother Paul says we've been trying to get our feet back
on the ground our whole lives.

MARVALYN: Oh.

STEVE: Yeah, it takes some people longer to do that than others . . .

MARVALYN: Yeah. *(Beat.)*

STEVE: You guys are loud.

MARVALYN: Huh?

STEVE: You and Eric. You yell and bang. We're right below you.

MARVALYN: Oh. Sorry about that. We're goin' through a rough patch. Happens. Sorry. *(Beat. Then, changing the subject.)* What is it like?

STEVE: What?

MARVALYN: To not feel pain.

STEVE: I don't know. I don't know what it's like to hurt, so . . . I don't know.
I don't really feel.

MARVALYN: Is this . . . how you were born?

STEVE: Yeah. I don't have fully developed pain sensors. They're immature, my brother Paul says //, and because they're immature —

MARVALYN: How does he know that?

STEVE: Oh, he *reads,* >

MARVALYN: But —

STEVE: and because they're immature, my development as a human being has been retarded, he says, >

MARVALYN: But —

STEVE: but he teaches me what hurts, though.

MARVALYN: Why??

STEVE: So I won't ruin myself. I have to know what hurts, so I know when to be afraid. See, my mind can't tell me when to be afraid, 'cause my body doesn't know what being hurt is, so I have to memorize what might hurt.

MARVALYN: OK . . .

STEVE: And I have to memorize what to be afraid of. *(Referring to his book.)* Things like bears. And guns and knives. And fire. And fear — I should fear fear itself, and pretty girls . . .

MARVALYN: Pretty girls?

STEVE: *(He thinks she's pretty.)* Yeah.

MARVALYN: Why should you be afraid of pretty girls?

STEVE: Well, 'cause my brother Paul says they can hurt you 'cause they make you love them, and that's something I'm supposed to be afraid of, too — love — but Paul says that I'm really lucky, 'cause I'll probably never have to deal with love, because I have a lot of deficiencies and not very many capacities as a result of the congenital analgesia.

MARVALYN: Wait, what do you mean you're never gonna have to deal with love //, why —

STEVE: 'Cause I'm never gonna know what it feels like, Paul says.

MARVALYN: Well, how does he know that?

STEVE: 'Cause it hurts.

MARVALYN: It shouldn't.

STEVE: And, plus, I have a lot of deficiencies and not very many capacities.

MARVALYN: You know what, a lot of people do. *(She kisses him. At first, it's just Marvalyn kissing Steve, but, eventually, Steve participates. Then, Marvalyn breaks away.)* I'm sorry. I'm sorry. Are you all right? I'm sorry I did that. You're just . . . very sweet.
(Beat.)

STEVE: *(Trying to make sense of what just happened.)* But . . . you have a boyfriend and you love him very much.

MARVALYN: *(She begins gathering her stuff.)* Yes I do. And yes I do.

STEVE: And you just kissed me.

MARVALYN: Yes I did.

STEVE: And it's Friday night and you're doing your laundry.

MARVALYN: Yes I am.

STEVE: And people who are in love with each other, they don't kiss other people and do their laundry on Friday nights, I've learned that. People who are in love with each other, they go to the Moose Paddy on Friday nights, or they go dancing together, or they go skating. And they kiss each other. They don't kiss other people — you know what? I don't think that's love, // what you and your boyfriend have —

MARVALYN: *(Deflecting, preparing to leave.)* I've been down here longer than I said I would be and he doesn't like that.

STEVE: Who?

MARVALYN: My boyfriend.

STEVE: Who you love very much.

MARVALYN: Yes.

STEVE: Even though you kissed me?

MARVALYN: Yes.

STEVE: Wow, I'm going to have to talk to my brother Paul about this —

MARVALYN: No! Don't talk to your brother Paul about this. Tell him to stop teaching you.

STEVE: What?

MARVALYN: Whatever he's teaching you. Tell him to stop. What he's teaching you isn't something you wanna know.

STEVE: But I have to learn from him —

MARVALYN: Look: I was gonna be a nurse, so I know: You need to go to a doctor, and not have your brother read whatever it is he reads.

STEVE: But —

MARVALYN: You know what, I gotta go.

STEVE: *(He sits down on the bench.)* Right. You gotta go. You're — you're leaving. I knew you would. That's what people do.

MARVALYN: No, I just have to — . I told you, Eric // doesn't like it if —

STEVE: Your boyfriend?

MARVALYN: Yeah, he doesn't like it if I'm down here longer than I said I'd be, and I've been down here longer than I said I'd be . . . *(On this line, Marvalyn picks up the ironing board. Then, as she goes to put it away, she accidentally swings it around and hits Steve in the head, just as she did at the beginning of the episode. Steve gets knocked off the bench.)*

MARVALYN: Oh! I'm sorry!

STEVE: OW!

MARVALYN: I'm so sorry!, are you all right? I can't believe I just did that to you again!

STEVE: OW!!

MARVALYN: *(She goes to help him, then stops.)* Wait — : What did you just say?

STEVE: *(As he rubs his head, he realizes what he just said. He looks at her, tells her plainly:)* Ow.

(Music. Marvalyn and Steve just look at each other. Utter uncertainty. This is scary. And wonderful. But mostly scary — because who knows what's next. Lights fade. Transitional aurora. End of "This Hurts." After the lights have faded, and "This Hurts" is over, we begin Episode Four, which is entitled . . .

GETTING IT BACK

Music fades. We hear someone — Gayle — pounding on a door.)

GAYLE: Lendall! *(More pounding.)* Lendall! *(More pounding.)* Lendall!

(Lights up on the living room of a small home in Almost, Maine. It is furnished with a comfortable chair and an end table. Lendall, who has been woken up, enters and crosses through his living room to answer the door. Gayle is still pounding on the door.)

LENDALL: OK! Gayle! Shhh! I'm comin', I'm comin'.

GAYLE: Lendall!

LENDALL: Hey, hey, hey. Shh! *(Lendall exits stage left to answer the door.)*

GAYLE: *(Blowing by him.)* Lendall —

LENDALL: *(Re-enters.)* What's the matter?, what's goin' on?

(Beat. Gayle is stewing.)

LENDALL: What?

GAYLE: *(She's been in a bit of a state, but she collects herself.)* I want it back.

LENDALL: What?

GAYLE: I want it back.

LENDALL: What?

GAYLE: All the love I gave to you?, I want it back.

LENDALL: What?

GAYLE: *Now.*

LENDALL: Why?

GAYLE: I've got yours in the car.

LENDALL: What?

GAYLE: All the love you gave to me?, I've got it in the car.

LENDALL: Well, wh —

GAYLE: I don't want it anymore.

LENDALL: Why?

GAYLE: I've made a decision: We're done.

LENDALL: What?!

GAYLE: We're done. I've decided. And, so, I've brought all the love you gave to me back to you. It's the right thing to do.

LENDALL: *(Bewildered.)* Um, I —

GAYLE: It's in the car.

LENDALL: You said. *(Beat. He's kind of paralyzed trying to figure this out.)*

GAYLE: *(Waiting for him to take some action, and go get the love.)* I can get it *for* you, or . . . *you* can get it.

LENDALL: Well, I don't want it back. I don't need it —

GAYLE: Well, *I* don't want it. What am I supposed to do with all of it, now that I don't want it?

LENDALL: Well, I don't know . . .

GAYLE: Well, under the circumstances //, it doesn't seem right for me to keep it, so I'm gonna give it back. *(She leaves.)*

LENDALL: Under what circumstances? *(Calling to her.)* Gayle — what are — ? I don't understand what — . . . What are you doing?

GAYLE: *(From offstage.)* I told you. I'm getting all the love you gave to me and I'm giving it back to you.

LENDALL: *(Calling to her.)* Well, I'm not sure I want it — whoah! Need help?

GAYLE: Nope. I got it. It's not heavy. *(She returns with a huge, red bag full of love. The bag should be filled with foam or pillow stuffing — something that is soundless. She places it on the floor.)* Here you go.

LENDALL: *(Truly puzzled, referring to the bag of love.)* And this is . . . ?

GAYLE: *(Starts off again.)* All the love you gave me, yeah.

LENDALL: Wow. *(Beat.)* That's a *lot.*

GAYLE: *(Returning with more bags of love.)* Yeah. *(She exits.)*

LENDALL: Whole lot.

GAYLE: Yeah. *(She returns with even more bags of love. There is now a HUGE pile of love on the floor.)*

LENDALL: Wow. What the heck am I gonna do with all that? I mean . . . I don't know if I have room.

GAYLE: *(Upset.)* I'm sure you'll find a place for it *(i.e., another woman)* . . . And now, I think it's only fair for you to give me mine back because . . . I want it back. *(Beat.)* All the love I gave to you?

LENDALL: Yeah?

GAYLE: I want it back. *(Beat.)* So go get it. *(Lendall doesn't move. He's probably trying to figure out what is happening and why it is happening.)*

GAYLE: Lendall, go get it. *(Lendall doesn't go.)* Please. *(Lendall still doesn't go.)* Now!!!

LENDALL: *(At a loss.)* OK. *(He exits.)*

(Gayle sits in the chair and waits. She is still in a state. Long beat. Lendall slowly returns . . . with a teeny-tiny little bag — a little pouch — and places it on a little table next to the chair. They look at the little bag. The bag should be between Lendall and Gayle. And Gayle should be between the many bags of love and the little bag of love.)

GAYLE: What is that?

LENDALL: *(It's obvious — it's exactly what she asked for.)* It's all the love you gave me.

GAYLE: That's — ? . . . That is *not* — . There is no way — . . . That is *not* — . *(Mortified.)* Is that all I gave you?

LENDALL: It's all I could find . . .

GAYLE: Oh. OK. *(Taking in the little bag . . . and then, all the big bags of love.)* OK. *(And she's crying.)*

LENDALL: Gayle . . . What's goin' on, here?

GAYLE: I told you: We're done.

LENDALL: Why do you keep saying that? —

GAYLE: Because — *(Very hard to say, but has to be said.).* Because when I asked you if you ever thought we were gonna get married — remember when I asked you that? In December? . . . It was snowing? . . .

LENDALL: Yeah.

GAYLE: Yeah, well, when I asked you . . . *that,* you got so . . . *quiet.* And everybody said that that right there // shoulda told me everything —

LENDALL: Everybody *who?*

GAYLE: Everybody!

LENDALL: Who?

GAYLE: . . . Marvalyn >

LENDALL: *Marvalyn?!?* Marvalyn said that — like she's an expert? — . . .

GAYLE: said — yes, Marvalyn, yes, said that how quiet you got was all I needed to know, and she's right: You don't love me.

LENDALL: What — ? Gayle, no!

GAYLE: Shh! And I've been trying to fix that, I've tried to *make* you love me by giving you every bit of love I had, and now . . . I don't have any love for *me* left, and that's . . . that's not good for a person . . . and . . . that's why I want all the love I gave you back, because I wanna bring it with me.

LENDALL: Where are you going?

GAYLE: I need to get away from things.

LENDALL: What — ? What things?! There aren't any things in this town to get away from!

GAYLE: Yes there are: you!

LENDALL: Me?

GAYLE: Yes. *You* are the things in this town I need to get away from because I have to think and start over, and so: All the love I gave to you? I want it back, in case I need it. Because I can't very well go around giving *your* love — 'cause that's all I have right now, is the love *you* gave *me* — I can't very well go around giving *your* love to other guys, 'cause // that just doesn't seem right —

LENDALL: Other *guys?* There are other guys?!?

GAYLE: No, not yet, but I'm assuming there will be.

LENDALL: Gayle —

GAYLE: Shh! So I think — . I think that, since I know now that you're not ready to do what comes next for people who have been together for quite a long time *(i.e., get married)*, I think we're gonna be done, >

LENDALL: Why? Gayle — !

GAYLE: and so, I think the best thing we can do now, is just return the love we gave to each other, and call it . . . *(Taking in the bags — the pathetic one that contains the love she gave him, and the awesome several that contain the love he gave her.)* . . . even *(It's not "even" at all.)* . . . Oh, Jeezum Crow, is that really all the love I gave you, Lendall? I mean, I thought — . I mean what kind of person am I if this is all the love I gave y — . . . No . . . n-n-no . . . *(Fiercely.)* I *know* I gave you more than that, Lendall, I *know* it! *(She thinks. Collects herself. New attack.)* Did you lose it?

LENDALL: No, Gayle —

GAYLE: Did you lose it, Lendall? 'Cause I know I gave you more than that, and I think you're pulling something on me, and this is not a good time to be pulling something on me!

LENDALL: I'm not. Pulling something on you. I wouldn't do that to you . . . Just — I think — . . . Gosh . . . *(Not mean; simply at a loss.)* I think you should just take what you came for, and I guess I'll see you later. *(This is pretty final. He exits into the rest of the house.)*

GAYLE: *(Realization of the finality. Calls him, weakly.)* Lendall . . . Lendall . . . *(Now Gayle is at a loss. But this is what she wants. She looks at the little bag, takes it, and is about to leave. But curiosity stops her. She sits in the chair, opens the bag . . . and examines what's inside.)* Lendall!? What is this? What the heck is this, Lendall? This is *not* the love I gave you, Lendall; at least have the decency to give me back what — . Lendall, what is this?

LENDALL: *(Returning.)* It's a ring, Gayle.

GAYLE: What?

LENDALL: It's a ring.

GAYLE: What? Well, what the — ? *(She takes what is in the bag out of the bag.)* This isn't — . This is *not* — . . . *(Realizes it's a ring box.)* Oh, Lendall, this is a ring! Is this a . . . *ring?* A ring that you give to someone you've been with for quite a long time if you want to let them know that you're ready for what comes next for people who have been together for quite a long time . . . ?

LENDALL: Mmhmm.

GAYLE: Oh . . . *(She opens the box, sees the ring.)* Oh! *(Beat.)* But . . . all the love I gave to you? Where is it?

LENDALL: It's right there, Gayle. *(Referring to the ring.)*

GAYLE: But —

LENDALL: It's right there.

GAYLE: But —

LENDALL: It *is*. That's it. Right there. There was so much of it — you gave me so much, over the years —

GAYLE: *Eleven.*

LENDALL: — over the eleven years —

GAYLE: *Eleven,* yeah.

LENDALL: — yeah, you gave me so much . . . that I didn't know what to do with it all. I had to put some in the garage, some in the shed. I asked my dad if he had any suggestions what to do with it all, and he said, "You got a ring yet?" I said, "No." And he said, "Get her one. It's time. When there's that much of that stuff comin' in, that's about the only place you can put it." *(Beat.)* He said it'd all fit *(i.e., in the ring)*. *(Beat.)* And he was right. *(Beat. They look at the ring. Then, simply:)* That thing is a lot bigger than it looks . . . *(Beat.)* So, there it is. All the love you gave to me. Just not in the same . . . form as when you gave it.

GAYLE: Yeah. *(Beat.)*

LENDALL: You still want it back?

GAYLE: Yes. I do.

LENDALL: Well, then . . . take it.

GAYLE: *(She takes the ring out of the box. Then, referring to the laundry bags full of love:)* Can I keep all that?

LENDALL: It's yours.

GAYLE: Thank you.

(Lendall puts the ring on Gayle's finger. Music.)

GAYLE: Lendall — . . . You didn't have to get me a ring. That's not what I was asking —

LENDALL: Yes I did. It was time. And it's honorable.

GAYLE: Well . . . it's very beautiful. *(Beat.)* Lendall — . . . I'm sorry. It's just — it's a Friday night, and I was sittin' home all by myself, and I started thinkin', and —

LENDALL: Shh. *(Into a kiss. He takes Gayle's hand. Maybe he gets her out of her coat. And hat. Maybe they dance. Lights fade. Transitional aurora. End of "Getting It Back." End of ACT I. Fade to black. Intermission. After the intermission, we move to what I'm calling the . . .*

INTERLOGUE

Music. Lights up on Pete, from the Prologue. He is simply waiting for Ginette. His snowball is on the bench next to him. He looks offstage left, to where Ginette exited. He looks at his snowball. He looks out. He bundles up against the cold. Lights fade, and we begin . . .

ACT II

with Episode Five, which is entitled . . .

THEY FELL

Music fades. Lights up on Randy and Chad — two "County boys" — hanging out in a potato field in Almost, Maine. They're probably drinkin' some beers — Natural Lite, if you can get it. They're in mid-conversation.)

CHAD: I believe you, I'm just sayin' —

RANDY: It was bad, Chad. Bad.

CHAD: I hear ya, b//ut —

RANDY: But you're not listenin', // Chad: It was bad! >

CHAD: No, *you're* not listenin', 'cause >

RANDY: Real bad.

CHAD: *(Topping Randy.)* I'm tryin' to tell you that I had a pretty bad time *myself !!!*

RANDY: *(Taking this in; then:)* No. There's no way! —

CHAD: It was pretty bad, Randy.

RANDY: Really?

CHAD: Yeah.

RANDY: OK: go. [Let's hear it.]

CHAD: *(This is a little painful.)* She — . . . She said she didn't like the way I smelled.

RANDY: What?

CHAD: Sally told me she didn't like the way I smelled. Never has.

RANDY: *(Taking this in.)* Sally Dunleavy *(Say, "DUN-luv-ee.")* told you that she didn't // like the way you — . . . ?

CHAD: Yeah.

RANDY: When?

CHAD: When I picked her up. She got in the truck, we were backin' outta her driveway, and all of a sudden, she started breathin' hard and asked me to stop and she got outta the truck and said she was sorry but she couldn't go out with me because she didn't like the way I smelled, never had! >

RANDY: What?

CHAD: Said she thought she was gonna be able to overlook it, the way that I smelled, but that that wasn't gonna be possible after all, and she slammed the door on me and left me sittin' right there in her driveway.

RANDY: *(Taking this in.)* 'Cause she didn't like the way you smelled?

CHAD: Yeah.

RANDY: Well what kinda — . . . ? *(Beat.)* I don't mind the way you smell.

CHAD: Thanks.

RANDY: Jeez.

CHAD: Yeah . . . *(Beat.)* Told you it was bad.

RANDY: More than bad, Chad. That's sad.

CHAD: Yeah. *(Beat.)* So, I'm guessin' I'm the big winner tonight, huh? So . . . I get to pick tomorrow, and I pick bowlin'. We'll go bowlin', supper at the snowmobile club . . . coupla beers at the Moose Paddy . . . and just hang out.

RANDY: *(Looks at Chad. Beat.)* I didn't say you're the big winner, >

CHAD: What?

RANDY: did I say you're the big winner?

CHAD: No —

RANDY: No. All that's pretty sad, Chad, and bad, but you didn't win.

CHAD: What do you mean?

RANDY: You didn't win.

CHAD: You can beat bein' told you smelled bad?

RANDY: Yeah.

CHAD: Well, then . . . [Let's hear it.]

RANDY: *(This is difficult to share.)* Mine's face broke.

CHAD: What?

RANDY: Her face broke.

CHAD: *(Taking this in.)* Her — . . . ?

RANDY: Only get one chance with a girl like Yvonne LaFrance, *(LaFrance rhymes with "pants.")* and her face broke. *(Beat.)* Told you it was bad. *(Beat.)*

CHAD: How did her face break?

RANDY: When we were dancin'.

CHAD: *Dancin'? (These guys don't dance.)*

RANDY: Yup.

CHAD: Why were you *dancin'?*

RANDY: 'Cause that's what she wanted to do. On our date. So I took her. Took her dancin' down to the rec center. You pay, then you get a lesson, then you dance all night. They teach "together dancing," how to dance together, and we learned that thing where you throw the girl up and over, and, Yvonne — well, she's pretty small . . . and I'm pretty strong. And I threw her up and over, and, well . . . I threw her . . . *over* . . . over. *(Beat.)* And she landed on her face. *(Beat.)* And it broke. *(Beat.)* Had to take her to the emergency room. *(Long beat. Then, finally:)*

CHAD: That's a drive.

RANDY: Thirty-eight miles.

CHAD: Yup. *(Beat.)*

RANDY: *(Disgusted.)* And she cried.

CHAD: Hate that.

RANDY: Whole way. *(Beat.)* Then had me call her old boyfriend to come get her.

CHAD: Ooh.

RANDY: He did. Asked me to "please leave." *(Beat.)* He's small as she is. *(They laugh. Beat. Chad laughs.)*

RANDY: What?

CHAD: That's just — pretty bad.

RANDY: Yup.

CHAD: And sad.

RANDY: Yup.

CHAD: So . . . I guess you win.

RANDY: Yup.

CHAD: That right there might make you the big winner of all time!

RANDY: Yup.

CHAD: "Baddest-date-guy" of all time!

RANDY: Yup.

CHAD: Congratulations!

RANDY: Thank you.

CHAD: So what do you pick tomorrow?

RANDY: Bowlin'. Supper at the snowmobile club. Coupla beers at the Moose
Paddy. Hang out.

CHAD: Good.

*(Beat. They drink their beers, crush the cans, which they throw offstage right
into a potato barrel, maybe, like they're shooting baskets. Randy sits. Chad
laughs.)*

RANDY: What?

CHAD: *(Sitting.)* I don't know. Just sometimes . . . I don't know why I bother
goin' "out." I don't like it, Randy. I hate it. I hate goin' out on these dates.
I mean, why do I wanna spend my Friday night with some girl I might
maybe like, when I could be spendin' it hangin' out with someone I *know*
I like, like you, you know?

RANDY: Yeah.

CHAD: I mean . . . that was rough tonight. In the middle of Sally tellin' me
how she didn't like the way I smelled . . . . I got real sad, >

RANDY: Aw, buddy —

CHAD: and all I could think about was how not much in this world makes me
feel good or makes much sense anymore, and I got really scared 'cause
there's gotta be something that makes you feel good or at least makes
sense in this world, or what's the point, right? And then I kinda came out
of bein' sad, and actually felt OK, 'cause I realized that there *is* one thing
in this world that makes me feel really good and that *does* make sense,
and it's you.

*(Everything stops. Chad isn't quite sure what he has just said. Randy isn't
quite sure what he has just heard. Long, long beat of these guys sorting out
what was said and heard.)*

RANDY: *(Quickly getting up to escape the discomfort.)* Well, I'm gonna head. *(He
starts to leave.)* >

CHAD: *(Probably just glad that Randy broke the silence.)* Yeah . . .

RANDY: *(Deflecting throughout the following.)* I gotta work in the mornin' . . .

CHAD: Well, I'm just supervising first shift at the mill, so I can pick you up anytime after three —

RANDY: Oh, I don't know, Chad: Me and Lendall, we got a long day tomorrow — we're still catchin' up, fixin' roofs from all the snow in December, // gotta do Marvalyn and Eric's, and —

CHAD: Well, four // or five?

RANDY: Could take all day, I don't know when we'll be // done.

CHAD: Well, you just // say when —

RANDY: I don't know, I don't know!, so, >

CHAD: Well —

RANDY: *(Putting a stop to this — he wants outta there.)* HEY!! I'll see ya later! *(Leaving.)*

CHAD: Yeah. Yeah-yeah-yeah . . . *(Chad watches Randy go. Then:)* Hey, Randy! — *(Suddenly, Chad completely falls down on the ground.)*

RANDY: *(Rushing back, seeing Chad on the ground.)* Whoah! Chad! You OK?

CHAD: Yeah . . .

RANDY: What the — . . . Here . . . *(Helps Chad up.)*

CHAD: Thanks. Umm . . .

RANDY: What was that? You OK? What just happened there?

CHAD: *(Trying to figure this out.)* Umm . . . I just fell . . .

RANDY: Well, I figured that out . . .

CHAD: No — . . . I just — . *(Beat.)* I think I just fell in love with you there, Randy. *(Randy is silent. What has Chad just said? What has Randy just heard? Chad looks at Randy, then suddenly and completely falls down again.)*

RANDY/CHAD: Ho!

CHAD: *(On the ground.)* Yup. That's what that was. *(Getting up.)* Me falling in love with you . . . *(He looks at Randy, and falls down again, suddenly and completely.)*

RANDY: Chad: What are you doin'? Come on, get up! *(Randy gets Chad up, roughly.)*

CHAD: Randy — *(Chad immediately falls down again.)* Whoah . . .

RANDY: *(Fiercely.)* Would you cut that out?!?

CHAD: *(Fiercely, right back, and from the ground.)* Well, I can't help it!! It just kinda came over me!! *(Angry.)* I've fallen in love with ya, here!

RANDY: *(Takes this in. Confused, scared. Long beat. Then:)* Chad: I'm your best buddy in the whole world . . . and I don't quite know what you're doin' or what you're goin' on about . . . but *(Angry.)* — what the heck is your problem?!? What the heck are you doin'?!? Jeezum Crow, you're my best friend, >

CHAD: Yeah —

RANDY: and that's — . . . That's a thing you don't mess with. And you messed with it. And you don't do that. *(He starts to go. Stops. Then:)* 'Cause, you know somethin', you're about the only thing that feels really good and makes sense in this world to me, too, and then you go and foul it up, by doin' this *(i.e., falling down)* and tellin' me *that (i.e., that you're in love with me),* and now it just doesn't make any sense at all. And it doesn't feel good. *(Starts to leave again. Stops. Turns to Chad.)* You've done a real number on a good thing, here, buddy, 'cause we're friends, and there's a line when you're friends that you can't cross. And you crossed it! *(Randy is now on the opposite side of the stage from Chad. Beat. Suddenly, he completely falls down. Beat. Randy and Chad just stare at each other. They are far away from each other. This is about as scary — and wonderful — as it gets. A moment of realization. Then, the guys try to get up to get to each other. But they suddenly and completely fall down. They try to get up; they fall down. They get up; they fall down. This happens as many times as it takes for Randy and Chad to realize that they're not gonna get anywhere — they're just gonna keep falling. Beat. Music. They just look at each other. It's all scary and thrilling and unknown. It's going to be wonderful. Just not quite yet. Lights fade. Transitional aurora. End of "They Fell." After the lights have faded, and "They Fell" is over, we begin Episode Six, which is entitled . . .*

WHERE IT WENT

Music fades. Lights up on Phil and Marci, who have just been ice-skating on Echo Pond in Almost, Maine. They are undoing their skates, putting on their boots/shoes. Phil has hockey skates; Marci has figure skates. Marci has one shoe on, one skate on. Note: Marci should be wearing a winter shoe — like an L.L. Bean hunting shoe, or a suede-like winter shoe — not a boot. Beat.)

PHIL: It still feels like you're mad.

MARCI: *(Undoing her skate.)* I'm not mad, // I just said I wish >

PHIL: But you were, you *are,* >

MARCI: you'd pay more attention lately.

PHIL: you're mad.

MARCI: I'm not mad! I was having fun, I thought. I had fun tonight. Did you?

PHIL: Yeah.

MARCI: Good. *(Smiles, continues to undo her skates; is puzzled by something.)*

PHIL: *(Beat. Then, continuing his defense:)* I mean, Chad called me in to the mill, I had to work.

MARCI: *(Looking for something.)* I'm not mad at you, Phil, you had to work, // I get it.

PHIL: I did!

MARCI: Phil *(Now actively looking for something.)*, where's my shoe?

PHIL: What?

MARCI: Where's my shoe, I can't find it.

PHIL: Well, it's gotta be here . . .

MARCI: Where is it?!?

(They look for her shoe. Beat.)

MARCI: Is this you being funny?

PHIL: No.

MARCI: 'Cause it's not funny.

PHIL: I —

MARCI: It's cold out here.

PHIL: Well, you're the one that wanted to go skating!

MARCI: Phil!

PHIL: *(Angry — a bit of an explosion.)* We'll find it! It's gotta be here! *(Beat.)*

MARCI: I'm not mad. I was never mad. *(Re-lacing her skate — too cold for stocking feet. Beat.)* I was disappointed. But now I'm // done.

PHIL: Marce! —

MARCI: I had fun tonight! Skating. I thought it would be fun >

PHIL: It *was* . . .

MARCI: forget all the . . . stuff. Get us away from the kids, get us back to where we used to be. We went skating . . . first time you kissed me, on a Friday night just like this one. 'Member? Right here . . . *(She touches Phil in some way — maybe rubs his back.)* Echo Pond —

PHIL: *(Subtly/subconsciously shaking off Marci's touch.)* I know where we are, where the heck is your shoe? *(Going off to look for it.)* Maybe it's — maybe it's in the car. Did you — . . . Where'd you put your skates on, out here or in the car? *(We hear him open the doors and trunk of the car.)*

MARCI: *(Dealing with the fact that Phil won't let her touch him.)* I put them on with you. Right here. *(Beat. She looks to the sky for answers.)*

PHIL: *(Returning.)* Well, it's not // in the car —

MARCI: *(She sees a shooting star.)* Oh-oh-oh!!! Shooting star! *(She closes her eyes, and makes a wish.)*

PHIL: Wha — // Where, where?!? *(He looks for it.)*

MARCI: *(Eyes closed.)* Shh!! I'm wishing, I'm wishing!

PHIL: *(Keeps looking, and then:)* Oh, I missed it.

MARCI: *(She just looks at him.)* Yeah, you did.

PHIL: What's that supposed to mean?

MARCI: *(Finishes re-lacing her skate, eventually gets up to look for her shoe.)* Nothin' — it's just . . . not really all that surprising >

PHIL: What?

MARCI: that you didn't see it.

PHIL: What?

MARCI: The shooting star.

PHIL: Why?

MARCI: You don't pay attention, Phil. *(Beat.)*

PHIL: See, when you say things like that, I feel like you're still mad.

MARCI: I'm not.

PHIL: Marce —

MARCI: I wasn't mad, *(Frustrated by a lot more than her missing shoe.)* WHERE is my *shoe?!?!* Gosh, maybe it *is* in the car. *(Going offstage, to the car, to look for her other shoe.)* I mean, >

PHIL: It's not in the car . . .

MARCI: *(From offstage.)* I have one shoe on already. I *know* I didn't put my skates on in the car, 'cause the shoe I have on was out there . . . I changed out there, didn't I? With you? Phil? >

(Phil doesn't answer. He is trying to sort out what's going with him, his wife. He's sad.)

MARCI: *(From offstage.)* Phil? I put my shoes right next to yours, after we put our skates on, but it's not . . . there . . . This is the weirdest thing. *(Returning.)* It's not in the car, I mean, I'm not gonna put one skate on in the car, the other one on out here — . *(Sees how sad Phil is.)* What's wrong?

PHIL: *(Covering — he may have been crying.)* Huh? Oh. I'm . . . making a wish of my own. On a regular one.

MARCI: Oh.

PHIL: Wanna wish on it with me?

MARCI: Yeah. Yeah, that'd be nice. Which one?

PHIL: See Hedgehog Mountain?

MARCI: Uh-huh.

PHIL: Straight up, right above it.

MARCI: The bright one?

PHIL: Yeah.

MARCI: That one?

PHIL: Yeah.

MARCI: Right there?

PHIL: Yeah.

MARCI: Phil:

PHIL: Yeah?

MARCI: That's a planet.

PHIL: What?

MARCI: That's a planet. You're wishing on a planet.

PHIL: That's a — ?

MARCI: Yeah, >

PHIL: Well, how do you know?

MARCI: and it's *(Sings.)* ". . . When you wish upon a star," not ". . . when you wish upon a *planet //* or *Saturn* — "

PHIL: I know, I know! How do you know?

MARCI: Said on the weather, Phil. Saturn's the brightest object in the sky this month. It'll be sitting right above Hedgehog Mountain over the next bunch of weeks. They've been sayin' it on the weather all week. And your wish is never gonna come true if you're wishing on a planet.

PHIL: Well —

MARCI: You gotta pay attention.

PHIL: Why do you keep sayin' that?

MARCI: What?

PHIL: That I gotta pay attention?

MARCI: 'Cause you don't.

PHIL: What are you talkin' about? —

MARCI: Phil: Happy Anniversary.

PHIL: Huh?

MARCI: Happy Anniversary. That's what I'm talkin' about. *(Beat.)*

PHIL: I'm —. *(Can't quite say he's sorry. Beat. Then, instead of apologizing:)* I knew you were mad.

MARCI: I'm not mad, // Phil!

PHIL: You're mad at me, and pretty soon, outta nowhere, it's gonna get ugly. >

MARCI: Phil, I'm not mad, I'm —

PHIL: I mean, Marce: I'm *sorry!!* I know I missed some things, but I gotta work! I gotta take a double when Chad needs me at the mill, he's helpin' me — *us* — out, you know, // offering me the overtime!

MARCI: I know, I know —

PHIL: No, you *don't* know: Me workin' is for *us*, and the kids, and it's a lot sometimes and it messes me up!

MARCI: Phil! I'm not mad about you workin'. You gotta work. I understand that. What I don't understand is why I'm lonely, Phil. I got a husband and a coupla great kids. And I'm lonely. *(Beat.)* You just — . . . you don't pay attention anymore. You go away. And I don't know where you go, but you go somewhere where you can't pay attention and you forget your son's first hockey game and // you forget Missy's birthday and >

PHIL: Hockey equipment costs money!

MARCI: you forget your *anniversary!* I mean I brought you here hoping you'd remember about us. But you didn't. And that makes me so mad I don't know what to do anymore . . . *(Beat.)*

PHIL: You *lie.*

MARCI: What?

PHIL: You lie so bad.

MARCI: What?

PHIL: You're mad at me. But you don't *tell* me — even when I ask you over and over —

MARCI: Because *you* wouldn't pay // attention if I did tell you —

PHIL: No! No! No! Because *you* don't know how to tell me what you feel like about me, so I never know where I am, where I stand! Maybe that's why I go away. So I can know where I am for a second! And you know what, it's lonely there too, where I go. And you sent me there. You went away a long time before I did. And now all's you do is lie.

MARCI: I don't lie!

PHIL: Yes you do! You say you're not mad, but you're mad. You say you have fun, but you didn't. You didn't have fun tonight, did you?

MARCI: No.

PHIL: But you kept sayin' you did.

MARCI: I didn't. I didn't have fun, Phil. I don't have fun with you anymore. *(Beat.)* Did you?

PHIL: No. I had a rotten, lousy time. *(Beat.)*

MARCI: Well, then . . . what are we doin'? What are we waiting for? *(And then . . . a shoe that looks exactly like Marci's other shoe drops from the sky, right between Marci and Phil. Marci and Phil survey the sky, trying to figure out what just happened. Music. Phil retrieves the shoe and gives it to Marci, who puts it on. Marci gets up. She then takes the car keys out of her pocket, exits, and we hear her start the car and drive away. Phil is alone. A shooting star cuts across the night sky on the field of stars. Phil sees it. Lights fade. Transitional aurora. End of "Where It Went." After the lights have faded, and "Where It Went" is over, we begin Episode Seven, which is entitled . . .*

STORY OF HOPE

Music fades. Sound of a car approaching, idling. A car door opens, then closes. Sound of car leaving. Sound of fancy-shoed footsteps in snow approaching. Doorbell. Lights up on a woman standing on the front porch of a small home in Almost, Maine. She carries a suitcase and a purse. Note: The actor playing the man must be short or thin. This is crucial to the magic of the story. "Story of Hope" is a story of loss, and a physical manifestation of loss in the man is key — lost height [again, this is best!], lost weight — because this man is literally half the man he used to be because he has lost so much hope. You'll be surprised by how magical and heartbreaking and funny this episode is when the physical manifestation of the man's loss is crystal clear.)

MAN: *(From offstage.)* Just a minute . . . *(The lights come on in the house; then a porch light comes on. A man who is not the man he used to be answers the door a bit cautiously. Nine o'clock at night is, after all, the middle of the night. He's in pajamas and a bathrobe. He enters and stops cold. He knows this woman.)*

WOMAN: *(So absorbed in what she has to say and in what she has come to do, that she really doesn't take in the man.)* I know this isn't going to be very easy, but I was just out there all alone in the world, and I got so scared, because all I could think about was how I had no place in this world, but then I just outta nowhere realized that there was one place in this world that I did have, and that was with you, so I flew and I took a taxi to get to you, I just had to come see you, *(Finally really looking at him.)* thank God you're — . . . *(The man is not who she thought he'd be.)* Oh — . . . Wait — . . . I'm sorry. You're not — . . . I'm — . . . *(Checking to make sure she's at the right place.)* This is the house — . . . I'm so sorry — . . . Does Daniel Harding live here?, I'm looking for Daniel Harding.

MAN: You're // looking for —

WOMAN: Looking for Daniel Harding, yeah. He *lives* here. I thought. But . . . *(Off the man's confused state, realizing.)* . . . ooooh . . . he doesn't, does he? Oooh. I am so sorry. *(The woman gathers her bags, preparing to leave.)* I'm so embarrassed. "Who is this woman and what is she doing here?" *(Beat.)* I just honestly thought he'd be here. I always thought he'd be here.

Always. *(Beat.)* Do you know him? Big guy, big tall guy. Played basketball, all-Eastern Maine, center? *Strong.* Do you know him? // Hockey, too? >

MAN: Well . . . —

WOMAN: Oh, don't even answer that. That was — . I know that's a horrible question to ask a person who lives in a small town, as if everybody in small towns knows everybody else, agh!, can't believe I asked that. I don't live here anymore, but when I did, I hated it when people assumed I knew everybody in town just because it was small. It was worse than when they'd ask if we had " . . . plumbing way up there?," 'cause, you know, people in small towns really don't know each other any better than in big towns, you know that? I mean, you know who you know, and you don't know who you don't know, just like anywhere else. *(Beat.)* I'm so sorry to have bothered you. I was just so sure — . When his parents passed away, he kept the house, I heard. He lived here. He stayed here, I thought. He was one of the ones who stayed. *(Beat.)* I didn't stay. I went away.

MAN: Most people do.

WOMAN: Yeah. And I guess he did too. I never thought he would. I guess I lost track. You gotta hold onto people or you lose 'em. Wish there was something you could keep 'em in for when you need 'em . . . *(Trying to make light, she "looks for him," and "finds him" in her purse.)* Oh, there he is, perfect! *(She laughs. Not much of a response from the man. Beat. She starts to go. Stops.)* Boy it's cold. I forgot.

MAN: Yeah. *(Beat.)*

WOMAN: *(Starts to go. Stops.)* I can't *believe* — . . . ! I took a taxi here. From Bangor. *(Say, "BANG-gore." Bangor is Maine's third largest city, pop. 31,000. It is 163 miles south of Almost, Maine.)* To see him.

MAN: *(Beat. She took a taxi 163 miles.)* That's far.

WOMAN: Yeah.

MAN: That's 163 miles.

WOMAN: Yeah. This place is a little farther away from things than I remember.

MAN: Why did you do that?

WOMAN: Because I could only fly as close as Bangor and I needed to get to him as fast as I could.

MAN: Why?

WOMAN: Because I want to answer a question he asked me.

MAN: Oh?

WOMAN: The last time I saw him, he asked me a very important question and I didn't answer it, and that's just not a very nice thing to do to a person.

MAN: Well, that's bein' a little hard on yourself, don't you th//ink?

WOMAN: He asked me to marry him.

MAN: Oh. *(Beat.)* And you . . .

WOMAN: Didn't answer him. No.

MAN: *(Whistles.)*

WOMAN: Yeah. And that's why I'm here. To answer him. *(Beat. Then, realizing she probably ought to defend herself.)* I mean, I didn't answer him in the first place because I didn't *have* an answer at the time. I mean, I was going to *college,* and then . . . the *night* before I'm about to go off into the world to do what I hope and dream, he asks me, "Will you marry me?," I mean, come on! I was leaving in the morning . . . What was I supposed to do?

MAN: I don't know.

WOMAN: *(Defending herself.)* I mean, I *told* him I'd have to think about it, that I'd think it over overnight and that I'd be back before the sun came up with an answer . . . and . . . then I left. Left him standing right . . . *(Where the man is standing.)* . . . there . . . and then . . . I didn't make it back with an answer before the sun came up or . . . at all.

MAN: That sounds like an answer to me.

WOMAN: No! That wasn't my answer! I just . . . went off into the world and that's not an answer, and I think — . . .

MAN: What?

WOMAN: I think he thought I'd say, "Yes."

MAN: Well, a guy's probably not gonna ask a girl that question unless he thinks she's gonna say, "Yes. "

WOMAN: I know, and . . . I'm afraid he probably waited up all night, hoping for me to come by and I just want to tell him that I know now that you just can't do a thing like not answer a question like the one he asked me, you can't do that to a person. Especially to someone you love.

MAN: *(Taking this in.)* You loved him?

WOMAN: *(Whoah.)* Well — . I don't know if — . I mean, we were kids. *(She considers. Then, honest and true:)* Yes. I did. I do. *(Beat.)* I feel like I dashed his hopes and dreams.

MAN: *(This speech is not an attack. It's more of a rumination — one that doesn't do much to make the woman feel better.)* Oh, come on. You give yourself too much credit. He was young. That's all you need to get your hopes dashed: Be young. And everybody starts out young, so . . . everybody gets their hopes dashed, and besides . . . I don't think you really *dashed* his hopes. 'Cause if you *dash* somebody's hopes — well that's . . . kind of a nice way to let 'em down, 'cause it *hurts* . . . but it's quick. If you'd have said, "No," *that* woulda been "dashing his hopes." *(Beat. Maybe a little pointed here.)* But you didn't say, "No." You said nothin'. You just didn't answer him. At all. And that's . . . killin' hope the long, slow, painful way, 'cause it's still there, just hangin' on, never really goes away. And that's . . . kinda like givin' somebody a little less air to breathe every day. Till they die.

WOMAN: *(Well that certainly wasn't helpful.)* Yeah . . . *(Beat. At a loss:)* Well . . . thank you.

MAN: For what?

WOMAN: *(Considers. Then, honestly:)* I don't know. *(She starts to leave.)*

MAN: *(After a beat.)* Good-bye, Hope.

HOPE: Good-bye. *(Stopping.)* Agh!, I'm so . . . sorry to have bothered you . . . It's just, I was all alone out there in the world with no place in it, and I realized what I'd done to him, to Danny, and that with him was my place in the world — . . . Wait . . . *(Realization.)* You called me Hope. How did you know my name? *(The man gently presents himself, and the woman recognizes him: He's Daniel Harding.)* Danny?!?

DANIEL: Hello, Hope.

HOPE: *(In a bit of a spin.)* Danny . . . I didn't // rec — >

DANIEL: I know.

HOPE: I didn't // rec — >

DANIEL: I know.

HOPE: I didn't even // recognize you!

DANIEL: I know.

HOPE: You're so . . .

DANIEL: I know.

HOPE: . . . small.

DANIEL: Yeah . . . I, uh, lost a lotta hope. That'll do a number on you.
(Long beat. They don't hug. Or greet each other physically. It should be awful.)

HOPE: Danny: I'm so sorry I never —

DANIEL: Shh. It's OK . . . 'cause, you know somethin'? You're early.

HOPE: What?

DANNY: You're early! You said you'd be back with an answer to my question before the sun came up, and Jeezum Crow, the sun's not even close to being up yet! It only went down a few hours ago. Look how early you are! That's good of you. *(Beat. They enjoy his goodness.)*

DANNY: So, a taxi all the way from Bangor.

HOPE: Yup.

DANNY: To tell me . . . ?

(Hope is about to say, "Yes," when she is interrupted by:)

SUZETTE: *(From offstage.)* Honey? Dan? Hon? Who's there?

DANNY: *(Beat.)* Just somebody . . . needs directions.

SUZETTE: It's awful late for directions.

DANNY: Yeah — Suzette, listen . . . *(Beat.)* . . . I'll be right in.

SUZETTE: OK . . . *(Long beat.)*

DANNY: I — . . .

HOPE: What?

DANNY: *(Simple — not precious.)* I hope you find it, Hope. Your place in this world. *(Beat.)* Bye.

HOPE: Good-bye, Danny. *(Danny goes inside. Hope lingers — she is at a loss. Finally — after all these years — she answers Danny. She knows he won't hear her. She knows it wouldn't matter if he did. But she answers him anyway.)* Yes. *(Beat. Then, smaller and to herself:)* Yes.

(Music. Hope starts to go; she turns back. The porch light goes out. Lights fade. Transitional aurora. End of "Story of Hope." As the lights fade, and "Story of Hope" is over, we begin Episode Eight, which is entitled . . .

SEEING THE THING

Music fades. Sound of two snowmobiles approaching and parking. The lights from their headlights can be seen offstage left as they approach. Lights up on the winterized porch of a small shack, in the middle of nowhere — but still within the "town" limits of Almost, Maine. Rhonda and Dave — the snowmobilers — enter, kicking the snow off their boots. They are carrying their snowmobile helmets and are dressed in layer upon layer upon layer of snowmobile/winter clothing. Note to actors: "Arctic Cat" and "Polaris" [Say, "pull-AIR-iss."] are snowmobile brands. Dave has a present — a wrapped painting — behind his back. Beat.)

RHONDA: OK. This is it. You're in. You're inside.

DAVE: This is the porch. *(He'd like to go farther inside.)*

RHONDA: It's winterized. *(This is as far as he's getting. Beat.)* So, Dave: *What?!* What do you gotta do in here that you couldn't do outside?

DAVE: Well, I got somethin', here, for ya, here. *(He presents his wrapped gift, creating "awkward present beat #1.")*

RHONDA: What's this?

DAVE: It's — . It's — . It's — . *(Changing the subject.)* Boy, that was fun, tonight, Rhonda! >

RHONDA: Yeah, was!

DAVE: I mean, twenty miles out there, >

RHONDA: Yeah!

DAVE: beans and franks at the Snowmobile Club, >

RHONDA: Yeah!

DAVE: twenty miles back, coupla beers at the Moose Paddy!

RHONDA: Awesome!

DAVE: Yeah, and, boy, you flew on your new sled, // man!

RHONDA: It's a Polaris, man!

DAVE: I know and you whupped *("Whupped" sounds like "looked" or "cooked.")* my butt!

RHONDA: Yeah! That's what you get for ridin' an Arctic Cat: *(Really takin' it to him.)* Ya get yer butt whupped! And I whupped it!

DAVE: I know!

RHONDA: Whupped your butt! >

DAVE: I know!

RHONDA: Whupped it! >

DAVE: I know!

RHONDA: Whupped your butt, Arctic-Cat man!!

DAVE: I know, I know, I'm not sayin' ya didn't!

RHONDA: *(Settling down.)* That was fun. *(Beat. Everything stops again. They look at the wrapped gift. Call this "awkward present beat #2.")*

DAVE: So, this is, um . . . Well, we been . . . together now —

RHONDA: *(Scoffing.)* Together?

DAVE: Well —

RHONDA: *Together?* What are you *talkin'* about, "together???" >

DAVE: Well, we been friends for quite a few years now, and, well —

RHONDA: You gettin' all girl on me?

DAVE: — shh! — and, and, and — . . . And, here. *(He presents her with his present.)*

RHONDA: *(These two don't give each other presents.)* What are you doin' here, bud?

DAVE: Open it.

RHONDA: "Together." Hmm. I don't know about this . . .

DAVE: Just open it.

RHONDA: *(She opens the present downstage center. The present — a wrapped canvas painting — must be opened in such a way that the audience cannot see what it is. Once Rhonda opens it, she props the painting up against a crate — still so that the audience can't see it. She has no idea what it is a painting is of. Beat.)* What is it?

DAVE: What do you mean, what is it? Can't you . . . see what // it is —

RHONDA: It's a picture . . .

DAVE: Yeah . . .

RHONDA: A paintin'.

DAVE: Yeah.

RHONDA: Where'd you get this? It looks homemade.

DAVE: What do you mean, it looks homemade?

RHONDA: Looks like someone really painted it.

DAVE: Well, someone really *did* paint it.

RHONDA: *(Realizing.)* Did you paint this?

DAVE: Yeah.

RHONDA: For me?

DAVE: Yeah.

RHONDA: Oh . . . *(She has no idea what it is, what to make of it.)* Why?

DAVE: *(Sad.)* Well . . . *(He painted it 'cause he thinks the whole world of her.)*

RHONDA: I mean . . . thank you! // Thank you, thanks, yeah.

DAVE: There you go!, that's what people say!, there you go! . . . You're welcome.

RHONDA: *(Sitting in chair, center, staring at her painting.)* So, Dave . . . I didn't know you *painted.*

DAVE: Yeah . . . This is — . . . *(He adjusts the painting, because she propped it up wrong. Then:)* I'm takin' adult ed art. At nights. Merle Haslem over at the high school's teachin' it, it's real good. And this is my version of one of those stare-at-it-until-you-see-the-thing things. Ever seen one of these? Some of the old painters did it with dots. They called it — *(Searches, but can't come up with, "pointillism.")* . . . somethin' . . . but I did it with a buncha little blocks of colors, see, and if you just look at the blocks of colors, it's just colors, but if you step back and look at the whole thing, it's not just little blocks of colors, it's a picture of something.

RHONDA: Picture of what?

DAVE: I'm not gonna tell you, you have to figure it out.

RHONDA: Oh, come on, Dave!

DAVE: No, it takes a little time, it can be a little frustrating.

RHONDA: Well, why would you give me somethin' that's gonna *frustrate?!?*

DAVE: No, no, no, I just mean you gotta not *try* to look for anything, that's what'll frustrate you. You gotta just *kinda* look at it, so it doesn't *know* that you're lookin' at it.

RHONDA: What're you talkin' about?

DAVE: You gotta trick it! *(Demonstrates "tricking it.")* Trick it! See? Gotta not let it know! And hopefully you'll eventually see what it is. It's a common thing, it's somethin' everybody knows.
(Rhonda tries "tricking it.")

DAVE: There ya go, there ya go!

RHONDA: *(Gives up on "tricking it.")* This is stupid. I don't see anything.

DAVE: No, you were doin' good!

RHONDA: Dave!

DAVE: All right, all right, then, do this: Do what you usually do around the house at night and check it out real casual-like, *(He demonstrates "checking the painting out real casual-like.")* and —

RHONDA: I usually have a Bud and talk to you on the phone.

DAVE: Well, do that. Where's the kitchen? *(Starting into the house.)* // I'll get you a Bud, and you can talk to me —

RHONDA: *(Stopping him — she doesn't want him going inside.)* N-n-n-n-no! >

DAVE: What?

RHONDA: I'm outta Bud. Only got Natty Lite.

DAVE: *(Starting back into the house.)* All right, I'll get you a Natty Lite, // and you can have your beer and talk to me —

RHONDA: *(Stopping him.)* N-n-no!

DAVE: Why not? Come on, let's go inside and get us a coupla beers! >

RHONDA: No! *(Back to the painting.)* We gotta trick this thing, right? See? I'm trickin' it, I'm trickin' it! // Trickin' it! Trickin' it!

DAVE: It's what people who've known each other for a long time do. *Come on!!* HEY!!! *(Stopping her "trickin' it" routine.)* Quit it! How many years I know ya, I come all the way out here every Friday night, and I never been inside your house for beers?! That's unnatural. It's unnatural, // Rhonda! So let's do what's the *natural* thing to do and go inside and have some beers —

RHONDA: I don't care what it is, I gotta trick this thing. Hey! Hey-hey-hey, *DAVE!!* Quit runnin' your suck! I gotta look. At this thing. *(She sits; stares straight at the painting, which frustrates Dave.)*

DAVE: You're doin' it wrong!

RHONDA: Shh!

DAVE: You gotta trick it, you gotta trick it! —

RHONDA: Hey-hey-hey!, OK, OK!! I got somethin'!

DAVE: Yeah?

RHONDA: Yeah! Yeah-yeah-yeah: roadkill.

DAVE: What?

RHONDA: Roadkill. Dead raccoon in the middle of the road.

DAVE: What? No! That's not what it is! —

RHONDA: OK. Deer. Dead bloody deer // in the middle of the road —

DAVE: What? No! Rhonda! It's not // a dead deer in the middle of the road!

RHONDA: OK: moose. >

DAVE: What?

RHONDA: Dead bloody moose in the middle of the road.

DAVE: RHONDA!! No!! No!! That's not somethin' I'd wanna paint!!!, // That's not even close to what it is! Dead moose?!? Come on!!! >

RHONDA: Well, that's what I see, I don't know what it is, // don't get *mad*, Jeezum Crow!?!?

DAVE: You don't see what it is?!?

RHONDA: No.

DAVE: Well, can I give you a hint?

RHONDA: Yeah!

(Dave kisses her right on the mouth. That's the hint. She immediately gets up/pulls away. Then, angry/flustered:)

RHONDA: What are you doin'?!? *(Little beat.)* What was that?!? Why did you do that?!?

DAVE: 'Cause I was giving you a hint — . . .

RHONDA: Don't ever do that again. *Ever!* AND GET OUTTA HERE! *(She storms off into the house. Beat.)*

DAVE: *(Gathering his things. To himself:)* Jeezum Crow . . . *(Then, exploding:)* HEY, RHONDA!!

RHONDA: What?

DAVE: YOU REALLY ARE WHAT THEY SAY!!

RHONDA: What? What do they say?

DAVE: THAT YOU'RE A LITTLE HUNG UP, THERE!!!

RHONDA: *(Re-entering forcefully.)* Who says that?!?

DAVE: *(Retreating — she's tough.)* Everybody.

RHONDA: *(Continuing to advance.)* Everybody who?

DAVE: *(Retreating.)* Everybody, Rhonda. It's what people in town say . . .

RHONDA: When?

DAVE: When they're *talkin'.* They say that you're a little hung up, there, so I gotta be a little persistent, there, they say, and, boy, they were right!

RHONDA: Who says?

DAVE: *(Tough question to answer, 'cause these are their best buds.)* Suzette.

RHONDA: *Suzette?*

DAVE: Yeah, and Dan . . .

RHONDA: *(Disbelief.)* Suzette and Dan *Harding* say that I'm a little hung up, there, and that you gotta be a little persistent there . . . ???

DAVE: Yeah.

RHONDA: Well, who else?

DAVE: Marci . . .

RHONDA: *Marci?!?*

DAVE: Yeah, and Phil, // and — >

RHONDA: Marci and *Phil?!?* —

DAVE: — yeah — and Randy and Chad, and >

RHONDA: *Randy and Chad?!?* —

DAVE: Lendall and Gayle and >

RHONDA: *Gayle?* —

DAVE: Marvalyn and Eric and >

RHONDA: Marvalyn . . . ?

DAVE: and Jimmy, and Sandrine, and East, and >

RHONDA: *East??*

DAVE: that's just to name a few . . .

RHONDA: *(Deeply, deeply hurt.)* Well, why would they — . . . ? I love those guys. I'm good to those guys. Why would they say that about me? That's talkin' about me. That's mean.

DAVE: No — . I don't think they're bein' mean, Rhonda. I think they said that *(i.e., that "you're a little hung up there")* to me about you to kinda warn me what I was gettin' myself into with you. 'Cause they like you. And me. Us. They're rootin' fer us, Rhonda.

RHONDA: Who's rootin' fer us?

DAVE: Everybody! East and Gayle and Lendall and Randy and Chad —

RHONDA: Well, they never told me that, that they're "rootin'" fer us —

DAVE: Well, that's 'cause you're a little hung up, there, Rhonda! *(Beat. He has scraped something deep inside Rhonda.)* Just — . . . I'm sorry if I made you mad. I don't know what I did wrong. I just gave you a kiss. I mean, just . . . why not give me one back? It's the polite thing to do, you know, get a kiss/give a kiss, very fair. Just . . . give me a kiss, Rhonda . . . *(Beat.)*

RHONDA: I don't know how.

DAVE: What do you mean?

RHONDA: I don't know how. I've never done it before.

DAVE: You never . . . kissed?

RHONDA: I won arm wrestling at every Winter Carnival from fifth grade on and I work in plywood at Bushey's Lumber Mill, and that's not what most men wanna . . . want.

DAVE: Oh, now, where do you get that?

RHONDA: From *everybody.*

DAVE: Well then . . . you got it wrong, Rhonda, 'cause I gotta tell you, there's a lotta guys, that take good, long looks at you! *(Beat.)* Holy Cow: So, you never — you never [kissed . . . or had . . . relations] . . . ?

RHONDA: No.

DAVE: Well, gosh, I think that's kinda neat. *(Beat.)* You know what?, do me a favor: Try givin' me a kiss and see what happens. And I'm not gonna make fun of you or nothin' bad like that, I promise . . .

RHONDA: *(Sitting in her chair.)* No . . . No . . . No . . . Let's do the *(Back to the painting.)* this: Is it apples? Cherries? Big open-faced strawberry rhubarb pie —

(Dave kisses Rhonda. For a while. Eventually, Dave gently breaks the kiss, checks on her. She's OK. Looks she liked it this time. The painting should be in Rhonda' eye line during/after this kiss, because now . . . she's finally going to be able to see what Dave has painted for her.)

RHONDA: Oh, Dave . . . I see it! It's a — . I see it. It's — . . . *(Getting up from her chair and getting the painting — so the audience can't see it.)* It's nice. That's really nice. It's good. You're good at this! *(She clutches the painting to her chest — the audience still can't see it.)*

DAVE: Yeah?

RHONDA: Yeah.

DAVE: *(Kisses Rhonda. The painting is squished between their bodies — audience still can't see what it is!)* And *you* are very good at *this* . . .

RHONDA: *(Kisses Dave hard — and she really is very good at it, which catches Dave by surprise.)* I thought it'd be hard! *(She kisses him again, fast and hard.)* And it's not!!! *(She kisses him again, fast and hard.)* At all . . . *(The painting — now an afterthought — ends up facing upstage in Rhonda's chair; the audience still hasn't seen it.)* And I feel like I wanna do it for a long time, but I also feel like I wanna do somethin' else . . . next . . . *(Rhonda is just about jumping out of her skin, dying to know what's next.)* but I don't know what that is.

DAVE: I do.

(Music. The anticipation is killing them both. But finally, Dave musters his courage, and shows Rhonda what they might wanna do next . . . by gently unzipping her jacket and taking it off. He then unzips his jacket — with her

help! — and takes it off. Then he takes off his boots; indicates that Rhonda should do the same. And Rhonda does. Dave then takes off his snowmobile pants; Rhonda takes off hers. And then Rhonda and Dave start to take off layer after layer after layer [the more layers the better — and funnier] of snowmobile/winter clothes, which they do more and more rapidly and with more and more intention until it's a bit of a frenzy, and we end up with two people from Northern Maine facing each other in only their long johns . . . and a great big pile of winter clothes on the ground between them. Beat. They're dying for each other, breathing heavily.)

DAVE: You wanna know what comes next-next?

RHONDA: Yeah.

DAVE: Why don't we go inside . . . and I'll show you . . .

RHONDA: Well, how long is it gonna take?

DAVE: Well . . . it could take all night. Maybe longer . . .

RHONDA: Well, wait *(Music fades.)* — we're workin' tomorrow, first shift.

DAVE: Says who? *(Beat. He shrugs — he has an idea.)*

RHONDA: *(Gets what he's saying!)* You mean call in? We're callin' in?!? *(Music. This is a very exciting idea — because these people never call in!)* We're callin' in!!! *(Very excited!)* We're callin' Chad!!! *(Very, very excited!)* 'Cause you and me, we're not working first shift or *any* shift tomorrow. *(Still very, very excited, Rhonda starts to exit into the house; stops — and this is Rhonda's own special brand of seduction:)* You get yourself *inside*, here, Mister Arctic-Cat Man and show me what's *next! (She raucously exits into the house.)*

(Beat. Dave is amazed — a bit stunned. The way this has panned out is far beyond his wildest dreams!! And it's because of his painting, which he now picks up — still so the audience can't see it — and has a moment with. He looks at it, clutches it, and gives thanks! He is interrupted by:)

RHONDA: *DAVE!*

(Snapped out of his reverie, Dave exits, to live out this dream. As he does this, he casually puts the painting on the chair so it's propped up on the chair's arms, against the chair's back so that the audience can finally see that it is a painting of a HEART — just a big, plain, red HEART on a white background. Lights fade. The HEART remains lit. Music up. End of "Seeing the Thing." After the lights have faded on "Seeing the Thing," the painting of the heart remains brilliantly lit. It seems to glow brighter for a while, and then, suddenly — music ends/blackout/transitional aurora, and we move to the . . .

EPILOGUE

Music. Lights up to reveal Pete, still exactly where we left him in the Inter-logue: sitting on his bench, looking off left to where Ginette exited. His snow-ball is still sitting next to him. Pete gets up, taking his snowball with him, and goes toward where Ginette went off, to see if he can see her. And then . . . there's a wonderful little swell in the music as . . . Ginette slowly — maybe a little wearily — enters from the other side of the stage, stage right! It starts to SNOW! Pete senses Ginette; turns to her; starts toward her — but stops and, first, nonverbally asks, using the snowball, if she's been all the way around the world . . . and she nods, "Yes," because she has! She's been all the way around the world and she's back — and she's "close" again. Pete tosses his snowball behind him, and Ginette and Pete run to each other and hug. They go to the bench, sit, and, on the last chord of the music, resume looking at the stars. The northern lights appear. Music ends. Lights fade to black.)

END OF PLAY

WAR IN PARAMUS

Barbara Dana

for my mother and father

PLAYWRIGHT'S BIOGRAPHY

Barbara Dana is an award-winning author of books for children and young adults. Her books include *Zucchini* (Washington Irving Children's Book Choice Award; Maude Hart Lovelace Award; Land of Enchantment Children's Book Choice Award), *Zucchini Out West, Necessary Parties* (ALA Best Book), *Crazy Eights, Rutgers and the Water Snouts,* and *Young Joan,* a novel based on the life of Joan of Arc. She cowrote the award-winning screen version of her novel, *Necessary Parties* (International Monitor Award), aired on PBS. Other screenplays include *Chu-Chu and the Philly Flash,* and the short film *T.G.I.F,* honored at the New York Film Festival. Barbara is an actor as well as a writer, having appeared on stage, in films, and on television since the age of sixteen. She is a member of the Dramatists Guild. *War in Paramus* is her first play.

ORIGINAL PRODUCTION

The world premiere of *War in Paramus* took place on October 11, 2005 at Abingdon Theatre Company in New York City. The cast was as follows, in order of appearance:

THELMA GARDNER	Anne Letscher
KEVIN PARNELL	Jeremy Beiler
VIOLET GARDNER	Kate Bushmann
WILLIAM GARDNER JR.	Matthew Arkin
HARRY TORONTO	Gene Gallerano
PHILIP RISER	David McElfresh

The play was directed by Austin Pendleton. Scenic Design, Michael Schweikhardt; Costume Design, Wade Laboissonniere; Lighting Design, David Castaneda; Sound Design, David Margolin Lawson; Fight Choreographer, Rick Sodelet; Production Stage Manager, Mary E. Leach; Production Manager, Gabriel Hainer Evansohn; Press Representative, Shirley Herz Associates; Casting, William Schill. Abingdon Theatre Company: Artistic Directors, Jan Buttram, Pamela Paul; Managing Director, Samuel J. Bellinger; Associate Artistic Director, Kim T. Sharp.

NOTE: The premiere production of *War in Paramus* at Abingdon Theatre Company was performed without an intermission.

PLAYWRIGHT'S NOTE
War in Paramus: Where did it come from?

In the fall of 1999, after moving to a new house, unopened cardboard boxes remained stacked on the floor of my study for months. I was working on a couple of things at the time, a novel and a play, with a fast-approaching deadline for the novel, so I just left the boxes to fend for themselves and worked around them. When I finally found the time to deal with them I discovered, among the old tax returns, acting résumés, headshots and banking statements, the first draft of a play. I had written it thirty years before and had pretty much forgotten about it. It had needed work, but I hadn't done it, opting instead to tell a version of the story in a novel for young adults. I took the play out of the box, remembering having written it for myself, Austin Pendleton, Elizabeth Wilson, and Rochelle Oliver.

"I wonder if this is any good," I thought.

Being in a family of actors, I called my sons to see if we could have a reading of the play so I could hear it. A few weeks later we sat around the table in my son Anthony's Brooklyn loft with a bunch of actor friends. As I listened to them read, I got excited about the idea of working on the play. Then Kate Bushmann, who read the part I had written for Elizabeth Wilson, asked if she could show it to Abingdon Theatre Company, and Sam Groom, who read the Father, asked if he could show it to HB Playwrights.

Many readings followed. The second draft was read at Abingdon, the third received a staged reading at Hudson Stage Company in Westchester and was directed by Austin, who worked with me on the play after each of several subsequent readings, which he also directed. In 2003 the play was done in workshop at HB Playwrights, directed by Billy Carden, where further work was done on the script.

I had a thrill during auditions for the premiere production at Abingdon when Austin read the part of "Kevin" in a scene I had written for him all those years ago. He was, of course, wonderful.

My thanks to Austin, Billy Carden, HB Playwrights, Abingdon Theatre Company, Hudson Stage Company, my sons Anthony and Matthew Arkin, who acted in the productions, my daughters-in-law, Amelia Campbell and Pamela Newkirk-Arkin, who did many readings of the play, my granddaughter, Molly Arkin, who played "Thelma" in a benefit performance, Sam Groom, Kate Bushmann, Elizabeth Wilson, Rochelle Oliver, Jean Schneider, my agents, Phyllis Wender and Sonia Pabley, all the wonderful actors who helped develop the play and to Judith Schmidt who helped me get the play out of the box.

CHARACTERS

THELMA GARDNER: fifteen, a rebel

KEVIN PARNELL: middle twenties, a law student, earnest, likable, a bit shy

VIOLET GARDNER: an attractive woman in her forties, a housewife, bright, energetic, often feels overqualified for her job

WILLIAM GARDNER JR.: about fifty, gentle, with the soul of an artist, designs boxes

JENNIFER GARDNER: twenty-two, a delicate beauty, about to be married

HARRY TORONTO: seventeen, charismatic, with a genuine sweetness and a dangerous edge

PHILIP RISER: sixteen, loyal, a follower

SETTING

Paramus, New Jersey, 1970.

WAR IN PARAMUS

ACT I
SCENE ONE

A Friday evening in October.

Lights up revealing two rooms of the Gardner home, a modest apartment in a development of two-story garden apartments. The main area, the living room, is prominent. Thelma's bedroom, upstage, right of center, is raised a couple of steps, as is the hallway stage right, leading to the bathroom, den, and additional bedrooms. The living room furnishings seem to have been ordered from the pages of a Sears catalogue. The effect is unartistic and conventional, with many lace curtains, knick-knacks and pictures of fruit. There is a couch, a coffee table, a large chair, a desk, a hutch, TV, etc. Several model boats are displayed. The front door is upstage, left of center; the swinging kitchen door, stage left. Thelma's room is a mess. The bed is unmade. Clothes, stuffed animals, a football, movie magazines, shoes, and records seem to be overflowing. The bureau drawers are open, with clothes pouring forth. There is a portable record player on the floor. A handwritten sign is taped to the wall above the bureau: "DON'T COMPROMISE YOURSELF. YOU'RE ALL YOU'VE GOT," it says in large, black letters. A poster of Janis Joplin is taped to the wall above the bed.

Thelma Gardner and Kevin Parnell are seated in the living room. Thelma is fifteen, angry, restless, imaginative, honest, with innate sensitivity and strength, part child, part fiery young woman. She wears torn jeans and a rumpled army shirt. She sits on the floor, staring at Kevin, who is in the large upholstered chair. Kevin is in his mid-twenties, earnest, intelligent, and a bit shy. He handles details with meticulous care, while keeping his distance from the deeper mysteries of life. Thelma studies him as she might if he were an intriguing exhibit in an anthropology class.

THELMA: You don't say much, do you?

KEVIN: Hm? . . . what?

THELMA: You don't say much, do you. You don't talk an awful lot.

KEVIN: Oh. Well. No, actually I don't, I guess. I guess that's true. I don't talk an awful lot.

THELMA: You certainly don't. What are you, shy, or what?

KEVIN: I wouldn't say that. It's just that I . . . Well, yes. I guess I am a little shy.

THELMA: That's a shame.

KEVIN: I don't know if it's a shame. It's, ah, not, ah . . . Well.

(Kevin looks toward the hallway.)

THELMA: My sister's not ready.

KEVIN: I can see that.

THELMA: *(Grim.)* I'm entertaining you until she's ready.

KEVIN: That's nice.

THELMA: It certainly is. What do you want to do?

KEVIN: I don't know. Just sit here, I guess. She'll be along any minute, won't she?

THELMA: No. It will be quite some time. Want to play Monopoly?

KEVIN: I don't think so.

THELMA: I'll give you Boardwalk and Park Place.

KEVIN: No.

THELMA: That was a good offer. You were pretty stupid to turn that down.

KEVIN: I don't feel like playing Monopoly now.

THELMA: No problem.

KEVIN: *(A beat.)* How's school?

THELMA: I don't go.

KEVIN: You don't go to school?

THELMA: I haven't been feeling well.

KEVIN: I'm sorry.

THELMA: It's not your fault.

(Kevin looks for Jennifer.)

THELMA: *(Continuing.)* Jennifer's not ready yet.

KEVIN: Right.

THELMA: You want to watch TV?

KEVIN: No.

THELMA: That's good.

KEVIN: Why?

THELMA: It's broken.

KEVIN: Oh. Well.

(Attempting comraderie.)

It's a good thing I wasn't counting on watching a program.

THELMA: I'll say! My God! You don't know how good! . . . The TV repairman's truck broke down.

KEVIN: Huh.

THELMA: Want to hear the radio?

KEVIN: I'm fine just sitting here.

THELMA: Bet you a dollar it's the news. Want to bet?

KEVIN: Not really.

(Thelma turns on the radio.)

RADIO ANNOUNCER: . . . just weeks after it was revealed that the United States Air Force had secretly bombed Cambodia. Reports followed that the Air Force, along with the Department of Defense, had falsified reports to hide the fact. National Security Council head, Henry Kissinger, urged Americans to . . .

(Thelma shuts off the radio.)

THELMA: You owe me a dollar.

KEVIN: We didn't bet.

THELMA: How come you're not over there decimating poor innocent villagers?

KEVIN: Just lucky, I guess.

THELMA: Do you have some kind of congenital weakness?

KEVIN: Not really.

THELMA: What do you have?

KEVIN: Nothing much.

THELMA: You're hiding something.

KEVIN: No, I'm not.

THELMA: You are. I can tell.

KEVIN: I have flat feet.

THELMA: What is that?

KEVIN: It doesn't matter.

THELMA: What do you do, Kevin?

KEVIN: I'm going for my law degree at Columbia.

THELMA: Well, that helps with the draft.

KEVIN: Who knows these days.

THELMA: Who knows anything, ever, when you come down to it, right?

KEVIN: I don't know about that.

THELMA: You prove my point.

(Kevin looks for Jennifer.)

THELMA: (Continuing.) Jennifer's not ready yet. You work, or anything, or are you just a student?

KEVIN: No, I work. I'm a clerk.

THELMA: A clerk! No kidding! (A beat.) What does that mean?

KEVIN: It means I'm not in charge.

THELMA: Oh, that's too bad.

KEVIN: Well, no. It's not, really. I mean, someday I will. . . . Be.

THELMA: Patience, patience.

KEVIN: Yes.

THELMA: Did anyone ever tell you you look like a turtle?

KEVIN: Not until now.

THELMA: It's amazing! The more I look at you, the more you look like a turtle! *(Laughing.)* Oh, God, I can't stand it!

KEVIN: *(Not amused.)* That's funny.

THELMA: I love to do that, think of what animals people look like. My sister's a weasel.

KEVIN: A weasel?

THELMA: You can't trust her across the street.

KEVIN: Huh.

THELMA: My mother's a fox and my father's a slow loris.

KEVIN: What's that?

THELMA: A small, arborial, nocturnal primate with a vestigial tail.

KEVIN: What are you?

THELMA: I'm a tiger.

KEVIN: Ha.

THELMA: Don't laugh. I wouldn't kid you. Do you sleep with Jennifer?

KEVIN: Now, just a minute . . .

THELMA: Oh, I know something about you! Oh, you there, sitting right there, I know something about you . . .

KEVIN: Stop that.

THELMA: Oh, you there . . .

KEVIN: Don't do that. Stop it. Come on.

THELMA: I'm fifteen . . . It's an awful age, really. I don't know why people don't go crazy being this age, but there you are. Maybe they do. Maybe that's what's wrong. Maybe everybody goes crazy when they're fifteen. Something's certainly wrong. *(Cries out.)* Aaahhh!!! *(She falls to the floor.)* *(Kevin looks for Jennifer.)*

THELMA: *(Continuing.)* Jennifer's not ready yet.

KEVIN: Don't say that anymore, OK? I can see she's not ready. I see that.

THELMA: Fine. Where are you going tonight?

KEVIN: *(Mad now.)* We're going to a movie.

THELMA: What movie?

KEVIN: They're re-running *West Side Story.*

THELMA: Are you going to see it?

KEVIN: That's what I said, *West Side Story.*

THELMA: No, you didn't. You said they were re-running *West Side Story.* You didn't say you were going to see it.

KEVIN: Well, yes, we're going to see it.

THELMA: That's nice . . . Haven't you seen it?

KEVIN: No.

THELMA: It's not without violence.

KEVIN: We'll manage.

THELMA: There's a murder.

KEVIN: Don't tell me what happens!

(Violet Gardner enters from the kitchen with a glass of sherry. She is an attractive woman in her mid-forties. She is smart, with an energetic flair. She tries valiantly to lift the spirits of those around her, and, although she doesn't know it, most importantly her own. She calls back over her shoulder:)

VIOLET: . . . and soak the pots!

(On her way in:)

Whew!!!

(To Kevin; cheery.)

Well, that wasn't so bad. Dishes don't take long at all once you get to them. If there's something you don't want to do, get right to it! Isn't that right, Kevin?

KEVIN: Oh, yes.

VIOLET: Sorry to leave you alone.

KEVIN: *(A look to Thelma.)* I wasn't a . . . ah . . .

VIOLET: *(To Thelma; offhand.)* Get off the floor, dear. It isn't nice. *(To Kevin.)* Refresh your Tab?

KEVIN: I'm fine.

(Thelma crawls up the stairs to the hall and into her room. She falls on the bed, arms outstretched, lies motionless. Violet continues cheerfully and with purpose to Kevin.)

VIOLET: Well! . . . Jennifer's a bit tardy this evening, isn't she? *(Playful, flirtatious.)* Can you stand it?

KEVIN: Ha, ha. Oh, well.

VIOLET: *(Calls out toward kitchen.)* Just leave those dishes on the drainer, dear! You needn't dry those! *(To Kevin; extraordinary news.)* The invitations are ordered!

KEVIN: Oh, wonderful!

VIOLET: A June wedding! What could be nicer?

KEVIN: Nothing.

(William Gardner Jr. (Bill) enters from the kitchen. He is about fifty, soft-spoken, gentle, preoccupied, with the soul of an artist. The harsh realities of life have been too much for him. He views the world from inside the relative safety of his own world. He carries a dish towel.)

BILL: *(Entering.)* I'll dry the rest of them if you want me to.

VIOLET: No, dear, that's fine. You sit down and rest.

(Bill starts to sit, stops.)

BILL: *(The towel.)* I'll put this back.

VIOLET: You do that.

(Bill returns to the kitchen. Violet continues entertaining Kevin with what she considers to be a fascinating and overwhelmingly humorous story.)

VIOLET: *(Continuing.)* I cannot begin to tell you what I went through, Kevin. Would you like to hear? You probably wouldn't be interested in all this, but it's quite an amazing story.

KEVIN: No, I would.

VIOLET: It's amazing. The inefficiency of modern business, that's where it begins. That's right where it begins.

KEVIN: Oh, yes.

VIOLET: *(Confidential.)* I never did like Bloomingdale's.

KEVIN: No?

VIOLET: I never did like it. It has been highly recommended, but I never did like it.

KEVIN: Well, it's not much of a store.

(Bill enters from the kitchen, whistling. He passes through the living room on his way to the hall.)

VIOLET: Where are you going?

BILL: I'm just going in here for a minute.

(He exits, hallway.)

VIOLET: It's hard to imagine. It is hard to imagine that modern business can be run in such a slipshod fashion. I was quite put off I can tell you.

KEVIN: I can imagine.

VIOLET: I was. Let me begin at the beginning. I went in and of course stopped at information to ask where the invitations would be.

KEVIN: Of course.

VIOLET: Well, she sent me to the wrong floor!

KEVIN: No.

VIOLET: She did! Can you imagine? In a growing concern like Bloomingdale's? I was taken aback.

KEVIN: Of course.

VIOLET: I was. Well. That's just the beginning! There was nothing even resembling an invitation on the sixth floor, which is where she sent me, so I finally asked someone in GARDEN FURNITURE!

KEVIN: *(Losing interest.)* Wow.

VIOLET: Well, what was I to do? . . . So . . . I asked someone in garden furniture where the wedding invitations would be and he said he had always been under the impression that they were in stationery on the first!

KEVIN: No.

VIOLET: How do you like that? After going up the six floors, you're told to go back to the main. Well, that was enough right there.

KEVIN: Of course.

VIOLET: Well, to make a long story short, he was right, the invitations were in stationery on the main, blessed be the man in garden furniture, and I went back down the six floors and sat myself at the selection counter.

KEVIN: Good for you.

VIOLET: Yes! But do you think I got waited on? Twelve minutes I counted on my watch before service was given.

KEVIN: Really?

VIOLET: Twelve minutes! Well, I wasn't even in the mood by that time, but I had come this far . . . *(Laughing now.)* . . . and I wasn't about to turn back now!

KEVIN: *(Laughing too.)* No!

VIOLET: Ha, ha. *(She sighs.)* Oh, dear. Well. Anyway, my salesgirl was some student from Hunter, part-time too, I'd wager, and I could see right away that I was in for something.

KEVIN: Oh, yes!

VIOLET: Phew!

(Violet moves to the hutch to refresh her sherry.)

KEVIN: What were you in for?

VIOLET: *(The most amazing story ever told.)* She showed me some of the most awful wedding invitations I have ever seen and I said, "Come now, you must have something else." Well, she didn't think so and she didn't know and one thing and another and finally she said she had one more book, she didn't think it was any good, but she'd show it to me anyway. Well, they were lovely!

KEVIN: *(Squirming with boredom.)* Huh.

VIOLET: Lovely! Any one of them you would be happy to send. Can you believe it? But don't think we're through yet. Ha, ha. Isn't this something?

KEVIN: Ha, ha. I should say.

VIOLET: Ha, ha. Oh, my. *(Gains composure.)* Well. I finally made my selection and she said, "Oh, dear, they've stopped making that!" No more to be had! Can you imagine? Anyway, she pointed out a nice one that they were making and then, get this, she proceeded to tell me I could have it in six months! Six months! Well, I told her that was too long. Too long! I was getting angry.

KEVIN: And rightly so.

VIOLET: I should say! Well! Listen to this. She made out the order in her relief girl's order book, or something and I can tell you what I did then.

KEVIN: What did you do?

VIOLET: I called the manager.

KEVIN: Of course.

VIOLET: I said, "GET ME THE MANAGER!" I said it loud. Just like that! "GET ME THE MANAGER!"

KEVIN: Good for you.

VIOLET: Yes. Well. He got it all straightened out and as I said in prefacing my little story, the invitations are ordered, but, ha, ha, I'll believe it when I see them. Isn't that something?!

KEVIN: It certainly is!

(In her room, Thelma turns on her record player. Janis Joplin sings loudly, "Tell Mama." Thelma jumps onto the bed and begins dancing.)

VIOLET: *(Calls.)* Thelma! Turn off that music! . . . Thelma!! *(Rising; politely to Kevin.)* Excuse me.

(Violet crosses to hallway steps, right, and up to Thelma's room. She bursts in.)

VIOLET: *(Continuing; to Thelma.)* Turn it off!!!

(Alone in the living room, Kevin vents his pent-up boredom in a silent scream, ending in a tiny peep, or perhaps by banging his head against the wall. Thelma shuts off the music. Violet returns to the living room.)

VIOLET: *(Continuing; to Kevin.)* So!

(An awkward beat. Thelma enters the living room.)

THELMA: Where's Jennifer?

VIOLET: Don't interrupt.

THELMA: She'll be late for the rumble.

(Thelma sits on the floor.)

VIOLET: Don't sit on the floor, dear. Did you clean your room?

THELMA: I forgot.

VIOLET: And check the chart. It's your night for garbage.

THELMA: *(Sings loudly.)* Garbage!

VIOLET: *(Sweetly, to Kevin.)* We have a chart, Kevin, you may have noticed, which hangs in the kitchen.

(Thelma picks up a magazine, reads.)

VIOLET: *(Continuing.)* Don't read in front of company, Thelma, you've been told.

(Violet takes magazine from Thelma.)

VIOLET: *(Continuing; to Kevin.)* We rotate our assignments. *(Playful, flirtatious.)* Mother can't be everywhere, can she?

KEVIN: Oh, no.

VIOLET: That's right. I'll tell you one thing, Kevin, your future bride has a fine record. She gets a star each week which means she has never once been asked to tend to her duties. Thelma doesn't do a thing.

(Jennifer enters from the hall. She is twenty-two and very beautiful. She wears high heels and a cocktail dress and carries a purse. She is thin, delicate, and pale.)

JENNIFER: *(Entering.)* I'm ready.

THELMA: *(Pretending to throw up.)* Buuhllhhaaa!!!

VIOLET: Thelma!

(Thelma lies on the floor.)

JENNIFER: *(To Kevin.)* Forgive my relatives.

KEVIN: Oh, no.

JENNIFER: We're, early, aren't we?

KEVIN: Yes, we are, a bit.

VIOLET: Well, why don't you sit right here? I have some things to do, so I won't be bothering you. *(To Kevin, playful; flirty.)* You don't want me around.

KEVIN: *(Protesting.)* Oh, no . . .

JENNIFER: I bet I know what you were talking about.

VIOLET: What's that, dear?

JENNIFER: Bloomingdale's.

KEVIN: That's right, we were! Isn't that amazing? How did you know that?

JENNIFER: I just had a feeling. Sometimes I think I'd like to sneak off and forget the whole thing.

KEVIN: What?!

VIOLET: Jennifer!

JENNIFER: Not the marriage, just the wedding.

KEVIN: Oh.

VIOLET: She's kidding. *(Admonishing.)* Jennifer. *(To Kevin.)* That would never do, would it, Kevin?

KEVIN: Oh, no.

VIOLET: I should say not. Ethical Culture calls! Excuse me. *(Calls out to hall:)* Dear! Would you come in here for a minute? *(To Kevin.)* I'm going to make a peach pie first thing in the morning and I don't have any peaches!

KEVIN: *(Mustering enthusiasm.)* Oh.

(Bill enters from the hall, with a model boat.)

BILL: Did you call me?

VIOLET: Dear, would you run across to Edith's and borrow some peaches?

BILL: Peaches?

VIOLET: Yes, dear. *(To Kevin.)* Bill's a dreamer.

(Thelma heads for her room.)

THELMA: *(Sings; opera.)* Peaches!

(Thelma falls on her bed as before.)

BILL: *(To Kevin.)* Hello!

KEVIN: *(Apologetic.)* I've been here.

BILL: Oh . . . Just stepping out for a minute. Peaches.

(Exits.)

VIOLET: *(Cheerfully.)* Well, then!

(Thelma turns on Janis Joplin. Violet heads back to Thelma's room.)

VIOLET: *(Continuing.)* Turn off the music!!!

(Thelma shuts off music. Violet returns to the living room. Thelma throws herself on her bed.)

VIOLET: *(Continuing; to Jennifer.)* Are you feeling all right, dear?

JENNIFER: I'm fine.

KEVIN: Is she sick?

VIOLET: She didn't eat any dinner.

JENNIFER: I'm fine, Mother. Don't worry about it.

VIOLET: I think your dieting may weaken you a bit, dear. You know how I feel about that.

JENNIFER: I'm fine.

VIOLET: I don't think she needs to diet, do you, Kevin?

KEVIN: Ha, ha. Oh, no.

VIOLET: *(To Jennifer.)* There! You see? *(To Kevin.)* Jennifer's always been frail, you know, a delicate beauty. *(Proud.)* There was a time she tended towards anemia.

KEVIN: I didn't know that.

VIOLET: Oh, yes. Well!

(Thelma falls onto her back on her bed, lies staring at the ceiling.)

VIOLET: *(Continuing.)* I'm just going into the kitchen for a minute and then

I'll be quietly situated in my room and you can have the living room all to yourselves.

(Violet starts off.)

KEVIN: That's not . . .

VIOLET: *(Flirtatious.)* Oh, now.

(Violet exits into the kitchen.)

KEVIN: Hi.

JENNIFER: Hi.

(They kiss.)

JENNIFER: *(Continuing.)* We can go now if you want to. We don't have to sit here.

KEVIN: Are you all right?

JENNIFER: I'm fine. I just had a lousy day, that's all. My boss kept screaming at me.

KEVIN: That's not nice.

JENNIFER: *(Not upset.)* All I can do is cry. It's very embarrassing.

(Violet comes in from the kitchen, heads for the hall.)

VIOLET: *(Cheerful.)* Just passing through.

(Exits, hallway.)

JENNIFER: I shouldn't get so upset about it.

KEVIN: Well, it's hard when someone screams at you like that.

JENNIFER: *(Not important.)* I hate my job. It's so boring.

KEVIN: Well, leave. It's not as if you had to work.

JENNIFER: It's something to do. I hate not having anything to do.

KEVIN: Don't worry about it. Soon we'll be married and you won't have to do a thing. It's time for the surprise!

JENNIFER: What surprise?

KEVIN: We're moving to Cleveland!

JENNIFER: What do you mean?

KEVIN: The job came through!

JENNIFER: You didn't tell me.

KEVIN: I'm telling you now. The job came through and not only that . . . but . . . this very morning I put a down payment on a house!

JENNIFER: Oh.

KEVIN: Is something wrong?

JENNIFER: I'm just surprised.

KEVIN: *(Proud.)* I knew you would be. I just put down the down payment and that was that.

JENNIFER: Well. *(Crying.)* We have a house.

KEVIN: What do you think?

JENNIFER: I'm surprised.

KEVIN: You don't seem very happy about it.

JENNIFER: *(Still crying.)* I'm just surprised.

KEVIN: I thought you'd be thrilled. I mean it wasn't as if we hadn't discussed it. We discussed Cleveland and the job and the house. I don't know what's the matter with you.

JENNIFER: I HATE CLEVELAND!!!

(In her room, Thelma rises, crosses to her door, stands listening.)

KEVIN: Well, this is news to me.

JENNIFER: I HATE IT! I CAN'T STAND IT!

KEVIN: Jennifer, this is not like you.

JENNIFER: I HATE IT!!

KEVIN: Since when don't you like Cleveland, may I ask?

JENNIFER: Since always. I HATE IT!

KEVIN: You could have told me. All this time we've talked about Cleveland, never once did you indicate you didn't like it.

JENNIFER: I HATE IT!

KEVIN: You've made that clear!

JENNIFER: It's too far away.

KEVIN: Far away from what?

JENNIFER: Just never mind!

KEVIN: Well, I must say you're a fine one. You don't give me a hint. You never say what you feel. How the hell am I supposed to know? You'll pardon my language there, but really! What am I supposed to be, a mind reader? *(Thelma leaves her room, crosses through the living room on her way to the kitchen.)*

THELMA: If you're screwing pretend I'm not here.

(Exits, kitchen.)

JENNIFER: I was afraid.

KEVIN: *(Impatient.)* Oh, well, fine. That's fine.

JENNIFER: I knew I'd get around to telling you. I just didn't want to make you mad if I didn't have to and I thought it would work out.

KEVIN: Yes, well you can see how well it's worked out.

(Thelma enters from the kitchen with a piece of cake. She stands, eating.)

JENNIFER: *(Vicious.)* Will you get out of here with that cake?!

(Thelma goes into her room, sits on the bed, eats, feeds her stuffed bear.)

KEVIN: Well, here we are in a fine pickle, aren't we?

(Jennifer closes her eyes.)

KEVIN: *(Continuing.)* What are you doing?

JENNIFER: I'm sitting on the couch.

KEVIN: I can see that, but is the discussion over. We have quite a little problem here and I'd like some help in solving it if that's not asking too much.

JENNIFER: I don't know what to do. I just feel very unhappy.

(Thelma leaves her room, heads for the kitchen.)

THELMA: I have to have a banana.

JENNIFER: *(Quickly.)* You come through again and I'll kill you!

THELMA: This will be my last trip.

(Exits.)

JENNIFER: I'll kill her!

KEVIN: Jennifer, for heavens sake.

(Violet enters from the hallway.)

VIOLET: *(Cheerful.)* Don't let me bother you. I just need some papers from the desk and I shall disappear. It's about time for your movie, isn't it?

KEVIN: Ah . . . Oh. Yes. I guess it is.

(Jennifer takes a pair of sunglasses from her purse, puts them on. Violet gathers papers.)

VIOLET: Accounts, accounts. I used to leave them to Bill, but they never got done. He's so vague.

(Bill comes through the front door. He carries a brown paper bag.)

BILL: I'm back.

KEVIN: *(Attempting politeness.)* Oh!

BILL: Nothing like a walk. Summer hasn't given up yet. Winter may be coming, but she's having a hard time chasing old summer away.

KEVIN: Ha, ha, oh, yes.

VIOLET: Did you get the peaches?

BILL: Uh-oh.

VIOLET: What.

BILL: I didn't get the peaches.

VIOLET: I asked you to get them.

BILL: Golly.

VIOLET: What have you got in that bag? I'll bet you've got them in there.

BILL: No. This is my glue. *(To Kevin.)* For my boats.

KEVIN: Oh.

BILL: I'll go back.

(Doesn't move.)

VIOLET: *(Annoyed.)* Well, go.

(Thelma enters from the kitchen with a banana.)

VIOLET: *(Continuing; to Thelma.)* Have you forgotten the garbage?

THELMA: Did I forget? Could I have been dreaming?

BILL: *(To Kevin.)* It's just across the street.

> *(Kevin nods. Bill heads for the front door. He stops, turns, heads for the kitchen.)*

VIOLET: *(To Bill.)* Where are you going?

BILL: *(Holds up bag.)* I'll leave this.

> *(Thelma blocks her father's way, points the banana at him.)*

THELMA: Drop that bag. Put your hands in the air.

BILL: There's a girl.

THELMA: There'll be no peaches tonight!

VIOLET: Thelma, go to your room!

THELMA: And forsake my garbage take-out?

> *(No answer from Vi. Thelma sits on the floor. Bill exits, kitchen, whistling tunelessly.)*

VIOLET: *(To Jennifer.)* Won't you be late?

KEVIN: *(To Jennifer.)* We'd better go.

> *(Jennifer sits motionless behind her sunglasses. Bill enters from the kitchen, crosses to the front door.)*

BILL: *(To Kevin.)* I'll be back in a minute with the peaches.

> *(Kevin nods. Bill exits, whistling. Thelma reaches for magazine, reads.)*

KEVIN: *(To Jennifer.)* We can still make it if you want to go.

VIOLET: Of course she wants to go. *(To Jennifer.)* You're not sick, are you?

JENNIFER: *(A zombie.)* I'm fine.

VIOLET: Jennifer sometimes gets sick to her stomach, you know.

KEVIN: Oh?

VIOLET: *(Proud.)* Yes, indeed!

KEVIN: Well . . . Maybe we should go.

> *(Jennifer rises as if a trance.)*

VIOLET: Have a wonderful time!

> *(Kevin steers Jennifer toward the front door.)*

KEVIN: Yes. Thank you. Good night, Mrs. Gardner.

VIOLET: *(Flirtatious.)* Now that you're engaged I want you to call me Vi. No more of this "Mrs. Gardner."

KEVIN: Ha, ha, oh, yes. Well . . . Good night . . . Vi.

> *(Kevin and Jennifer exit. Violet watches Thelma. A beat.)*

VIOLET: Thelma, you will put down that magazine. Perhaps you didn't hear me, Thelma. You will put down that magazine.

> *(Violet grabs the magazine from Thelma.)*

VIOLET: *(Continuing.)* You will go to your room and you will stay there until you can behave like a human being . . . Now!

(Thelma goes into her room, falls face down on her bed. Violet collects her papers as Bill enters through the front door with a sack of peaches.)

BILL: I've got them this time.

VIOLET: *(On her way out; grouchy.)* Good.

(Violet exits, hallway. Bill whistles as he exits into the kitchen with the peaches. Thelma gets onto her hands and knees on the bed, begins rocking back and forth. Bill re-enters from the kitchen almost immediately, still whistling, having left the peaches. He starts for the hallway.)

BILL: My boat, my boat. *(Crosses to the desk, picks up model.)* Glue. *(Carries the model into the kitchen, re-enters with a tube of glue.)* Why do I always run out when I need it? It's lack of proper planning, that's what it is.

THELMA: AAAHHH!

BILL: What's that now? *(Looks to Thelma's room.)* Thelma?

(Bill crosses to Thelma's room, peers in. Thelma is on all fours on her bed, head down, rocking.)

BILL: *(Continuing.)* What are you doing there?

THELMA: Leave me alone.

BILL: *(Entering her room.)* How about a game of Tug?

THELMA: War, Dad. Tug of War.

BILL: A quick round?

THELMA: No.

BILL: I Packed My Grandmother's Bag!

THELMA: Get out of my room!

BILL: I packed my grandmother's bag and in it I put a grapefruit.

THELMA: Get out!

(Bill closes the door. Moves farther into the room, as Violet comes down the hall, wearing a sweater, carrying her purse. She stands outside Thelma's door listening.)

BILL: Did something go wrong at school?

THELMA: I haven't been to school in a week.

BILL: Why haven't you been to school?

THELMA: I have a sore throat.

(Bill sits on her bed, holding the model.)

BILL: This is going to be a beauty.

(Thelma sits abruptly on her knees, falls to the bed on her back.)

THELMA: Shit!

BILL: A hobby is a wonderful thing. I had a hobby when I was a little boy.

I used to collect those chocolate papers. The ones you put the chocolates in? Like a cup, brown with those ridges. I don't remember what I did with them. I think I made stacks. Grandmother used to say, "Save the wrappers for Billy!" She called it out so everyone could hear. "Save the wrappers for Billy!" Now, that's a hobby for you. Not useful, but that's what makes it relaxing. Work can get routine.

THELMA: Shut up!

BILL: Thelma.

THELMA: I'm sorry. I don't know what's the matter with me. I think I'm going crazy. I feel so mean all the time.

BILL: You're not going crazy.

THELMA: I'm not so sure.

BILL: *(A beat.)* Edith was wearing a hat.

THELMA: What?

BILL: When I went to get the peaches. She was sitting by the radio, wearing a hat.

THELMA: Why?

BILL: *(Mock intrigue.)* I don't know. *(Informative.)* It had a cherry on it.

THELMA: A cherry?

BILL: I kid you not.

THELMA: Maybe she was getting ready for Halloween.

BILL: Could be.

THELMA: Was she wearing a mask?

BILL: *(In mock amazement.)* No.

(Bill chuckles. Thelma smiles. A shared sense of humor.)

BILL: *(Continuing.)* Oh, dear. Halloween . . . Jennifer wore that little pinafore one year. Remember?

THELMA: No.

BILL: It was so cute. With that . . . what do you call that thing? That front piece?

THELMA: Bib?

BILL: Bib. That's right. You don't remember that?

THELMA: No.

BILL: Oh, what's the matter with me? You weren't born yet.

THELMA: That's probably why I don't remember.

BILL: Of course.

(Thelma picks up her football, slams it into the floor.)

BILL: *(Continuing.)* I was thinking of naming this one after you.

THELMA: What?

BILL: The boat.

THELMA: The boat? Why?

BILL: I was thinking of it.

THELMA: I have a headache.

BILL: Uh-oh. Did you take an aspirin?

THELMA: No.

BILL: Better get busy if I want to get anything done. Your mother and I are going out.

THELMA: *(Rising.)* That's what I'm going to do.

BILL: What?

THELMA: Go out.

BILL: Out?

THELMA: Out. O-u-t. Out.

BILL: Oh, don't go out now. You're not feeling well. I'll get you an aspirin.

THELMA: I don't want an aspirin! What the hell is there to do around here? I'd like to play some football!

BILL: When I have a headache I just lie back.

THELMA: What's the matter with me? I'm going crazy.

BILL: I lie back and close my eyes.

THELMA: I can't breathe. Why is it so hot in here?

BILL: Is it hot?

THELMA: I don't know. Maybe it's cold. Something's wrong.

BILL: I feel comfortable.

THELMA: You do?

BILL: Yes.

THELMA: I don't know what's the matter with me. I certainly don't.

BILL: Do you have a fever?

THELMA: I'm dying.

BILL: I thought I was catching a fever last week. It was that beautiful day. What was it, Thursday? Or Wednesday? Thursday, I think. I think it was Thursday. That beautiful spring-like day, whenever it was. I was going to take my sandwich to the park and eat it there, but I felt this sore throat coming on and I didn't go. If I had I might be sick today. Change of weather is always difficult. Have you been going out without your coat?

THELMA: I've been inside all week.

BILL: Don't go out without your coat. Not in this pesky weather.

THELMA: Dad?

BILL: It's not summer anymore.

THELMA: Dad?

BILL: Summer is past.

THELMA: I need to talk to someone.

BILL: I'm all ears.

THELMA: Doesn't it bother you that I'm dying?

BILL: I'll get you an aspirin.

THELMA: AAAHHH!!!

BILL: Oh. There's a girl.

THELMA: *(Intense; worried.)* Did you get the letter?

BILL: What letter?

THELMA: The school thinks I should go to a psychiatrist.

BILL: What?

THELMA: They were going to send you a letter. You didn't get it?

BILL: No. Why do they think you should go to a psychiatrist?

THELMA: They seem to think I'm troubled. I don't know why. Just because I'm depressed all the time and scared and I don't see the point of living and I can't get along with anyone and I'm always sick and I lie and I can't function in school and I hate myself, I mean, that's no reason, would you say?

BILL: You're fine.

THELMA: I'm not fine!

BILL: You have your life ahead of you.

THELMA: I'm a mess!

BILL: I wish I were in your shoes.

THELMA: No, you don't.

BILL: My life is at a different stage, but you . . . the world is your oyster! I was talking to a bus driver yesterday . . .

THELMA: Crap on that bus driver! I don't want to hear about it! You go off in your damn dream world. I can't stand it!

(Violet opens Thelma's door.)

VIOLET: I heard screaming.

BILL: We were just having a talk.

(Thelma pushes past her mother, heads for the front door. Violet and Bill follow.)

VIOLET: Where do you think you're going?

THELMA: Out!

VIOLET: No, you're not!

(Thelma exits, slamming the door.)

BILL: She didn't take her coat.

VIOLET: She'll live.

BILL: Golly.

VIOLET: I'm at my wit's end.

BILL: *(Worried.)* The school said she should go to a psychiatrist.

VIOLET: I know.

(Begins straightening up the living room.)

BILL: You do?

VIOLET: *(Not important.)* They sent us a letter.

BILL: I didn't see it.

VIOLET: It's on the desk.

BILL: Why didn't you tell me?

VIOLET: It came this morning! Open your eyes!

BILL: *(Anxious.)* A psychiatrist.

VIOLET: It's ridiculous!

BILL: I don't know if it's ridiculous.

VIOLET: Of course, it is.

BILL: She's upset.

VIOLET: I can see that!

BILL: She needs our support.

VIOLET: What's that supposed to mean?

BILL: Nothing. I, ah . . .

VIOLET: What?!

BILL: I just . . .

VIOLET: You think I don't support her?

BILL: I didn't say that!

VIOLET: Say what you mean!

BILL: Well, you're at her too much.

VIOLET: Oh, fine!

BILL: You have to . . .

VIOLET: So, it's my fault!

BILL: Now, Vi . . .

VIOLET: Everything I do is wrong!

BILL: That's not . . .

VIOLET: I'm going to put away the peaches!

(She heads for the kitchen.)

BILL: Wait a minute! . . . Vi?!

(Violet exits kitchen.)

(Blackout.)

SCENE TWO

Later that night. Rock music blasts in the darkness. Lights up. Harry Toronto and Philip Riser are sprawled in the living room. Harry, seventeen, is in the downstage chair, drinking beer. There is a genuine sweetness about him, with, at times, a violent edge. He is smart, a leader. Philip is sixteen, but looks younger. While Harry is prominent in a room, Philip is often over-looked. He is small and rodent-like with long hair and beady eyes. He sits on the floor in a corner, surrounded by magazines that he reads throughout. He rarely smiles. Thelma is in her room. She kneels by her record player, putting a record into its cover, as the rock music blasts forth. She rises, leaves her room, and hurries through the living room on her way to the kitchen, exits. Harry beats time to the music, drinks. Philip is laughing as he reads a magazine.

HARRY: *(Distracted.)* What.

PHILIP: *(Shouts over music.)* This guy got locked in a refrigerator!

(Harry crosses to the hutch to get a shot of liquor. Philip laughs hysterically.)

PHILIP: *(Continuing; choked with laughter.)* Look! . . . This dumb jerk! His hair froze!

(Harry looks at the picture.)

HARRY: It's not that funny.

PHILIP: *(Hysterical.)* He looks demented! Look at his hair sticking out! I can't stand it!

(Harry looks at the picture. He tries to keep a straight face, but can't. Both boys roll on the floor in hysterical laughter. Slowly, their laughter subsides. The music ends. They lie, motionless.)

HARRY: Oh, God, that's funny.

(Harry sits up, tears the picture out of the magazine.)

HARRY: *(Continuing.)* I have to put this up in my room.

PHILIP: You don't have a room . . . You still crashing at Sheldon's?

HARRY: Yeah. Did you find your mother?

PHILIP: She was in Maine.

HARRY: What was she doing in Maine??

PHILIP: Who knows. She's been asleep for two days.

(Philip resumes reading. Harry takes a hunting knife out of his pocket.)

HARRY: Did I show you my knife?

PHILIP: Five times you showed me that stupid knife.

HARRY: I ought to go camping, or something.

PHILIP: So, are we going to do it?

HARRY: I said we were.

PHILIP: When?

HARRY: I'll let you know.

PHILIP: When?

HARRY: What?

PHILIP: When will you let me know?

HARRY: Just cool it!

PHILIP: Tonight?

(Harry grabs Philip. They wrestle, play fighting vigorously as Thelma enters with a jar of peanut butter and a bag of pretzel sticks. She steps around them as they fight.)

THELMA: Did you know flat feet can get you out of the draft?

HARRY: No.

PHILIP: What are flat feet?

THELMA: You should check it out.

PHILIP: Aren't everybody's feet flat?

(The boys stop wrestling.)

HARRY: *(To Thelma.)* That's ridiculous. There's a million things you could do.

PHILIP: What are flat feet?

HARRY: You could drive a truck. You could distribute bandages.

(Thelma tosses the bag of pretzels to Harry, sits. Harry hands Thelma a pretzel that she dips into the peanut butter jar and returns to him. There is a sense of attraction between them. For Thelma it's a crush. For Harry, a fondness one might have for a mascot.)

HARRY: *(Continuing.)* This is a wonderful combination.

PHILIP: Let me have some.

(Harry throws the bag to Philip, who catches it without looking.)

PHILIP: *(Continuing.)* And the peanut butter!

(Thelma pushes the peanut butter jar across the floor to Philip who prepares his snack while reading.)

THELMA: We need some Janis.

(Thelma puts her pretzel in her mouth, heads for her room. Harry calls after her.)

HARRY: I'm gonna keep flunking out until the war is over!

THELMA: Can you do that?

HARRY: Watch me.

THELMA: *(Selecting a record; calls to Harry.)* I think you should look into this flat feet thing!

HARRY: Forget it.

PHILIP: I'm going to Canada.

HARRY: That's crazy.

PHILIP: My cousin makes lobster traps.

> *(Philip reads. Thelma puts on Janis Joplin, "Piece of My Heart." She re-enters the living room, sings along with Janis to Harry, who ignores her.)*

HARRY: Hey, Philip. Toss me the bag.

> *(Thelma sits. Philip tosses the pretzel bag back to Harry without looking.)*

HARRY: *(Continuing; impatient.)* And the peanut butter!

> *(Philip shoves the jar back to Harry. They shout the following over the loud music.)*

THELMA: I can't believe she's dead.

PHILIP: She was mourning Jimi.

THELMA: That wasn't the whole reason.

HARRY: Who said it was?

PHILIP: Twenty-seven is the age to die.

THELMA: That's true.

PHILIP: *(Ominous.)* The curse of twenty-seven.

THELMA: I don't want to live past twenty-seven. It seems disrespectful.

> *(Harry rises, crosses to Thelma's room.)*

THELMA: *(Continuing.)* I miss her so much.

> *(Harry shuts off Janis, returns to the living room.)*

HARRY: You've got to let up on this Janis thing. It's been a week.

THELMA: I feel like I lost my sister.

HARRY: There's always Jennifer.

THELMA: Thanks anyway. An insane person! She's marrying this guy? She doesn't even know if she likes him. And this thing . . . God. I didn't tell you about this. This thing about the silver bowls!

HARRY: What's that?

THELMA: She's all excited because her friend, Bev, got these wedding presents, a whole bunch of shit, including seven silver bowls! She registered at Orbachs you may be interested to know.

PHILIP: I'm not.

THELMA: Why Orbachs didn't come clean and say Bev didn't need so many silver bowls I couldn't tell you. Anyway, Jennifer thinks these bowls are the best things in the history of recorded time. It doesn't matter that Bev didn't know who the hell she was marrying, or why. She got seven silver bowls!

PHILIP: When does this story begin?

THELMA: If you're not interested, don't listen! *(To Harry.)* So now she's a slave. She has to thank the seven people who sent the silver bowls she doesn't want and doesn't need. That's only polite. She has to buy the stationery, which has to be engraved with her new name because her old name isn't any good anymore because now she belongs to somebody else, she has to write the seven thank-you notes, she has to mail the seven thank-you notes, and then . . . Care of the bowls!

PHILIP: This is getting good.

THELMA: She has to polish these stupid bowls she doesn't want and doesn't need. That means getting the money to buy the polish, and replacing the T-shirt she tore up to make the rag she used to do the polishing. *(With growing intensity.)* See, it's not just the bowls. This kind of thing passes for life and it gives me the creeps. I get hamsters in my veins.

PHILIP: I hate that.

THELMA: Bev's life! I'd rather kill myself! But that's what Jennifer wants . . . or thinks she wants. She doesn't have a clue. She's shrivelled and died inside her idea of herself like a rotten walnut in its shell.

HARRY: I heard about this guy on the radio this morning who shot his parents . . . Moonbeam Henderson.

THELMA: An odd name.

HARRY: He shot them before breakfast and went to school.

THELMA: Jesus.

HARRY: They bled all over the carpet while he slept through algebra.

THELMA: *(Sits up.)* Jesus! Where was this?

HARRY: Nebraska.

THELMA: My God.

PHILIP: *(Stops reading.)* He confessed?

HARRY: He said they wouldn't let him have the car.

THELMA: There must have been another reason.

HARRY: I could understand doing that.

THELMA: You could?

HARRY: Yeah. It really scared me. I thought, right, yeah. Just tune out and have a regular day.

THELMA: You could kill your parents?

HARRY: If they crapped on me enough I could. Who knows what went on in that house. You don't know.

THELMA: That's true.

HARRY: Moonbeam Henderson. That should tell you something. *(A beat.)* I wanted to kill my old man last week. I hate him and his idiot wife.

THELMA: Why do you hate her?

HARRY: She collects paperweights with snow and plates from every city she's ever been to. They're on shelves all over the house, hideous plates . . . disgusting, with pictures of capital buildings and regional birds.

THELMA: You hate her because she collects plates?

PHILIP: You haven't seen them.

HARRY: It's not just the plates. She's schizophrenic and she hates me. I can't believe I have to live with her.

THELMA: You don't anymore.

HARRY: That's true. I hate the paperweights most of all. Thomas Jefferson, Benjamin Franklin, Tony Orlando and Dawn, all in snow.

THELMA: God. When did your dad kick you out?

HARRY: Last week. I took a gold coin out of Michelle's underwear drawer.

PHILIP: She collects those too.

HARRY: I was going to return it. I needed some pot. Dad gave me this knife. Now I want to stab it through his heart.

(Thelma stares at the knife.)

THELMA: Did you ever want to cut yourself?

HARRY: No. Did you?

THELMA: Yeah.

PHILIP: *(Stops reading.)* On purpose?

HARRY: When?

PHILIP: You wanted to cut yourself on purpose?

HARRY: Like when?

THELMA: Never mind.

HARRY: Like now. I can tell. You need help.

PHILIP: So, what's the plan?

THELMA: What plan?

PHILIP: We're going to rob Jiffy Donut.

THELMA: Why are you going to rob Jiffy Donut? That's a pitiful idea.

HARRY: It's not Jiffy Donut so much as the guy who works there.

THELMA: Sean? That guy with the vampire teeth?

PHILIP: He stole some pictures out of Harry's locker.

THELMA: What kind of pictures?

HARRY: Pictures of my mother in Utah with my dog.

PHILIP: Truth is stranger than fiction.

THELMA: Why would Sean want to steal pictures of your mother in Utah with your dog?

HARRY: Because they mean a lot to me.

THELMA: That's sick.

HARRY: You want to help us?

THELMA: What. Rob Jiffy Donut?

HARRY: Yeah.

THELMA: No.

HARRY: We need a lookout.

THELMA: Forget it. I'm going to get some Fruit Loops.

(Thelma goes into the kitchen. Harry puts the knife back into its sheath.)

PHILIP: Wanna watch TV?

HARRY: It's broken.

PHILIP: Bummer . . . *The Partridge Family*'s on.

HARRY: Why do you like that stupid show?

PHILIP: *(Offended.)* It's not stupid.

(The front door opens. Kevin enters carrying Jennifer, who is unconscious.)

KEVIN: Uh . . . hello.

(Kevin moves a step or two into the room. Jennifer's weight is too much for him. He adjusts her to a half-standing position. Philip looks up from his magazine.)

KEVIN: *(Continuing.)* Ah . . . hi! . . . Ah, excuse me, but Jennifer's sick here.

(Harry and Philip stare at Kevin.)

KEVIN: *(Continuing.)* Hi. I don't know you, but you see she's sick here. She fainted.

HARRY: Who are you?

KEVIN: *(Struggling with Jennifer.)* Oh, dear. I'm Kevin. Can you help me get her to the couch? She's heavy.

HARRY: *(To Philip.)* You know this man?

PHILIP: No.

KEVIN: I'm Kevin. I'm Jennifer's fiancé. *(Nearly drops her; desperate.)* PLEASE! Help me get her to the couch.

(Harry helps Kevin carry Jennifer to the couch.)

HARRY: Is she dead?

KEVIN: Of course she's not dead. She's breathing. She just fainted.

HARRY: She looks terrible.

KEVIN: I know.

HARRY: What are you going to do with her now?

KEVIN: Who cares!

HARRY: That's not very nice.

KEVIN: *(Fussy.)* Oh, shut up and mind your own business.

HARRY: *(With an edge.)* Now, just a minute. Don't talk to me like that. You understand?

KEVIN: I'm sorry.

HARRY: All right . . . Now, do you know where she lives.

KEVIN: *(Confused.)* Where she . . . Oh. Well. Oh . . . she lives . . . ah . . . she lives here.

HARRY: I never saw her before in my life.

KEVIN: Oh, hi! I mean, who are you?

HARRY: I should ask you that question. You're the one who came barging in here.

KEVIN: I didn't barge.

HARRY: You certainly did.

KEVIN: I did not barge!

HARRY: You didn't knock. You didn't ring the bell. You should be more careful.

KEVIN: This is Jennifer's house! What's the matter with you? . . . Are you a robber?

HARRY: Are you?

KEVIN: Don't be cute.

HARRY: I don't think I'm cute. Do you Philip?

PHILIP: A little bit.

(Thelma enters from the kitchen with a box of Fruit Loops.)

THELMA: *(To Kevin.)* What are you doing here?

KEVIN: She fainted.

THELMA: Well, put her in her room. You're interrupting our party.

JENNIFER: *(Stirring.)* Ugh.

KEVIN: I'll get you some brandy.

THELMA: Does she have to stay on the couch?

(Ignoring Thelma, Kevin rises, gets brandy from hutch.)

HARRY: *(To Thelma.)* She's all right there.

(Pissed off, Thelma sits on the floor. Philip takes Fruit Loops from Thelma, eats.)

HARRY: *(Continuing; to Kevin.)* Listen, I'm sorry about before. I guess it wasn't the best time for jokes.

(Kevin moves to Jennifer with the brandy.)

KEVIN: I should say it wasn't. *(To Jennifer.)* Here. Take a little of this brandy.

HARRY: Do you forgive me?

KEVIN: I forgive you.

HARRY: No, you don't.

KEVIN: *(Annoyed.)* I do. I forgive you.

HARRY: No, you don't. I can tell.

KEVIN: I do! For heaven's sake! I forgive you!

HARRY: Now you're really mad.

KEVIN: Will you just leave me alone?!

(Jennifer is spilling the brandy.)

KEVIN: *(Continuing; to Jennifer.)* Here. Drink this yourself.

(Jennifer takes a long drink, puts the empty glass on the floor.)

JENNIFER: I'm going to sleep.

THELMA: *(To Kevin.)* Get her out of here!

HARRY: Let her stay.

(Thelma looks daggers at Harry. Jennifer dozes. Kevin sits.)

HARRY: *(Continuing.)* I'm sorry. Really.

KEVIN: I forgive you.

HARRY: It must have been a drag.

KEVIN: She was so sick. It was awful.

HARRY: What happened?

THELMA: The story of Jennifer's death.

(Thelma goes into her room, falls on the bed.)

KEVIN: I was in the powder room.

HARRY: You were in the powder room?

KEVIN: No. I wasn't in the powder room. She was in the powder room. I was in the lounge.

HARRY: Oh. You were in the lounge and she was in the powder room.

KEVIN: That's right. I waited an hour.

HARRY: In the lounge.

KEVIN: Yes. I waited an hour in the lounge and she didn't come out.

HARRY: And you thought something might be wrong.

KEVIN: That's right.

HARRY: How long does it take to pee.

KEVIN: That's right . . . No. I just thought it was a little long.

PHILIP: It was.

KEVIN: Yes. So when this lady came by and started towards the powder room I asked her to check.

HARRY: To check on Jennifer.

KEVIN: That's right, and she checked.

HARRY: And she was dead.

KEVIN: That's right.

HARRY: That's too bad.

KEVIN: No, she wasn't dead. She was just lying on the floor.

HARRY: In a dead position.

KEVIN: Well, yes, in a way. I thought she was dead.

HARRY: It must have been a shock.

KEVIN: It certainly was. And there I was in the powder room!

HARRY: You barged in there too.

KEVIN: Well, no, I didn't barge. I mean, I asked this lady.

HARRY: The same lady who checked on Jennifer.

KEVIN: The same one. I asked her to tell the people, the ladies, I mean, that it was an emergency and I had to go in.

HARRY: So they went out.

KEVIN: They went out and I went in and there was Jennifer.

HARRY: Dead.

KEVIN: It was awful.

HARRY: I can imagine.

KEVIN: I raised my voice. I remember I said, *(Yells.)* Jennifer, are you all right? *(Quieter.)* I said it just like that. Very loud, but she didn't move, so I started pulling on her.

HARRY: You wanted to leave the powder room.

KEVIN: Wouldn't you?

HARRY: I certainly would. All that powder.

KEVIN: That's right. As I was pulling on her she woke up.

HARRY: And here you are.

KEVIN: That's right. I brought her home. There was no point in staying for the movie.

HARRY: In her condition.

KEVIN: That's right.

(Thelma rises, exits her room, stands at the top of the hallway steps, watching the others. Kevin looks at Jennifer who is dozing, an arm hanging off the side of the couch.)

KEVIN: *(Continuing.)* Do you think she's all right?

HARRY: How would I know? She's your fiancée. Does she look like that often?

KEVIN: No, never. She almost fainted once before. That was at Lincoln Center, but she put her head between her legs and we stayed for the second act.

HARRY: I hope she could see that way.

KEVIN: I don't know what to do. I hate to leave her like that. *(To Thelma.)* I wish your parents were here.

THELMA: I don't.

JENNIFER: What's happening?

HARRY: Good morning.

JENNIFER: Who are you?

HARRY: I'm Harry.

JENNIFER: Hello, Harry!

THELMA: All right, she's up! You can catch the second show!

KEVIN: Jennifer, you scared me to death.

THELMA: Leave!

KEVIN: I thought you were dead.

THELMA: You're ruining my party!

HARRY: I don't want her to leave.

> (*Thelma goes into her room, gets her football, re-enters living room. She tosses the football to Philip. They play catch.*)

JENNIFER: I need a drink.

KEVIN: *(Fussy.)* You already had one.

HARRY: She wants another one.

JENNIFER: *(Party mood.)* That's right! I want another one!

KEVIN: You've still got some.

> (*Jennifer looks for her glass, picks it up, holds it out to Harry.*)

JENNIFER: Cheers, Harry!

> (*Jennifer finishes drink in one gulp. Holds glass out to Kevin.*)

JENNIFER: *(Continuing; tough.)* Get me some more.

KEVIN: Jennifer, you've had plenty. That was a full glass.

HARRY: She wants some more.

JENNIFER: That's right. I want some more.

KEVIN: *(To Jennifer.)* You look terrible.

JENNIFER: That's not very nice.

HARRY: I think she looks great.

THELMA: Another county heard from.

JENNIFER: *(To Harry; moved.)* Thank you.

KEVIN: Listen, Jennifer, do you want me to stay until you're parents come back?

> (*Harry pours brandy into Jennifer's glass, looking into her eyes.*)

HARRY: We'll be fine.

JENNIFER: That's right! We'll be fine!

KEVIN: I'll stay.

JENNIFER: *(To Harry, a toast.)* Touché!

KEVIN: What the hell does that mean, Jennifer? Get a hold of yourself.

> (*Jennifer downs the drink. Harry sits next to Jennifer on the couch.*)

HARRY: Would you like a massage? I give a great massage.

KEVIN: She doesn't need any massage.

JENNIFER: *(To Harry.)* Thank you. That would be lovely.

HARRY: Put down your glass.

> *(Jennifer puts glass on the floor.)*

HARRY: *(Continuing.)* Lie down.

> *(Thelma folds her arms around her head, covering her ears. Jennifer lies on her stomach.)*

KEVIN: Jennifer, you don't need any massage.

HARRY: Shut up.

KEVIN: I beg your pardon?

HARRY: *(Massaging Jennifer.)* I said, shut up.

KEVIN: That's no way to talk to me.

HARRY: Fuck off.

JENNIFER: That's right. Fuck off!

KEVIN: Jennifer!

JENNIFER: You talk too much.

KEVIN: Jennifer, what is wrong with you?! I don't know you anymore.

JENNIFER: I don't know you and you don't know me . . .

HARRY: *(Intimate.)* I'd like to know you.

PHILIP: In the Biblical sense.

JENNIFER: *(Childlike; petulant.)* I don't like the Bible.

> *(Harry's massage gets more familiar. Jennifer squeals with laughter.)*

KEVIN: Jennifer, will you tell him to stop that?!

JENNIFER: I like it!

HARRY: She likes it.

KEVIN: Jennifer, stop this!

JENNIFER: You're no fun at a party.

KEVIN: This is not a party, Jennifer.

THELMA: Not anymore!

KEVIN: Now, come to your senses.

JENNIFER: I don't like you.

KEVIN: All right. That's enough. Get your hands off my fiancée.

HARRY: Make me.

KEVIN: Listen, buster, don't get smart with me!

HARRY: Go to hell.

KEVIN: *(Attempting assertiveness.)* That's it.

THELMA: Doesn't look like it to me.

KEVIN: You're asking for it, buster. I'm losing my temper.

HARRY: Go for it.

KEVIN: Get away from her!

HARRY: Make me.

KEVIN: Get away!!!

(Kevin pushes Harry.)

HARRY: I wouldn't do that.

JENNIFER: Who said they liked the Bible? Who was it?

KEVIN: *(To Harry.)* Now you're supposed to leave.

(Harry doesn't move.)

KEVIN: *(Continuing.)* Leave!!! *(Shoves Harry again.)* You get out of here.

(Harry pulls out his knife.)

HARRY: You see this?

THELMA: Jesus, Harry!

KEVIN: *(To Harry; re knife.)* You put that away.

HARRY: Make me.

PHILIP: Let's go, Harry. Come on.

KEVIN: Just put that away now.

HARRY: Make me.

KEVIN: You put that away, or I'll have to call the police.

HARRY: Try it.

PHILIP: Come on, Harry.

JENNIFER: You stopped my massage. Why did you stop my massage?

KEVIN: Jennifer, this boy is a lunatic!

HARRY: *(Menacing.)* Don't call me names. Don't do that.

THELMA: Forget it, Harry!

PHILIP: Come on!

JENNIFER: I want my massage.

KEVIN: I'm calling the police.

(Kevin makes a move toward the phone. Harry intercepts him. They struggle. Kevin cries out in pain. He slumps over.)

THELMA: Jesus, Harry!

PHILIP: Let's go!

THELMA: *(To Kevin.)* Are you all right?

KEVIN: I'm bleeding!

(Kevin heads for Thelma's room. Thelma follows.)

PHILIP: Let's get out of here!

THELMA: Are you all right??!!

KEVIN: Oh, God!

JENNIFER: *(In her own world.)* I don't like the Bible.

KEVIN: My arm!

THELMA: Let me see!

(Kevin sits on Thelma's bed, rocking.)

KEVIN: I'm going to faint. I know it.

HARRY: Put your head between your legs. Everybody's doing it.

(Philip grabs a doily as he follows Harry into Thelma's room.)

THELMA: It's bleeding. I can't see.

PHILIP: (Offering doily.) Here.

(Thelma takes the doily, wipes the wound.)

KEVIN: (Ominous.) I have that dizzy feeling.

HARRY: Do you want me to bite you in the ear?

KEVIN: No.

HARRY: That's what they do with cows when they brand them. They bite them in the ear so they don't feel the pain of the iron.

KEVIN: No, thank you.

HARRY: You're not a cow.

KEVIN: No, I'm not.

THELMA: (The wound.) I think it's OK.

(Thelma ties the doily around Kevin's arm like a tourniquet. Kevin rocks back and forth.)

HARRY: Like I said, I'm sorry. I didn't mean to hurt you . . . HEY! It's only a small cut.

KEVIN: I don't like cuts.

HARRY: You'll get over it.

KEVIN: No cuts of any kind.

HARRY: Come on now. It's not that bad. I lost the end of my finger once.

KEVIN: Please . . .

THELMA: Don't tell that now!

HARRY: I cut it right off.

THELMA: Jesus, Harry! (To Kevin.) Why don't you leave?

KEVIN: I can't drive. I have an arm!

HARRY: I was fooling with this mechanical saw, you know, the kind with the blade that spins around?

THELMA: I'm calling a cab.

(Thelma leaves room, runs to phone on the hutch, dials.)

HARRY: Anyway, I felt it cut . . . God, it was awful. I felt this slice and it went numb.

KEVIN: (Faint.) Could we not listen to this now?

THELMA: (On phone.) We need a taxi. Meadow Green Apartments. 4 Maple Grove. Gardner.

HARRY: I knew something bad had happened. I didn't want to look because I thought maybe my whole finger was cut off.

KEVIN: Please!

(Kevin dashes from the room, heads for the kitchen. Harry and Philip follow.)

PHILIP: *(On the run.)* That's disgusting.

HARRY: I finally looked down and saw that the tip of my finger was lying there, separate from the rest of my hand.

KEVIN: Jesus!

(Kevin escapes into the kitchen. Harry and Philip follow.)

THELMA: I'm not listening to this.

(Thelma goes into her room, throws herself on the bed, covers her head with the pillow as Kevin runs from the kitchen, heads for the phone, followed by Harry and Philip.)

HARRY: I screamed so loud! I was with these people, this guy and this girl and they came running in and the guy wrapped his handkerchief around my finger. Luckily there was a hospital a block away so we rushed over there, but the weird thing was . . . this really blows my mind . . . the weird thing was the doctor sent the guy back to get the rest of my finger.

KEVIN: Stop!

(Kevin crumbles by the phone, sinking to his knees. Thelma hangs her head off the side of the bed, eyes wide, mouth open, a silent scream.)

HARRY: Anyway, they sewed it back on and it's fine now. *(Holds up index finger.)* I don't have any feeling in the very tip, but otherwise it's OK.

(Kevin sinks further, lies on the floor.)

HARRY: *(Continuing; a beat.)* Would you like to lie down?

KEVIN: Yes.

PHILIP: I hate that story. Why do you tell it?

HARRY: *(To Jennifer.)* Excuse me.

(Harry dumps Jennifer onto the floor.)

JENNIFER: *(Tiny sound.)* Ooh.

KEVIN: Don't do that!

HARRY: She doesn't care.

(Harry and Philip help Kevin to the couch.)

KEVIN: This is terrible.

HARRY: Your taxi'll be here any minute.

(Thelma leaves her room, stands on the landing steps, watching the others.)

HARRY: *(Continuing.)* I'm really sorry.

KEVIN: That's OK. Maybe I need an ambulance.

HARRY: We'll check it out. *(Heads for front door.)* Come on, Philip. *(To Kevin.)* Sit tight. *(To Thelma.)* Jiffy Donut. Ten fifteen.

(Harry and Philip start out. Philip waves to Kevin.)

PHILIP: Bye.

(They exit.)

KEVIN: *(A beat.)* This day has not gone well.

(Thelma returns to her room, falls on her bed.)

JENNIFER: *(Stirring.)* Who put me on the floor?

KEVIN: Not her again!

(Jennifer tries to get up. Kevin pretends to sleep.)

JENNIFER: Who's in charge? *(Rises with difficulty; spots Kevin.)* You're a sleeping man. *(Steadies herself.)* You sleep and I sleep.

(Jennifer lies on the floor in the middle of the room, sleeps. Thelma grabs the hair on both sides of her head, pulls it straight out on either side, her face contorted in pent up frustration. She gets on all fours, head down, rocks, then collapses in "child's pose," hunched in a tight ball.)

KEVIN: I'll probably die. I've heard you can die from cutting yourself with a razor. It's the germs! *(Rocking.)* Oh, don't let me die! I did what they told me. Marks in the nineties. I obeyed all the rules. I joined all the committees. Maybe not all the teams, but all the committees! I stepped on bugs, but that's not so bad. Everybody steps on bugs. THEY'RE SO SMALL!!

JENNIFER: *(Wakes.)* I need my sleeping pillow.

KEVIN: I threw water on my camp counselor. That wasn't nice. But the whole table did it.

(Jennifer crawls up the landing stairs and exits down the hallway.)

KEVIN: *(Continuing.)* I was good! Top of the bunk. I raised the flag! Best all around camper of '54! I lost the ring. But that was me!!! Oh, God, why did this happen?

(A key is heard in the front door. Kevin appears not to notice.)

KEVIN: *(Continuing.)* It's not fair! *(As the door opens.)* Goddamn it to hell!!!

(Violet and Bill stand in the doorway.)

BILL: It's Kevin.

KEVIN: Oh!

VIOLET: *(Flat; disapproving.)* You were dreaming.

KEVIN: Hello.

BILL: Howdy-doo.

VIOLET: What happened to your arm?

KEVIN: What? . . . Oh, yes. Ow! It hurts.

VIOLET: What happened?

BILL: Golly.

KEVIN: It's . . . ah . . .

BILL: Oh, my.

VIOLET: *(To Bill.)* Let him talk!

KEVIN: . . . A cut. I cut myself. It was accident.

VIOLET: Where's Jennifer?

KEVIN: She's . . . I think she's in bed. She was sick.

> *(Violet exits quickly, hallway.)*

KEVIN: *(Continuing.)* It's not serious. She fainted. She's awake now . . . or she may be asleep. But not from fainting. I mean she woke up from fainting, but she may be asleep from sleeping. Pretend I'm not here.

BILL: Golly.

KEVIN: Oh, God.

BILL: What happened?

KEVIN: I was . . . I was ah . . . cutting a . . . ah . . . peach. I was cutting a peach and the knife slipped. It's nothing really. They're getting an ambulance.

BILL: An ambulance, golly. Are you going to the hospital?

KEVIN: I don't know where I'm going.

BILL: Golly.

KEVIN: I don't know who I am.

BILL: The hospital. That's not good.

> *(A car horn is heard. Thelma sits up, checks her watch. Horn sounds again.)*

KEVIN: That's for me.

BILL: Let me help you.

KEVIN: I have to go.

> *(Doesn't move.)*

BILL: All righty then. We're off.

> *(Car horn sounds again. Thelma leaves her room, stands on landing stairs, watching the men.)*

BILL: *(Continuing.)* There's the door.

> *(Kevin still doesn't move.)*

BILL: *(Continuing.)* Maybe someone should go with you.

KEVIN: To the door?

BILL: No, no. To the hospital.

KEVIN: It's not necessary.

BILL: Here we go.

> *(Bill helps Kevin to the door.)*

KEVIN: I'm fine.

BILL: There's a boy.

(Horn sounds again. Kevin exits. Bill shuts door.)

BILL: *(Continuing.)* Oh, dear.

THELMA: It was just a scratch.

BILL: *(Anxious.)* He said ambulance.

THELMA: He didn't mean it.

BILL: He cut himself on a peach.

THELMA: Don't worry about it.

BILL: *(Anxiety mounting.)* Was he going to the hospital?

THELMA: Who knows.

BILL: My mother died in a hospital.

(Bill is weak. He sits on the couch.)

THELMA: You told me.

BILL: They called me at Pratt.

THELMA: I know.

BILL: That's probably why I don't like them.

THELMA: Dad.

BILL: She wrote me every day.

THELMA: You told me.

BILL: I can still see her on the porch. I used to climb up from the outside to talk to her through the screen. When I was a little boy. We couldn't touch her.

THELMA: Dad?

BILL: They said she shouldn't have had another child.

THELMA: Dad.

BILL: Her health couldn't take it.

THELMA: I need to talk to you.

BILL: Why did they tell me that?!

THELMA: Dad!

BILL: Stupid bastards!

THELMA: Listen to me!

BILL: *(Bent over; holding his head.)* No help telling me a thing like that!

THELMA: Listen, goddamnit!

BILL: Thelma!

THELMA: I don't care about your mother and the porch and the screen! I don't even care that she died! I have my own problems! . . . Don't look at the floor!

BILL: Thelma . . .

THELMA: Don't look at the floor!! I have to talk to you!!

BILL: What is it?

THELMA: It's important!

(Bill looks up.)

BILL: Tell me.

THELMA: OK. Are you listening?

BILL: Yes.

THELMA: I was watching Jennifer . . .

BILL: Jennifer?

THELMA: My sister.

BILL: Of course.

THELMA: I was watching her and she was acting . . . don't know . . . awful.

BILL: Jennifer?

THELMA: Jennifer! Yes! I was watching her, and it was awful. I didn't want to be like that!

BILL: Golly.

THELMA: I didn't want to be her! It was a shock because I always did!

BILL: Really?

THELMA: You didn't know that?

BILL: No.

THELMA: It makes me insane! She's beautiful, she's smart, she's thin . . .

BILL: She's a great girl.

THELMA: It kills me! I used to ask myself, why does it torment me that I'm not like Jennifer when I hate the way she is? What's so great about having nice hair?

BILL: Well . . .

THELMA: But I would look at myself and there would be this crazy, wild person, this stupid person with dirty hair and split ends . . . and then there would be "Jennifer"!

BILL: Golly.

THELMA: I know what it is.

BILL: What?

THELMA: I keep thinking if I'm like Jennifer, you and Mom will love me.

BILL: Oh, Thelma. We love you.

THELMA: I don't think you do.

BILL: We love both our girls. You with your . . . bicycle . . . and your . . . stuffed animals, and Jennifer with her dancing. I'll never forget "Brownies Dancing Tiptoe."

THELMA: What?

BILL: It was a recital at dancing school. She played a brownie, a little sprite. There was a group of them. Little brownies. They had these peaked caps.

That was the number they did, "Brownies Dancing Tiptoe." She was so beautiful. Like a little angel.

(Thelma screams, a primal scream.)

BILL: *(Continuing.)* Thelma!

THELMA: SHUT UP ABOUT JENNIFER! I HATE HER! I HATE YOU! I HAVE TO GET OUT OF THIS HOUSE!!

(Thelma runs into her room, grabs her coat. Bill follows.)

BILL: You don't . . .

THELMA: Don't tell me I don't mean it!

BILL: You don't mean it.

THELMA: You don't care about me! All you care about is yourself and your boats and your mother dying on the porch and Jennifer and the shitty Brownies Dancing Tiptoe!

BILL: That's not true.

THELMA: It is!

BILL: You're under pressure.

THELMA: Damn right!

BILL: You had a hard week at school.

THELMA: I wasn't in school this week! DON'T YOU EVER LISTEN TO A THING I SAY?

BILL: I listen.

THELMA: Try this!

BILL: I always listen.

THELMA: You know where I'm going?

BILL: Now?

THELMA: Yes, now! Do you know where I'm going now!

BILL: It's late.

THELMA: I'm going downtown and I'm going to meet my friends and we're going to rob Jiffy Donut.

BILL: What?

THELMA: You heard me.

BILL: *(Distraught.)* You're not going to rob Jiffy Donut!

THELMA: I knew you'd say that.

BILL: Don't be silly!

THELMA: We'll be armed and dangerous. My friend has a knife!

(Bill appears faint. He quickly leaves the room. Thelma follows.)

BILL: You're not going to rob Jiffy . . .

THELMA: Stop me!

BILL: . . . Donut!

(Bill sinks to the couch. Thelma stops on landing stairs.)

THELMA: . . . Stop me!!

BILL: *(Head down.)* You'll feel better in the morning.

THELMA: I dare you!!

BILL: There's a girl.

THELMA: STOP ME!!! DON'T LOOK AT THE FLOOR!!!

(Bill does not look up.)

THELMA: *(Continuing; shuts off.)* All right. Fine. Forget it.

BILL: Thelma . . .

THELMA: Maybe you'll look at me in jail.

(Bill appears sick to his stomach. He hurries toward the hall.)

BILL: You're not going to be in any jail!

(Bill exits, hallway. Thelma moves to the couch, sits, motionless. A long beat. In one violent gesture she sweeps the beer cans and magazines off the coffee table and runs out the front door.)

(Blackout.)

ACT II
SCENE ONE

The next morning. Thelma's room is empty. Violet is seated in the living room, studying decorating pamphlets. Last night's beer cans and magazines remain strewn about. She seems oblivious to the mess surrounding her.

VIOLET: Beige, beige, beige! Beige, or taupe. Beige, or tan. And then there's green. I won't like the green, I can tell. I will not be happy with it, so there's no point in going on! Cancel the green!!
(Bill enters from the hallway, in bathrobe and pajamas.)
BILL: I'm half asleep.
VIOLET: You overslept.
BILL: How did I do that?
VIOLET: How would I know?
BILL: What time is it?
VIOLET: It's after ten.
BILL: Is it really?
VIOLET: It is.
BILL: I hardly ever do that.
VIOLET: Well, you've done it now.
BILL: Boy, oh, boy.
VIOLET: *(Studying pamphlets.)* Beige, beige, beige.
BILL: Orange juice.
(Bill rises, heads for the kitchen.)
VIOLET: What do you think about beige for the den?
BILL: What?
(Exits, kitchen.)
VIOLET: I said . . . Oh, you're gone.
(Bill re-enters with a glass of juice.)
BILL: You had it all poured and waiting for me. How thoughtful.
VIOLET: My pleasure. It's probably warm by now anyway.
BILL: How thoughtful.
VIOLET: My pleasure.
(Bill sits, drinks.)
VIOLET: *(Continuing.)* I've been thinking about beige for the den.
BILL: *(Appreciating juice.)* Mmm.
VIOLET: What do you think about that?
BILL: What?

VIOLET: Beige.

BILL: What about beige?

VIOLET: For the den. I've been thinking about beige for the den.

BILL: Did the paper come?

VIOLET: *(Pointing vaguely.)* It's over there.

 (Bill looks for the paper.)

VIOLET: *(Continuing.)* Do you like that idea?

BILL: What idea?

VIOLET: Beige . . . .Beige, beige, beige! Beige for the den!

BILL: It sounds nice.

VIOLET: I think so. But if you don't like it, we won't have it, will we?

 (Bill finds the paper, picks it up.)

BILL: No.

VIOLET: Certainly not!

BILL: Where are the girls?

VIOLET: Still asleep. Jennifer was sick last night.

BILL: Oh, dear. Is she all right now?

VIOLET: How would I know? She's asleep.

BILL: Oh.

 (Bill sits, reads paper. Violet begins cleaning up the living room.)

BILL: *(Continuing.)* Kevin had an accident.

VIOLET: I know.

BILL: He cut himself on a peach.

VIOLET: On a peach?!

BILL: No, not on a peach. I mean he was cutting a peach. He cut himself on a knife while he was cutting a peach.

VIOLET: I hope they didn't eat up all my peaches. I need them for my pie.

BILL: I'm worried about Thelma.

VIOLET: Don't be silly.

BILL: The school said she should go to a psychiatrist.

VIOLET: I guess we all know about that! I don't know what the world is coming to. Taking good people's money for nothing. You could talk to a chair.

BILL: What do you mean, talk to a chair?

VIOLET: They don't talk to people, those doctors. It's shameful. If you can't help yourself, nobody else can do it for you. Whatever happened to willpower? You don't hear about it these days. It's out of fashion.

BILL: Well, now . . .

VIOLET: Oh, you don't know anything. You're like a child. I swear to God. Forgive me, dear, but it's true.

BILL: Well . . .

VIOLET: Still looking for your mother.

BILL: I don't . . .

VIOLET: We all have our troubles.

BILL: My mother died of tuberculosis!

VIOLET: Thirty years ago! Get over it!

BILL: I still want to do something for Thelma. Maybe I should check on her.

VIOLET: Check on her?

BILL: See if she's all right.

VIOLET: Of course she's all right. She's asleep.

BILL: She was upset last night. Maybe I should bring her some juice.

VIOLET: Leave her alone.

BILL: I worry about her.

(Bill heads for Thelma's room. Violet follows.)

VIOLET: It's the age.

BILL: I don't remember Jennifer having trouble.

VIOLET: We were lucky with Jennifer. It's in the genes.

(They stop outside Thelma's door.)

BILL: There are other things to consider.

VIOLET: Consider your life away.

BILL: Now, Vi, you have to look at all sides of the picture.

VIOLET: Oh, please! I swear to God, if you want to complicate a thing, you're the one for the job!

BILL: *(Theoretical.)* Don't minimize what I have to say.

VIOLET: Very few people are helped by psychiatrists and you know it.

BILL: I'm not so sure.

VIOLET: Going over and over your problems! Hell's bells! Look at the positive! Open your eyes!

BILL: It's not that simple, Vi.

VIOLET: Of course it is. How do you think I felt when my brother choked on that nut?

BILL: Awful?

VIOLET: You think I didn't want to talk about it? I longed to talk about it. After the funeral I asked Mother if Beau could breathe in heaven.

BILL: What did she say?

VIOLET: She didn't answer me.

(Violet heads for the living room. Bill follows.)

BILL: She should have.

VIOLET: No! His name was never mentioned in our house again. And that saved us.

BILL: I'm not so sure.

VIOLET: Talk, talk talk! I swear to God. You'll hash a thing over 'til the cows come home.

(Violet resumes straightening up the room.)

BILL: That's unfair.

VIOLET: Move on! People are stronger than you think.

BILL: That's not the point.

VIOLET: Have a little faith in your own daughter.

BILL: I have faith in her.

VIOLET: A little patience goes a long way.

BILL: I just don't like to see her unhappy. It makes me uncomfortable.

(Violet is on her hands and knees, picking up pretzel crumbs from underneath the coffee table.)

VIOLET: *(Irritable.)* It's generally by doing the thing we don't want to do that we gain the most happiness. Self-respect is a wonderful thing.

BILL: *(A beat.)* I lost an account yesterday.

(Violet stops cleaning.)

VIOLET: How did that happen?

BILL: I'm not sure.

VIOLET: You design better boxes than anyone in the firm.

BILL: Sid's better than I am. He's younger.

VIOLET: He may be younger, but he's not better. He couldn't be.

BILL: He is.

VIOLET: After fifteen years of service.

BILL: They don't care about that.

VIOLET: Well, they should. You're an excellent designer!

BILL: Thank you. I just wish other people felt that way. But it's all right. I have a nice job, not too hard, and it leaves me time for my boats.

VIOLET: *(With irritation.)* Your boats.

BILL: A hobby is nice. *(A beat.)* Did we fail?

VIOLET: With what?

BILL: With everything. I don't know.

VIOLET: You're depressed because you lost the account. You never know if you do the right thing. You do your best. Please, don't think about it. You'll get yourself upset. *(Brightens suddenly; holds up a pamphlet.)* I'm going to hold this up against the wall, that's what! Beige or tan. There's a difference you know.

BILL: Is there?

VIOLET: There certainly is!

(Violet exits, hallway. Bill opens his newspaper, whistles as he reads. After a few beats he disapproves of something in the paper, stops whistling.)

BILL: Tch, tch, tch. That war. Boy, oh, boy.

(Bill takes a deep breath, makes popping noises, blowing air through his lips. He looks toward Thelma's room, rises, hesitates, then crosses to her door. He puts his ear to the door, hears nothing, knocks, listens, knocks again.)

BILL: *(Continuing.)* Thelma? . . . It's high time! . . . Thelma? . . . High time! . . . How about some scrambles? . . . Thelma? *(Opens door.)* Uh-oh.

(The doorbell rings.)

BILL: *(Continuing.)* Uh-oh!

(Bill shuts Thelma's door, heads for the front door, stops, concerned.)

BILL: *(Continuing.)* I'm in my robe.

(He resumes his trip to the front door, opens it. Kevin is in the doorway. He is unshaven, wears rumpled clothes from the night before. His arm is in a sling.)

BILL: *(Continuing.)* It's Kevin! Here's a surprise.

(Kevin enters. Bill shuts door.)

KEVIN: Excuse me for coming so early, Mr. Gardner.

BILL: No, no. I'm in my robe. I shouldn't be.

KEVIN: Is Jennifer here?

BILL: I overslept.

KEVIN: Is Jennifer here. Is she up?

BILL: Up? Oh, golly. I don't think so.

KEVIN: I'd like to wait if it's all right.

BILL: Of course.

(Notices sling.)

Oh, dear. How's your arm?

KEVIN: All right. This isn't necessary. It's a sling.

BILL: Oh.

KEVIN: I went to the emergency room. They put a bandage on it and gave me a tetanus shot.

BILL: Oh, dear.

(They sit. Pause.)

KEVIN: I hope you don't mind my waiting.

BILL: Of course not. Our house is your house. Well. *(A pause.)* Thelma's not in her room.

KEVIN: Oh.

BILL: I wonder where she is.

KEVIN: The kitchen?

BILL: I don't think so. Vi . . . ah, Mrs. Gardner.

KEVIN: Right.

BILL: . . . Vi, ah . . . said she was asleep.

KEVIN: But she's not.

BILL: No . . . It's a mystery. I'm a little worried.

KEVIN: She'll turn up.

BILL: Mm.

(Pause.)

KEVIN: How's the paper box business?

BILL: It's seen better days.

KEVIN: Sorry to hear it.

BILL: It's true.

KEVIN: There'll always be boxes.

BILL: I guess.

KEVIN: Of course.

BILL: Plastics have interfered.

KEVIN: They would.

BILL: No matter what they say.

KEVIN: Of course. *(A beat.)* Do they say otherwise?

BILL: Some do.

KEVIN: Well, they couldn't help but interfere. Another container.

BILL: I know.

(Pause.)

KEVIN: You were reading the paper. Don't let me disturb you.

BILL: No, no. Bad news, always bad news.

KEVIN: I know. It's terrible.

BILL: I just read where a lady in the Bronx fell out of a window.

KEVIN: Oh, my.

BILL: Two ladies in Brooklyn fell out of a truck.

KEVIN: Oh, my.

BILL: Not to mention our foreign policy . . . Kevin, Kevin, what's wrong with the world?

KEVIN: I don't know.

(Thelma enters through the front door. Her shirt is torn, her clothes, filthy.

Her face is streaked with soot. Agitated, exhausted, her breathing is irregular. She appears frightened, suspicious. She looks about the room as if seeking an answer to some crucial question.)

BILL: Oh, Thelma! There you are!

(Thelma looks to the phone. She looks to the kitchen. Listens.)

BILL: Where were you? I thought you were asleep. I checked on you, but you weren't there.

(Thelma tries to steady her breathing. She covers her eyes with her hands.)

BILL: *(Continuing.)* How 'bout some scrambles?

(Thelma shivers, cold. Disoriented, she moves to her room. Bill follows.)

BILL: *(Continuing.)* Krispies! Snap, crackle and pop!

(Thelma goes into her room, slams the door. She leans on it, breathing heavily. Bill moves back toward the living room.)

KEVIN: . . . I guess not.

(Bill returns to the couch, sits.)

BILL: So! . . . You're marrying my little girl! Isn't that something?

(Thelma, pulls a sweatshirt from a pile of clothes on the floor. She puts it on, shivering. She pulls a jacket from the pile, puts that on too. She holds it closed. She sits on the floor, her back against the bureau, her arms around her knees.)

BILL: *(Continuing.)* It's funny to have a daughter getting married. I've thought about it, you know, pictured it. And here it is. I think I first thought about it when she was seven. I think that's when it was. I don't know. Was it six? Six or seven, I don't remember. Six or seven, something like that . . . Maybe eight.

KEVIN: Ah-huh.

BILL: Golly.

KEVIN: Wow.

BILL: "Brownies Dancing Tiptoe."

KEVIN: What?

BILL: *(Edgy.)* "Brownies Dancing Tiptoe!" It was a recital. At dancing school.

KEVIN: Oh.

(Bill looks to Thelma's room, concerned, then back to Kevin.)

BILL: Where was I? Oh, yes, "Brownies Dancing Tiptoe." I looked at her and I said to myself, "She'll be getting married some day." It came as a shock. It's not so bad, really, but it came faster than I thought it would, I can tell you that. You'll take good care of her, won't you? Of course you will, what a silly question. I know you will.

(Jennifer enters from the hallway in a housecoat. She has a hangover, moves carefully to reduce the pain.)

BILL: *(Continuing.)* Here's Jennifer.

JENNIFER: You're still in your robe.

BILL: Yes. Yes, I am. I couldn't get started today.

JENNIFER: *(To Kevin.)* Good morning.

KEVIN: Good morning, Jennifer.

  (A beat.)

BILL: I need some orange juice. *(To Kevin.)* Do you want some?

KEVIN: No, thank you.

BILL: There's something about orange juice. Sometimes I feel like orange juice
  and nothing else will do. Do you ever feel that way?

KEVIN: I don't like orange juice.

BILL: You don't?

JENNIFER: Some people don't.

KEVIN: I don't.

BILL: Oh. Maybe I won't have any orange juice . . . My robe. I should get
  dressed. *(Starts for hall.)* I'm just going in here. *(Exits.)*
  *(Thelma climbs onto her bed. She lies in a fetal position, eyes wide, clutch-
  ing her pillow.)*

JENNIFER: *(In pain.)* My head.

KEVIN: I'm not surprised.

JENNIFER: What do you mean?

KEVIN: With all you drank last night.

JENNIFER: Did I drink a lot?

KEVIN: Ha!

JENNIFER: I didn't expect you this morning.

KEVIN: Well, here I am.

JENNIFER: What's the matter with your arm?

KEVIN: I don't expect you to remember that.

JENNIFER: I don't.

KEVIN: Last night was rather unpleasant . . . Jennifer . . . I have some things
  to say to you. It's not easy for me. I suppose you know that. I suppose
  you know me well enough by now to know that I don't assert myself easily. Assertion is not easy. I'm working on it. It's getting better, but it's still
  not easy . . . There have been things building up in me. That's what they
  do. They build up and I hide them from myself. I pretend they're not
  there, but they are, they're there and last night certain things became
  clear. Last night turned the trick you might say. Last night was the last
  straw, the one that broke the camel's back . . . Do you know what went
  on last night? . . . Well, I'll tell you. My fiancée provoked such

goings-on, we won't go into that now, but suffice it to say, such goings on were provoked that I ended up being stabbed in the arm by a lunatic! Half the night I spent in the emergency room, which was no picnic, I might add, and the other half I spent . . . shall I tell you where? . . . Well, I'll tell you! The other half I spent in the Port Authority Bus Terminal! That's right! You heard me! THE PORT AUTHORITY BUS TERMINAL! And I can safely say it will be my last night there! You brought me to a point of such tension and confusion, such frustration and anger, such aggravation and . . . heaven knows what, that I sat immobile in the Port Authority Bus Terminal for five hours! Five hours! Count them!

(Demonstrates with fingers.)

One, two, three, four, five!!! Five hours staring into space among the bums. Bums to the right of me, bums to the left, people in torment on every bench and a few who missed their connection. It was no picnic, I can tell you that. But I made myself sit there. I said, "Kevin, you are going to sit here until you come to a decision." And that's what I did. *(Holds up injured arm.)* Here you see an arm. This arm has been injured! Injured!! And I hold you responsible! The side of you that I saw last night, and drunk is no excuse, the side of you that I saw will take a long time to erase from my mind. The experience has shaken me greatly! I HAVEN'T SHAVED! . . . In addition to this, differences between us are slowly becoming apparent. Differences which create a gap too large for easy passage. The matter of our home, the matter of Cleveland. Could you be happy in the place I want to live, the surroundings I envision? I don't know. And in this state of turmoil and confusion, unrest and anxiety, mistrust and anger . . . in this state I will not enter matrimony. I may change, I may come to feel differently, but as things stand . . . as they stand now . . . That's it. *(Pause.)* What do you think?

(Jennifer is crying, silently.)

KEVIN: *(Continuing.)* Do you have anything to say?

JENNIFER: No.

KEVIN: Then I'll go.

JENNIFER: All right.

KEVIN: All right. Good-bye.

JENNIFER: Good-bye.

(Kevin exits. Violet calls from the hallway.)

VIOLET: *(Offstage.)* Kevin?!!

(Jennifer cries softly. Violet enters from the hallway with pamphlets.)

VIOLET: Has Kevin left?

JENNIFER: Yes.

VIOLET: What a shame. I wanted to ask his opinion on the den. Men like to feel needed.

(Violet picks up remaining beer cans, glasses, puts them on a tray.)

VIOLET: *(Continuing.)* Did you have your breakfast?

JENNIFER: No.

VIOLET: I've decided on beige anyway, so it doesn't matter.

JENNIFER: I'm not getting married.

VIOLET: It goes better with the carpet.

(Violet exits, kitchen, with tray.)

JENNIFER: I'm not getting married!

(Violet re-enters.)

VIOLET: What?

JENNIFER: The engagement is off.

VIOLET: What do you mean?

JENNIFER: He left.

VIOLET: Kevin?

JENNIFER: Who do you think?

VIOLET: What happened? . . . You had a fight . . . Oh, Jennifer. Don't be upset. All couples have their disagreements. It's nothing.

JENNIFER: He won't come back.

VIOLET: Of course he will.

JENNIFER: No, he won't.

VIOLET: Well, he'll never find a better wife. He'll come to his senses.

JENNIFER: It's probably just as well. I don't know if I want to get married anyway.

VIOLET: Of course you do. You're twenty-two years old! . . . Now, I tell you what. Calm yourself and when you're all pulled together you call him on the phone and tell him you're sorry.

JENNIFER: For what?

VIOLET: It doesn't matter. Just tell him you're sorry. Men like to feel they're in the right. You know in your own mind what you think. No one can change that, but let him think he's won. Men need that.

JENNIFER: I don't even know if if love him.

VIOLET: Love is a myth.

BILL: *(Offstage.)* *(Sings loudly; proud.)* "Who can I turn to when nobody needs me?"

VIOLET: I'm going to get the mail.

(Exits, front door.)

(Bill appears in the hallway, on his way to the desk.)

BILL: *(Sings.)* "My heart wants to know and so I must go where destiny leads me."

(Bill gets glue from desk, heads back down the hallway, patting Jennifer on the head as he passes.)

BILL: *(Continuing; sings.)* "With no one beside me and no one to guide me, I'll go on my way and after the day the darkness will hide me."

(Disappears down the hall.)

JENNIFER: OH, GOD, HE HATES ME!! WHAT AM I GOING TO DO??? OH, GOD, OH SHIT! OH, GODDDDDDD!!! HE HATES ME! I WISH I WAS DEAD!!!

(Violet enters front door with the mail.)

VIOLET: Why is there never any mail on Saturday?

(Violet notices Jennifer in a heap on the floor. Jennifer smiles, masking torment.)

VIOLET: *(Continuing.)* I don't think they sort it.

JENNIFER: *(Fake cheer.)* Junk, junk, junk!

(Violet exits, kitchen.)

JENNIFER: *(Continuing.)* AAAHHHH!!! HE HATES MY GUTS!! I'M GOING TO KILL MYSELF!!! OH, GOD! OH, SHIT! OH,GOD!!!!

(Violet re-enters.)

VIOLET: The crust is made!

(Jennifer starts for the hall.)

VIOLET: *(Continuing.)* Where are you going?

JENNIFER: A bath. *(Stops.)* I'm going to try that new bubble gel. "Essence of Lavender." *(Honest.)* I always used to wonder what it would feel like to know what I wanted.

(Starts down hallway.)

VIOLET: Jennifer, wait!

JENNIFER: What is it?!

VIOLET: Ethical Culture called yesterday. The wedding date is confirmed!

JENNIFER: Great.

(Jennifer continues down the hall. Thelma pulls herself up, crawls under the bed covers as Bill comes down the hallway, passing Jennifer.)

BILL: *(To Jennifer.)* I'm going to get Thelma some breakfast.

VIOLET: Let her get her own breakfast!

BILL: She had a rough night.

VIOLET: Who's fault was that?!

(Violet heads for Thelma's room.)

BILL: Cereal.

(Exits, kitchen.)

(Violet bursts into Thelma's room, throws off Thelma's covers.)

VIOLET: Get up! I've had it with you, Missy! GET UP! You will clean your room, you will wash your clothes, you will do your homework and you will go to school, or there will be hell to pay on Monday! GET UP!!

(Thelma sits up.)

VIOLET: *(Continuing.)* What happened to you? You're filthy!

(Thelma gets out of bed, scared, angry, violent. She leaves her room, heads down the hallway to the bathroom. Violet follows.)

VIOLET: *(Continuing.)* Don't leave the room when I'm talking to you!

(Thelma pounds on the bathroom door.)

JENNIFER: *(Offstage.)* I'M IN HERE!

(Thelma whips past her mother.)

THELMA: LEAVE ME ALONE!

(Violet follows Thelma into the living room. Bill enters from the kitchen with a bowl of cereal, sits on the couch.)

VIOLET: Tell me what happened!

THELMA: NO!

BILL: What's going on?

VIOLET: TELL ME NOW!

THELMA: LEAVE ME ALONE!

BILL: Let's calm down.

VIOLET: WHAT HAPPENED??!

JENNIFER: *(Offstage.)* CAN A PERSON TAKE A BATH IN THIS HOUSE?! WHY IS THERE ALWAYS SCREAMING??!!!

BILL: *(Calls.)* That's all right! There's just a little problem!

JENNIFER: *(Offstage.)* JESUS CHRIST! IT'S A MAD HOUSE!

(Jennifer enters from the hall, wrapped in a towel.)

VIOLET: WHAT HAPPENED TO YOU??!!!

THELMA: I set fire to Ethical Culture.

VIOLET: WHAT?!

THELMA: I SET FIRE TO ETHICAL CULTURE!!!

VIOLET: You set fire to Ethical culture?!

THELMA: I SET FIRE TO IT!

BILL: There's a girl.

VIOLET: What are you talking about??!!

JENNIFER: You set fire to Ethical Culture?

THELMA: Shut up, Jennifer!

BILL: Easy now.

VIOLET: You tell me what really happened, and tell me now, Missy!

THELMA: WHY DOESN'T ANYBODY BELIEVE ME??!!

BILL: Let's just . . .

THELMA: I BURNED DOWN THE FUCKING BUILDING!! YOU GOT THAT??!!

VIOLET: You're making it up!

THELMA: Don't you wish!

JENNIFER: You're crazy.

BILL: We need to, ah . . .

THELMA: I BURNED IT DOWN!! I wanted to burn it down and than I didn't, but it was too late! OH, SHIT!

JENNIFER: She really did it.

VIOLET: Did anyone see you?

THELMA: What difference does it make?! I DID IT!!! *(Suddenly edgy.)* Did the police call?

VIOLET: You left the house . . . you went to Ethical Culture . . . AND BURNED IT DOWN??!!

THELMA: No.

VIOLET: What?!!

THELMA: I went to rob Jiffy Donut.

JENNIFER: Is this a joke?

THELMA: IT'S REAL!!! I met my friends at Jiffy Donut . . . sound familiar, Dad? . . . so we could rob it!

VIOLET: Rob it?!!

THELMA: You heard me! My friend had a knife.

VIOLET: A knife??!!

THELMA: He nearly slit a guy's throat.

VIOLET: What guy??!!

THELMA: Sean! Red hair! Teeth like a vampire!

VIOLET: Who's Sean??!!!

THELMA: *(Fast; intense.)* Sean Neverman! He works there! Nights! I was the lookout! This man came by with a dog so we couldn't do it! I was in the alley and my friends were there and Philip was throwing up and there was vomit and the dumpster and this starving cat was pacing around, and . . .

VIOLET: What?!!

THELMA: I wanted to die! . . . My friends left . . . I didn't know what do to. I wished I had Harry's knife so I could slit my wrists! It was hours . . . I was there and . . . I don't know, it was freezing and it smelled like shit . . . the dumpster and Philip's vomit. Then I remembered the matches. I took them from the counter at Jiffy Donut . . . And I was walking, walking . . . streets, stores, houses, nothing. Empty, endless, nowhere. And there was Ethical Culture. I looked at the building. I noticed how it's wood, like a house. That's good, I thought. Wood burns. I climbed the tree. I wanted to get on the roof. That's where I started the fire.

JENNIFER: Jesus.

THELMA: *(Suddenly worried.)* Did the police call? I know they're going to call. They're going to call, or come to the door. I don't know why they're not here yet . . . Mr. Lombardi saw me. My gym teacher. He was putting out the trash. He looked at me and I ran. I had to get away from the fire and the roof and the porch! There's a porch, the top of the porch, and the screen frame, and I had the lighter fluid. I stole it from the 7-Eleven. I tore my shirt on the nail. It was a rag. I put it down on the edge of the porch frame. I picked up the lighter fluid. I poured it on the rag. I took the matches out of my pocket. I struck a match . . . and held it by the rag. It caught. And the flames! Right away, and I jumped back! It spread so fast! I had to get down the tree and I fell and I got up and I ran to the bushes! I was hiding, and it wouldn't stop! It was beautiful! So . . . REAL! . . . But the people came and I ran! Mr. Lombardi and the trash and I was running, but I couldn't! My knees, and I collapsed. I was on the sidewalk. I just lay there.

(The phone rings. No one moves to answer it. It continues to ring. Thelma sinks to her knees, crying. The phone rings ten times, then stops. A long beat. Thelma's breathing becomes easier. She's calmer now.)

THELMA: *(Continuing.)* Later, I went back to see. The smoke and the firemen and the lights and the tape . . . the people, the police. A lot of it burned. A third of it . . . I don't know . . . a wing. The whole thing is wrecked. I hid in the shed. Then I came home. *(A long beat.)* So that's me, Mom. What do you think?

(The phone rings again. No one moves. Slowly, Thelma rises and exits down the hallway. Violet follows her, then Jennifer, then Bill. The phone continues ringing as the lights fade. The phone continues ringing in the darkness.)

SCENE TWO

Six weeks later. The stage is empty. There is a large duffle bag by the front door. Bill enters from the hallway in his pajamas, whistling "Strange Fruit." He stops, anxious, puts his hand to his throat. He moves to the radio on the upstage hutch, turns it on.

RADIO ANNOUNCER: . . . west of the Mekong Delta.
    (Bill exits into the kitchen.)
RADIO ANNOUNCER: *(Continuing.)* President Nixon was optimistic about the chances for further progress as more troops were dispatched to Saigon yesterday to bolster the number of military forces already in place.
    (Bill re-enters, whistling, with a glass of orange juice. He stops whistling, stands in the living room, anxiously clearing his throat. With his free hand he holds his neck.)
RADIO ANNOUNCER: *(Continuing.)* Several more incidents of individuals burning draft cards were reported last week in Texas, Louisiana, and upper New York State. The president is taking a hard line on . . .
    (Bill crosses to the radio, switching the station. We hear a scramble of various channels. He settles on Glenn Miller's band in a rousing swing number. He drinks his juice. The front door opens. Violet enters with a bag of groceries.)
VIOLET: I can't stand Glenn Miller.
BILL: I'll turn it off.
    (Bill shuts off the radio as Violet heads for the kitchen.)
VIOLET: We have to leave soon. You better get dressed.
    (Violet exits, kitchen. Bill takes a drink of juice. Once more, he anxiously clears his throat, then sits in downstage chair. He takes another drink of juice, resumes whistling. Violet enters from the kitchen, with a couple of rolls of toilet paper, heads for the hall.)
VIOLET: *(Continuing.)* I just put away what would spoil. I have to get Thelma's last minute things out of the dryer. Will you stop whistling?
BILL: Oh, I'm sorry. Does it bother you?
VIOLET: It's bothered me for twenty-three years.
BILL: You never told me.
VIOLET: I'm telling you now.
BILL: I'll watch it.
VIOLET: Thank you. Start the day, dear. Pajamas make you groggy. And would you put away the rest of the groceries? We have to leave if we're going to get there for lunch.

(Thelma comes down the hallway, enters her room. Her hair is wet and stringy. She is wrapped in a towel. Throughout the following she pulls underwear, jeans, and a sweatshirt from bureau and returns to the bathroom.)

BILL: I hope this is the right thing for her.

VIOLET: It's better than jail, wouldn't you say, thank your lucky stars. The judge was lenient.

BILL: Well, jail . . .

VIOLET: Be glad it's not a state school with juvenile delinquents roaming around. It's a perfectly decent place. "North Woods School offers troubled teens a structured framework, in a relaxed country setting with daily opportunities for healing and growth." You read the brochure.

BILL: I hope she'll be all right.

VIOLET: She'll be fine. I labeled all her clothes.

BILL: I liked that therapist. I know you don't like therapists, but I liked her.

VIOLET: Oh, I'm sure they have it well in hand.

BILL: Maybe it's a good thing.

VIOLET: What do you mean?

BILL: Maybe she needs to get away.

VIOLET: Why would she need to get away?

BILL: I don't know. I have a funny feeling it might be just the thing. That therapist made sense to me.

VIOLET: Then you have nothing to worry about. You're always worrying. Most of the things you worry about never happen.

BILL: Thelma needs a space of her own, where she feels safe. There's a lot of pressure here. I feel it.

VIOLET: Maybe you should go away to school.

BILL: Now, Vi, I'm only . . .
    (Trails off.)

VIOLET: What?

BILL: Maybe they can help her. We haven't been able to do it.

VIOLET: That's an understatement.

BILL: It's not an understatement, Vi. It's the truth.

VIOLET: I'm going to finish her packing. You better get dressed.
    (Violet heads up the landing steps toward hallway.)

BILL: I think I . . . ah . . . I don't . . . ah . . .

VIOLET: . . . What!!!!

BILL: I don't think I'll be going.

VIOLET: What do you mean, you won't be going?

BILL: I have a scratchy throat.

VIOLET: I've heard everything.

BILL: I better rest.

VIOLET: Your daughter is going away to reform school for God knows how long and you won't drive her because you have a SCRATCHY THROAT??!!

BILL: It's not a reform school.

VIOLET: You selfish bastard.

BILL: I have that tickle.

VIOLET: SHE'S YOUR DAUGHTER!!!

BILL: Vi . . .

VIOLET: . . . I CAN'T STAND IT ANYMORE!! . . .

BILL: . . . Calm yourself . . .

VIOLET: . . . I CAN'T STAND IT!!! . . .

BILL: . . . Now, Vi . . .

VIOLET: DON'T "NOW VI" ME, YOU SELF-CENTERED SON-OF-A-BITCH!! WHO MADE YOU THE MOST IMPORTANT PERSON IN THE WORLD??!!

BILL: I have a scratchy throat.

VIOLET: I'LL TELL YOU SOMETHING, MISTER! NOBODY CARES!!

BILL: . . . Calm down, Vi . . .

VIOLET: . . . YOU'RE NOT THAT FASCINATING!! . . .

BILL: . . . I just . . .

VIOLET: . . . YOUR SELFISHNESS DISGUSTS ME!! . . .

BILL: . . . Please . . .

VIOLET: . . . IF YOU WERE DYING IN THE GUTTER I WOULDN'T STOOP TO PICK YOU UP!!!

BILL: You don't mean that.

> *(Violet hurls a roll of toilet paper at Bill, hitting him hard, barely missing his head.)*

BILL: *(Continuing; forty years of rage.)* VIOLET!!!!!!!!

> *(Violet exits down the hall. A long beat. Bill clears his throat, picks up the toilet paper, his juice glass, stands, dazed, as Jennifer enters from the hallway in slacks and a sweater. She carries a clipboard, notes, and several magazines. Bill stands, watching Jennifer, who sits at the desk, consults her clipboard, picks up the phone, dials.)*

JENNIFER: *(On phone.)* . . . Hi. This is Jennifer Gardner. I'm calling about the tent . . . Tent . . . TENT! . . . that's right . . . Gardner, June 21st . . . Is this Rocco? *(Charming.)* . . . Oh, hi! . . . I thought it was you, but I wasn't sure. You and the other guy sound so much alike. What's his name . . .

Peewee! That's right, Peewee . . . Fine! . . . How are you? . . . Great! So, you were going to check on the cost of the larger tent. *(A major point.)* . . . Does that include the poles . . . That's too much . . . The other one is too small. I'm having a band.

(Bill exits, kitchen.)

JENNIFER: *(Continuing.)* . . . Of course I want them inside. What if it rains? You said it yourself, "You never know." You can quote yourself on that one! . . . Right . . . OK. Check with Peewee and let me know . . . Bye!

(Hangs up.)

Oh, God!

(Jennifer collects her things, moves to large chair, spreads things out on the ottoman in front of the chair, starts to sit, reconsiders.)

JENNIFER: *(Continuing.)* Coffee.

(Jennifer heads for the kitchen as Bill enters with a box of Ritz Crackers.)

BILL: Good morning!

JENNIFER: Good morning!

BILL: *(Holds up cracker box.)* Want a Ritz?

JENNIFER: No thanks. I need coffee.

(Jennifer exits into kitchen. Bill calls after her.)

BILL: A booster cup!

JENNIFER: *(Offstage.)* Right!

(Bill sits in the large chair, his arm around the cracker box. Thelma exits bathroom, enters her room. She is dressed in jeans and a sweatshirt. Throughout the following she moves slowly about her room, collecting things to take with her, a large stuffed animal, a football, a rubber snake, etc. She puts the smaller things in a gym bag. She climbs onto the bed and removes her Janis Joplin poster from the wall. She rolls it up, then sits on the bed. She puts on her sneakers and socks, then waits, sitting on the edge of the bed, holding the poster, staring out front.)

(Jennifer enters from the kitchen with a cup of coffee.)

BILL: It's always good to have a booster cup.

JENNIFER: Right.

BILL: I didn't have my booster cup this morning.

JENNIFER: That's unusual.

BILL: I didn't have coffee.

JENNIFER: Why not?

BILL: I have a scratchy throat.

JENNIFER: So you had tea.

BILL: I did.

JENNIFER: That's good.

(Jennifer stands by the ottoman and chair where Bill sits, waiting for Bill to notice her clipboard, etc. and give her the seat. Bill eats a cracker.)

BILL: Want a Ritz now?

JENNIFER: No.

BILL: Remember our Ritz and milk?

JENNIFER: I do.

BILL: Every night at the old apartment. I remember your little legs swinging off the Hitchcock chair. They didn't touch the floor.

JENNIFER: *(Edgy.)* That's right.

BILL: You and me . . . *(Regards clipboard; mystified.)* What are you doing there?

JENNIFER: Going over plans for the wedding.

BILL: Oh . . . Nobody else likes Ritz.

JENNIFER: Somebody must, or they wouldn't make them.

BILL: Oh. Yes . . . well . . . right. I meant in the family. Your mother doesn't like them. Thelma doesn't like them.

JENNIFER: *(Claustrophobic.)* Aren't you taking Thelma to school?

BILL: I have a scratchy throat.

JENNIFER: Oh, right. I forgot about that.

(Jennifer collects her things, moves to the couch. She spreads her notes and magazines out on the coffee table in front of her, studies her clipboard. Bill rises with crackers, moves to the coffee table, stacks crackers on top of her notes.)

BILL: Four Ritz for you, four Ritz for me. No butter, no jelly, no cheese. Can't taste the cracker with all that damn stuff. Four Ritz a piece and a half a glass of milk . . . Did you use to drink a whole glass?

JENNIFER: I don't remember.

BILL: I think you did.

JENNIFER: I might have.

BILL: I think you did.

JENNIFER: I need to concentrate on this right now, Dad, OK?

BILL: Oh, sure. Go right ahead. I think Thelma will be happy at school. Did you know they slide from floor to floor down laundry shoots?

JENNIFER: I didn't know that.

BILL: They do. They slide right down. It's a tough school, but they let them have a good time too. I guess a lot of them have problems.

JENNIFER: Most likely.

BILL: They take care of the pigs.

JENNIFER: What?

BILL: The pigs.

JENNIFER: Pigs?

BILL: They feed them.

JENNIFER: What pigs?

BILL: It's a farm.

JENNIFER: Oh.

BILL: Yup. They feed the pigs. They milk the cows. They plant things . . .

JENNIFER: . . . Right.

BILL: . . . And they have their classes. It's quite a school.

JENNIFER: Great.

> *(Shows her father the magazine.)*
>
> What do you think of this gown, Dad?

BILL: *(Intrigued.)* Hmm, well. Pretty bare on the shoulders there.

JENNIFER: I thought you'd say that.

> *(Violet comes down the hallway with a stack of Thelma's clothes.)*

VIOLET: Thelma! . . . Thelma, come and get your clothes! *(Stops at Thelma's door.)* We have to go! . . . Thelma?

> *(Thelma opens her door.)*

BILL: *(Considers cracker box; to Jennifer.)* I'll put this back.

> *(Bill exits, kitchen. Thelma takes the clothes from her mother.)*

VIOLET: Are you hungry?

THELMA: No.

VIOLET: I packed us a snack. Carrot sticks, celery spears, raisins, and a Clark Bar.

THELMA: Thank you.

VIOLET: *(With genuine warmth.)* I know you like Clark Bars.

THELMA: I love them.

VIOLET: I want you to think of us fondly. *(Sincere.)* Your mother loves you.

> *(A noise is heard from the kitchen. Violet heads for living room.)*

VIOLET: *(Continuing; calls out.)* What are you doing in the kitchen?!

BILL: *(Offstage.)* Groceries . . . there's a few more here . . . I'm just . . .

VIOLET: PUT THE TOOTHPICKS IN THE RABBIT!

BILL: *(Offstage.)* What's that?

VIOLET: PUT THE TOOTHPICKS IN THE RABBIT!! YOU KNOW, THE CHINA RABBIT BY THE TOASTER!! PICK UP THE EARS!!! *(To Jennifer.)* He'll never find it.

> *(Thelma puts the stack of clothes into the gym bag. She zips the bag, picks up her pea coat, stuffed animal, and her poster. She carries her things out into the hall, sets them on the landing.)*

VIOLET: *(Continuing; to Jennifer.)* How's it going dear? Are you choosing the chiffon?

JENNIFER: Dad wasn't pleased with the bare shoulders.

VIOLET: A jacket would be nice.

JENNIFER: I don't want to wear a jacket.

VIOLET: It's your wedding.

JENNIFER: I'm beginning to wonder. Do we really have to invite Kevin's cousin's half-sister and the seven godchildren?

VIOLET: Of course! No question there! *(Watches Thelma on the landing.)* . . . Well. I better get a move on.

(Violet exits down the hallway. Jennifer regards Thelma on the landing.)

JENNIFER: Do you need any help?

THELMA: That's why I'm leaving.

JENNIFER: Don't be smart. I asked a simple question.

THELMA: Which I answered.

JENNIFER: I meant help with your packing.

THELMA: I'm packed . . . As you can see.

(Jennifer studies her clipboard.)

THELMA: *(Continuing.)* You don't need any help, do you.

JENNIFER: With the wedding?

THELMA: With your life.

JENNIFER: It'll all fall into place once I order the tent.

THELMA: The tent. Oh, God, yes. That'll do it.

JENNIFER: *(Not hearing.)* Are you coming home for Christmas?

THELMA: I don't know.

JENNIFER: You'll miss a lot of stocking presents if you don't come home.

THELMA: You can't have everything.

JENNIFER: You better be at my wedding. That's June 21st. Do they let you out for the summer?

THELMA: I doubt it.

JENNIFER: Well, I want you at my wedding. You tell them that.

THELMA: OK.

JENNIFER: If you want to be there.

THELMA: Right.

JENNIFER: You don't give an inch, do you?

THELMA: Not unless I mean it.

JENNIFER: You're saying you don't want to come to my wedding.

THELMA: I'm saying I don't know if I want to come to your wedding.

JENNIFER: Fine.

THELMA: I tend to think I do, actually.

JENNIFER: Send me a card.

THELMA: OK.

> *(Sits on landing steps; a beat.)*

I'm sorry I set fire to Ethical Culture.

JENNIFER: Forget it.

THELMA: It was a cruel thing to do.

JENNIFER: It doesn't matter. I'd rather have the wedding at church.

THELMA: Why was it going to be at Ethical Culture?

JENNIFER: Kevin's resistant to Pastor St. Bernard. It's the whole Lutheran/Presbyterian thing. We're working it out.

THELMA: Let me know how it goes.

JENNIFER: I will. You take care of yourself.

THELMA: I'll try.

JENNIFER: Can we visit you?

THELMA: I don't know.

JENNIFER: You let me know about that and I'll let you know about the wedding.

THELMA: OK.

> *(Violet enters from the hall. She wears a coat, carries a purse. She hands Thelma her Janis poster and stuffed animal, picks up Thelma's pea coat and bag, crosses through the living room.)*

VIOLET: I'll get the snacks and we're off.

> *(Violet sets bag and coat by the front door. She starts into the kitchen as Bill enters from kitchen. There is awkward tension as they pass each other. Violet exits, kitchen.)*

BILL: You're leaving.

THELMA: Yes, Dad.

BILL: I ah . . . I'm not going with you. I have a, ah . . . scratchy throat.

THELMA: I wondered about the pajamas.

BILL: Oh. Right . . . I'll miss you.

> *(Thelma moves to hug him.)*

BILL: *(Continuing.)* I'd better not hug you. I don't want you to catch anything.

> *(Violet enters from the kitchen with the snacks.)*

VIOLET: Say your good-byes. There's construction on the thruway.

> *(Violet helps Thelma on with her coat, hands Thelma the poster and the stuffed animal.)*

BILL: You've got all that stuff.

THELMA: I'm leaving.

BILL: Golly . . . Good-bye, sweetheart.

THELMA: Good-bye, Dad.

BILL: *(A beat.)* Sorry I can't go with you . . . It's just this pesky tickle . . . I love you.

THELMA: I love you too, Dad.

VIOLET: *(On her way out.)* Defrost the fish sticks, Jennifer. I won't be home 'til six.

(Violet exits.)

JENNIFER: Good-bye, Thelma.

THELMA: Good-bye.

(Thelma looks about the room, a last look. She looks to her father. She tentatively starts out, stops, looks back at him, exits. A long beat. Bill looks at the floor.)

JENNIFER: Are you going to get dressed today?

BILL: I might as well.

(Bill starts toward the hallway. He pats Jennifer's shoulder on his way out.)

BILL: *(Continuing.)* Time passes.

(Bill exits down the hallway. Jennifer crosses to the phone, dials.)

JENNIFER: *(On phone.)* Hi, Kev, it's me . . . How's your neck? . . . Any change in the rash at all? . . . You can't expect it to heal overnight. Eczema takes a while . . . So, when is the closing? . . . Right . . . Oh, it's a lovely house. You can do a lot with a split level . . . OK. Sure. We'll go a few days early . . . The safe side. Absolutely. There could be a blizzard. February in Cleveland you never know . . . It's fine . . . Whatever you want. Anything is all right with me.

(The lights fade in living room. Light remains in Thelma's room. Lights out.)

END OF PLAY

BULRUSHER

Eisa Davis

PLAYWRIGHT'S BIOGRAPHY

Eisa Davis is the author of *Bulrusher* (Urban Stages), *Hip Hop Anansi* (Imagination Stage), *Angela's Mixtape, Paper Armor, Six Minutes, Umkovu,* and *The History of Light.* She is the winner of the Helen Merrill Award, the John Lippmann New Frontier Award, and she has received fellowships from the Mac-Dowell Colony, Cave Canem, and the Van Lier and Mellon Foundations. Her work has been developed by the Hip Hop Theater Festival, New York Theater Workshop, New York Stage and Film, The New Group, Soho Rep, The Flea, The Cherry Lane, Portland Center Stage, Hartford Stage, Cleveland Playhouse, Seattle Rep, Yale University, the Nuyorican Poets Café, the Schomburg Center for Black Research, and the Women's Project, among others. She is currently working on a screenplay based in part on her play *Angela's Mixtape.* Eisa's writing has been published in *American Theatre, The Source, To Be Real, Everything But The Burden, Step Into a World, Role Call,* and *Total Chaos.* As an actress, Eisa's recent work includes the films *Robot Stories, Confess,* and *The Architect,* television appearances on *The Wire* and *Law and Order,* and starring roles at the Public Theater, La Mama, and regional theaters around the country. She also acts in her own plays. Eisa has performed her original songs at venues including Joe's Pub, BAMCafé, the Whitney Museum, and as a musical guest on the Showtime series *Soul Food.* A graduate of Harvard and the Actors Studio/New School, Eisa is a member of New Dramatists and a native of Berkeley, California.

ORIGINAL PRODUCTION

In March 2006, *Bulrusher* received its world premiere at Urban Stages/Playwrights' Preview Productions in New York (Frances Hill, Artistic Director; Sonia Koslova, Managing Director; Lori Ann Laster, Program Director; Stanton Wood, Development Director). It was directed by Leah C. Gardiner. Scenic Design and Video/Projection Design: Dustin O'Neill; Lighting Design: Sarah Sidman; Costume Design: Kimberly Ann Glennon; Sound Design: Jill BC DuBoff; Original Songs Composed by Eisa Davis; Original Score Composed and Performed by Daniel T. Denver; Additional Guitar Music by Robert Beitzel; Choreography by Jennifer Harrison Newman; Fight Choreography by Denise Hurd; Stage Management and Board Op: Jana Llynn, Leisah Swenson, Sonia Koslova, Holly M. Kirk; Assistant Stage Manager: Stephen Riscica; Assistant Director: Ronald Francis Brescio; with the following cast, in order of appearance:

```
BULRUSHER . . . . . . . . . . . . . . Zabryna Guevara/Donna Duplantier
MADAME . . . . . . . . . . . . . . . . . . . . . . . . . . . . . . . . . .Charlotte Colavin
LOGGER . . . . . . . . . . . . . . . . . . . . . . . . . . . . . . . Guiesseppe Jones
SCHOOLCH . . . . . . . . . . . . . . . . . . . . Peter Bradbury/Darrill Rosen
BOY . . . . . . . . . . . . . . . . . . . . . . . . . . . . . . . . . . . . . Robert Beitzel
VERA . . . . . . . . . . . . . . . . . . . . . . . . . . . . . . . . . . Tinashe Kajese
```

Bulrusher was first developed in readings at New Dramatists directed by the author and later, by Seret Scott. Subsequent readings were hosted by The Cherry Lane (directed by Leah C. Gardiner), Hartford Stage (directed by Kate Whoriskey), Musefire (directed by Lorraine Robinson), and San Francisco Stage and Film (directed by Mark Routhier). Portland Center Stage workshopped the play in its JAW/West Festival, where it was directed by Valerie Curtis-Newton, with dramaturgy by Mead Hunter.

CHARACTERS

BULRUSHER

MADAME

LOGGER

SCHOOLCH

BOY

VERA

SETTING

Boonville, California, a small town in the Anderson Valley of Mendocino County, north of San Francisco. 1955.

NOTE

Actual Boonville residents developed their own dialect of over 1300 words and phrases at the turn of the last century. The language, called Boontling, was primarily devised to discuss taboo subjects and keep outsiders out. But Boontling also functioned to document town history, create unexpected value from the strange, and satisfy the residents' overriding love of inventive talk.

ACKNOWLEDGMENTS

Deep gratitude to the trees, rivers, and hills of Mendocino County, and to all the people who, voluntarily or involuntarily, served as midwives for this play: Daniel T. Denver, Nicole Ari Parker, Angela Davis, Fania Davis, Emily Morse, Mead Hunter, Leah C. Gardiner, Valerie Curtis-Newton, Ian Morgan, New Dramatists, the Helen Merrill Award committee, Marina Drummer, Robert Geary and his aunt, the last living speaker of Southeastern Pomo, Greg Tate, Adrienne Kennedy, August Wilson, and Sam Jordan. A special thank you to all of the actors who brought this play to life, particularly: Robert Beitzel, Peter Bradbury, Charlotte Colavin, Donna Duplantier, Matthew Grant, Zabryna Guevara, Adrienne Hurd, Michelle Hurd, Guiesseppe Jones, Tinashe Kajese, the late Margo Skinner, Keith Randolph Smith, Dale Soules, Ed Vassallo, and Michole Briana White.

BULRUSHER

ACT I

In the dark, the sound of dripping water — leaky faucet into a steel wash-tub. Then, a spot on Bulrusher, entirely wet, looking up into the sky. She wears a green dress. She talks to the river, reciting her first memory.

BULRUSHER: I float in a basket toward the Pacific, hands
    blue as huckleberries. This air is too sweet,
    this cold water a thin, foul milk.
    The woman who bore me wrapped me,
    gave me to the green of the Navarro,
    named me silence. She prays
    this river has studied time
    and will never turn back
    her secret skin, the mark
    that stretched into life.
    Forgiveness is an insect
    that may one day draw my blood.
    Catch me, I ask the power lines,
    defying the fog's quiet shroud. What is
    a motherless daughter but pure will?
    The river hears me and turns to molasses.
    With a sharp bank through high shams,
    I am born into a new language.
    (More drops falling quickly, becoming gradually slower as lights darken.)
MADAME: It's gonna happen.
    (Lights up on the back parlor of a brothel. A big sign is visible: NO SATIN, NO RED, NO LACE. Madame, Logger, and Schoolch are in the parlor. Madame wears a crucifix. Schoolch drinks tea. It is the Fourth of July.)
LOGGER: Oh you're just sayin' that.
MADAME: I'm gonna leave here, I tell you.
LOGGER: Say that every summer.
MADAME: I mean it too.
LOGGER: What about your business? What about alla us?
MADAME: Come the Apple Show, I'll stay through the prize giving and then
    I'm a leave.

LOGGER: Not even stayin' for the dance? You love the dance.

MADAME: It don't love me. End up hobbin' by myself 'cause no one's got the beans to say they know me. You, you don't come and Schoolch dance too fancy. What's for me.

LOGGER: The music. They hire that band from Frisk to show all the Boont tunesters how it's done.

MADAME: You never even been to the Apple Show dance!

LOGGER: I heard it's nice.

MADAME: From me! I'm the one told you it's nice. But I can't stay out my years here, Apple Show dance or not. Feel rain comin'?

LOGGER: Can't smell it.

MADAME: We'll ask Bulrusher when she get here what the river say.

LOGGER: I want me sweet Michelle today.

MADAME: Sweet Michelle is flattened with the influenzy.

LOGGER: Then young Elinor.

MADAME: She don't like you.

LOGGER: You don't like me with her 'cause she do like me.

MADAME: Elinor ain't the only one.

LOGGER: Well I asked for sweet Michelle. Who else you got? Cory?

MADAME: Her flag's out. She ain't workin' today.

LOGGER: You call yourself a businesswoman? Never give me what I want 'cause you like to see me scramble. You like watchin' the screw turn.

MADAME: Lucky I let you in here at all. You could have to go all the way into Ukiah for your geechin'.

LOGGER: Who left?

MADAME: Well. I suppose I could let you burlap Reina.

LOGGER: That Mexican gal. She so set in her ways. I like to experiment, move things around some. Don't like it the same way all the time.

MADAME: We make the rules around here. Do it the way we like or you can go to Ukiah.

LOGGER: I ain't got the gas.

MADAME: Then take it here the way we say! And you know you only get bahl girls here. Everybody says it and we know it's true. We are the best, because we do it our own way. You don't got no stringy hair and wrinkle socks here. If you want some low-quality diseased moldunes head up the pike and cool off in the oaks. But we are the softest madges you goin' to find. So is it the Spanish moss or my witch's butter?

LOGGER: I'm tryin' to enjoy myself. I'm tryin' to buy me some heel scratchin'. I got money and you got girls, so why you got to rout me each time?

MADAME: So you'll appreciate what you're gettin'. Reina's up front with the rest of the girls; let me tell her you want her.

LOGGER: I never said I wanted her.

MADAME: You didn't have to. She's the quiet one, don't harp much at all. And I can see you ain't in the mood for any more talkin'.

LOGGER: That's earth. You sure sulled me.

MADAME: Get your money together. You're payin' up front today.

LOGGER: Aw girl —

MADAME: No more credit for you. Can't have you old dehigged jackers tryin' to dish me. Makes me can-kicky.

(She exits.)

LOGGER: When we gon get you a girl up there Schoolch?

(Schoolch is silent, but Logger converses with him anyway, waiting for his responses in the pauses below.)

LOGGER: Let go a that teacher's English, talk a little how we talk. Harp the ling, and you can take one of these women for a ride. *(Pause.)* No? Well it's a shame you won't 'cause they all love it. *(Pause.)* You seein' the fireworks later? Nice out in the buzzchick field. Open view. *(Pause.)* You got any kids goin' on to high school in the fall? I thought goin' on to the upper school would be real special with all the readin' of books and poetry; get you some right romantic material. Only finished middle school myself but my daddy was awful proud. He ain't had but a little education so I read the Dunbar and Wheatley to him at night.

(Schoolch looks quizzical.)

LOGGER: Negro poets. Colored. Bookers who could write poems. *(Schoolch is unconvinced.)* They did. A whole bunch of 'em. Long poems too.

(As Madame re-enters:)

MADAME: Reina's in her room.

LOGGER: *(Continuing, to Schoolch.)* I feel poetical all the time 'cause I keep they verses in my head. *(To Madame.)* When you gonna get Schoolch in with one of your girls? He can't be a silent seeker all his life.

MADAME: He won't sleep with none of them, says he's waiting for me. I just think he's scared to roll somebody he taught long division to. Time to pay up now, Lucas.

LOGGER: *(To Madame.)* You ever heard of the colored poets they had in slavery days and right after?

MADAME: It's ten dollars. Don't try to shike me.

LOGGER: Wait now, ten dollars? I just got a phone line put in, so I'm watchin' my budget. How much a that do I get to keep?

MADAME: Pardon?

LOGGER: Ten dollars ain't what I pay. Now I 'spect some change.

MADAME: I only gave you a break way back when you were goin' with me. You go with her, your same money got two mouths to feed.

LOGGER: You always got two mouths and both of 'em always wide open.

MADAME: Listen booker tee, ain't no call for that sorta nonch harpin'. You can step right out and get your Fourth of Jeel jollies rubbin' up gainst some tree.

LOGGER: Hold up, you love my nonch harpin'.

MADAME: Only when I'm working.

LOGGER: Then what you doin' right now?

MADAME: Tryin' to get you to give me my ten dollars.

LOGGER: Oh girl, you ain't gonna leave this town.

(Bulrusher enters.)

BULRUSHER: Evenin' Schoolch. Madame. Mr. Jeans.

LOGGER: Evenin'. *(To Madame.)* Take your ten then. I need me a fresh-smellin' girl right now, fresh as a sprig of mint.

MADAME: We don't serve any other kind.

(Logger throws down a ten and heads up the stairs.)

MADAME: Don't tell me, Schoolch, I already know, don't let no booker tee back talk me. I know that's what you gonna say. He may not be as single-minded as you, but he's a man all the same, ain't no second-class citizen. Don't tell me otherwise not on no Fourth of Jeel. What the river say today Bulrusher?

BULRUSHER: Clear through midday tomorrow, some mornin' fog. Then a storm tomorrow evenin'.

MADAME: Rain? Now? Well that does my garden no good. All the rows I planted are already dead from heat.

BULRUSHER: Your ground cover and wildflowers should take to it. This kinda rain, they'll grow right over the bald patches.

MADAME: That river tells you everything, don't it. Schoolch, do you realize how much money you have lost over the last eighteen years letting this girl keep her future-readin' skills to herself? No excuse, just plain bad business. You raised her and won't let her pay you back. And you're not even religious! You don't even go to church! This is the only place you come to with any regularity besides the schoolhouse. You come here, don't even sleep with the beautiful whores I got workin' here, you just come and sit and drink tea with the madame of them all. You ain't a Christian, and you ain't a good businessman. Just a waste. And the real

shame is that you never get your sexual release. It ain't nothin' like tea
drinkin', I tell you.

BULRUSHER: Supper's in the oven, Schoolch. I done ate so you go head on, I'll
see you back at the house.

(Schoolch looks at Bulrusher.)

BULRUSHER: I'm just gon sit out a while, keep the sunset in view.

(Schoolch exits.)

MADAME: You still know how to tell people's futures?

BULRUSHER: I haven't for some time.

MADAME: I suppose everyone in this town asked you to read their bathwater
by now. No fortunes left to tell.

BULRUSHER: I've never read your water.

MADAME: And that's how it'll stay.

BULRUSHER: Yes'm.

(Sounds of lovemaking from upstairs.)

MADAME: Alright, time to set yourself spinnin'.

BULRUSHER: Alright then.

*(Bulrusher exits and lights change. She sits, looking into the sunset. Boy en-
ters. He looks at Bulrusher, then looks away. She opens a book.)*

BOY: Well we can't just sit here and not say nothin'.

BULRUSHER: I'm readin'.

BOY: No you're not, you're ignorin' me.

BULRUSHER: Just 'cause it's the Fourth of July don't mean we gotta talk.

(He is quiet for a moment, then flares.)

BOY: I'm done with women! They don't tell you what they mean! Hide the
truth of they feelin's, sweeten it up with rosewater perfume, then just
outta nowhere, plop. Splat. You are thrown over and no land for miles.

BULRUSHER: You didn't care about her no way.

BOY: What do you know?

BULRUSHER: She knew things weren't goin' nowhere with you and took the
words outta your mouth.

BOY: You know who I'm talkin' about?

BULRUSHER: You was goin' with the McGimsey girl.

BOY: She said somethin' 'bout me to you?

BULRUSHER: You know nobody talk to me.

BOY: You did some a your fortune tellin' on me, that's how you know?

BULRUSHER: I ain't never touched your water. I just used my eyes.

BOY: Ain't got no one to go to the fireworks with tonight. Out here talkin' to
you instead.

BULRUSHER: I told you, we ain't gotta talk. *(Pause.)* You ain't never talked to me before.

BOY: No one talk to you 'cause all you got is hard truth for people. If you was nice and not cocked darley all the time you might have you a pal.

BULRUSHER: Don't need no pal. Got the river.

BOY: Well I like bein' stuck on someone, I don't care how unnatural *you* are.

BULRUSHER: Let's make this our first and last conversation.

(Boy looks at her and smiles.)

BOY: You're gonna be my new girlfriend.

(He exits. Fireworks.)

(Bulrusher slams the book closed and talks to the river.)

BULRUSHER: They want to know who I am.

I don't. I want to swing, swing
over the scrub pine, the hens.
They want me to lend them my eyes.
I won't. I want to snake like ice grass,
thick as a future I can't see.
But at five, I knew it all,
I read it in their bathwater;
I met them in front of the general store.
I want to swing, swing
over the scrub pine, the poppies: be a meteor,
a perfume, love the fly on my tongue.

(Next morning. Schoolch's house.)

BULRUSHER: I packed a lemon for you to bring over to Madame, for tea. It's in your lunch basket.

(Schoolch is silent.)

BULRUSHER: Heard the Gschwends say Darlin ain't gonna make it to the library to help you today. He almost lost a thumb launchin' rockets in the field last night.

(Schoolch is silent.)

BULRUSHER: Have a good day now.

(Schoolch picks up his books and basket, exits.)

(Bulrusher plays with his water glass. Is about to put her fingers into it, then tosses the water out the window. She steps out onto the porch. Boy is stumbling down the road, hung over, trying to keep the sun out of his face. He gets to her porch and sinks onto it to rest. He doesn't acknowledge her as she looks at him a spell. Then she walks to the pump and pumps some water into a

bowl. She sets it by him on the step. Boy splashes water onto his face, drinks some, then plays in it, slapping it like a baby. Bulrusher sits on her chair.)

BOY: Where'd you get that moshe?

BULRUSHER: I ain't talkin' to you.

BOY: Your truck. Where'd you get it. Where'd you get it?

BULRUSHER: While back I got it.

BOY: I want me a truck. Always hitchin' a ride to see my ma in Mendocino — I want me a truck a my own.

BULRUSHER: Yeah, well.

BOY: You got one. I can do as good as you, or better. Get me a new one. God-damn I need a cigarette. You got a cigarette?

BULRUSHER: You want a cigarette?

BOY: Yeah.

BULRUSHER: They're inside the house.

BOY: Wait. I forgot. You my new girlfriend. I gotta be nice. I pretty please pretty face need a pretty cigarette. Please.

BULRUSHER: I'm getting 'em anyway. I'm headed into Cloverdale, pick up my oranges.

(She goes in, but peeks out at him through the window.)

BOY: *(Sings.)* Thorn, spine and thistle
Bramble, pennywhistle
Poisoned flowers on a vine
Sticky cockleburrs and pine
Sap that's sweet but never kind
Stuck like so much gristle
(Calls to her.)
I made that one up. What kinda perfume you use?

BULRUSHER: *(Offstage.)* I don't.

BOY: There's a smell I smell when I come near ya.

(She comes back onto porch. She has no cigarettes.)

BULRUSHER: Orange rind.

BOY: No, sweeter.

BULRUSHER: Algae.

BOY: Come on now, say something pretty.

BULRUSHER: Fresh out.

BOY: No pretty words and no cigs? Well. Just looking at you smokes me.

BULRUSHER: Be seein' ya.

BOY: Every Monday you head into Cloverdale. Pick up your oranges, sell 'em to the town. You must make you a lot of money. What you do with it?

BULRUSHER: Well I ain't givin' none to you. I'll be gettin' on the road.

BOY: The pike!

BULRUSHER: *Road.*

BOY: *Pike.* You harp the ling, maybe people would like you.

BULRUSHER: They buy my oranges. That's enough.

BOY: Schoolch won't let you talk the way we all talk, huh.

BULRUSHER: Don't need to.

BOY: You can't find out anything 'bout anyone in this town if you don't harp the ling. Like last night. I found out why that McGimsey girl went mossy on me — she's been bilchin' Tom Soo, and his ma is Chinese! That ain't so bad, but Tom Soo? Tom Soo from *Philo?* She ain't had a taste for any tarp but boarch, so I'm glad she got ink-standy with me. Can't have no applehead ruinin' my track record, sunderin' my reputation. I'm a standin' man.

BULRUSHER: I reckon.

BOY: I ain't afraid a talkin' to you. Hey, I just splashed in this bowl a water.

BULRUSHER: Yeah.

BOY: Means my fortune's in it. You could stick your fingers in there and tell what's gon happen to me. What's my life gonna feel like? What's it gonna feel like when I touch you?

(*He reaches for her arm. She lets him touch her, then pulls away.*)

BULRUSHER: I only tell the weather now. Ain't read nobody's bathwater in years. After the May Bloyd incident.

BOY: It was you brought that on May Bloyd?

BULRUSHER: I just told her it was coming.

BOY: And you never read nobody since.

BULRUSHER: Sometimes I get a little taste by accident. Like in the general store and one of the twins hand me a coke got beads of water on the bottle.

BOY: Con-den-sa-tion is the proper name.

BULRUSHER: Con-des-cen-sion, I'll try to remember that.

BOY: So you're smart too.

BULRUSHER: Don't try to school the schoolteacher's girl.

BOY: You're so smart, you oughta tell fortunes again. Get you a booth at the Apple Show.

BULRUSHER: I said I ain't done it in years.

BOY: So you can't do it anymore.

BULRUSHER: I'm at the peak of my perception! I can call rain a whole week off from it coming down. I'm the best I ever been.

BOY: And keepin' it all to yourself. People come from all over the county for the Apple Show. You could make a name with folks you never even met. You need you a manager, to publicize all your ventures. You could really make a killing.

BULRUSHER: For what?

BOY: I don't know. Why you think you got that power in the first place?

(Bulrusher starts to go.)

BOY: Look, you could just tell my fortune then.

BULRUSHER: I ain't putting my fingers in there. Or your bathwater.

BOY: What about spit? That's water, right? If you just kiss me you'll know everything there is to know.

BULRUSHER: One of your friends put you up to this? You messin' with me just 'cause everyone thinks you're cute? Just 'cause you can?

BOY: Tiger lily, manzanita, you're my girlfriend. *(Sings.)* Oh my girl —

BULRUSHER: If I'm your girlfriend, prove it. Give me something.

BOY: I ain't got much to offer a girl except my sensuality. We could take a walk through Fern Canyon, watch the salmon run —

BULRUSHER: It's summertime, ain't no salmon running the river.

BOY: There's always trout. Steelhead trout.

BULRUSHER: Take me somewhere where there's people and put your arm around me. Take me to the Anyhow.

BOY: The Anyhow Saloon? I just came from there.

BULRUSHER: And I'm leavin' here.

(Bulrusher opens the door to her truck and slams it.)

BOY: Bulrusher, be my fortune.

(Boy dumps the bowl of water on his head.)

(Sings.) Oh my girl, with the cattail curls, be mine, be mine, all mine.

(Rain. Bulrusher's truck is now filled with oranges. She sees a girl walking.)

BULRUSHER: Hey.

VERA: Hey.

BULRUSHER: You want a lift?

VERA: 'Preciate it.

(Vera gets into the truck with her suitcase, exhausted and soaking wet. She has covered her head in newspaper. When they see each other's faces, they are instantly struck but try to maintain their ease.)

BULRUSHER: You walked all the way from Cloverdale in this storm?

VERA: I didn't know what else to do. Gone so long without sleep can't tell night from day, rain from dry. I come all the way from Alabama on a Jim Crow train.

BULRUSHER: Is that a new model?

VERA: Afraid not. You never heard a Jim Crow?

BULRUSHER: Separately, but not together. Where you going to?

VERA: *(Removes newspaper.)* Some tiny town where my uncle live.

BULRUSHER: Got his name? I know everybody round here.

VERA: Don't care what name he answer to long as he give me a place to lay my head. Conductor wouldn't give me a berth for nothing. Southern route.

BULRUSHER: Why not?

VERA: If you don't know the answer to that I am pleased to meet you.

BULRUSHER: We'll find him. Where in Alabama you from?

VERA: Birmingham. The Magic City.

BULRUSHER: What's there?

VERA: Church. Iron ore. And a Vulcan that forges everything with fire.

BULRUSHER: You like it there?

VERA: Can't stand it and I can't stand rain. Guess I'm outta luck.

BULRUSHER: It'll stop tomorrow morning.

VERA: Hope so, I gotta find me some work in a jiffy. *(Realizes.)* How do you know the rain'll stop?

BULRUSHER: The river told me.

VERA: Huh. *(She takes this in.)* My name's Vera Blass.

BULRUSHER: Bulrusher.

VERA: What's your family name.

BULRUSHER: Ain't got family.

VERA: Dead?

BULRUSHER: Don't know. Was born somewhere far from where I live. And my mother tried to drown me when I got born, but I guess I wasn't ready to go.

VERA: She changed her mind?

BULRUSHER: No. She sent me down the Navarro River but someone found me in the weeds. The bulrushes.

VERA: Like Moses.

BULRUSHER: No. Like me.

VERA: You can have *my* mother if you want — she's too concerned with being a model Negro citizen to drown anyone. *(Vera yawns.)* Forgive me, I can barely keep my eyes open. You in school?

BULRUSHER: Naw. But I like books. Got learnt at home.

VERA: What are all these oranges for?

BULRUSHER: Sellin'.

VERA: So there's a street got colored merchants here? 'Cause I am howlin' hungry. Ain't had a thing to eat since Texas. Would love a plate of fried fish and biscuits, cornbread, and greens, ooh. *(Looks into sideview mirror.)* Look at my hair, oh Lord! I can't meet no one like this. Wrong as a wet cat. Why didn't you tell me?

BULRUSHER: You look beautiful to me.

VERA: Really.

BULRUSHER: Yeah.

(Silence.)

VERA: What kind of beauty shops in your town?

BULRUSHER: Mazie does hair.

VERA: Our kind of hair?

BULRUSHER: No. I do my own.

VERA: Looks — nice. But ain't no colored women to do it for you?

BULRUSHER: I'm the only one.

VERA: *(Panicking.)* What? My uncle live in a all-white town?

BULRUSHER: He look like you?

VERA: I don't know. I just know he's colored.

BULRUSHER: A logger lives downriver from the general store, maybe he's the one you mean.

VERA: He's the only Negro besides you?

BULRUSHER: Yeah. What's wrong? *(Vera is silent.)* Well how 'bout some Indians? We just passed the reservation. *(Vera is silent.)* If you hungry, I got an orange —

VERA: *(Suddenly.)* Let me out.

BULRUSHER: We're almost to Boonville.

VERA: Please.

BULRUSHER: You gotta find your uncle.

VERA: Let me out.

BULRUSHER: You can't walk back.

VERA: Don't tell me what I can't do.

BULRUSHER: Let's at least get you fed and dry.

VERA: I can take care of myself —

BULRUSHER: I can ride you back to the train station in the morning when the rain clears. Just get some rest tonight.

(Vera is silent. She leans her head back on the seat and closes her eyes. They ride.)

BULRUSHER: Alabama, huh. So is the dirt really red there?

VERA: Yeah.

(Silence.)

BULRUSHER: That must be confusing to all the honeybees. You got bees right?

VERA: Mm hm.

> *(Silence.)*

BULRUSHER: 'Cause you know they like red. Huh. Red dirt. You come from a place where the dirt looks like flowers?

> *(No response from Vera. Bulrusher turns to look at her — Vera is asleep. Bulrusher talks to the river, rapt. The storm rages.)*

BULRUSHER: Newspaper over
her head with the ink
just about run off.
In this dark light, I see her,
and build a pedestal
of water. She is the one,
the only one, nothing is caught
between us but my throat.
I want to say this
is a dream but it is true.
Do I know her? Is she the wet sight
of home?

> *(The brothel. Madame, Logger, Schoolch.)*

LOGGER: *(To Madame.)* I'll get Tuttle's tree up for you, but not tonight. It's a roger out there and I'm gittin' back to my mink. This Michelle gives me the fiddlers! *(Calls up the stairs.)* Michelle, I'm comin' to put in on you! Yes, I'm ready for my ricky chow!

> *(Logger heads up the stairs.)*

MADAME: His tree just fell on *my* property. And Tuttle has the nerve to say it is *my* responsibility to lift that log up. Isn't my tree, it's *his* tree — and I try my best to be patient — but the last time one of his trees fell in my yard, he left it layin' there for three whole months! I had to plant my flower garden around it. What sort of look is that? I try to build a little civilization here, I try. But people don't have the work ethic I do, they don't understand that adherin' to standards of behavior and so forth is fortifyin' to the morals. And I got morals. Keep the whole of my brothel with its eye on discipline. If you don't have that, you don't have nothing divine in your life. If you can't get up regular as the sun each day, no matter what sort of cloud is cloudin' ya, you ain't fit to meet God. And I'm a meet him. God will be my final savior and I will be comforted, and it won't be because I chose to give my body over to the menfolk, it won't be because I'm a businesswoman like Mary Magdalene — and Jesus *loved* her — but because I am disciplined and godlike in my approach to all things. I have nothing if not that foundation to stand upon. And so I will be revealed.

And still you judge me. What can I do to make you happy, Schoolch? How is it I can do right by God but never can do right by you? I gotta find a way to sell this place and leave this town for good. I have to see my mother's grave again. I gotta smell the grass growin' there.

(She goes to the window.)

Bulrush here with somebody. Ooh, but it is pearlin' out there.

(Schoolch looks as if he is getting ready to say something. Vera and Bulrusher enter.)

BULRUSHER: Evenin' Schoolch, Madame.

MADAME: Evenin'. Who's this now?

BULRUSHER: This Vera. She's looking for a relative of hers.

MADAME: Is it a man relative?

BULRUSHER: Uh huh.

MADAME: He ain't here.

BULRUSHER: What about the logger Mr. Jeans? If he ain't the man, he might know him.

MADAME: (To Vera.) Where you from?

VERA: Well, it's a little browner than here.

MADAME: Is it.

VERA: I'm from Alabam. We lost the war.

MADAME: We try to forget about that stuff round here. You'll get used to it.

(Sounds of Logger and Michelle's lovemaking.)

MADAME: Well you can't stay here. No offense darlin', but I don't take in no strays.

BULRUSHER: Schoolch, you go on home and eat — I'll make sure she's got a place to stay for the night.

VERA: It's alright.

BULRUSHER: If we can't find the logger you can have my bed.

(Schoolch looks at Bulrusher.)

BULRUSHER: It's my room. If she hasn't got a place to stay, I'm giving her my room.

(Schoolch looks.)

BULRUSHER: I'm eighteen now Schoolch, I got majority.

(Schoolch exits.)

MADAME: Ooh, he's upset. Well, let me call out to the logger's house then. It *is* late, you know. He most likely ain't in.

VERA: You don't have to call him. I'll find him on my own.

MADAME: It's raining child. The phone is drier and has a little less pride.

(Vera goes out and sits on the porch.)

BULRUSHER: *(Calling to her.)* Sit under the awning so you don't get wet.

MADAME: *(To herself.)* I'll be. Another piece of cut cabbage in this town. *(To Bulrusher.)* Tell her to stand on the side. Don't want her affiliated with my business.

(Madame picks up the phone, pretends to dial, harried.)

BULRUSHER: You got any fried fish or biscuits, cornbread, or greens?

MADAME: There's a plate a biscuits in the kitchen. None a that other stuff. What's it for? You can't eat my food for free now.

BULRUSHER: It's for Vera. I'll get it.

MADAME: The butter and preserves are in crocks by the icebox. But don't mess up the place now, and don't get any crumbs on the counter!

(Sounds of ceramic bumping around.)

MADAME: Don't doll around in there I said! Slice a ham in the box if you want it — but put the lid back on the container, don't let it go bad. *(Pretending to "end" her phone call.)* Well I just rang the logger and he ain't home. You all might want to hit that hotel.

(Bulrusher comes back out with a plate for Vera.)

BULRUSHER: *(Calling to Vera.)* I got some biscuits and ham for you Vera if you want to step in and have it at the table.

MADAME: No, you better wrap that gorm up and walk down to the hotel now; it's getting on into the night, wanna make sure she can get a room without any fuss. It's really not good for my business havin' you two round here on a rainy night like this.

BULRUSHER: Vera, don't bother 'bout comin' inside, I'm headed out there.

MADAME: That's right, use that common sense.

(Logger enters from a room upstairs. He wears only a woman's Chinese silk robe. Bulrusher sees him and stops.)

LOGGER: Heard some talk about biscuits —

MADAME: Oh limpin' Jesus —

LOGGER: — and had to get right up out of that bed and see what you was hiding from me. You know geechin' gets me scottied. Better give me some of those flories so I can go another round with Michelle —

MADAME: I just called you.

LOGGER: No you didn't, I didn't hear you say my name. Did you holler up to me, say, Lucas, come on down, I need you?

BULRUSHER: She called you on the phone. Called your house.

LOGGER: *(Proud.)* Yeah, I just got me a telephone. *(To Madame.)* But you knew I was here.

BULRUSHER: She did, huh.

LOGGER: Yeah. What you want me for? *(Takes a biscuit from Bulrusher.)* Think I'll have this biscuit right here.

BULRUSHER: I got a person for you to meet. Vera! Come inside and meet a Negro.

LOGGER: I always say colored. That other one's too easy to mispronounce.

(Vera comes inside.)

BULRUSHER: This Vera.

MADAME: She just came to town. I didn't want to disturb you.

VERA: Your name is Lucas?

LOGGER: Yes ma'am. Lucas Jeans.

VERA: I'm Ina's daughter Vera.

LOGGER: You Vera? *(Exuberant.)* Oh my goodness. Let me get my pants on. I didn't know you were coming here. Just let me splash a little water on and cleanse myself —

(He runs upstairs. Vera, Bulrusher, and Madame stand in silence as he fumbles around, noisily picking up his clothes. He runs down the stairs, still dressing, and hugs Vera.)

LOGGER: You look like Ina round the eyes, but you shaped different. I ain't seen your mother since we was kids. She here with you?

VERA: No, I'm by myself.

LOGGER: How is she?

VERA: She's doin' her best.

LOGGER: And did your daddy keep his job as a porter on the railroad?

VERA: He's at the steel mill now.

LOGGER: Well, you can only go so long bowing and scraping for people before it breaks your manhood, that's just how it is. I wish I'd a known you were comin'.

VERA: Didn't my mother send you a telegram?

LOGGER: Huh. Reckon she sent it to the sawmill. It's closed now, logging days are done. I just do odd jobs now, pickin' apples and hops, herdin' sheep and trainin' horses. But Lord you just in, you don't need to hear all this. Let's get you some food and into a warm bed.

VERA: Thank you.

LOGGER: You already grown, land's end. Why don't I drive you back over to my region. Make a pallet for myself and you can have the ticking and box spring, alright? You got your things, suitcase somewhere?

VERA: In Bulrusher's truck.

LOGGER: You got Vera from the station?

BULRUSHER: Saw her walking the road and gave her a lift.

LOGGER: My goodness, but that was Christian. I won't forget that, girl. Thank you for your trouble.

BULRUSHER: Alright. *(To Vera.)* Here's the food if you still want it.

LOGGER: *(To Madame.)* Let me give you toobs for it.

BULRUSHER: No, I got it. Here's a quarter.

MADAME: Let Lucas pay. He owes me a belhoon for leavin' early anyway.

LOGGER: You always trying to rooje me.

MADAME: You woulda spent at least that much on horn and chiggle if'n you kept your normal hours.

LOGGER: You ain't got one straw of kindness in that heart of hay do ya? I just want a tidrey of love. Just a tidrey.

(He throws a dollar on the pool table and leaves with Vera. Bulrusher walks out with them.)

LOGGER: Vera, that woman ain't representative. Got a lot of honest two-handed folks around here, they'll be happy to meetcha. Thanks again Bulrusher. You done a bahl thing. *(To Vera.)* You know I was the one told Bulrusher she was colored. She was five and didn't even know. My moshe is over here, I'll jape you home.

VERA: I don't know what that means.

LOGGER: You don't have to. Just another part of the scenery.

(He takes her bag to his car.)

BULRUSHER: If you need anything.

VERA: How 'bout an orange.

(Bulrusher throws her one.)

BULRUSHER: You gonna stay?

(Vera waves good-bye. Bulrusher stands and watches her go in the rain. Suddenly she realizes how wet she is and smiles. Heads inside.)

MADAME: Don't track mud in here, you're all wet.

BULRUSHER: You lied on the night of the only rain of the summer. The logger was here all the time.

MADAME: It's a habit Bulrusher. Think I would jenny on a customer that's got a woman asking for him? Woulda lost this madge house long ago if I was that tuddish. If you going to be a businesswoman — and I see you are enterprising with them oranges — you gotta be wise. Think on both sides of your head. Don't be afraid of anything anyone can ever say to you.

BULRUSHER: You woulda had us over to the hotel wasting good money on a room when he was here all the time.

MADAME: I woulda told him soon as you were out the door. He'd a come and found you — and didn't he? Find you? Don't judge me for what never happened.

BULRUSHER: I don't like to argue with Schoolch.

MADAME: When has he ever stayed mad with you? He can see what's going on.

BULRUSHER: What.

MADAME: You ain't never had a — a friend. You ain't never had somebody you can see yourself in.

BULRUSHER: I ain't like other folks, don't need no friends. I was born to read. Born to read water.

MADAME: Go see Schoolch before he goes to sleep. He'll steam you but you can take it.

BULRUSHER: I need a beer first.

(Bulrusher exits.)

MADAME: You left crumbs on my pool table.

(Bulrusher enters Schoolch's house. She is tipsy. Moves around the kitchen, soaking some beans. Distracted, she knocks over a bowl and it breaks. Schoolch comes down the stairs.)

SCHOOLCH: You'll replace that with your orange money.

BULRUSHER: Yes sir.

SCHOOLCH: Careless. But you eighteen! Got your majority! Telling me how old you are. I know how old you are. You are alive because of me.

BULRUSHER: Yes sir.

SCHOOLCH: You broke that on purpose to make your point?

BULRUSHER: No sir.

SCHOOLCH: Well you must want an ear settin' after all the backtalk you gave me tonight. In front of a stranger at that.

BULRUSHER: No sir.

SCHOOLCH: Then what's all this somersettin' for? I never expected to see you acting like this.

BULRUSHER: Yes sir.

SCHOOLCH: Like all the other children when their comb's gittin' red. I thought I trained you so you'd never jump track on me.

BULRUSHER: I've been good. I done everything you said. I stopped readin' water and tellin' fortunes, did all my lessons here at home so I wouldn't be 'taminated by the children at the school. I don't harp the ling with anybody and I save up all my money steada spendin' it in Cloverdale or Fort Bragg. All I do is show my 'preciation.

SCHOOLCH: More backtalk? My house, my rules. Break them, and you can leave here. But you won't. How many times do I have to tell you? When you were a baby, when you were just a few days old, your mama sent you down the river, sent you floating down to the brine. Wanted nothing to do with you. But you got yourself caught in some weeds and the Negro Jeans found you, brought you to the brothel tied up in his suede duster. Put you on the pool table and there you were, kicking up the smoky air. You didn't blink or cry under that hanging lamp, you just lay there kicking for your life. Madame, she ain't the kind to take pity, wasn't going to risk her business taking you in. But even if she said she wanted you, she would have had to fight me. I saw you and I felt like you had answered a question. Your eyes, the clay color of your legs, the curly hair on your head — you seemed like family, like mine. That if I had you, I'd be alright. And if you had me, you'd be alright. I knew I could protect you, I knew that you weren't supposed to be alive, that you weren't supposed to belong to me at all and that's why I needed you. That's why you fit. So there's no separating us Bulrusher, we are just like our names, bound to what we do and what's been done to us. Our names are our fates and our proper place. Don't forget that.

(Pause.)

BULRUSHER: Gotta clean this up.

(Schoolch starts up the stairs.)

BULRUSHER: Schoolch, I was Christened at the church, right?

(Schoolch stops.)

BULRUSHER: Did the reverend give me a name when he tapped me with the water? I got a Christian name, don't I?

(Pause.)

SCHOOLCH: Once we had another name for you, but I forget it now. You're Bulrusher to me.

(Next morning. Logger's house. He is tending a fire in the wood burning stove. He puts a few pieces of bread and a pot of water over the flames. Vera comes into the kitchen in a nightgown. It's too large; she has to pick up the hem to walk. The hem is splattered with a little mud.)

LOGGER: You look like you still sleep. *(Vera frowns, squinting.)* "Ere sleep comes down to soothe the weary eyes." That's Dunbar. You like the morning? *(Vera mumbles.)* Your mother would stay in bed all day if she wasn't colored. I can't imagine what she look like now, grown and running a house. See I was always the one up and getting breakfast on. She liked to sit in the bed and play with the strings from her blanket, talk a little 'bout her dreams from the night before. Stare out the window like a princess waiting for some magic. My sister.

VERA: It's cold.

LOGGER: Yeah, mornings are cool here then it heats up by midday — lot different than Birmingham. I tend to ride in the mornings, but I thought I'd stay in today, hear your news. *(A brief pause, then:)* I hope you brought a comb with you. I've tried not to say anything since we're just meeting but your hair looks like the burning bush.

VERA: Well if nobody does hair around here I don't know what I'm a do.

LOGGER: You don't do your own hair?

VERA: Mother always does it.

LOGGER: *(Looking at her.)* And it's thick too. Huh. I ain't got a pressing comb but I can plait it for you.

VERA: That's alright, I'll just get some rollers and smooth it down that way.

LOGGER: But you can't go in the store to buy rollers looking like that.

VERA: I'll wear a scarf.

LOGGER: Didn't Ina tell you always wear clean panties case you have an accident and have to get operated on in the hospital?

VERA: Yes.

LOGGER: Well why would you walk out the house with clean panties and a nappy head? That defies all reason, makes my mouth hurt to say it. I'm gonna plait your hair up before you even think about goin' outside. Sit down here. And bring the comb and grease from the dresser.
(He sits on a chair and opens his legs. Vera stands stock still.)

LOGGER: Come on. I don't care if you tenderheaded, it's gotta be done.

VERA: You gon braid my hair? You a man. You ain't s'posed to do that.

LOGGER: Used to do Ina's every Saturday night, with clean square parts. What am I doing explaining myself to you! Just set down.

VERA: You gon be careful?

LOGGER: No.

VERA: I'll just wear a scarf —

LOGGER: What did I just say to you? Now set!
(Vera gets comb and grease.)

LOGGER: Questioning your elders, mmph. I don't know how Ina raised you but no sellin' wolf tickets round here. You got you a job and your own place to stay, *then* we can put our conversation on an even plank.
(Vera is afraid to sit down.)

LOGGER: I ain't tellin' you again.

(Vera sits between his legs. He begins to comb and part Vera's hair.)

LOGGER: I'm gonna do it so you don't need no rollers. If you wet it and let it dry like this, when you take it out you'll have all the pincurls you need.

(He goes to work on two french braids. Silence.)

VERA: I do want to find me a job while I'm here.

LOGGER: Well, what can you do?

VERA: Type. File. Take minutes.

LOGGER: Nobody need none of that fingernail polish stuff round here. We'll find you something you can put your back into.

(He combs. She looks out the window.)

VERA: That Bulrusher girl said it would clear up this morning.

LOGGER: She's always right about the weather. You oughta pay her a visit today, thank her for her kindness.

VERA: Is she really the only Negro this way? I don't want to work for white people.

LOGGER: Used to be more of us here during boom time, but once the sawmills closed, everybody went south. Oakland, Fresno, Los Angeles.

VERA: But you stayed.

LOGGER: Keep your head still.

VERA: You like living with all these ofays?

LOGGER: It's alright. Indians are the colored folk here, what's left of 'em. They got it *bad.* All their land got took, they ain't allowed to go to school, and some of 'em can remember when they was legal slaves. So don't go lyin' and sayin' you're part Cherokee.

VERA: White folk just don't have no morals. And easy women too. Never thought I'd see a town a crackers let a buck into their bordello.

(Logger yanks her head to the side. She yells.)

LOGGER: I know we're just getting to know each other, but I have to ask. Why you here, Vera?

VERA: Mother sent me.

LOGGER: By yourself. In the middle of the summer.

VERA: She needed to get me off her hands for a while.

LOGGER: Lean forward. You done with school?

VERA: Graduated Parker High. I'm going to college.

LOGGER: *(Excited.)* That's all right! *(Hugs her head.)* Oh Vera, I'm proud. Proud of ya.

VERA: I just need a job so I can save up.

LOGGER: College! Pretty soon you'll be a teacher yourself, huh.

VERA: *(With real hope.)* Maybe.

LOGGER: Don't sell yourself short, now, you can do anything you put your mind to.

VERA: Mother always talks so fondly of you. Said you cut down fifty-foot trees all by yourself. That white men look up to you in California.

LOGGER: How is Birmingham doin' these days?

VERA: They only bomb our houses every *other* Sunday.

LOGGER: Yeah, I like these ofays a lot better than those. Listen Vera, you are family and you are welcome to stay. We'll find you a job, that's earth.

VERA: I won't be no trouble.

LOGGER: Love braidin' hair.

(Bulrusher talks to the river.)

BULRUSHER: She has tiny burns on her arm and on her ear and on her forehead near her hairline. Thin feathery scars, with crosshatching that looks like the teeth of a comb. All hot and fried and ironed — her smell begins with that — her hair, her clothes — all of her seems to have been cooked with corn oil and a strip of metal. Is it the smell of Birmingham, the steel pressing against her, burning her skin? Is that where her scars are from?

I want to dream of her.

(Schoolch's porch. Bulrusher is cleaning her shotgun. Vera enters.)

BULRUSHER: Hey.

VERA: Hey. It stopped raining.

BULRUSHER: Yeah. You sleep good?

VERA: No. After the rain it was too quiet. Silence in my ears all night.

BULRUSHER: You don't like it?

VERA: I just never heard darkness before. Is it too early to visit?

BULRUSHER: No. I been up, out in the woods, catching some dinner.

VERA: You used that gun?

BULRUSHER: Mm hm. Want to see what I shot?

VERA: That's alright.

BULRUSHER: Sure? I ain't cleaned her yet —

VERA: It's alright. Thanks again for helping me last night. Hope I didn't get you in trouble.

BULRUSHER: Well, Schoolch never speaks to me otherwise so I think of it as a special occasion.

VERA: I don't want to step on anybody's toes. Especially when I got to find a job.

BULRUSHER: I never even seen anyone like you.

VERA: We look just the same.

BULRUSHER: No we don't. You're pretty, like the kind you feel inside of your-self when you go to the movies and think you're in it?

VERA: Yeah? You never seen another colored girl before?

BULRUSHER: No. I had to drink some beer just to get over you.

VERA: Beer? But that's only for men! You'll grow hairs on your tongue you keep that up.

BULRUSHER: I been doin' it since I was twelve! Are there hairs?

(Bulrusher opens her mouth.)

VERA: Let me see your — open wider. *(She looks.)* Looks clean, but your tongue is real long. You have to be careful.

BULRUSHER: But I don't like whiskey. What else am I gonna drink at the Any-how?

VERA: The Anyhow?

BULRUSHER: Saloon.

VERA: They let you drink at a saloon?

BULRUSHER: Something wrong with that?

VERA: And you walk right in the front door?

BULRUSHER: Ain't no other door.

VERA: I used the front door once at Pizitz. Department store. We supposed to use the back entrance, in the alleyway, by the trash — but I strode right in the front.

BULRUSHER: Why are you supposed to use the back?

VERA: I went to buy some doughnuts and they came to throw me out. Back door, they said. My pocket got caught on the door handle when they were pushing me, and the whole front panel of my dress just came off. Came off right in this cracker's hand. And he got so red when he saw my stockings, he just walked off real fast. The bus wouldn't pick me up. Had to walk all the way home holding myself with newspaper.

(Bulrusher looks at her.)

And it's the dark that scares me, huh.

BULRUSHER: You gonna stay?

VERA: If you'll be my friend.

BULRUSHER: I'll take care of you, whatever you need.

VERA: *(Smiles.)* So what do y'all do around here? For fun?

BULRUSHER: Drink. The Apple Show is coming up though. Big dance for that.

VERA: Applesauce, huh.

(Boy enters.)

BOY: Whoa, seein' dubs. Whose sneeble are you?

(Bulrusher aims her gun at Boy's crotch.)

VERA: Bulrusher!

BULRUSHER: Show her some manners.

BOY: That thing ain't even loaded, you just cleaned it.

BULRUSHER: She ain't nobody's sneeble. Introduce yourself proper.

(She pokes him with the gun.)

BOY: Pleased to make your acquaintance.

VERA: I'm Vera, pleased to meet you.

BULRUSHER: Say *your* name.

BOY: Damn Bulrusher, take that highgun offa me!

BULRUSHER: Say it.

BOY: I'm Wilkerson, enchanté.

BULRUSHER: Your whole name.

BOY: Streebs Wilkerson —

BULRUSHER: Streebs, which means strawberries —

BOY: Don't tell her that —

BULRUSHER: — 'count of the red birthmark he got on his balls.

BOY: You supposed to be my girlfriend, don't go spreading lies. (To Vera.) She ain't even seen my privates.

BULRUSHER: Don't need to, as much as you talk about 'em. He says I'm his girlfriend but he didn't even talk to me last night at the Anyhow.

BOY: We're in the early phases of love. You all kin?

BULRUSHER: She kin to Mr. Jeans.   VERA: I'm kin to Mr. Jeans.

VERA: From Birmingham.

BOY: My great granddad died over you, tryin' to keep the Union together.

VERA: You think us colored folk are worth it?

BOY: What?

VERA: Death.

BOY: Haven't really sized up the race as a whole.

BULRUSHER: Yeah. We are.

BOY: You ain't colored, you a bulrusher and a fortune-teller. And you my girl-friend.

BULRUSHER: Just 'cause you say something don't make it true. Get off my porch 'fore I load up this gun and use it.

BOY: Aw, manzanita —

BULRUSHER: Off.

BOY: I'll stack your oranges for you nice and tight.

BULRUSHER: What did I say.

BOY: Don't be so teet lipped. Leavin' me all dove cooey. I just wanna see your golden eagles.

(Bulrusher chases him off. As he exits, he yells:)

BOY: You can't get rid of me, doolsey boo, no no! I'm gonna geech you!

VERA: What's a sneeble?

BULRUSHER: Like a snowball. It's the funny way to say Negro.

VERA: And you'd point a gun at a white man for that?

BULRUSHER: He's a boy. I won't have him treat you wrong.

VERA: Fred — my boyfriend at home — he'd never do what you just did. He
fears the Lord God. He did steal me a pickle dipped in Kool-Aid powder
from the store once, but that's about it. Sneebles. Why's everyone talk so
funny here?

BULRUSHER: They're harpin' the ling. Folks made it up a while ago to tell jokes
and secrets, to make everything they talk about something they own. I
can harp it but I don't. Made up my own way to talk instead, a way to
talk to the river. I tell stories, make poetry, like I'm writing my own book.
I tell things over and over so I can understand 'em. Hey, you really want
a job?

VERA: Yeah. Need one bad.

BULRUSHER: I'm thinking of expanding my business. Summertime and all, oranges always do good, but I thought I might sell some lemons.
(Vera laughs.)

BULRUSHER: What? If lemons don't please you, we could try pineapples. Or
bananas.

VERA: You want my help?

BULRUSHER: Sure. We could split our yield clear down the middle.

VERA: You sure? All I done is office work.

BULRUSHER: I'll teach you what you need to know. How to choose the ripe
ones, how much to charge on the road versus my regulars buy crates.
You're smart enough; you won't have to pay me no mind after the first
day.

VERA: *(Laughing.)* Applesauce *and* lemonade. And I thought California didn't
have nothing else in it but movie stars and palm trees.

BULRUSHER: You don't want to work with me?

VERA: Of course I do, I was just kidding you. It's how I say thanks.

BULRUSHER: I got a twang in my stomach when you walked up today. Then
it spread all over. Still feels like there's turpentine under my skin. You did
all that to me. Wait till I tell the river.

VERA: You something else.

*(The brothel porch. A month and a half later. Boy plays a few chords on his
guitar as Logger sings.)*

LOGGER: *(Sings.)* Oh she caned me with her look
She slayed me with her eye
But I had her sweet jerk once
And for it I would die
And for it I would die
And for it I would die
She turned me like a horse
She reined my wildness in
But every time she pats my rump
Oh Lord I want to sin
Oh Lord I want to sin
Oh Lord I wants to sin

BOY: That's an old song from the mill ain't it. Pa sang it different. You changed the words.

LOGGER: Naw, the song changed on *me*. I can't sing it like we used to 'cause I don't feel it that way anymore. I mean, they got electric saws now.

BOY: What's the electric saw got to do with a girl?

LOGGER: I'm saying! I mean, I came out here from Birmingham when I was about your age and that whole field in front of you was a stand of conifers. Used to ride my Appaloosa over that ridge with your pa, just take in the country. Built my own house. Not with siding, not with half logs. Tongue and grooved my own cabin all from redwood I felled myself. Now you're lucky if you see a pygmy tree.

BOY: Where's the girl in that?

LOGGER: Right! All through the valley, up and down the coast, the trees are gone and so is my youth — I have nothing left to destroy. Nothing fallin' around here but apples on sheep.

BOY: Yeah, I'm kinda weary of doing what all everyone else do. I mean I'm not different from nobody, I'm just not always the same. Hey, I got a new song to keep me company. You wanna hear it?

LOGGER: Not one of them lonesome tunes now.

BOY: Oh I can't write those. I just missed the draft to Korea, got all my days in front of me, so I think I got a right to be happy, to sing a happy song.

LOGGER: Alright. Ply it for me. But soft now. I don't want to get jangled. Too pretty an evening for nothing loud.

BOY: It's in a new key I found, real sweet. *(He plays a chord.)* Isn't that bahl.

LOGGER: See what'n all you got jacker, ply your song.

BOY: *(Sings.)* Twelve nights of hard liquor
Sent Rowan to his grave

He saw the lights of Galilee
And Mary just the same
And if you call for Rowan now
The road'll answer back
He's twelve nights gone to perfidy
Spread on a burlap sack
Oh save me in my nightly walk
Save me in my days
Don't want to go like Rowan Hale
I'll keep my goodly ways
Oh save me in my nightly walk
Save me in my days
Don't want to go like Rowan Hale
I'll keep my goodly ways
I'll keep my goodly ways

LOGGER: Huh. That's your happy song? You got kinda loud at the end there.

BOY: I didn't know what I was sayin' for a minute and I sang with my full power to get me through.

LOGGER: And you made that tune up.

BOY: Most of it.

LOGGER: Clearly, you been inspired — but stop that loud singing. It sounds like you wanna hurt somebody. Don't you got a gal?

BOY: Yeah, I'm getting her.

LOGGER: Well what you doing about it? You need to marry and set up house. That's what you oughta do since you ain't in the service or a travelin' man. Need you a wife.

BOY: You ain't had one.

(Madame enters with glasses on, reading a letter.)

MADAME: Are you comin' in today or are you just tryin' to hoot on me by sittin' on my stoop?

LOGGER: If you got any vision in that pinchy face of yours, you could see I am whittlin' and warblin' with this yink here.

MADAME: Yes but I don't see either a y'all payin' my loiterin' fee. If you gonna porch up and tell jonnems and wess all day, fine by me but you have got to give up some rent.

LOGGER: "There is a heaven, for ever, day by day,
The upward longing of my soul doth tell me so.
There is a hell, I'm quite as sure; for pray,
If there were not, where would my neighbours go?"

That's some Dunbar for ya Madame, Paul Laurence. Better get you some compassion 'fore you die.

BOY: I was playin' some songs on the guitar. You want to hear another one I wrote, Jeans?

LOGGER: Well, just play some chords, what all you strummed on that last one. None of them words, just the strings vibratin'. That's all I want to hear.

BOY: Airtight.

(Boy strums.)

LOGGER: Madame, you ain't been honest with me.

MADAME: What now.

LOGGER: You ain't always been this hard. You used to be another kind of woman, kind got gentleness swaying out her like a breeze.

MADAME: I am the same woman you have always known, Lucas, I still got wind for ya.

LOGGER: You would hold me before; before you wouldn't let me go with the other girls.

MADAME: *(Evasive.)* There's more paperwork now, I got more things to take care of.

LOGGER: You put me out. You had me in your arms and then you shunted me like I had the tuberculosis.

MADAME: Well, I started to lose my business sense with you comin' so regular — I had to draw a line just to clarify.

LOGGER: I ain't happy with the way my life looks. With Vera here got me thinking. I'm a forty-six-year-old grizz and I don't know what is ahead of me. Like this tweed here. He's comin' into his manliness and he got all sorts of gals to choose from for to make a future. My future is done. All I got left is the past.

MADAME: You still active in your daming. You don't miss a weekend here.

LOGGER: And that ain't appealin' to me no more. It feels like I'm just eatin' the same Thanksgiving meal over and over — I get all stuffed up and nothing tastes good enough anymore to be thankful for.

MADAME: So that's it? Tradin' in your riding crop for a chastity belt?

LOGGER: I just want to settle myself into somethin' more wholesome. I want to feel someone. The same someone every night.

MADAME: Pay me and I'll hold your hand.

LOGGER: I don't want it that way. I want it for real. I know Schoolch has been on you for the same thing but —

MADAME: What you askin' me, Lucas.

LOGGER: I don't know. You've been good to me, more than any other woman

I know — I just want a real home and a quiet con*tent* in the evenings steada all this skee swillin' and boisteration. I don't got a ring or nothin' like that —

MADAME: Oh you have lost your skull fillin' now.

LOGGER: I just want to give something over. I want to smush myself into you.

BOY: There's another song I got — I can play just the chords to that. Kinda gettin' tired of this one —

LOGGER: Well pluck another song then.

BOY: That's what I'll do.

MADAME: Lucas, I can't marry you.

LOGGER: That's just your knee jerking.

MADAME: Apple Show almost here. Just got this letter from someone who wants to buy this place, make me rich. How can I marry you when I'm leavin'?

LOGGER: You didn't even think about it.

MADAME: I have — for longer than you want to know.

LOGGER: You've been wanting this?

MADAME: I don't run my life by what I want, Lucas. That ain't my way.

(Lights shift to Bulrusher and Vera. Bulrusher talks to the river as Vera sings.)

BULRUSHER: She is a mirror.

VERA: *(Singing under Bulrusher's words.)* For all we know

BULRUSHER: A mirror. Schoolch never allowed any mirrors in the house.

VERA: This may only be a dream

BULRUSHER: I always think about touching her skin. It's just like mine only smoother.

VERA: We come and we go, like the ripples on a stream

BULRUSHER: She says that I am beautiful. She says she wants to stretch herself over me like taffy so everyone can see my sweetness. But I want to do that to her.

VERA: So love me tonight, tomorrow was made for some

BULRUSHER: I don't care about anything else.

VERA: Tomorrow may never come, for all we know

BULRUSHER: We sell fruit.

VERA: *(Speaking to unseen customer.)* They're sweet. Nickel a piece.

(As the scene continues, they do not speak to each other, but continue to be in their own separate worlds.)

BULRUSHER: I eat with her every day, pick her up from her uncle's house by Barney Flats.

VERA: I have never been served food by a white woman before. I sat at the table with my napkin folded in my lap and she poured milk into my glass.

BULRUSHER: I take her with me to Cloverdale and we buy oranges and lemons and bananas and she sings next to me in the truck. Once she put her fingers on my knee and spelled my name up my thigh.

VERA: Bulrusher, why don't we go to the beach? Can't you see us running along the sand and tearing off our stockings?

BULRUSHER: One day she kissed my cheek to say good-bye. I grabbed her hand.

VERA: I'm saving up my money. And I eat anything I want. Sometimes just bread with mustard.

BULRUSHER: She wants to go to the ocean with me but I don't like the ocean. That's where my mother wanted me to die. You're my river. I'll bring Vera to you instead.

(The river. Bulrusher and Vera now talk to each other.)

BULRUSHER: *(To Vera.)* I guess I can tell everybody else's futures because I don't know my own past. I was supposed to die, but I didn't, so I think I got an open ticket to the land of could be.

VERA: You like reading water?

BULRUSHER: Only if the person want to know the future. If she don't then it's all garbled up, can't read a thing. Image gets blurry, blinds me even. *(She picks up a twig and turns it on Vera.)* Sometimes I wish I did water witching instead 'cause no one ever minds finding water and water never minds being found.

(They laugh.)

BULRUSHER: Have you ever tried wild blackberries? Here.

VERA: They're sour.

BULRUSHER: They're almost ready.

VERA: What about these?

BULRUSHER: Poison.

VERA: And these? They smell like being sick.

BULRUSHER: Just juniper berries. If you're sick, you need these eucalyptus leaves. They'll cure anything that's hurtin' your chest from inside.

VERA: This water'll cure me!

(Vera takes off her clothes and jumps into the river in her slip.)

VERA: I just want to be clean. I'm clean here, right? You can see I'm clean.

BULRUSHER: Yeah, I can see.

VERA: Then why aren't you getting in?

BULRUSHER: I don't know.

VERA: There're fish!

BULRUSHER: Stand in the sand.

VERA: It's deep.

BULRUSHER: There's a branch above you, hold onto that.

VERA: Nobody else come down here?

BULRUSHER: Only me. This is my secret place on the river.

VERA: Your river. It's your diary, your church, your everything.

BULRUSHER: Yeah, has been.

VERA: Well, your river is making me cold, so you should get in.

BULRUSHER: It's not cold, you're in the sun.

VERA: I don't want to die in here.

BULRUSHER: Why would you die?

VERA: Because it's quiet. Everything's so quiet. It makes me want to cry.
    (Vera laughs.)

BULRUSHER: The river holds you. Anything that you are scared of, it'll hold
    for you. I asked the river to save me when I was a baby girl, and it
    held me.

VERA: Is that why you won't get in? You're scared your luck will run out?

BULRUSHER: I've just never taken anyone down to this water. I always come
    here alone to talk and listen and I don't know how to do that with you
    here too.
    (Vera starts to get out.)

BULRUSHER: No, you stay, I just can't get in with you.

VERA: I'm done. I got in and I'm gettin' out.

BULRUSHER: Stay in longer, it's only been a minute.

VERA: Nothing to do if you're not in with me. Can't splash, can't play — and
    I don't hear the river saying things like you do so I suppose I'm just a lit-
    tle less entertained.

BULRUSHER: Wait — don't get out. I'll put my feet in.

VERA: I'm naked as a plucked chicken in an apron! You take off your clothes
    too.

BULRUSHER: Why?

VERA: Because we're here together. So we're gonna do the same thing.
    *(Bulrusher takes off her shoes. She takes off her shirt and then Vera pulls off
    her trousers for her. Bulrush is startled then begins to laugh. She dives in
    wearing her undershirt and bloomers.)*

VERA: You don't wear a bra?

BULRUSHER: What's that?

VERA: For to keep your chest up. They'll start draggin' in the dust if you don't strap those things.

BULRUSHER: I didn't know you were supposed wear anything else.

VERA: You have been raised by wolves and none of 'em female.

(Bulrusher touches one of Vera's tiny scars.)

BULRUSHER: What are these scars?

VERA: From my mama tryin' ta straighten my hair with a hot comb. But I'm a country girl now. Can get my hair wet as I want. Handstand!

(When Vera comes up, Bulrusher touches Vera's neck. Vera holds Bulrusher's hand to her wet neck and collarbone.)

VERA: Have you ever noticed that white people smell like mayonnaise?

BULRUSHER: You don't want to go back to Birmingham.

VERA: Some days I could kill them all.

BULRUSHER: You're scared.

VERA: White folks are the ones should be scared 'cause we ain't takin' what they're servin' much longer. If they'd just read the Bible sometime they'd see what's coming for 'em.

BULRUSHER: Your mother misses you; she will cut her finger on the edge of a letter. But it isn't from you, it's a notice from a contest at the radio station.

VERA: I entered it in May.

BULRUSHER: You'll win a year supply of Dixie Peach Pomade and a subscription to *Jet* magazine. What's all that?

(Vera takes Bulrusher's hand off of her neck.)

BULRUSHER: I'm sorry.

VERA: You didn't ask if you could do that.

BULRUSHER: I didn't mean to.

VERA: That wasn't fair. I can't see *your* future.

BULRUSHER: It just happened. I couldn't read if you didn't want me to. I just wanted to touch your skin — like you wanted me to.

VERA: So what? So my mother didn't send me here. So I came here on my own. But that isn't all you saw.

BULRUSHER: No.

VERA: Then say it. Say what I already know.

BULRUSHER: It doesn't matter.

VERA: I wanna hear you say it.

BULRUSHER: I said I'd take care of you, that ain't gonna change now.

VERA: Say it.

BULRUSHER: I'll start tellin' fortunes again, make us some more money — you
   don't have to worry 'bout nothin'.

VERA: You can't fix everything! Some things are just wrong and always will be.

BULRUSHER: Not you.

VERA: Yeah me.

BULRUSHER: So that's why you're here.

VERA: Don't make me explain. Just say it. Say it.

BULRUSHER: You're gonna have a baby. A boy.

VERA: A boy?

BULRUSHER: But I won't let you stand up to work, I'll do all the lifting. You
   can just sit and count the money.

VERA: I'm not gonna have a boy. Or a girl.

BULRUSHER: Yes you are. And he's gonna be as pretty as you.

VERA: I don't want it. All I need is the money to get rid of it.

BULRUSHER: He's yours. Don't say that.

VERA: Then you don't really want to help me.

BULRUSHER: Why would you want to get rid of a child?

VERA: You don't know where it came from.

BULRUSHER: But he's in you now.

VERA: I don't care 'cause I'll never love it.

BULRUSHER: You can just give him to me.

VERA: No! I never want to see its face! If you don't want to help me, that's fine.
   That's fine.

   (Vera gets out of the water. Bulrusher follows her, quiet.)

VERA: If you tell anybody —

BULRUSHER: I won't.

   (Bulrusher turns away from Vera. They both put on their clothes in silence.)

VERA: Bulrusher.

   *(Bulrusher turns toward her and Vera buttons Bulrusher's shirt. Vera kisses
   her.)*

VERA: I guess I can't hide anything from you, huh.

   *(She kisses Bulrusher again. Bulrusher falls against Vera, crying. Vera kisses
   Bulrusher's tears.)*

ACT II

Same evening. The brothel. Boy, Madame, and Logger are drunk by now and Schoolch, sober, has joined them. Boy continues to play his guitar.

LOGGER: See this woman is an artisan. Don't you remember when you used to have me in your boudoir, this is years ago, boom time, and serve me some of that pecan coffee cake? Sometimes had raspberries too. 'Course you got the berries from Gowan's since everything dies in your garden, but that made sense to me. Seems if you are running a brothel proper, it should look real inviting but not feel like you could really live there. The kinda place you can't wait to get back to but so intense you can't stay? That's 'cause you are an artisan. And trained all your women good.

MADAME: Well I also train the men. If he's afraid of the woman in front of him, if he thinks he makes the rules, if he don't listen, he can't get nowhere with me. If I see a man got potential, I'll send him to one of the other girls, watch how he touch her. If he is the slightest bit distracted, that is his downfall. I'll tell him. You're distracted. Downfall of mankind! I'll come out and show him what he ought to do and how. Most men ain't used to that — having someone take enough of an interest to increase their skills. But I'm an artisan and on occasion a man can arouse me into my creativity.

LOGGER: You never had to teach me nothin'.

MADAME: Yeah, you were probably practicing on them horses.

LOGGER: I'm a natural, honey, and you know it. Why? Because I know how to talk. And I know how to listen. You used to take me in, 'stead of sendin' me with the other girls, 'cause with me you could empty yourself out. Tell me all kinds of stories 'bout yourself. And after that, I'd slip you out of your bodice and let you lay there. I could see all your moles and freckles, the streaks and scars and blushes. I wanted to turn your bright skin red, from inside. Have it run at top speed, have your heart race your own curves. You were open and draped in those smooth sheets — and I don't know if I was feelin' love, but when I look back, I sure want to call it that.

MADAME: Huh. You hear that, Schoolch? And this is the one talking 'bout marrying me. Bragging on himself steada begging on his knees.

BOY: How 'bout we sing the Wabash Cannonball?

LOGGER: Ain't braggin'. Tellin' the truth. You want me so much it makes *my* bones ache.

MADAME: Ha! I don't want you! I'm sellin' and I'm gone. I'm like Schoolch here — kept my feelings in the cupboard so long I don't need 'em. You're just like old china. Never gonna use you.

BOY: You know Schoolch actually taught us the Wabash Cannonball in class, stood up on his desk and looked right at us and his eyes filled up when he sang. He sang so strong, his hair moved, like he was standing on the top of a real cannonball train. And if that train was real, I figured my daddy had to be on it, that he'd left me and my ma on a machine so fast people had to sing about it.

LOGGER: Oh I miss your pa. You know I was there when you were born. Your pa cut your umbilical with my barlow when the midwife got ridgy. Yeah, we felled plenty pine together. How's your ma?

BOY: Still working at the hotel in Mendocino.

MADAME: When you gonna get yourself grown and start taking care of her?

BOY: I don't know.

(He strums his guitar. As Vera and Bulrusher enter:)

BOY: If I had me a wife, I could do anything.

LOGGER: If I had me a wife.

MADAME: Where you two been?

BULRUSHER: Went swimming down on the river.

BOY: *(Almost singing, to Bulrusher.)* If I had me a wife . . .

MADAME: Well, you look distracted. And you don't need to stand that close to each other.

LOGGER: Like two redwood saplings. Vera here going to college, and Bulrusher got her business? They *should* stand close to each other.

BULRUSHER: I like standing here.

(Pause.)

VERA: I'm feeling pretty tired.

LOGGER: Well then we'll say good night to Madame here. And don't slip and call her Madam — 'cause she will curse you out in French.

BULRUSHER: I can take Vera home.

LOGGER: That's alright. It's on my way. So Madame, you think about what I asked you.

MADAME: I told you, I'm signing this place away. Settlin' accounts with the girls and leavin' soon as the cash is in my palm. None of those plans include you.

LOGGER: You know you ain't left town since that year your mother passed. Unless you got another mother you been hiding from us, you staying put.

BOY: Before you go, I want to say something.

LOGGER: I'm sure you do.

BOY: It's a public announcement and it's got to be made. *(To Bulrusher.)* I'm ready to put my arm around you, Bulrusher.

LOGGER: This a new song you wrote?

BOY: I'm gonna put my arm around you where the people can see. I'll take you to the Anyhow and stand by you. I'll never leave you.

MADAME: See what you started Lucas?

BULRUSHER: Why? Why you wanta stand by me?

BOY: I told you I'm a standin' man. I've known you all my life.

BULRUSHER: But you ain't never talked to me till last month.

BOY: I was shy.

BULRUSHER: You didn't want to put your arm around me because I'm colored.

BOY: What? No. I just thought you were a witch! Everybody says you don't have no ma, you just got spit out the river by the devil's tongue.

BULRUSHER: And who said that about me? White people.

LOGGER: Listen now, you can't say that Bulrusher. You know the reason no one talks to you is 'cause you ain't got no family. Whoever gave birth to you didn't care nothing for you, but this white gentleman Schoolch has cared and cared hard.

BULRUSHER: So this Boy wants to be like Schoolch, wants to save me?

BOY: I figure if he lets me be with you, if you let a bloocher like me into your pasture, that's proof I can do anything in this world.

BULRUSHER: You don't even know what you want to do.

BOY: I want to choose you. You pulled a gun on me. It wasn't loaded, but it was passionate. No girl's ever done that to me before.

BULRUSHER: I'll do it again.

BOY: See? Some people don't need reasons — they just know. They just have hearts and certainty. That's what's happening here. And it may seem strange to you because you ain't inside my heart and feeling it pound, but some things are just for sure. You are that. You are my for sure.

BULRUSHER: What are you talking about?

BOY: I'm choosing you! The witch! Why can't you just be chosen? Sometimes that's all people need. To be chosen, to be the only one. I'm a do that for you. You don't have to do it for me if you don't want to, but I'll make it easy for you to change your mind.

MADAME: Lucas, you taking notes? This boy's got the goods.

BULRUSHER: I don't need you. I don't need *you*. I might have, but now I got me this one. I got Vera. And I'm a take care a her.

LOGGER: That's different than what he's talking about Bulrush. She's your friend and he's talking romantic.

MADAME: But they standin' too close together! I've seen this before, two girls stand too close, then they get distracted, and blow apart. If you're a woman, you can't fall in love, not with a man or with your friend. You just can't afford to. Schoolch, tell her.

(Schoolch is silent.)

BULRUSHER: Vera will tell you. I'm a take care of her. I don't want nobody else.

LOGGER: Vera, what you say about all this?

VERA: She's a good friend.

LOGGER: That's all?

BULRUSHER: She kissed me. That's what I know. She kissed me and that means we are meant for each other, don't it?

BOY: You're a witch, a bulrusher, a colored girl, and a degenerate too? Oh I've got to save you with my songs of mercy. You don't want her, I'm tellin' you you don't.

LOGGER: Vera, ain't there something you got to tell us?

VERA: I don't think so.

LOGGER: I realize it's early on and all so I've been letting you cavort and take in your last bit of childhood, but I know what you come here for. I'm up earlier than you, honey. I know you get tongue-cuppy in the mornings out back, and it's every morning, so I know. But we're still gonna get you to that college, believe you me.

BOY: You mean this girl is lizzied? Lews 'n larmers. Well congratulations to the man who got you heisted. See Bulrusher? That's just what I wanna do with you.

(Bulrusher punches Boy. They struggle.)

MADAME: No upper-cuttin' on my premises!

LOGGER: Let 'em fight it out. I wanna see who they are.

(Bulrusher is strong, but Boy is a more experienced fighter. He pins her arm behind her back and holds her down.)

BOY: You still feel like hittin' me?

BULRUSHER: Yes!

VERA: Stop it!

BOY: I'm asking you true, that's what you want?

BULRUSHER: Yes!

BOY: You think you can hurt me that way?

BULRUSHER: I hope so!

BOY: Then try.

(He lets go and lies down, face up. She gets on top of him. A moment of reckoning — then she starts pummeling him.)

BULRUSHER: *(Punching with each word.)* You don't want me.

MADAME: Lucas, I'll jump in there myself if you don't!

BULRUSHER: You don't know me.

VERA: He's bleeding!

BULRUSHER: He's drunk, he won't even notice.

MADAME: Bulrusher, stop this now!

(Bulrusher continues to hit him, focus intensified.)

VERA: Why are you doing this?

MADAME: You may not listen, but you can feel.

(Madame tries to drag Bulrusher off of him but Bulrusher hits Madame, knocking her to the floor.)

SCHOOLCH: Bulrusher.

(At the sound of his soft voice, everything stops.)

SCHOOLCH: That's enough.

(Schoolch and Logger both move to help Madame — an awkward moment that evolves into a silent showdown. Finally, Logger helps her up. Bulrusher gets off of Boy slowly and stands, suddenly aware of what she has done.)

SCHOOLCH: Go home, Bulrusher.

(Bulrusher looks at Vera, then runs out, driving off in her truck. Madame is already cleaning.)

LOGGER: Madame, you hurt?

MADAME: I'm mad, that's all. Look at the blood on my floor.

LOGGER: You alright son? Ooh, she Joe Macked you.

BOY: Got a tooth loose.

(Madame hands him a hot towel.)

MADAME: Here's some brandy if you need it.

(He drinks some.)

BOY: I hope Bulrusher will forgive me. You think she will?

LOGGER: I'll take you home, Boy. Let's go Vera.

MADAME: What do you want a baby for.

LOGGER: Let's go.

(Logger, Vera, and Boy exit.)

(Split scene: Madame and Schoolch continue to talk in the brothel parlor while Bulrusher talks to the river.)

MADAME: Damn babies. They grow up and make more. Grow up and serve nothing but hurt. Why did you take that girl in?

BULRUSHER: I float in a basket toward the Pacific, hands blue as huckleberries.

MADAME: How did Lucas find her in the weeds? Why did he bring that weese here?

BULRUSHER: The woman who bore me named me silence.

MADAME: He knew a baby in a brothel takes away more customers than war. The girls would hear her squall and remember they're women.

BULRUSHER: Who is a motherless daughter but pure will?

MADAME: She seemed like she was trying to fit in, but now she's a walking curse. Why did you take her in?

BULRUSHER: I want to swing, swing, over the green grapes, the fir trees, ride the wind, find my home, go all the way home.

SCHOOLCH: When your mother passed, you left town. You left me, you left Lucas.

BULRUSHER: Home.

SCHOOLCH: You stayed away a long time, but you came back.

BULRUSHER: Home. And I am . . .

SCHOOLCH: You know how I feel about you. Why'd you come back? Was it for me? Or him?

BULRUSHER: Who?

SCHOOLCH: Me? Or him?

BULRUSHER: Who.

SCHOOLCH: And who are you leaving now? Me? Or him.

BULRUSHER: Who?

SCHOOLCH: Madame? You answer me!

(Long pause.)

MADAME: There's blood on my floor.

(Split scene ends — lights out on Bulrusher. Madame stoops to clean up the floor with her towel, but Schoolch takes it and wipes the floor for her. He hands her the bloody towel.)

SCHOOLCH: Cory up there?

MADAME: She's in the front with the men on the monthly plan. What, you want me to send her up?

SCHOOLCH: On the Wabash Cannonball.

(He throws ten dollars on the pool table and goes up the stairs. Madame, shocked, sits.)

(Next morning. Bulrusher enters the brothel. Madame has not moved since the night before.)

BULRUSHER: Mornin'.

MADAME: Looks the same to me.

BULRUSHER: I can open your shades for you.

MADAME: No thanks. Don't need any more heat in this room. And that sun bleaches my upholstery.

BULRUSHER: You seen Schoolch? I been worried. Couldn't sleep.

MADAME: Me neither.

BULRUSHER: He didn't come home last night.

MADAME: Don't trouble yourself about him.

BULRUSHER: You know where he is?

MADAME: He's here.

BULRUSHER: Here? Upstairs?

MADAME: That's right. Historic, ain't it? Schoolch finally getting his equipment serviced.

BULRUSHER: He — he really —

MADAME: Yes. It is natural, you know.

BULRUSHER: It's my fault. I'm sorry.

MADAME: It ain't your fault. Ain't your fault at all.

BULRUSHER: He's never gonna come home now. He's punishing me.

MADAME: You don't know that.

BULRUSHER: It's because of what I said and did last night that's pushed him over —

MADAME: No, child, he's punishing me.

BULRUSHER: Why?

MADAME: We've known each other a long long time. Know things about the other no one else knows. He's just angry that I'm leavin' town.

BULRUSHER: You say you're leavin' every summer.

MADAME: Well maybe he was mad at me for being so easy on you! When you knocked me over, you cracked my porcelain spittoon!

BULRUSHER: I apologize for that too.

MADAME: You better!

BULRUSHER: I mean to work it all off. Maybe I can help you with your business here, take in some clients for you.

MADAME: What? Work a bed for me?

BULRUSHER: I mean — well, during the Apple Show — if you're short staffed.

MADAME: You ain't even had your cherry popped.

BULRUSHER: What do you mean?

MADAME: My point exactly. You can't just fling yourself into this profession! It's gotta be part of a plan. And I don't want you disrespecting the solicitors I represent with your lack of training and experience. You'd probably get knocked up, like that Vera girl, the love of your life.

BULRUSHER: You don't know how I feel about her.

MADAME: I know she's a girl. And she's pregnant. Soon she'll be a woman, with a baby, and she's gonna need more than you can give.

BULRUSHER: What can't I give? You think she want somebody who talk all that talk about "you are my for sure" like Boy did last night? He's probably been practicing them lines on every girl he know for the last ten years. He'd say that to a whore.

(Madame's look stops Bulrusher cold.)

BULRUSHER: *(Explains.)* You don't know what that Boy and his friends used to do to me.

MADAME: He's trying to give something to you and she's trying to take something from you. You got to choose wisely.

BULRUSHER: You're just sticking up for him 'cause you're both white people.

MADAME: That girl has put so much hate into you. *(Pause.)* You shouldn't see her for a little while.

BULRUSHER: Did you talk to her?

MADAME: I talked to Lucas. He called this morning.

BULRUSHER: What'd he say?

MADAME: Said you needed to cool off.

BULRUSHER: I am cool.

MADAME: You meant to hurt Boy last night, and you did.

BULRUSHER: But Boy don't care what I do. Nothing I do can change him.

MADAME: That's just not how you treat people.

BULRUSHER: I'm sorry. I did it for Vera.

MADAME: And you better cool offa her too.

BULRUSHER: Can't I apologize?

MADAME: Lucas don't want you seein' Vera no more.

BULRUSHER: I don't need to kiss her, that was what she did to me. Once. We can just talk.

MADAME: He says no.

BULRUSHER: But I said I'd take care of her and the boy when he's born.

MADAME: A boy?

BULRUSHER: I read her water. It was an accident.

MADAME: What do you want with her baby?

BULRUSHER: I ain't never had a family. So maybe with her, I can make my own.

MADAME: I've got to have clean lines in my life, nothing blurry. Gotta keep all the food on my plate in separate heaps, can't put on my knickers if they haven't been ironed. Anything unexpected, anything messy, I clean it up. My path has always been clear in front of me . . . but I can't see it anymore. Somebody wants to buy this place for more money than I ever expected to see in my life, and I should be happy, but between that and you and Lucas and Schoolch I feel like something's choking me . . . I want that man, but how can I have him? . . . There's something I'm supposed to do but I don't know what it is. Do you?

BULRUSHER: You're shaking, Madame.

MADAME: I feel like I'm having a greeney. I need to know something. I need to know what I'm supposed to do.

BULRUSHER: Why are you asking me?

(Madame walks into the kitchen and brings back a bowl of water. She plunges her hands into it and splashes it onto her face.)

MADAME: Can't you see it on my face? I'm not breathing right. Nothing I plant ever grows in my garden . . . If I could just smell the grass on my mother's grave, smell the grass growing there —

BULRUSHER: What for?

MADAME: Read my water.

BULRUSHER: Schoolch.

MADAME: I'll worry about him.

BULRUSHER: I said I wouldn't read again, unless Vera wanted me to.

MADAME: I need you to tell me what to do. Tell me what to do.

BULRUSHER: I want to see Vera.

MADAME: I told you Lucas said no.

BULRUSHER: I'll read your water if you arrange for us to meet.

MADAME: You can't love that girl!

BULRUSHER: Call him. Or I won't read.

(Madame picks up the phone to call Logger. She begins to cry as she talks.)

MADAME: Lucas, how you doin'. No, I'm fine, was just calling about Vera. She's got to get over to the doctor, you know. Make sure she and that baby are alright. I can take her when I go into Mendocino. No, I'll do it. I've done it before. She needs a woman around for that kind of thing. Enough lying on a cold metal table and showing yourself to a man with bad breath. What? No, nothing's wrong with me. No, I'm not crying. It's just hot in here. I'll call you later.

(She hangs up.)

MADAME: There.

(She pushes the bowl of water to Bulrusher.)

BULRUSHER: Don't let Vera get rid of the baby.

MADAME: Don't push it. I asked you to read my water, not hers.

BULRUSHER: I can't guarantee I'll see something you want to see.

MADAME: Just hurry.

BULRUSHER: This could be like May Bloyd.

MADAME: May had that coming to her. She wasn't the saint she made herself out to be.

BULRUSHER: If you cry, cry over the bowl, I'll get a stronger signal that way.

MADAME: Can you see the past?

BULRUSHER: Water has a current. I follow where it goes. Hands in the water.

(Bulrusher puts her hands into the water with Madame's. She closes her eyes. After several beats, she pulls Madame's hands out, holding them over the bowl. Schoolch comes down the stairs, unseen.)

BULRUSHER: Don't see anything but you in a blue hat.

MADAME: That's it?

BULRUSHER: Yeah — it just looks all the same from here on. Two pillows on your bed, and a blue hat.

MADAME: That's how soon from now?

(Bulrusher opens her eyes.)

BULRUSHER: I don't get time, I get pictures. That's the only one coming through.

MADAME: How is that supposed to help me? You sure ain't what you advertise.

SCHOOLCH: Mornin'.

(Bulrusher drops Madame's hands, wiping her own on her pants.)

BULRUSHER: Mornin'. I came to find you.

MADAME: Schoolch, she didn't see nothin'.

SCHOOLCH: You asked her to read when you know she's wiped her hands of fortune?

MADAME: How can she wipe her hands of themselves?

SCHOOLCH: You don't mind them calling her a witch then. Well I do. You ain't never loved her. Never loved anybody. Well I do.

BULRUSHER: I made you some spoonbread, Schoolch. I didn't know where you were.

SCHOOLCH: I was setting myself free. You can't be bound to people who don't know how to love.

BULRUSHER: You didn't come home. Don't do that again without telling me.

(Schoolch laughs. Bulrusher smiles.)

MADAME: Schoolch. I don't know what I'm supposed to do.

(Schoolch pulls out a leather envelope thick with money.)

SCHOOLCH: This should help.

MADAME: *(Pulling money from envelope, realizing.)* You wrote me that letter? *You* wanna buy me out? Why?

SCHOOLCH: I want you to leave. I don't care if it costs my life savings. If you ain't gonna set things right, you gotta leave. I'm tired of waitin' and I'm tired of bein' tired. Make up your mind.

(Schoolch and Bulrusher exit. Madame sits.)

(Lights change. The river. One week later. Bulrusher and Vera are in the water. They are not actually touching, but can feel every movement made by the other — they are making love. Bulrusher speaks to the river. Vera cannot hear her.)

BULRUSHER: Pampas grass, Swiss chard,
waterfall, chipmunk.
And vines, vines, growing in the hill.
Monkeyflower and jackrabbits,
a roll dipped in apricot jam,
fresh cream turns to butter in the churn.
I swing, swing, over the poppies,
the scrub pine: I'm a meteor, its trail,
hold a star on my tongue.

(They come out of the water and begin putting their clothes back on. They are strangely awkward with each other — their lovemaking wasn't what they thought it would be. Vera is a bit faraway; Bulrusher looks to her for cues.)

VERA: Hey.

BULRUSHER: Hey.

VERA: I missed you.

BULRUSHER: You got a new dress.

VERA: Madame gave it to me. I put it on in the doctor's office. I guess I'm supposed to grow into it.

BULRUSHER: So the baby's . . . ?

VERA: Still there.

BULRUSHER: Good. Does your uncle talk bad about me?

VERA: Mainly he sings songs to my stomach. He's been real nice to me.

BULRUSHER: He's a good man.

VERA: He made friends with a long distance operator and called my mother. Now she knows everything.

BULRUSHER: Are you going back?

(Pause.)

VERA: A white man did this to me. A policeman. I typed reports for him in the front office.

BULRUSHER: Do you love him?

VERA: He raped me. And my boyfriend is studying to be a pastor.

BULRUSHER: Do you want me to kill him?

VERA: That's so sweet.

BULRUSHER: Then I'll do it.

VERA: I don't want him dead, I want him to change. *(To herself.)* All of 'em gotta change . . .

BULRUSHER: I thought you wanted all white people murdered. I'd do that for you. As many as I could.

VERA: Bulrusher, don't say that. I was just talking.

BULRUSHER: Maybe the same thing happened to you happened to my mother. Maybe that's why she got rid of me.

VERA: No, I can tell you were made from love. So you shouldn't go beating people up.

BULRUSHER: We've saved up a lot of money. That plus the Apple Show, we can go away somewhere. Drive the truck down to Mexico. No one will know where the baby comes from.

VERA: And you'd leave Schoolch?

BULRUSHER: I'd have food sent to him from the hotel.

VERA: But you'd be OK without him?

BULRUSHER: Mm hm.

VERA: He's white, you could just kill him.

BULRUSHER: I could.

VERA: *(Laughing.)* You couldn't. You sure don't know how to lie.

BULRUSHER: Is your boyfriend gonna be mad that you ran off with me?

VERA: Fred? He doesn't get mad, he prays. "What you do to the least you do to me," something like that. And sometimes he believes the things he says. At least I hope so. What about Boy? He's gonna be awful teary if you go.

BULRUSHER: I don't understand him. His friends used to lift up my shirt and wouldn't let me go till I said I had goat titties. Boy wouldn't do nothing but watch and laugh. Now I'm the sparkle of his eye?

VERA: Well you probably *did* have goat titties back then. You don't anymore.

BULRUSHER: Isn't that the same as what the policeman did to you?

VERA: You already broke the boy's face in, what else do you want?
    (Madame enters.)

MADAME: You still have your clothes on, that's good news. Wrap it up now, I don't want to put Lucas on the wonder.

VERA: Just a few more minutes, ma'am.

MADAME: You want me to wait until you go into labor? I got things to do.

VERA: We won't be long.

MADAME: I'm going to sit in the car. Don't make me have to come and get you again.

BULRUSHER: A few more minutes.

(Madame exits.)

BULRUSHER: Should we take off our clothes again just to show her?

VERA: No.

BULRUSHER: I did get that turpentine feeling under my skin again. But your lips were — cold.

VERA: What did you see when you kissed me? Did you see my future?

BULRUSHER: I thought I would, but I didn't. You were blurry, like when a person doesn't want me to read. Maybe kissing makes a different kind of water? 'Cause all I felt — was your mouth. Cold.

VERA: You didn't like it.

BULRUSHER: Um . . . I think so.

VERA: You didn't. I know you didn't. It's OK though. Find the right person I guess, and everything'll fall into place.

BULRUSHER: What about you? You could teach me.

VERA: There's feeling *(She places her hands over her own and Bulrusher's heart.)* and touching. *(She palms Bulrusher's hip.)* Sometimes they both come in the same person and sometimes they don't. I think you like Boy. That's who you're meant for.

BULRUSHER: He's not pretty.

VERA: But he's cute.

BULRUSHER: And I said I'd take care of you.

VERA: Woman of your word.

BULRUSHER: Everything will be fine when we go away together. We'll just have to find a town with a river.

VERA: My mother sent the first *Jet* magazine I won.

BULRUSHER: And the pomade?

VERA: She kept that. There's a picture in here I want you to see.

(Vera shows her the magazine.)

BULRUSHER: Is that a dead boy?

VERA: That's what the headline says.

BULRUSHER: But his head looks like a football with gravel glued on. There's no nose, eyes, mouth — he doesn't have a face left.

VERA: They killed him and drowned him in a river for whistling at a white woman.

BULRUSHER: This happened in your town?

VERA: Close enough.

BULRUSHER: Why do colored people even live where these things happen?

VERA: Because we're done runnin' . . . done bein' ashamed. We didn't do nothing wrong but get born.

BULRUSHER: Why didn't the river save him?

VERA: I guess so we could save ourselves. When I watched you beat that Boy up, I suddenly knew right then and there that I couldn't undo my own hurt by making more. One day I'm gonna be a teacher and I'm 'n a say what I know. That we can take our hate and let it open us so wide we can love anybody. That we can stand in the face of violence and say I can take that, I'm bigger than that.

BULRUSHER: Bigger than the white people.

VERA: Bigger than our own small fists.

MADAME: *(Calling from offstage.)* Vera now, let's move it.

BULRUSHER: So I'll see you at the Apple Show.

VERA: *(Laughing.)* We'll disappear after the dance. We'll drive off into the sunset, won't we?

BULRUSHER: And the love songs will come on the radio and they'll be about us. *(Vera is silent.)*

BULRUSHER: Did *you* like it? Kissing me?

VERA: This is for you. Got it in Mendocino.

(Vera hands Bulrusher a small pewter hand mirror engraved with flowers.)

VERA: I wanted to kiss you all over from the moment I met you. I don't know why. Never felt like that about a girl, ever. But then when we do kiss, it's like — it's like you said. It's cold, like I'm pressing my lips to a mirror, like it's just me again and again, over and over. I don't know why *that* is either. Each time, cold kisses, cold rain. *(She touches Bulrusher's cheek.)* And we can't do nothin' about the weather. *(She stands.)* Just take this — and remember me when you look at your own face.

BULRUSHER: It's nice, but I don't need it. I'll be seeing you all the time.

VERA: Keep it anyway.

(As Vera begins to leave, she leans down to the water and whispers to it.)

VERA: *(To river, softly.)* Thank you.

BULRUSHER: I'll meet you after the Apple Show dance.

VERA: Bulrusher.

BULRUSHER: What.

VERA: Don't learn how to lie.

(Suddenly Madame is there.)

MADAME: *(To Vera.)* In the car.

(Vera hesitates, looking at Bulrusher. Then, she goes.)

MADAME: *(To Bulrusher.)* Bulrush, Schoolch says someone's coming to see you.

BULRUSHER: Who?

MADAME: He says he heard from your mother, up by Clear Lake. She wants to do penance. Huh. 'Bout time. She'll meet you Sunday dusk by Wharf Rock.

BULRUSHER: My mother? But Sunday is the Apple Show dance.

MADAME: So? You want to meet her, don't you?

BULRUSHER: I guess.

MADAME: Sunday by Wharf Rock.

(Lights change. Bulrusher talks to the river as the Apple Show begins. Music.)

BULRUSHER: Dusk, Sunday.

Dusk, Sunday.
Schoolch says my mother
will meet me: dusk,
Sunday, by Wharf Rock.
What will I do with
my hands? Will she push
me into the ocean?
Throw herself to the tide?
O river,
tell me, tell me:
will I kill her?

(The Apple Show. Everyone dances as Boy calls it from the grandstand. Madame leads Logger, who does not know how to dance, and Schoolch and Bulrusher dance with great flourish. Stomping, clapping.)

BOY: Headgents give right hands across and balance four in line
Back with the left and don't get lost and mind your steps and time
Swing your partner halfway round and balance there again
Swing your partner to her place and those two ladies chain
Rat a tat tat, rat a tat tat, rat a tat tat
Rat a tat tat, rat a tat tat, rat a tat tat

LOGGER: I told you you'd stay for the dance.

MADAME: Only because you said you'd come.

LOGGER: Can't believe you actually drug me to a dance. I don't do things I ain't good at.

MADAME: You're tripping over your shoelaces pretty well.

(They dance. Bulrusher, now in her booth, reads water for unseen townspeople.)

BULRUSHER: It's fifty cents for one image of your future. Please pay before you place your hand in the water sir. Thank you. Relax your arm. Alright. *(A few beats.)* Your sheep are going to be attacked by bobcats. Next. *(Boy walks up.)*

BOY: Will you tell our future?

BULRUSHER: Step aside, I'm only taking paying customers. It's fifty cents, ma'am.

BOY: I want you to be in my future.

BULRUSHER: Let me get this bowl refreshed.

BOY: I wrote songs for you and everything.

BULRUSHER: Relax your arm. You will purchase a pair of socks that are very intriguing to a person whose sex is difficult to ascertain. No, thank *you*.

BOY: You're still sore over hitting me the other night?

BULRUSHER: You'd like two dollars worth of images? Yes sir, I'll give you your money's worth — and add one more for free!

BOY: You got my jaw real good. I can't eat any of these crunchy apples.

BULRUSHER: Very relaxed arm, that's a good sign. Your gonorrhea will clear up and be less of a hindrance in your adultery. You will oversleep and miss your mother's funeral. You will leave the Anyhow Saloon drunk and crash your truck into Petrified Gulch, where your tires will calcify before you can tow it out. You will — you sure? But you get two more, we ain't done. Well at least take a complimentary navel orange.

BOY: I know I can't make up your mind for you, but won't you give me a little somethin'?

BULRUSHER: I'm working, Boy. And then I'm leaving.

BOY: How 'bout a dance before you go?

BULRUSHER: Just stop bothering me! Look, I'm sorry I broke in your face.

BOY: I'm sorry for not talking to you till — lately.

BULRUSHER: And.

BOY: I'm sorry for not putting my arm around you in the Anyhow.

BULRUSHER: And.

BOY: I'm sorry for laughing at your goat titties.

BULRUSHER: So we're square. Listen, I've got to get to Wharf Rock by dusk but I need you to keep an eye out for Vera.

BOY: You're still stuck on her.

BULRUSHER: I'm taking care of her.

BOY: That's different. Means I still got a chance. Did you ever read that love letter I wrote you when we was twelve?

BULRUSHER: I took it to the outhouse and threw it down.

BOY: *(Smiles.)* I always knew you liked me.

BULRUSHER: Tell Vera to wait for me if you see her.

BOY: If you'll give me a dance.

BULRUSHER: Trade.

BOY: *(A whoop.)* Eeeee tah! What you going to Wharf Rock for?

BULRUSHER: To meet my mother.

(Schoolch walks up to Bulrusher's booth.)

BOY: Afternoon. Bulrusher's gonna dance with me.

(Boy walks away. Bulrusher starts to gather up her money.)

BULRUSHER: Schoolch.

SCHOOLCH: Bulrush.

BULRUSHER: You mind me reading fortunes?

SCHOOLCH: No, never. Just minded what all these people had to say about you when you did.

BULRUSHER: I can take it.

SCHOOLCH: I believe you.

BULRUSHER: Thanks for taking care of me Schoolch.

SCHOOLCH: So you're gonna kill your mother and run off with Vera. You got your majority, you can do what you want. I just wanted to make sure that was your plan.

BULRUSHER: I was gonna have your food sent from the hotel.

SCHOOLCH: Where's the shotgun.

BULRUSHER: I'll bring it back. I'm just afraid she's gonna try and kill me again.

SCHOOLCH: You didn't need that gun when you were a baby.

BULRUSHER: Why did she say we had to meet by the ocean? That's where she sent me to die. I've never been there and I don't want to go. If I even look at the ocean, it might take away all my river power — it could still kill me.

SCHOOLCH: You can tell everybody else's fortunes, but you could never tell your own.

(Schoolch watches Madame and Logger dance. Madame notices him and stops, leaving her hand in Logger's. Schoolch bows to her, and exits. Madame and Logger begin to dance again with Bulrusher and Boy.)

MADAME: Fancy footwork, Boy. Keep it loose 'cause she might split your lip on the next beat.

LOGGER: Mm, she's starting to look reformed to me. Got a sense of purpose about her.

MADAME: You want her to read your fortune?

LOGGER: Nope. Holding it right here in my hands.

(Madame and Logger dance off the stage.)

BOY: Schoolch taught you all this?

BULRUSHER: Yup. He even gets a periodical sent to him from Kansas City with pictures of the new steps.

BOY: Let me hold you like this. *(He puts his hand on her hip.)* Your hip feels kinda hard. Is that all the money you made?

BULRUSHER: And saved. What. You don't like how hard work feels?

BOY: Well maybe if you'd just — dance a little closer. A little slower. Yeah, like that.

(Bulrusher moves in and takes his tempo for a few measures. Fireworks — but this time, inside them. She stops dancing.)

BULRUSHER: Alright, that's enough.

BOY: You liked dancing with me! I could feel it.

BULRUSHER: Keep an eye for Vera. And Boy —

(Bulrusher kisses him on the cheek. Then she walks away. Boy hops onto the grandstand.)

BOY: And this song is for Boonville's own Bulrusher, who has come out of early retirement to tell our fortunes again. I don't know about you, but doesn't that make you feel more secure? Ain't it swell to know where you're going?

(Stomping and clapping again, he calls:)

Apples in a pot

Apples in a pot

Skin is getting hot

Skin is getting hot

Lemon

sugar

brown

(Wharf Rock. Ocean waves crashing. Bulrusher hugs the shotgun to herself. She is unsteady and chants to tame the ocean of her nerves.)

BULRUSHER: *(Eyes closed.)* Seaspray,

dress me in white mist,

hide me from her.

(No response from the ocean.)

Seaspray, white mist,

clothe me in salt.

(No response. She opens her eyes.)

You're not like the river. You

won't listen. But you will not have me.

You are the mother I refuse.

I will live, and live,
live, and live,
without the terror of your love.
(*Madame appears in a blue hat.*)

MADAME: We don't look nothing alike.
(*Bulrusher spins around to her.*)

BULRUSHER: Blue hat.

MADAME: Is that gun for me?

BULRUSHER: Madame.

MADAME: Yeah. Don't call me anything different.

BULRUSHER: Madame.

MADAME: A gun. Where'd you get all these violent impulses?

BULRUSHER: Madame?

MADAME: Yeah. (*Pause.*) Well don't stand there dumb, let's us have a conversation. Ain't you saved up some questions for me?
(*Pause.*)

BULRUSHER: No.

MADAME: I know you got some curiosity.
(*Pause.*)

BULRUSHER: When you leaving?

MADAME: You know I say that every summer when the heat gets to me. Gave Schoolch his money back. I can't leave none a you. So you glad it's me? Coulda been someone you couldn't relate to, somebody lacking morals and accountability.

BULRUSHER: I just — what you —

MADAME: Spit it out.

BULRUSHER: How could — I don't — this ocean air is trying to kill me —

MADAME: No it ain't. You can talk.

BULRUSHER: I don't got any questions. I got to go.

MADAME: Bulrush, hold on. We don't gotta change nothing, let's just talk a while.

BULRUSHER: I got to go. Vera.

MADAME: I still have that basket I wove you. Went down and picked it up after Lucas found you. Wove it from reeds and rushes I found near Clear Lake when my ma was sick. You kept growin' in me, she passed, then you were born. Thought it would be nice for you to float in that basket and look up at the sky. But I was greedy. I had to spend a while with you before I sent you off; had to see what of Lucas made it into you.

BULRUSHER: Vera and I are cousins?

MADAME: Kiss kiss.

BULRUSHER: I've got to tell her.

MADAME: Bulrush —

BULRUSHER: I'm going!

(Madame grabs Bulrusher by the shoulders.)

MADAME: Lucas took Vera to the train. She's going back to Birmingham.

BULRUSHER: I can catch her.

MADAME: No you can't.

BULRUSHER: Why not?

MADAME: The train left yesterday.

BULRUSHER: What about the baby.

MADAME: What about it. It's up to her.

(Bulrusher pulls all the money out of her pockets and throws it into the ocean.)

MADAME: Now what did you do that for?

BULRUSHER: You made Vera go away.

MADAME: No.

BULRUSHER: You sent me down the river like I wasn't nothing but shorn hair. White whore didn't want her colored baby.

MADAME: I ain't white, my ma's a Pomo Indian. The rest I hope you'll let me make up for.

BULRUSHER: I always wished you were my ma. But why should I want you now?

MADAME: You don't have to.

BULRUSHER: I got plenty of shame. Plenty. And now you want to scrape some more off your shoe and rub it on me. You ain't nothing. Nothing but shame.

MADAME: That's right. Think my mother wanted me to be a businesswoman? Think I could have kept my business with folks knowing I was Indian? I made my choice, stuck to it by her deathbed. Wasn't going to put you through all that I knew. Wasn't going to have no customer's baby. And I wasn't tryin' to lose no customer named Lucas.

BULRUSHER: You told Lucas the truth, that I'm his?

MADAME: No, I told him I would marry him.

BULRUSHER: He wouldn't marry you if he knew about me.

MADAME: I guess I wanted to clear it with you — see if you want another father.

BULRUSHER: I ain't givin' up Schoolch.

MADAME: You don't have to.

BULRUSHER: You already turned Schoolch down. He should have somebody in this world.

MADAME: He has what he's always had. I wish I wanted Schoolch, 'cause he never wanted to be a customer. And he never used you against me. Raised you with pure intent, followed you like a calling.

BULRUSHER: *You* didn't follow *me* down the river, I did that by myself.

MADAME: What do you want me to say?

BULRUSHER: I want you to apologize for trying to kill me.

MADAME: I didn't want you dead.

BULRUSHER: Then why did you get rid of me like that? I was floating for an eternity.

MADAME: You can't remember that.

BULRUSHER: Yes I can. Yes I can. I remember floating in the night, the fog and the coyotes — didn't know what that sound was then but I do now. Mr. Jeans found me at Barney Flats, but I was there for days. I begged to be found. I talked to the sun with my fingers, kept closing my fist around it every time it went down trying to keep it with me. But the night would always come. And the river was so thin there, deep as a teardrop — but I kept myself alive. Why? To find you? To lose the only one who ever really touched me? Schoolch never did, he doesn't know how. Only told me to sit up straight. Vera touched me, gave me softness and you made her leave. You knew she was going when I saw her last, didn't you. *(Madame is silent.)* Of course you did. So is she gonna kill the baby or be the preacher's wife who got raped by a cop?

MADAME: You're angry with me.

BULRUSHER: I'm not angry. I'm gonna kill you. I want to kill something. Walk toward the edge of that bluff. Do it.

(Madame doesn't move and Bulrusher aims her shotgun.)

BULRUSHER: Back to me. Go to the ocean and look at it.

(Madame walks to the edge of the cliff.)

BULRUSHER: See it gnashing its teeth? It wants you. Didn't want me. But it still wants to eat. Salt gonna sting your eyes, gonna burn you. All that seaweed down there is gonna grab you and drown you.

MADAME: Bulrusher.

BULRUSHER: You already dead, ever since you tried to kill me. You been dead.

MADAME: Bulrush —

BULRUSHER: Dead for money. Wanted some damn money steada me. Well go get it. I threw it in there for you. It's all yours.

MADAME: Bulrusher, I named you.

BULRUSHER: Bulrusher, caught in the bulrushes, abandoned to the weeds. I'm a weed.

MADAME: You got a name. You ain't a weed.

BULRUSHER: Jeans? Whore? Sneeble? Witch?

MADAME: You got my mama's name. You got your grandma's name just like she wanted you to have it.

BULRUSHER: Pomo? Indian? I don't want it.

MADAME: You got her name. It's Xa-wena. Means on the water.

BULRUSHER: You called me that once. One day.

MADAME: You remember.

BULRUSHER: I remember everything.

MADAME: *(Chants softly.)* O beda-Xa, a thi shishkith, ometh ele'le'. Xa-wéna ewé-ba ke katsilith'ba ele'ledith. O beda-Xa, a thi boshtotsith.

> *(Speaks.)* River water, I ask you, protect her, help her. Take her to your bosom. Save her from the night and cold, river water, protect her. I thank you.

> *(Madame turns around. Bulrusher has lowered her shotgun.)*

> I prayed for you in your basket. And your river listened. She listened. The river's your mother. I throw stones into it every day to thank her for caring for you.

(Madame kneels and hugs Bulrusher's legs.)

MADAME: See? I got softness.

(Pause.)

BULRUSHER: Xa-wena.

MADAME: Yes?

BULRUSHER: I was just sayin' it.

MADAME: Oh.

> *(Lights fade. Madame exits. Spot on Bulrusher holding the mirror Vera gave her. She can barely speak as she tries to find her bearings in the things she knows.)*

BULRUSHER: Chaparral, dust, frogs, cicadas, bay trees, sequoias, pine cones, horse shit, lizards, hummingbirds, ravines, ferns, eucalyptus, woodchips, wild rose, full moon in clouds, exposed roots, skunks, hawks, poppies, driftwood fences, yellow hills, cormorants, spiderwebs, all blown dandelion zero.

> *(Two weeks later. Bulrusher sits on the porch with Schoolch. During the following lines, Logger enters and puts his foot up on the porch. Bulrusher does not talk to the river, but to the audience. She is easy, calm.)*

BULRUSHER: This town is a byway, a traveler's raincoat

folded away from sight. People need
something stop here. They smell it, take it,
and pass through. I sell oranges, balls
of sun. You eat them in sections like a heart
torn from the spine. When they're gone,
I lie in my red flatbed and watch the stars
fall without pity.

LOGGER: *(Lively.)* So Madame and I talkin' 'bout getting locked real soon, October, when the sun fades some and we can have a party in her garden. Both of you invited of course, I'll even braid your hair special Bulrush if you want me to.

BULRUSHER: Schoolch and I smoke cigarettes
by the duck pond, I peel bark
from the madrone tree and rub
the smooth beneath.

LOGGER: Schoolch, hope you don't mind that I won Madame after all these years you been courtin'. But you know, the woman's got her own mind and well, she made it up. Two pillows on her bed now. And Bulrush, you got every right to stay on here with Schoolch, but you just let me know if you need anything, not that Schoolch wouldn't already have it to give, but you know, if you need anything, uh, the family history and so forth, I got a lot a stories, uh, diseases you might be prone to, uh, and the like, of that nature.

BULRUSHER: Soon it will be colder than ever.
In the garden my collards will be pregnant with ice.
But an early frost makes the greens taste sweeter.

LOGGER: You woulda died in them weeds if I hadn't found ya. And then Schoolch was good enough to raise you up. Well, can't judge Madame for what never happened. *(Bright.)* Got a letter today, from Birmingham. Your cousin Vera wrote you a note. I hear she's gettin' married soon too. *(He gives the letter to Bulrusher.)*

Gotta have you a family and a church to lean on in a city like that. It's just been sounding worse and worse down there ever since that boy got . . . what they did to him . . . But you can't just take what pain life has to give you, you gotta make something out of it too. People see you got that kinda strength, they can't deny you. No sirree.

SCHOOLCH: When I finally took away Bulrusher's bottle she cried and cried all night. "I want my bah-ul! I want my bah-ul!" Come the next morning she didn't need it no more. But she had turned and turned so in the crib her hair got matted into chunks. It was like she had a hat on made of steel wool. I tried to comb through it, poured baby oil all over it, dunked her in a big vat of lard, but those tangles wouldn't come out.

LOGGER: Is that the truth.

SCHOOLCH: So I had to cut it all off. Cut it all off.

(Pause.)

LOGGER: Did you. *(Laughing.)* Well Bulrusher you must have cried all that next night too!

(Logger hugs Bulrusher with one arm.)

SCHOOLCH: She did. I sat by her crib. Didn't hold her but she knew I was there.

(Bulrusher looks at Schoolch, then puts the letter into a bowl of water. She lifts up the paper and lets the ink run. She sinks it back in, and tries to get a signal. Nothing. She pulls her hand out, then puts it back in. Nothing. Once more she tries, hand in, then out —)

LOGGER: So how is Vera?

BULRUSHER: I can't tell.

LOGGER: Oh, you don't read off of paper. Uh huh.

BULRUSHER: No, anything somebody touch I can read from once it's in water. Maybe I can't read *her* anymore. Or maybe I can't read at all.

LOGGER: Now don't say "can't." You can do anything you want if you put your mind to it. Schoolch, you thought about installing a phone here? I put one in and now I can't live without it.

(Boy enters, plucking his guitar. He sits next to Bulrusher.)

BOY: I got a new song for you.

BULRUSHER: I got a new name.

BOY: What is it?

(She turns the bowl onto its rim and the water runs out. She looks at him gently. Blackout.)

END OF PLAY

A GLOSSARY FOR THE CURIOUS from *Boontling: An American Lingo* by Charles C. Adams, Mountain House Press, 1990

airtight: no problem, also name for a sawmill
applehead: girl, girlfriend
bahl: good
barlow: pocketknife
belhoon: a dollar
bilchin': having sex with
bloocher: one who chatters aimlessly or masturbates
boarch: Chinese male
booker tee: black man
bookers: black people
bow for: have sex with (*bow* is pronounced like a violin bow)
Bulrusher: foundling, illegitimate child
burlap: have sex with
buzzchick: baseball
can-kicky: angry
chucks: dull or unruly children
cocked darley: habitually angry
comb's gettin red: puberty
cut cabbage: a black woman, the feeling of her vagina
daming: womanizing
dehigged: broke, without money
dish: cheat
doolsey boo: sweet potato
dove cooey: lonely
dubs: double
ear settin': a lecture
fiddlers: delirium tremens
flag's out: menstruating
flattened: sick
flories: biscuits
Fourth of Jeel: Fourth of July
geechin': penetration
golden eagles: underwear (made from Golden Eagle brand flour sacks)
gorm: food
greeney: a fit, a strange feeling associated with sudden awakening
grizz: old bachelor

harp: talk
heel scratchin': sex
heisted: pregnant
highgun: shotgun
high shams: thick brush
hobbin': dancing
hoot: laugh
horn and chiggle: food and drink (the verb *horn* means "to drink")
ink-standy: tired
jackers: young men who masturbate
jape: drive
jenny: snitch
jimhead: confused
Joe Mack: to beat someone up
jonnems: tall tales
lews 'n larmers: gossip
ling: Boontling
lizzied: pregnant
locked: married
madges: prostitutes
mink: woman (of easy morals, well-dressed enough to afford mink*)*
moldunes: breasts
moshe: automobile
mossy: change the subject
Navarro: Bulrusher's river; main waterway west to the ocean
nonch harpin': dirty talk
pearlin': raining
Philo: a neighboring rival town
pike: road
put in on: to court
ricky chow: sexual intercourse
ridgy: backwoodsy
roger: storm
rooje: cheat
rout: scold
Schoolch: short for school teacher
scottied: hungry
shike: beat someone in a deal
sneeble: black person

silent seeker: quiet, unobtrusive seducer
skee: whiskey
somersettin': to become emotionally upset
stringy hair and wrinkle socks: an unkempt woman
sulled: angered
tarp: pudendum of either sex
teet lipped: angry
that's earth: that's the truth
tidrey: a little bit
tongue-cuppy: nauseous, to vomit
toobs: two bits, a quarter
tweed: child
tuddish: mentally disabled
upper-cuttin': fist fight
warblin': singing
weese: infant
wess: exaggerate
whittlin': politicking
yink: young man

PRONUNCIATION

Ina: EYE-nuh
Madame: muh-DAMN
McGimsey: mick-JIM-zee
Philo: FY-low
Pizitz: puh-ZITS
Ukiah: yoo-KAI-yuh
Xa-wena: ha-WAY-nah

Pomo Chant *(Courtesy of Robert Geary)*:
Oh buh-DAH-hah, ah tee-SHEESH-keeth, oh met eh-LAY-lay. Ha-WAY-nah ay-WAY-bah kay kaht-SEE-leet-bah ay-LAY-lay-deeth. Oh buh-DAH-hah, ah tee BOSH-toe seeth.

Note: The "th" sounds at the ends of words are very lightly aspirated.

INDOOR/OUTDOOR

Kenny Finkle

for M.T.M., Beverly, and of course the real Samantha

PLAYWRIGHT'S BIOGRAPHY

Kenny Finkle's play *Indoor/Outdoor* has been produced at theaters around the country, including Trinity Repertory in Providence, R.I., Hangar Theatre, and the DR2 (Off-Broadway). In August 2005, *Bridezilla Strikes Back* (co-written with Cynthia Silver) played in the N.Y. Fringe Festival and received the "Best Solo Performance" Award. In 2002 his play *Transatlantica* premiered at the Flea Theatre in Tribeca. His play *Josh Keenan Comes Out to the World*, was presented as part of Philadelphia's Gay and Lesbian Theatre Festival (2004) and toured schools in upstate New York (2003, produced by the Hangar Theatre, directed by Kevin Moriarty). He is a recipient of a NYFA fellowship, was awarded University of Illinois' Inner Voices prize and has received commissions from the Hangar Theatre in Ithaca, N.Y. and Ford's Theatre in Washington, D.C. Kenny is a graduate of Columbia University's MFA Playwriting program and is a member of the Dramatists Guild.

ORIGINAL PRODUCTION

Indoor/Outdoor was originally produced by the Hangar Theatre in Ithaca, N.Y. (Artistic Director: Kevin Moriarty; Executive Director: Lisa Bushlow). Opening night was July 21, 2004. Directed by Kevin Moriarty with the following cast:

SAMANTHA	Jenny Maguire
SHUMAN	Michael Bakkensen
MATILDA	Brandy Zarle
OSCAR	Tommy Schrider
Set Design:	Beowolf Boritt
Costume Design	Greg Robbins
Sound Design	Ryan Rummery
Lighting Design	Jeff Croiter
Stage Manager	Monika Tandon

Off-Broadway production by DR2 Theatre in New York, N.Y.* Produced by Daryl Roth, Margo Lion, Hal Luftig in association with Lily Hung. Opening night was February 22, 2006. Directed by Daniel Goldstein with the following cast:

SAMANTHA	Emily Cass McDonnell
SHUMAN	Brian Hutchison
MATILDA	Keira Naughton
OSCAR	Mario Campanaro

Set Design .... David Korins
Costume Design .... Michael Krass
Sound Design .... Walter Trarbach and Tony Smolenski IV
Lighting Design .... Ben Stanton
Stage Manager .... Brian Maschka

originally produced in NYC at the Summer Play Festival July 2005

CHARACTERS

SAMANTHA: a cat
SHUMAN: the man who brings her home
MATILDA: receptionist at the Vet and a burgeoning Cat Therapist
 (This actor should also play Mom.)
OSCAR: another cat *(This actor plays all other characters.)*

SETTING
The majority of action takes place in and around Shuman's house.

AUTHOR'S NOTE
Both Samantha and Oscar should not be played with any physical indication that they are cats.

INDOOR/OUTDOOR

Lights up on Samantha sitting by herself on the edge of the stage.

SAMANTHA: *(To audience.)* Hi. My name's Samantha and these are my memoirs.

(Just then Shuman appears on stage, looking for Samantha.)

SHUMAN: Samantha? SAMANTHA??

(He wanders off.)

SAMANTHA: That's Shuman. I live with him. He's looking for me right now. We'll get to him in a minute. First though, you need to know me. OK. From the beginning. This is how I was born.

(Mom appears and stands with her legs wide open. She grunts. And grunts again. And then screams. On the scream Samantha slides in between her legs with her eyes closed. She screams too. Then looks around.)

SAMANTHA: Wow! I'm alive! Finally! Oh wow, I'm tired. Hi, you must be my mom. I'd recognize you anywhere.

MOM: Listen darling, I'd love to chat right now but I've got twenty more of you coming.

(Mom starts to grunt again. Samantha moves out of the way and Mom leaves.)

SAMANTHA: *(To audience.)* I suppose this is as good a time as any to tell you . . . I'm a cat. Hence the twenty siblings. I hated them all. Mostly because they were all mean to me and wouldn't let me eat. After a few months of this I was really really thin and sickly. I was probably on my last leg.

Think Ben Kingsley in Gandhi when he's close to the end of the hunger strike . . .

What? You think just because I'm a cat I can't make cultural references? Hello! I sit in front of the TV 90 percent of my life, what do you expect?

Anyway, all my brothers and sisters had been given away but because I was so little and scrawny nobody wanted me.

This was fine by me because it meant I had my mom all to myself.

But as it turned out, Mom always seemed to be busy with the people of the house.

Then one night, Mom came to find me.

(Mom appears. She's slightly out of breath.)

MOM: There you are. I've been looking all over for you.

SAMANTHA: Mom! Hey!

MOM: Shhh . . . Keep your voice down.

SAMANTHA: Sorry.

MOM: Listen . . . I got a lot to tell you and a little bit of time to do it. The woman of the house expects me in the master bedroom in five minutes to watch *Cybil* on the O Channel. And if I'm not there, she'll start to get suspicious.

SAMANTHA: OK.

MOM: First, I want apologize for not being a good mother.

SAMANTHA: No, you're a great —

MOM: No I'm not. I'm not a good mother. But I need you to understand I'm a prisoner here. Practically every second of my day is tied up with this family's lives and schedules. And I hate this family. I've tried my whole life get away from them but never been able to. They are not nice people. They have terrible taste in furnishings. And they've never let me keep one kitten from any of my litters. Not one!

SAMANTHA: But I'm still with you so maybe that means they've changed.

MOM: They haven't.

SAMANTHA: But I don't understand —

MOM: Have they named you?

SAMANTHA: What do you mean?

MOM: Have they given you a name?

SAMANTHA: No. I don't think so. Not yet.

MOM: If they were going to keep you, trust me you'd have a name by now.

SAMANTHA: But what's gonna happen to me?

MOM: You're going to be sent to the Animal Shelter.

SAMANTHA: The Animal Shelter? Don't they, you know k-kill cats at the shelter?

MOM: You get five days there. Five days to find someone. And then . . . Let's not think about that.

SAMANTHA: Oh my God!

MOM: Shhh . . . Stay positive.

SAMANTHA: How am I supposed to stay positive about this?

MOM: I need you think about this as an opportunity to better your life. You have a chance to find someone who will truly love you.

SAMANTHA: How am I going to do that?

MOM: You are simply not going to settle for anything less. The biggest regret of my life is that when I was sent to the shelter, I was so terrified that I jumped at the first chance to get out. And now look at me. I'm trapped here. With people that don't know the difference between 100 and 800 thread counts! I have refined tastes! I want better for you. I want you to find what I couldn't. True love.

Promise me you won't settle for anything less.

SAMANTHA: But —

MOM: Promise me. Please.

(Beat.)

SAMANTHA: I promise.

MOM: Oh good. Good! This is good.

(Just then the theme song from Cybil *plays in the background.)*

MOM: Oh crap, *Cybil* is starting. I hate that show!

(Mom exits.)

SAMANTHA: *(To audience.)* The next day like Mom predicted I was sent to the Animal Shelter. It was totally horrible.

Think *Amistad* meets *Schindler's List.*

I wanted to live up to my promise and find true love. But I didn't know how to go about it. How do you find your true love? Especially in an animal shelter where you only have five days to do it. But I tried not to think about this and instead focused on my goal. Find true love! Find true love! Find true love. The first time someone came by my cage, this is what happened.

(A Southern Woman comes up to Samantha's cage.)

SOUTHERN WOMAN: *(With a southern accent.)* As God as my witness I do declare I've never seen a more precious lil kitten in all the land.

SAMANTHA: I am precious! I'm yours! I love you! You love me! You're my true love! Take me home! I want to live every second of my life by your side!

SOUTHERN WOMAN: Heavens to Betsy, you simply won't do. I'm looking for a more self-sufficient cat. One that won't get in the way while I'm drinking my mint juleps.

(The Southern Woman exits.)

SAMANTHA: *(To audience.)* Self-sufficient. OK. I can be self-sufficient. I decided that the next time I'd show the person how self-sufficient I am.

(A Fabulous Man comes by Samantha's cage.)

FABULOUS MAN: Girl! You are one fierce little kitten! Work it girl!

SAMANTHA: Thanks, but I don't really need you to tell me to work it. I'll work it all on my own.

FABULOUS MAN: Oh no! No, no no! You will not do! In my Technicolor world I need a cat that needs me to tell it what to do!

(With a snap of the fingers, Fabulous Man exits.)

SAMANTHA: *(To audience.)* OK, so I can't be too needy, I need to be somewhat self-sufficient but also wanting to be told what to do. OK, I can do this. I know I can.

(A Depressed Woman enters.)

SAMANTHA: Hi, I'm looking for my one true love but if I don't find my one true love I'll be OK on my own unless you tell me you want me to be upset or something. I'll be whatever you want me to be, but only when it suits me . . . and you of course, I'll always take into consideration your feelings and —

DEPRESSED WOMAN: My life has no meaning.

SAMANTHA: I don't think this is really going to work out. *(To audience.)* I was distraught. This was only my first day! After several more days of fruitless attempts, I was at my wit's end, maybe my mom was wrong, maybe I shouldn't have been so intent on finding true love. The thought just made me burst into tears. And it was at that exact moment that Shuman fell into my life.

I don't mean to be dramatic, well yes I do, but this would be a good time for really romantic music. A great love song please.

(Wildly inappropriate music plays. Think . . . "Baby Got Back" or "Who Let the Dogs Out.")

SAMANTHA: Hey! HEY!

(The record should probably scratch here.)

SAMANTHA: That's not even a love song! Can we try that again please?

A great love song please.

(The chorus of Olivia Newton John's "I Honestly Love You" plays.)

SAMANTHA: Hey!

(The record scratches again.)

SAMANTHA: So yes, that's a great love song but it's a little too slow and sappy for this moment. I think it should be a great love song that's happy and fun and thrilling! Got it? OK, one more time. A great love song please!

(Paul McCartney's "Silly Love Song" plays.)

SAMANTHA: That'll do. Thanks. *(To audience.)* Anyway, OK, this is what happened. Shuman walked in.

(Shuman enters.)

SAMANTHA: *(To audience.)* From across the crowded shelter our eyes met.

(He sees Samantha. They look at each other.)

SAMANTHA: *(To audience.)* BAM! A connection! It knocked us both off our feet! Like so.

(They both fall backwards.)

SAMANTHA: *(To audience.)* Then, he got up, walked to my cage, the door miraculously opened and a second later I was in his arms. He was so warm and strong. And then he put his hand under my chin and started scratching and I, for the first time in my life, started to purr.

SHUMAN: You're purring. Are you happy?

SAMANTHA: Yes very. *(To audience.)* And if I didn't know then that he was my true love. What he said next sealed the deal.

SHUMAN: Hi. I guess you're coming home with me. You're beautiful. Your name is . . . *(He looks deep into her eyes for a moment.)* Samantha. I know it is.

SAMANTHA: *(To audience.)* Shuman named me.

SHUMAN: You don't have to be scared anymore, I'll love you like you are supposed to be loved until the day I die.

SAMANTHA: *(To audience.)* And with that I dug my claws deep into his sweater and wouldn't let go. And Shuman took me to his home.

(Shuman takes Samantha into his house — very "carried over the doorway" to the opening of ABC's "Be Near Me.")

SAMANTHA: *(To audience.)* Shuman's house sits deep in a forest and from every window in every room all you can see are trees and sky and grass.

SHUMAN: So this is home.

SAMANTHA: I love it Shuman!

SHUMAN: I'm so happy you're here!

(Shuman rushes off.)

SAMANTHA: *(To audience.)* And Shuman became my true love. And it was everything I dreamed it would be. For a while at least. But we'll get to that later.

(We are now in Shuman's house. In his bedroom. In his bed, for that matter.)

SAMANTHA: This is Shuman's bed.

From the very first night I was home, I slept in it with Shuman. Some of you may think this was really quick, but it just felt so natural. Here's how it happened.

(Shuman appears and gets into the bed. Samantha stands in the doorway. The two look at each other. Then —)

SHUMAN: Hey.

SAMANTHA: Hey.

SHUMAN: I'm going to sleep.

(She stares. Beat.)

SHUMAN: Well . . . uh, good night.

SAMANTHA: Good night.

(He turns off the light. Beat. He turns the light back on. The two stare at each other another moment. Then —)

SHUMAN: Hey.

SAMANTHA: Hey.

SHUMAN: Uh — do you want to — uh —

SAMANTHA: *(To audience.)* And before he even finished his sentence, I jumped onto the bed and crawled right in the crook of his arm, aka, armpit.

(She places herself under Shuman's armpit.)

SAMANTHA: *(To audience.)* And he turned off the light and we went to sleep. Here's what happened in the morning.

(It's now morning. Samantha watches Shuman sleep.)

SAMANTHA: *(To Shuman.)* You sleep restless. You look ugly in the morning. You have terrible breath. You hog the sheets. And the bed . . . At least you don't fart.

(He farts.)

SAMANTHA: Ew . . . You're warm though. I like this bed. The sheets are comfy and really bright. They make me want to dig my claws into them. And into you. I'm so into you. You're cool. Do you like me? You can't hear me. You're not listening. Oh look at your hair, it's so clean and nice. I'm gonna lick your hair. Is that OK? I don't care. I want to and I'm going to. I'm going to lick your hair with flair.

(She does.)

SAMANTHA: Hmmm. Salty . . . Thick . . . I wanna lick it flat. Oh wow yeah. Oh yeah.

(Suddenly the alarm clock goes off. It's really loud, abrasive.)

SAMANTHA: AH!!

(She literally jumps away.)

SHUMAN: Ah alarm!

SAMANTHA: Good morning.

SHUMAN: Hey there Samantha.

SAMANTHA: Hey.

(He turns over, going back to sleep.)

SAMANTHA: You're going back to sleep? You just got up and I'm hungry!

SHUMAN: Shhh.

SAMANTHA: Shhh? I'm hungry! Get up!

SHUMAN: Samantha, relax. Come here.

SAMANTHA: No.

SHUMAN: Come on.

(He grabs her and pulls her into him.)

SAMANTHA: But I'm hungry.

SHUMAN: Shhh . . . .

SAMANTHA: Oh you feel good. I love the way you touch me. You've got great hands.

(Samantha rolls over on to her back. He rubs her belly and legs.)

SHUMAN: You little slut.

SAMANTHA: Shut up, it feels good.

SHUMAN: Shhh. Sleep. Sleep.

SAMANTHA: OK, just keep touching me and I'll –

(She falls immediately sleep. Beat. Then she opens her eyes and turns to the audience.)

SAMANTHA: Before we go any further, I think that this may be a good time to tell you more on Shuman, the man.

(We are now in Shuman's office.)

Shuman works from home, doing Web design, which sounds interesting and boring at the same time. In case you didn't notice, Shuman is very sensitive and cries over almost anything. Like so.

(Shuman at his computer.)

SHUMAN: Save. Save! SAVE! SAVE!!!! Why won't you save? I, I, I, I —

(He starts crying hysterically.)

SAMANTHA: Every morning Shuman gets up and talks to himself in the mirror. Like so.

(Shuman stands looking at himself in the mirror.)

SHUMAN: I am worthy of success. I am worthy of love. I am worthy of solitude. I am worthy of hope. I am worthy of dreams. I am worthy of time. I am worthy of Samantha. I am worthy of this day. Good morning.

SAMANTHA: And at night he has to brush his hair 100 times before going to sleep. Like so.

(Shuman stands looking at himself in the mirror and brushing his hair. Samantha watches in awe.)

SHUMAN: 98, 99, 100. There. One hundred strokes. Good night.

SAMANTHA: *(To audience.)* A big thing to Shuman is music. He loves it. And plays it in the house all the time. He only seems to like to play British pop songs from the 80s — Culture Club, Thompson Twins, Howard Jones, and every other one- or two-hit wonder that tried to make it big in America. Anyway, one of Shuman's favorite things to do is put on music really loud and sing and dance to it. I am his audience and biggest fan. Sometimes he even lets me dance with him. Like so.

(Shuman enters.)

SHUMAN: Everybody dance!

(Shuman performs an excerpt from Madness' song "Our House." By the end of the song, Shuman has Samantha in his arms and the two are dancing together.)

SHUMAN: Our house in the middle of our street

Our house in the middle of our . . .

Our house . . .

SAMANTHA: *(To audience.)* I guess the first time I noticed something wasn't quite right between Shuman and me was over dinner a couple months after I moved in.

(The two sit across from each other at a table.)

SHUMAN: You look pretty tonight.

SAMANTHA: Thanks Shuman. You look very nice too.

SHUMAN: After dinner do you wanna cuddle up in front of the TV and watch a movie?

SAMANTHA: OK.

SHUMAN: *Breakfast at Tiffany's* is on AMC tonight. I love that movie. I saw that with my mom . . . before she died. Not right before she died, not on her deathbed or anything. When I was little, she took me, to a revival of it. But she's dead now. All my relatives are dead. Dead, dead, dead, dead, dead, dead, dead.

SAMANTHA: I'm sorry Shuman.

(Shuman begins to cry. Samantha goes to comfort Shuman.)

SHUMAN: Oh Sammy! You are the greatest thing that's ever happened to me!

SAMANTHA: *(To audience.)* And it was at this exact moment that I noticed Shuman had a crumb of food on his upper lip. Shuman noticed me staring at him and then he started staring at me and then he said –

SHUMAN: I wonder what you're thinking . . .

SAMANTHA: You have a crumb sticking on your upper lip.

(Shuman stares at Samantha intently.)

SHUMAN: You're trying to look into my soul aren't you?

SAMANTHA: No . . . I'm not. *(To audience.)* So then I tried to wipe it off with my paw. And Shuman said —

(She tries to wipe it off by rubbing his face with her paw.)

SHUMAN: Well I love you too.

(Shuman then grabs Samantha's paw and kisses it.)

SAMANTHA: Ew.

(She pulls away.)

SHUMAN: Alright, play coy Miss Sammy, I know you love me.

SAMANTHA: Well I do love you but the point is you have a crumb on your lip and it's driving me crazy! . . . *(To audience.)* And for the first time I realized that maybe Shuman didn't always understand me.

Just as clarification, I think I should say, I don't really speak in English. I speak in Cat. This is what I really sound like.

Meow wowo, memeo, meowwww, moeoem, moew.

So I suppose it shouldn't be all that surprising that Shuman didn't always understand me but still, sometimes he'd be so far off the mark it'd be shocking!

Like this one time, Shuman was working at his desk and I was so upset by something I saw on TV and needed to talk to him about it. Here's what happened.

(Shuman is at his desk. Samantha is at the door.)

SAMANTHA: Hey.

SHUMAN: Hey Sammy.

SAMANTHA: This show I just saw was really disturbing.

(No response from Shuman who keeps working.)

SAMANTHA: It was on IFC or Sundance or Bravo — I can't tell the difference, I'm just a cat, and was a documentary about this filmmaker —

SHUMAN: I already fed you Sammy.

SAMANTHA: I know you fed me. Can you listen to me though for a sec? The filmmaker was trying to raise money for a film and kept running into all these problems and —

SHUMAN: Sammy! I can't play right now.

SAMANTHA: I know you can't play, I just want you to —

SHUMAN: SHHH!!!!

SAMANTHA: Don't shush me! I'm really upset!

SHUMAN: Sammy, I'm working!

SAMANTHA: Don't take that tone with me!

SHUMAN: Do you need to take a nap?

SAMANTHA: No.

SHUMAN: Do you have a hairball?

SAMANTHA: No! God! It's not a hairball!

SHUMAN: Hmmm . . . You look OK.

SAMANTHA: I am OK. My body is OK. It's my mind. I'm very emotional right now. I just need to talk.

SHUMAN: Sammy if you can't be quiet, I'm going to have to close the door.

SAMANTHA: Don't close the door. Just listen to me. Let me just tell you about this documentary —

SHUMAN: I'm sorry Sammy but I'm trying to work.

(Shuman shuts the door on Samantha.)

SAMANTHA: Let me in Shuman. Shuman? Please? I just want to talk. Why won't you talk to me? Shuman? SHUMAN? . . .

And soon other things became complicated for me as well — like when he'd go out for long periods of time without any real explanation.

(Shuman exits.)

And I wouldn't know when he'd be back or if he was coming back at all. The first few times he came back, I tried to act cool about it.

(Shuman walks through the door.)

SHUMAN: Hey Sammy.

SAMANTHA: Oh hey. Didn't hear you come in. Yeah, I was real busy by myself, uh huh. *(To audience.)* But when he didn't tell me where he'd been or why he'd left, I'd want to lash out at him. But since he hadn't done anything wrong I had no reason to lash out, so I wouldn't. But then it happened again. And again. And again. Until one day, he walked in the door and I couldn't hold back anymore.

(Shuman walks through the door.)

SHUMAN: Hey Sammy.

SAMANTHA: Where were you? What were you doing? Who were you with? Why were you gone so long? Why didn't you take me? Why did you need to leave? I've been so scared and lonely and I thought you'd left me and were never coming back and I hate being alone even for a minute, you know that. You just left. Tell me where you went. Tell me!!!!!

SHUMAN: Someone sure is talkative today!

(Shuman kisses Samantha on the head and exits.)

SAMANTHA: The next time he went out, I worked myself into such a frenzy that I started to feel really sick. My stomach hurt and my head ached and my legs felt all shaky and I was having a hard time breathing . . .

Think Julia Roberts in *Steel Magnolias* right before she has her first seizure.

Shuman found me later that day.

(Shuman enters.)

SHUMAN: There you are. I've been looking all over for you.

SAMANTHA: You have?

SHUMAN: Come on Sammy, let's go in the other room.

(Shuman tries to pick Samantha up. She won't budge.)

SAMANTHA: I don't want to go anywhere. Leave me alone.

SHUMAN: Come on. Let me pick you up.

SAMANTHA: No.

SHUMAN: Why won't you let me pick you up?

SAMANTHA: Because I want to stay here.

SHUMAN: Are you OK?

SAMANTHA: No. I'm not OK. Go away.

(Shuman looks at Samantha.)

SHUMAN: You're heart is racing Sammy, you're breathing is strange, you're, oh my God, you're sick! Oh Sammy! I - I - I - I don't know what to do, I — I — I — I think we're going to have to take you to the vet. I don't have a vet. I'll find a vet. Don't worry, I'll find someone to take care of you.

(He's crying and then tries to pick Samantha up.)

SAMANTHA: No. No vet. Just leave me alone for awhile, I'll be fine.

SHUMAN: Shhh . . . They'll take care of you. Come on.

(Shuman finally lifts Samantha into his arms.)

SAMANTHA: *(To audience.)* So Shuman took me to the vet and that's where we met Matilda.

(Matilda sits at a desk on the phone. She's on the verge of tears.)

MATILDA: *(Talking on the phone.)* The thing is, Dr. Schaeffer, I just feel so lost. So terribly terribly lost. OK. I'll try that.

(Shuman and Samantha enter the vet's office.)

MATILDA: Right now? But — OK, *(Reciting a mantra.)* "I trust in the universe to guide me." I did too mean it. OK. "I trust in the universe to guide me." OK. Yes. That felt a little better. Thank you. *(She hangs up. Turning to Shuman.)* Hello. How can I help you?

SHUMAN: — uh — Hello. My cat is sick and I don't know what to do.

MATILDA: Of course you don't. That's why you're here. At the vet. We take care of sick animals here.

SHUMAN: I know.

MATILDA: Good! That's the first step. Knowing. So just fill out this paperwork *(Matilda hands Shuman a clipboard.)* and when it's complete, bring it back to me. And then we'll go from there.

SHUMAN: OK . . .

(Shuman sits with Samantha and starts doing paperwork.)

MATILDA: *(To herself.)* I trust in the universe to guide me. I trust in the universe to guide me.

SAMANTHA: I want to go Shuman.

SHUMAN: Sammy shh . . .

SAMANTHA: I'm fine. I'll be fine.

SHUMAN: Sammy!

SAMANTHA: Please Shuman, just take me home!

MATILDA: It won't be that bad sweetie, I promise.

SHUMAN AND SAMANTHA: Thanks.

SHUMAN: I am a little nervous. I guess I —

MATILDA: Actually I was talking to your cat. Oh my God, I was talking to your cat! *(To Samantha.)* Hi! I think I heard you. But to be sure can you speak again?

SAMANTHA: What should I say?

MATILDA: Anything you want to. Oh. Oh my, I heard you!

SAMANTHA: You did! *(To audience.)* She did! Matilda could hear me! I liked her immediately.

MATILDA: My dream! This is — wow! That mantra really worked quick!

SHUMAN: Uh —

MATILDA AND SAMANTHA: Shhh . . .

SHUMAN: But —

MATILDA: Hi, I'm Matilda.

SAMANTHA: I'm Samantha.

SHUMAN: I'm Shuman.

MATILDA: What's the matter sweetheart?

SAMANTHA: Well, I don't know, I'm just feeling really sick to my stomach and a little out of control. It's really complicated and I feel a little weird talking about it in front of *him,* if you know what I mean.

MATILDA: Yes I do know exactly what you mean Samantha. Hold on. *(To Shuman.)* Well Shuman, it's clear that Samantha is going to have to stay overnight so you can just go now and I'll —

SHUMAN: Overnight?

MATILDA: Yes.

SHUMAN: But what's wrong?

MATILDA: I'm not at liberty to say. But it looks serious.

SAMANTHA: Serious?

MATILDA: Shh!

SHUMAN: You didn't even examine her. How do you know something's wrong? Are you the doctor?

MATILDA: Well, no I'm not the doctor. I'm the front desk girl, woman, womangirl. The doctor is out of the office this afternoon, in a "meeting" if you catch my drift, very inappropriate, but who am I to judge? No one apparently, just the front desk womangirl, I have no opinions. Oh no, not Matilda. No, I'm just here to serve you, you selfish son of a —

Anyway, he'll be back later. So I can just check Samantha in and then he'll see her later and examine her and determine precisely what's wrong.

SHUMAN: But she has to stay all night?

MATILDA: Yes.

SHUMAN: But we've never spent a night apart. I don't want her to be traumatized by it. Maybe I could stay and wait for the doctor.

MATILDA: It'll be hours before he gets back.

SHUMAN: That's OK.

MATILDA: He works alone.

SHUMAN: I won't stand over him.

MATILDA: He doesn't like to be pressured.

SHUMAN: Maybe I should get a second opinion.

MATILDA: On what?

SHUMAN: On whether she should stay or not.

MATILDA: Samantha must stay.

SHUMAN: I just don't — I — well, I, I, I –

(Beat. Shuman starts to cry.)

MATILDA: Oh my. It's OK. Let it all out. It's OK.

SHUMAN: This is just — she's never been away from the house for the night and I don't want her to be lonely and sad and . . . I just love her so much and I don't want to lose her and –

MATILDA: Shuman, you're not going to lose her tonight, OK? I promise. I really want you to take a leap of faith here, OK?

(Beat.)

SHUMAN: OK.

MATILDA: OK. Good.

Now, have you finished filling out that paperwork?

(Shuman bends down to fill out the paperwork.)

SAMANTHA: *(To audience.)* As soon as Shuman was gone, Matilda turned to me and said —

MATILDA: The doctor is gone for the rest of the night. I lied to Shuman. I wanted to be alone with you.

You see, Samantha, I've been having this recurring dream that I can speak to cats. For almost two years. Every night, the same dream. I'm sitting across from a cat having a delicious Nicoise Salad and we're talking and I'm giving the cat really smart advice. But I never understood why.

And then you come in today, and I can hear you speak and I think you're what I've been waiting for and I think I'm here to help you.

And I'd like to help you, if you'd let me.

SAMANTHA: I'd like that.

MATILDA: Oh! Good! OK! OK! Good! Now! TELL ME EVERYTHING!!!!

SAMANTHA: *(To audience.)* And so I did. And we stayed up all night, talking about Shuman and Matilda helped me see that maybe I wasn't overreacting at all but that maybe — well, it's better when she says it. Listen.

MATILDA: I just think Samantha that you've made Shuman too much of your life. You have to take space for yourself. You have to find out who you are, you know? He'll love you more if you do. Trust me, I know this from experience. Like that guy Anthony, the one I told you about? He loved me more when I stopped dressing like him, calling him ten times a day, and peering into his windows with my high-tech binoculars. Sure, it took a restraining order to enforce that, but I know deep down, he loves me more and to this day, I know he wants me, he just hasn't been able to say it yet. But he will say it. One day. I'm certain of it. And until then I just have to keep breathing. Oh Anthony. Oh my, I've got to breathe. *(Does Lamaze breathing.)* I'm taking Lamaze classes for the breathing exercises. I have a hard time breathing sometimes . . . I thought Lamaze would help, but I'm not sure if it is.

SAMANTHA: *(To audience.)* Matilda really made sense. I mean, really, I really did consume myself with Shuman's life. I made a vow then and there that when I got back home I would work really hard at finding out who I was and what made me tick and stop worrying so much about him.

In the morning when Shuman came to pick me up, Matilda stood by my side in a show of fierce sisterhood.

(Shuman enters.)

SHUMAN: Samantha! I missed you so much!

SAMANTHA: I missed you too!

MATILDA: Samantha!

SAMANTHA: But not as much as I thought I would.

MATILDA: Good girl. *(To Shuman.)* Good morning Shuman.

SHUMAN: Hi.

MATILDA: You'll be pleased to know Samantha is all better.

SHUMAN: Oh that's great. What was wrong?

MATILDA: Well as it turns out, it seems Samantha's problems were mostly mental.

SHUMAN: I'm sorry?

MATILDA: Mental. As in "of the mind." You see, Shuman, Samantha and I spoke at length about this last night and well, this is awkward but she feels, Shuman, that you don't always listen to her.

SHUMAN: Uh — OK, I —

MATILDA: Actually, I wanted to give you my card, in case you wanted me to come work with you both, to work through your issues.

(Matilda hands Shuman a card. He looks it over.)

SHUMAN: Cat therapist? I didn't know there was such a thing.

MATILDA: It's a legitimate career path! *(Referring to the card.)* Do you like the little flowers I put around the edges?

SHUMAN: Uh —

MATILDA: Don't answer that. I put all my various numbers, e-mails and my home address on the card for your and Samantha's convenience. I highly recommend therapy Shuman. I'd hate to see things fall apart.

SAMANTHA: She's really smart Shuman.

MATILDA: Oh that's so sweet Samantha! Thank you!

SHUMAN: What'd she say?

MATILDA: She said I was really smart.

SHUMAN: . . . Right. OK, thanks for the card.

MATILDA: Please, I'm available any time. Any time at all. And I make house calls of course. So call me. This is the time to address these issues. Not later. Oh! That sounds so official!

SHUMAN: Uh — OK.

MATILDA: OK. Good. Very good. So I'll be hearing from you both soon, I'm sure.

SHUMAN: Right.

(Shuman picks up Samantha.)

MATILDA: Good-bye Samantha. Remember everything we talked about!

(Matilda grabs Samantha and hugs her.)

SAMANTHA: *(To audience.)* And then we left. And came home. And I knew I had to stick to my vow and really give myself the space I needed. During the day, I was fine, nights though were really hard. We'd get into bed together like we always had before.

(They get into bed. Samantha under Shuman's arm.)

SAMANTHA: And within seconds, Shuman would be fast asleep and I would be so wide awake I didn't know what to do with myself. With his arm around me I felt completely trapped. I could barely breathe. I wanted out of there immediately. So I'd try to move.

(She tries to move. Shuman won't let go.)

SAMANTHA: But the more I'd move the tighter his grip seemed to get.

Then one night, I heard a rustling in the kitchen and I had to see who or what it was. After several failed attempts, I finally got out from under Shuman's arm and ran into the kitchen and found a *mouse* rifling through the cabinets.

(A Mouse appears. Think . . . Speedy Gonzalez.)

MOUSE: Oh shit, a cat.

SAMANTHA: *(To audience.)* No one had ever told me about mice before, but somehow I instinctively knew that mice were evil and that I was to rid the house of them. So that's what I did. Or attempted to do. All night long. Like so.

(Samantha chases the Mouse all around the house to a fabulous and energetic soundtrack.)

SAMANTHA: *(To audience.)* Finally after much back and forth, I got the mouse under my paw, like so.

MOUSE: Ow.

SAMANTHA: Shut up. *(To audience.)* And I started toying with it. Like so. *(To Mouse.)* Should I let you go?

MOUSE: Yes, please, I didn't mean to be here anyway, I must have taken a wrong turn in Albuquerque —

SAMANTHA: OK.

MOUSE: Oh thank you. Thank you.

(Mouse starts to go.)

SAMANTHA: Naw, changed my mind.

MOUSE: NO!!!!!

SAMANTHA: YES!!!!! *(To audience.)* For those of you that are weak of heart, I'll refrain from illustrating the rest of what happened. For those of you that aren't weak of heart, think *Texas Chain Saw Massacre* meets *Nightmare on Elm Street's 1, 2, 3, 4* and . . . *6!*

(The Mouse disappears.)

However, suffice it to say, eventually I killed it. This was an entirely new experience for me. Killing. Chasing. Using my instincts like that. It came so naturally. And it felt so good! I mean, really good! I felt like a wild tigress! And I never wanted to feel any different!

The whole next day I carried the mouse around with me. The mouse changed everything about me. I started to walk with more confidence. Like so.

(Confident and Sexy and Sassy music plays think Right Said Fred's "I'm Too Sexy." Samantha shows us her more confident walk.)

SAMANTHA: *(To audience.)* And then I noticed that my voice changed too. Like so. *(In her "stronger" voice, the mouse is now tucked under her arm.)*

I AM TIGRESS HEAR ME ROAR!!!! ROAR!!!! ROAROW!!!!!! *(To audience.)* Later that day, I decided to show the new me to Shuman.

(Samantha enters Shuman's office, mouse in mouth. She struts in.)

SAMANTHA: Shuman! Turn around and look at me I say!

SHUMAN: I'm working Sammy.

SAMANTHA: Turn around I say! ROAROW!!! ROAROW!!!!!!

SHUMAN: Sammy!

SAMANTHA: Fine! I'll come to you then.

(Samantha gets onto his desk, mouse in hand, so to speak.)

SHUMAN: What are you holding?

SAMANTHA: It's a mouse Shuman. My first! I killed it, violently last night, in a horrible bloody fight that took all night. Would you like to see it?

(Samantha puts it on the desk so Shuman can examine it.)

SHUMAN: Oh Sammy . . .

SAMANTHA: Isn't it just divine?

SHUMAN: Oh my God . . .

SAMANTHA: I know. I know.

SHUMAN: This is so . . . disgusting.

SAMANTHA: What?

SHUMAN: Ew. Oh my God. Ew. Ew. Ew. I, I, I, I, I, —

(Shuman starts to slide the mouse off the desk, presumably into a trash can. Samantha blocks him.)

SAMANTHA: What are you doing?

SHUMAN: Sammy, let go, the mouse has to be thrown away.

SAMANTHA: NO!

SHUMAN: Samantha, let go of the mouse.

SAMANTHA: No! The mouse is mine. I killed it. You can't just throw it away. It's mine! MINE!

(Shuman then picks Samantha up and moves her. She flails.)

SAMANTHA: No! SHUMAN GET OFF ME! LET ME GO! THE MOUSE IS MINE! GIVE ME BACK MY MOUSE! *(To audience.)* But he didn't listen to me and he threw the mouse away. After that I snuck out of bed every night and roamed the house looking for danger or excitement or both.

And then one night, while stalking through the kitchen, the very thing I'd been looking for found me. And his name was Oscar the cat.

(Oscar the Cat appears in a haze of smoke. He is one cool cat. Sexy R&B plays [think R. Kelly].)

SAMANTHA: *(To audience.)* I first spotted him through the sliding glass door. I was frozen to the spot. I couldn't move. I couldn't breathe.

OSCAR: Hey . . . sup sweetheart?

SAMANTHA: *(To audience.)* I couldn't speak. All I could do was watch and listen.

OSCAR: What's the matter cat got your tongue? . . . Hey . . . I'm Oscar. I'm an alley cat. Moved up here from the city a few years back. All the hustle and bustle just got to me one day and I took off. It's nice up here. Quiet. But I'll tell you what . . . a little boring. That is until I spotted you. Yeah, I'm not ashamed to admit it. I've had my eye on you for a while now. You are one sexy kitten. I've been trying to figure out how old you are. I'm guessing, a year? Am I right? Maybe a little less? Wanna give me a hint here? . . . So are you acting cool or are you shy? I hope you're shy 'cause I hate cool. I'm not into playing games. I just say what I feel . . . how about you? Nothing huh?

Well I tried. How about I come by tomorrow and try again? Say, same place, same time? . . . I'll take that for a yes. Later baby.

(Oscar exits.)

SAMANTHA: *(To audience.)* And we fell into a pattern. Every night Oscar would show up, try to get me to talk, he'd fail, he'd talk about himself and then leave. I'd be breathless for him the whole next day and then one night, a few weeks later he took things to a new level.

(Oscar appears again.)

OSCAR: So . . . do you ever speak? I think you do. But if you didn't I'd still like you. Yeah OK, I like you. So what? I like you. Do you like me?

SAMANTHA: *(To audience.)* I wanted to answer but I was scared.

OSCAR: You could at least nod your head or something. Up and down if you like me, side to side if you don't.

SAMANTHA: *(To audience.)* So I nodded my head up and down, like so.

(She does.)

OSCAR: I knew it! . . . I mean, that's cool . . . No I don't, I mean — COOL! You're cool. Do you like living inside? I've never done it. Can't imagine what's it like. Outside is the only place I've ever lived. Born and bred. If you ever got out here, I'd show you all these cool places around here. Like there's a little garden just down the road that I like to stalk in. And around the corner over there, there's the most comfortable patch of grass. In the afternoon I lay out there and get sun. Have you ever felt sun on your coat? It's heaven. I can't imagine not having felt that. You have to feel that. It's natural. It's what you're supposed to feel. I'm babbling. I'm gonna go.

(Oscar leaves. Then re-enters.)

OSCAR: See ya tomorrow sweetheart.

(Oscar leaves again.)

SAMANTHA: *(To audience.)* After he left all I could think about was what it must be like to feel the sun on your coat. And I started to wonder why hadn't Shuman ever taken me outside? Why was I an indoor cat? The next night Oscar talked more about his life outside.

OSCAR: Don't get me wrong. It's not always a picnic out here. I mean, tornadoes are no joke. But for the most part it's like a giant playground. Oh, which reminds me. I brought you a present. *(He takes out a gift-wrapped box.)* Just a little plaything, something I saw and made me think of you. Nothing really. It's not a big deal or anything, just, alright I'm shutting up now . . . Well . . . Open it! That's a joke. I know you can't open it. What's that? Oh you want me to open it for you? Well if you insist. OK. *(He opens the gift. He pulls out a pinecone.)*

OSCAR: It's a pinecone. They fall from those trees over there. They're really fun to knock around. *(He demonstrates.)* I mean I don't know if you like knocking things around but I do and I figured maybe you did too but I don't really know but if you do, and if you ever were to come outside you could knock this around. Anyway, I'm just gonna leave it here for you.

SAMANTHA: *(To audience.)* I'd never gotten a present before. Shuman never bought me anything, except things I needed. He would never think of just getting me something for fun. Or to show me how he felt about me. But Oscar. Oscar thought of me and got me something. Just for me. And if this wasn't enough, then he said something that really got to me.

OSCAR: You know where I wish I could take you? The beach. Do you know it's only sand and water? Nothing else for as far as the eye can see. Can you imagine that? Just water and sand. It's like a giant litter box. And sand, oh man, sand is supposed to feel like heaven underneath your paws. I'm dying to feel that. Sure during the day people are around but at night, it'd be ours.

SAMANTHA: *(To audience.)* Ours. He said ours. I'd never thought of there being another "ours" besides me and Shuman and then there was Oscar saying "ours" and I couldn't help but think that it sounded right. Like I was really supposed to be with Oscar outside and not with Shuman inside. That Oscar and I were the right "ours" and Shuman and I weren't.

With Shuman love had always felt like a comfortable blanket

wrapped around me. But with Oscar, it was inside me. Deep inside all the way to the core of me and was filling me up and any minute I was going to explode from it.

I wanted to give myself over to Oscar. I wanted to speak to Oscar. But I lived with Shuman. I loved Shuman. Or maybe I didn't. I didn't know anymore. I didn't feel like I knew anything anymore. I needed help. I needed clarity. I needed guidance. I needed . . . Matilda! Matilda would know what to do. But how was I going to get to her? And then I remembered that Matilda gave Shuman her card and I knew Shuman had put it on his desk when we got home that day.

So first I got her card off Shuman's desk. Then I knocked the phone out of its holder.

(She does all these things.)

Then, the tricky part. Dialing the number. Paws are great for a lot of things but they aren't exactly precise. Here's my first attempt at calling Matilda.

(Samantha attempts to dial the number. We hear the phone ringing. Lights up on a Woman in Amsterdam.)

AMSTERDAM WOMAN: Hallo! Leibenstrasse Huis!

SAMANTHA: Matilda?

AMSTERDAM WOMAN: Is dit een kattenkopje beslagen en zoeterd?

SAMANTHA: Uh . . . wrong number. *(To audience.)* So I tried again. I tried to dial the right numbers this time.

(Phone rings again. Lights up on Michael Jackson.)

MICHAEL JACKSON: Hello?

SAMANTHA: Matilda?

MICHAEL JACKSON: This is Michael Jackson. Is this a little kitty cat?

SAMANTHA: Uh . . . yes, but I think I have the wrong number.

MICHAEL JACKSON: Do you — I got it Tito — do you want to come to Neverland? I'm so lonely right now.

SAMANTHA: Uh — No!

(Samantha quickly hangs up.)

SAMANTHA: *(To audience.)* This was really starting to stress me out. I decided to try one more time. *(Samantha dials again.)*

(Phone rings again. Lights up on Matilda!!!!)

MATILDA: Hello?

SAMANTHA: Matilda?

MATILDA: Samantha?

SAMANTHA: Matilda! Yes! It's me Samantha!

MATILDA: Oh Samantha! You have been on my mind so much lately! WHO IS RASPUTIN?

SAMANTHA: What? Uh — I don't know, I —

MATILDA: Oh no, sorry Samantha, I'm watching *Jeopardy* and sometimes I yell out the answers. Sorry. I'm turning the TV off now. OK . . . I'm here for you now. What's going on Samantha?

SAMANTHA: Well Matilda I have a really big problem and I need your advice. It's about Shuman and —

(Just then Shuman walks in.)

SHUMAN: Sammy? What are you doing?

SAMANTHA: Uh —

MATILDA: It's about Shuman and . . . what Samantha?

SHUMAN: How did you get the phone?

(Shuman goes to pick up the phone. Samantha tries to stop him.)
(Note: For the sake of rhythm, lines here should overlap.)

SAMANTHA: Shuman, no!

SHUMAN: Sammy! Shhh! *(Into the phone.)* Hello?

MATILDA: Put Samantha on the phone please.

SHUMAN: Excuse me.

SAMANTHA: Give me the phone!

MATILDA: Hello Shuman, this is Matilda, please put Samantha back on the phone.

SHUMAN: Matilda from the vet's office?

MATILDA: That's right.

SAMANTHA: Let me speak to her.

SHUMAN: *(To Samantha.)* Shhh . . . *(To Matilda.)* I don't understand what's going on here.

MATILDA: Samantha called me, she needed to talk and —

SHUMAN: Uh — Samantha's — a cat.

MATILDA: Yes, and?

SAMANTHA: Shuman!!!

SHUMAN: *(To Samantha.)* Shhh! *(To Matilda.)* She doesn't talk on the phone. She can't call people on the phone.

SAMANTHA: Yes I can, I did! Please Shuman! Just leave us alone for a few minutes!

SHUMAN: SAMMY! SHUT UP!

MATILDA: Don't you dare yell at her!

SHUMAN: I'm not.

MATILDA: Yes you are!

SHUMAN: She just — listen I have to go.

MATILDA: I'm concerned Shuman, I'm very —

SHUMAN: Right, good talking to you.

MATILDA: I WILL NOT SIT IDLY BY —

(Shuman hangs up before Matilda finishes. She disappears.)

SAMANTHA: Why wouldn't you let me talk to her? I needed to talk to her! Why do you always butt in on everything? Why can't you just give me space!

SHUMAN: Sammy —

(The phone starts ringing again. Shuman lets it ring. Then he looks at Samantha and moves the phone far out of her reach.)

SAMANTHA: Answer it! It's Matilda! Answer it, so I can speak to her! Answer the phone.

SHUMAN: Sammy calm down.

SAMANTHA: Don't tell me to calm down, I want to speak to Matilda, please, she's calling for me. I need her. You don't understand. You don't understand anything about me!

SHUMAN: Just, Sammy, please, just be quiet. Quiet down. Please.

SAMANTHA: NO!!!!

SHUMAN: Jesus! Samantha what's the matter with you?

SAMANTHA: What's the matter with me? What's the matter with me? Everything's the matter! You're the matter!

SHUMAN: Are you sick or something?

SAMANTHA: UH!!!! Why won't you listen to me? Listen to me! Ugh! Just forget it!

(Samantha turns away from him.)

SHUMAN: Please don't ignore me. Please.

SAMANTHA: I'm ignoring you.

SHUMAN: Please. Samantha! Please!

SAMANTHA: I said, I'm ignoring you!

SHUMAN: Fine . . . Then . . . I'm going out!

SAMANTHA: Fine!

SHUMAN: Fine!

(Shuman storms out.)

SAMANTHA: *(To audience.)* As soon as he left, I went and found Oscar.

(Oscar appears.)

SAMANTHA: I CAN SPEAK!!!!!

OSCAR: I knew it! I knew you did! Say some more.

SAMANTHA: What should I say?

OSCAR: I don't care. Recite the alphabet twenty times. Count backwards from a billion. Anything. Say anything.

SAMANTHA: Uh — hi.

OSCAR: That'll work.

SAMANTHA: My name's Samantha.

OSCAR: Samantha. Sa-man-tha. I like that. Samantha . . . Hi Samantha. I'm Oscar. You already know that. You know practically everything about me already. I guess I've been talking a lot. But I haven't had much choice have I? You got a lot of catching up to do.

SAMANTHA: Where should I start?

OSCAR: Wherever you want to.

(Beat.)

SAMANTHA: Uh — I don't know. Ask me some questions.

OSCAR: What's your favorite position . . . to nap in . . . ?

SAMANTHA: I like to curl up in a ball on the sofa.

OSCAR: I like to do that too! Not on the sofa, I mean there aren't any sofas out here, but I like to curl up in a ball too. That's how I take my naps. Just like that, in a ball. What else?

SAMANTHA: I killed a mouse once.

OSCAR: You're a beast! You're a goddess! You're a tigress! You're — you're so unbelievable! You're — Oh this is just too much! I'm overwhelmed here! I'm freaking out Samantha! I'm freaking out. That's it. I'm out of control. I gotta sing. I just gotta!

SAMANTHA: Sing?

OSCAR: I always sing when I'm freaking out. It . . . focuses me. One! Two! One, two, three, four!!!!!

(Oscar bursts into Lenny Kravitz's "Fly Away.")

OSCAR: *(Singing:) I wish that I could fly*
Into the sky
So very high
Just like a dragonfly
I fly above the trees
Over the seas
To all degrees
To anywhere I please
Oh I want to get away
I want to Fly Away
Yeah yeah yeah!
I want to get away

I want to fly away
Yeah yeah yeah!
(Suddenly Shuman enters the kitchen. He flips on a light.)

SHUMAN: Samantha?

SAMANTHA: Uh — uh — uh —

SHUMAN: Who's this? What's going on?

SAMANTHA: Go away! Get out of here.

OSCAR: Who me?

SAMANTHA: No, not you Oscar! Him!

SHUMAN: Where'd she come from?

OSCAR AND SAMANTHA: She?

SHUMAN: You two friends?

SAMANTHA: We're more than just friends. We're —

SHUMAN: That's so sweet.

SAMANTHA: It's not sweet, it's —

SHUMAN: OK Sammy, say good night to your little friend.

OSCAR: Little? I'm not little, I'm —

SHUMAN: Come on, let's go to bed.

SAMANTHA: No.

SHUMAN: Night night little cutie!

SAMANTHA: I'm not going to bed with you Shuman.

SHUMAN: You want me to pick you up? OK.

(Shuman picks Samantha up in his arms.)

SAMANTHA: Put me down. I want to stay here. I want to stay with Oscar!

SHUMAN: Calm down Sammy. Sammy stop wriggling. Sammy!

SAMANTHA: *(To audience.)* And I was so angry at him for picking me up and
   disturbing me and Oscar that I — well I did something I'd never done
   before . . . I bit him. Hard. Like so.

(Samantha bites Shuman's arm.)

SHUMAN: OW!!!! GODDAMN IT!!!!!! OW!!!!!

(Samantha jumps out of Shuman's arms.)

SAMANTHA: *(To Shuman.)* HA! You deserve it! You, you, you!!!!

SHUMAN: I — I — I — I — I — I —

SAMANTHA: *(Hissing at Shuman.)* GET OUT OF HERE NOW!!!!!!

SHUMAN: Samantha, I — I — I —

SAMANTHA: *(Still hissing.)* NOW!!!!!!!

SHUMAN: I can't believe you bit me! Bad girl! Bad BAD GIRL! You will not
   be allowed in bed tonight! You can stay out here and think about what
   you did!

(Shuman exits. Samantha turns to Oscar.)

SAMANTHA: So, where were we?

OSCAR: . . . I should probably go.

SAMANTHA: Oh.

OSCAR: I shouldn't be here right now.

SAMANTHA: Well I — no. I don't want you to, I —

OSCAR: Look, save your breath. I'm an alley cat, OK? I know how this goes. So I'm just gonna back away now. Real slow. And then it'll be like I wasn't ever here and it'll all be cool. I mean it won't be cool. It'll stink but I'll be fine. Eventually.

(Oscar starts to leave.)

SAMANTHA: No! Oscar! I love you.

OSCAR: You do?

SAMANTHA: Yes . . . I do. I love you! I LOVE YOU! Do you love me?

OSCAR: Have since the moment I caught a glimpse of that tail of yours. Love everything about you. Every little hair and paw. Can't get enough of you. You got me pussy whipped Samantha, excuse my vulgarity.

SAMANTHA: I kind of like it when you talk like that. It makes me feel . . . wild. So wild that I can't stay inside anymore. Oscar I want to bust out of here and live with you for the rest of my life.

OSCAR: You do?

SAMANTHA: Yes! I'm nothing inside. I need to get to you!

OSCAR: You're not playing a game are you?

SAMANTHA: No. I mean it. Do you want me to be with you?

OSCAR: More than anything. I want you here with me. I want you to be outside.

SAMANTHA: I'm going to get to you.

OSCAR: But how?

SAMANTHA: I don't know yet. But I'm going to figure something out. I promise I am. *(To audience.)* And the whole time, he would look at me with those eyes! Those eyes that made me feel like I was a beautiful wild tigress. I could feel it in me, my wildness, like my blood, coursing through me.

And then that made me think that maybe if I started to act wild around the house, Shuman would get the idea and let me out.

So I started doing these really complex and bizarre running patterns all around the living room. Like so.

(Samantha indeed does a bizarre running pattern. Shuman follows, talking as he runs.)

SHUMAN: Sammy? Sammy! Stop! Hey!

(Samantha as she continues to run, speaks to the audience.)

SAMANTHA: I then proceeded to destroy everything I possibly could. Like so.

(As she continues to run, Samantha starts knocking off plants, books, tables, chairs — anything and everything in her way. Shuman attempts to pick up the pieces behind her.)

SHUMAN: Stop it Sammy! SAMANTHA! I — I — I — I — Hey! No! That's expensive! Why are you doing this? Stop it! STOP IT SAMANTHA!!!! Oh. OK. OK. You win. OK? You win! Just go ahead. I'll clean up later. I — I need to sit. I need to sit and . . . breathe. Oh God, do I need to breathe.

(Shuman sits and breathes.)

SAMANTHA: *(To audience.)* I knew I had to take things further if I wanted Shuman to kick me out, but I didn't know how to. How much more wild could I get? I racked my brain over this for days and then finally one morning while in my litter box, it hit me or rather, dropped out of me. If you catch my drift . . .

I decided that the best place to do it would be on his computer. After all he spent so much time there and it was his money line and he couldn't just wash it in the washing machine. If I really did it right, he would possibly have to get a whole new computer. So first, I ate a lot of food in the kitchen and then waited until I felt like I needed to go to the bathroom. Then I waited until Shuman took a break to watch TV. His computer was on and open and then I stood on top of it and — well, here's exactly what I was thinking, in the moment.

(To herself.) OK Sammy. This is it. Just relax and dump. Come on. Relax. Breathe in. Breathe out. Come on Sammy. Just release. Release! Release! *(To audience.)* But I couldn't release. I couldn't stop thinking about how much it was going to hurt Shuman and how much I didn't want to hurt him. How all I wanted to do was to be outside and why did that mean that I had to hurt Shuman? And then I guess because I wasn't thinking about going to the bathroom, I started to. Right there. On the computer. And it was one of those things that once I started I couldn't stop. And so I just steeled myself and let it rip. Afterwards, I hid in a cabinet in the kitchen and waited. And soon enough, Shuman discovered it.

(Shuman enters and sees the computer.)

SHUMAN: No. Ew. SAMMY!!!!!??? I, I, I, I, I,!!!!!!

SAMANTHA: *(To audience.)* So I left my hiding place and went right up to him and stared at him with a look of defiance.

(Shuman picks Samantha up.)

SHUMAN: I've had it with you. Do you hear me? I've had it! I hate you Samantha! I hate you! You've destroyed everything in this house! You've practically destroyed me! I'm throwing you out. Out into the forest so you can get attacked and killed and eaten by wild animals. So, good-bye! Good-bye! And don't come back asking for food. Because I'm not giving you any. I can only take so much and I've taken a lot from you Samantha! A lot. But this, this was it! So . . . Good-bye. Good-bye!

(Shuman goes to open the door.)

SAMANTHA: *(To audience.)* We were so close. And then Shuman opened the door and —

(Shuman opens the door. Matilda (dressed in cycling gear — helmet, knee pads, etc.) who has been eavesdropping at the door falls into the house.)

MATILDA: Whoa! Good thing I was wearing my helmet!

SAMANTHA AND SHUMAN: Matilda!

MATILDA: That's right. It's me. Matilda. I told you I would not sit idly by! OK, it's obvious from what I could hear just now that there's been a complete breakdown in communication here. Do you both agree?

(No answer.)

MATILDA: I said do you both agree?

SHUMAN AND SAMANTHA: Yes.

MATILDA: Good. Common ground has been established.

OK. We're going to do an exercise to help us, us meaning you two, start to communicate to each other. The exercise is called "I Feel" and it's really very simple. Both of you are going to sit in these two chairs I've placed opposite each other and one of you is going to start and simply say, "I Feel" and then add an emotion onto the end. Then the other says, "I feel" and says what they feel, OK?

SHUMAN: How am I going to know what Samantha's saying?

MATILDA: You are going to listen.

SHUMAN: But —

MATILDA: I said Shuman that you are going to listen!

SHUMAN: OK. Fine. Whatever.

MATILDA: Fine. Now both of you have a seat please.

(They do.)

MATILDA: Good. And who would like to start. No, scratch that, Shuman you start.

(Silence.)

SHUMAN: Matilda, this is stupid —

MATILDA: Uh uh, turn to Samantha and tell her how you feel. No emotion is wrong.

SHUMAN: Fine. I feel stupid.

MATILDA: Good Shuman! Good! Samantha?

SAMANTHA: I feel . . . impatient.

MATILDA: Good Samantha.

SHUMAN: What'd she say?

MATILDA: Listen to her. Samantha repeat yourself.

SAMANTHA: But I feel differently now.

MATILDA: Then say whatever you feel.

SAMANTHA: I feel frustrated.

MATILDA: Good. Shuman?

SHUMAN: I still don't understand.

MATILDA: Very well, I'll help you along for a bit. She said she feels frustrated.

SHUMAN: Why?

MATILDA: Uh uh, "I feel . . . "

SHUMAN: I feel confused.

MATILDA: Good.

SAMANTHA: I feel trapped.

MATILDA: Try to stick with emotions. She said she feels trapped.

SHUMAN: I feel confused still.

SAMANTHA: I feel insignificant.

MATILDA: She feels insignificant.

SHUMAN: Why?

MATILDA: I feel . . .

SHUMAN: I feel questioning?

MATILDA: That'll work.

SAMANTHA: I feel unknown.

MATILDA: She said she feels unknown.

SHUMAN: I feel confused.

SAMANTHA: I feel you don't listen.

MATILDA: She feels you don't listen.

SHUMAN: Am I supposed to listen to her?

SAMANTHA: I feel like you refuse to know me.

MATILDA: She said she feels like you refuse to know her.

SHUMAN: Does she need to be known?

SAMANTHA: Yes.

MATILDA: Stick with "I feels" . . . Shuman, start us up again.

SHUMAN: I feel like you think you can talk to cats!

MATILDA: I feel like I can. But this isn't about me.

SHUMAN: I feel like you should leave my house!

MATILDA: I feel like you're wrong. But again, this isn't about me.

SHUMAN: You can't just stay when I ask you to leave.

MATILDA: Yes I can. Continue please.

SHUMAN: I feel like this was fine without you here.

MATILDA: I feel like had I not arrived when I did, you would have thrown Samantha out of your house.

SHUMAN: I feel like that's my prerogative. Besides I would never have left her outside.

SAMANTHA: I feel like I would have been happy outside.

MATILDA: I feel like you don't know what you're talking about.

SHUMAN AND SAMANTHA: Yes I do.

MATILDA: I feel confused.

SHUMAN: I feel out of the loop.

MATILDA: I feel like Samantha needs to clarify.

SAMANTHA: I wanted to get outside. I've been trying to get outside.

MATILDA: Why?

SAMANTHA: To be with Oscar.

MATILDA: Who's Oscar?

SHUMAN: Oscar?

MATILDA: Shhh.

SHUMAN: Who's Oscar?

MATILDA: Shuman, I'm putting you on time out.

SHUMAN: OK, this is it. Out! Get out of my house! I've tried. I don't know why but I tried. I tried to cooperate. You saw me cooperate right? I tried. But this is just absolutely ridiculous, you're talking to my cat. You're trying to get me to talk to my cat.

MATILDA: And that makes you feel — ?

SHUMAN: Silly! I feel silly!

MATILDA: Because?

SHUMAN: Because — she's — she's a cat! She doesn't — she's not supposed to have all this stuff going on in her. She's supposed to be simple. That's why I got a cat! I wanted simple. I'm good at simple. I'm not good at the other stuff. I can't. I can't give more than that. I'm incapable of it. I've tried. I can't.

MATILDA: Good. I'm sensing anger.

SHUMAN: You're damn right your sensing anger! You! You come in here! And take everything over and tell me what I can and can't do and what's going on with my cat! MY CAT! You have no right!

MATILDA: Good, go with this Shuman, let it all out!

SHUMAN: And I don't think you know anything! I think you're making it all up! I think you're a looney tune! YOU'RE A LOONEY TUNE DO YOU HEAR ME? I hate you! I hate you Matilda! I hate you!

MATILDA: Well I hate you too! You're selfish! You're over emotional and yet somehow insensitive! You're a complete mess! A complete and utter mess! I've hated you since the minute I met you!

SHUMAN: The feeling's mutual.

MATILDA: Oh yeah?

SHUMAN: Yeah!

(Beat. The two stare at each other. Fireworks.)

MATILDA: Good. OK. Good. Good. So now Shuman I'm putting you on time out. OK?

SHUMAN: OK.

MATILDA: OK. Samantha, private conference with me over here.

(Samantha follows Matilda to another side of the room.)

MATILDA: Now, Samantha, where were we?

SAMANTHA: We were talking about Oscar.

MATILDA: Oscar. Right. Who's Oscar?

SAMANTHA: An alley cat. We're in love.

MATILDA: Oh my.

SAMANTHA: As soon as I get out of here, we're going away together. You ruined everything when you showed up. Shuman was just about to throw me out.

MATILDA: Oh my.

SAMANTHA: I'm not happy here Matilda. I don't want to make this work. I'm not meant to be an indoor cat. I'm an outdoor cat.

MATILDA: But how do you know?

SAMANTHA: I killed a mouse. I — I'm a wild tigress. I'm —

MATILDA: Oh my.

SAMANTHA: So you have to help me Matilda. You have to help me get out of here. Distract Shuman or something. Open the door for me. Let me be free to be with the cat I love! To be my true self. To love! To Live!

MATILDA: But what about Shuman?

SAMANTHA: I've been trying to get away from him ever since I got back from meeting you. He's bad for me. He doesn't care for me. He doesn't know me. I need to be known. I need to be —

MATILDA: Oh my.

SAMANTHA: So will you help me get out of here?

>   *(Beat.)*

MATILDA: No. No Samantha I won't help you leave.

SAMANTHA: You won't?

MATILDA: No, I'm going to help you stay.

SAMANTHA: Why?

MATILDA: Because there's something worth fighting for here.

SAMANTHA: How can you say that? You have no idea what Oscar makes me feel, you have no idea how I've felt here. I feel compromised, I feel like — like I've settled. I don't want to settle Matilda.

MATILDA: How is staying and letting yourself be known to Shuman settling?

SAMANTHA: I feel like you don't understand me.

MATILDA: I feel like maybe you don't understand yourself.

>   *(Quite suddenly, Samantha bites Matilda . . . Hard.)*

MATILDA: OW!!!! Oh! You little . . . Samantha! Oh!!!!!

SHUMAN: What happened?

MATILDA: She bit me! Samantha you bit me!

SHUMAN: Samantha! Bad girl! Bad bad girl!

MATILDA: Yes bad girl. No. Not bad girl. That's bad to say. You're not a bad girl. You're just confused. You're lost. You're — I'm — I'm — I must, I must breathe. Breathe Matilda. *(She does some of the Lamaze breathing.)* Let's just get this all out in the open. Shuman, Samantha is in love with an alley cat named Oscar.

SHUMAN: What?

SAMANTHA: Matilda!

MATILDA: And she wants to live outside with him. How does that make you feel? Tell Samantha.

SHUMAN: I feel . . . confused. Overwhelmed. Unsure. Is this true? Samantha? I — I — I —

SAMANTHA: It's true.

MATILDA: She said it's true.

SHUMAN: When did this happen? Where did you meet? How could this happen?

SAMANTHA: It all just happened. It felt . . . natural.

MATILDA: She doesn't know how it happened.

SHUMAN: And you love him?

SAMANTHA: Yes.

MATILDA: She said yes.

SHUMAN: More than me?

SAMANTHA: I think so.

MATILDA: She said she thinks so.

SHUMAN: I feel like I don't understand.

SAMANTHA: I feel like you don't want to understand.

MATILDA: She feels you don't want to understand.

SHUMAN: If I knew you needed to be understood I would have tried.

SAMANTHA: How could you think I didn't need to be?

MATILDA: How could you think she didn't need to be?

SHUMAN: I just thought she was simple.

SAMANTHA: I don't feel simple.

MATILDA: She doesn't feel simple.

SHUMAN: I feel bad.

SAMANTHA: I feel bad.

MATILDA: She said she feels —

> (Shuman stops Matilda with his hand. Beat. Shuman really looks at Samantha, he can hear her.)

SHUMAN: I feel like I'm not enough.

SAMANTHA: I feel like I'm too much.

SHUMAN: I feel like no matter what I do you're not happy.

SAMANTHA: I feel like you never listen to me.

SHUMAN: I feel like I try to.

SAMANTHA: I feel like you do sometimes.

SHUMAN: I feel like sometimes I don't want to.

SAMANTHA: I feel like you're being honest.

SHUMAN: I feel like sometimes I get afraid.

SAMANTHA: I feel like sometimes I want more than you could give.

SHUMAN: I feel like I want to give you everything but don't know how to.

SAMANTHA: I feel like I want to give some things to myself.

SHUMAN: I feel like I never knew that.

SAMANTHA: I feel like I need to be known.

SHUMAN: I feel like I want to know you.

SAMANTHA: I feel like you can't ever know me.

SHUMAN: I feel like I'd like to try.

SAMANTHA: I feel like it's too late.

SHUMAN: I feel like you're wrong.

SAMANTHA: I feel like you're wrong.

SHUMAN: I feel like you're being stubborn.

SAMANTHA: I feel like you're not listening to me.

SHUMAN: I feel like you're not letting me in.

SAMANTHA: I feel like you want to smother me.

SHUMAN: I feel like I just want to hold you.

SAMANTHA: I feel like I don't want to be held.

SHUMAN: I feel like you're afraid.

SAMANTHA: I feel like you're wrong.

SHUMAN: I feel like you want something from me I can't give you.

SAMANTHA: I feel like you could give it to me if you wanted.

SHUMAN: I feel like you want me to let you leave.

SAMANTHA: I do.

SHUMAN: I won't do that.

SAMANTHA: But that's what I want.

SHUMAN: I don't think you know what you want.

SAMANTHA: I don't think you know me well enough to know.

SHUMAN: I feel like we have a history together.

SAMANTHA: I feel like you want to live in the past.

SHUMAN: I feel like you want to live in the future.

SAMANTHA: I want to live with Oscar.

SHUMAN: I want to live with you.

SAMANTHA: I feel like Oscar knows me.

SHUMAN: I feel like I know you.

SAMANTHA: I feel like if you did, you wouldn't have thrown my mouse away!

SHUMAN: Your mouse?

SAMANTHA: Yes my mouse! I killed that!

SHUMAN: I know you killed it. It was going to start smelling so I threw it away.

SAMANTHA: It was mine.

SHUMAN: It was dead!

SAMANTHA: I loved that I killed that mouse and if you knew me at all you would have known that.

SHUMAN: How could I have possibly known that?

SAMANTHA: I told you.

SHUMAN: I feel like you didn't.

SAMANTHA: I feel like you weren't listening.

SHUMAN: I feel like you didn't try hard enough.

SAMANTHA: I feel like I did.

SHUMAN: Did you?

SAMANTHA: I did.

MATILDA: Did you?

SAMANTHA: Why are you taking his side?

MATILDA: I'm not taking anyone's side.

SAMANTHA: I feel like you're taking his side.

MATILDA: I feel like you're being resistant.

SAMANTHA: I feel like no one's listening to me.

MATILDA: I feel like you're not listening to yourself.

SHUMAN: I feel like I want to hold you Samantha.

SAMANTHA: I don't want you to.

SHUMAN: I feel like it's for your own good.

SAMANTHA: You don't know what's good for me. You don't know me.

SHUMAN: Let me know you.

SAMANTHA: You can't know me.

SHUMAN: I can if you let me.

MATILDA: He's right Samantha.

SAMANTHA: No he's not. He thinks I'm simple! I'm not simple! I'm complicated. He doesn't want to know that about me! He wants me to be simple! SIMPLE! SIMPLE! SIMPLE!!!!!

SHUMAN: I — I — I — I —

MATILDA: It's OK Shuman, let it out. Let it all out!

SAMANTHA: He's manipulating this! He's trying to —

SHUMAN: I love you Samantha. I love you!

MATILDA: Good Shuman. Good!

SAMANTHA: Don't coddle him. You wouldn't coddle me!

MATILDA: I'm not coddling him.

SHUMAN: I'm not being coddled.

MATILDA: I'm just trying to encourage him to express what he feels.

SHUMAN: No one coddles me.

SAMANTHA: No you coddle yourself.

SHUMAN: I do not. I — I — I —

SAMANTHA: There you go coddling yourself again!

SHUMAN: I'm not coddling myself. I'm starting to cry.

SAMANTHA: I feel like your crying isn't real. I feel like you're a fake. I feel like you have no backbone. I feel like you live in fear. I feel like you are a miserable lonely person.

SHUMAN: I feel like I don't know who you are.

SAMANTHA: I feel like that's what I've been trying to tell you.

SHUMAN: I feel disgusted by you.

SAMANTHA: I feel like I hate you.

SHUMAN: I hate you!

SAMANTHA: Then let me leave!

SHUMAN: Fine!

(Shuman starts to walk to the door. Matilda gets up and rushes to the door, blocking Shuman's way.)

MATILDA: No!

SHUMAN: Get out of my way Matilda.

SAMANTHA: Get out of his way Matilda.

MATILDA: No.

SHUMAN AND SAMANTHA: Yes!

MATILDA: You are not going to open that door Shuman.

SHUMAN: Yes I am.

MATILDA: I said no.

SHUMAN: But this is my house.

MATILDA: This is my session. And if I say you are not going to open this door. You are not going to open this door.

SHUMAN: I'll move you.

MATILDA: Try me. I know karate!

SHUMAN: I — I — I — I —

MATILDA: Shuman you will not let Samantha leave. That is not an option. Shuman you must stay strong. Tell me you are strong.

SHUMAN: I am strong.

MATILDA: Say it again and this time, mean it!

SHUMAN: I am strong!

MATILDA: Better. Again.

SHUMAN: I AM STRONG!!!!!

MATILDA: Good! GOOD!!! That's a breakthrough Shuman! Good! Here have a snack!

(She throws him a snack. He catches it and eats it.)

SAMANTHA: Why are you helping him Matilda? You don't even like Shuman!

MATILDA: I do like Shuman.

SAMANTHA AND SHUMAN: You do?

MATILDA: I do?

MATILDA: I do.

SAMANTHA: Well if you like Shuman so much why don't you stay with him!

SHUMAN: What is she saying? I can't understand her. I just could but now I can't.

MATILDA: Samantha I told you before, it's because I care for *you* that I'm making you stay. Please, you're mixing the issues, you're —

SAMANTHA: You're making no sense.

MATILDA: What?

SAMANTHA: I said, that you're making no sense!

MATILDA: You want me to get you a glass of water?

SAMANTHA: No I don't want water. I want you to stop caring about Shuman!

MATILDA: I — did you just ask me to get you a plane ticket?

SHUMAN: Plane ticket? Where's she going?

MATILDA AND SAMANTHA: SHHH!!!

SAMANTHA: Listen to me!

MATILDA: Samantha, I can't — I don't understand what you're saying. Are you alright?

SAMANTHA: No I'm not alright! I'm livid! STOP TAKING SHUMAN'S SIDE!!!!!

MATILDA: A bologna sandwich? What?

SAMANTHA: UH!!! Will you listen to me? Please! I —

SHUMAN: What's she saying?

MATILDA: I don't know, I — I don't know.

SHUMAN: What do you mean you don't know?

MATILDA: I — I lost my connection, I — I — I can't understand her. I — Samantha? Are you hungry? Are you tired? Are you cold? Are you — uh — I don't know what to say. I'm failing! Oh God! I'm failing! Someone help me! I mean, I need to help you! I can help you. I think I can I think I can I think I can. I — *(She starts doing the Lamaze breathing.)* I'm getting ahead of myself, my therapist tells me that's my fatal flaw, getting ahead of myself, but sometimes I just can't help it. Maybe I got ahead of myself by coming here today. I shouldn't have come. But you two need me! I know you do. And I know I was making progress, we just got derailed, we have to get back on track and then I can solve this and then I won't be so afraid to pursue my dream and I'll be a cat therapist full-time and I won't have to work in that stupid vet's office or moonlight at Hooters and I'll save cats everywhere and I'll be fulfilled and loved. Sometimes though I have a hard time believing anyone can ever love me. Sometimes I think that I'm going to die alone and no one will know me and I'll be found in a spider web of my own macramé and it'll take them four days to dig me out of it — And I don't want to die that way! I CAN'T DIE THAT WAY! OH GOD, I DON'T WANT TO DIE! I WANT TO LIVE FOREVER! I WANT TO BE A VAMPIRE! LIKE DRACULA! NO I DON'T! WHAT AM I SAYING? WHAT'S HAPPENING TO ME? I — I — I'm having a hard time breathing. Breathe Matilda, BREATHE!!!!

(Just then there's a crash. Oscar falls into the room from the ceiling. Everyone turns.)

SAMANTHA: OSCAR?

OSCAR: SAMANTHA!

SAMANTHA: Oscar, how did you get —

OSCAR: I broke the skylight. I couldn't wait another minute outside. I need to be with you. I need you with me.

SAMANTHA: Oh Oscar! Take me! Take me away!

(Oscar starts to rush Samantha. Shuman gets in the way.)

(Note: For rhythm's sake, lines can overlap in this section.)

SHUMAN: Get away from her.

OSCAR: Don't tell me what to do.

SHUMAN: Get out of here! Get! NOW!!!

OSCAR: Not until Samantha leaves with me.

SHUMAN: Samantha is my cat!

SAMANTHA: You were just going to let me go!

SHUMAN: She stays here with me!

SAMANTHA: You can't do that.

SHUMAN: And she'll always stay here!

OSCAR: You're going to let us out of here buddy or else.

SHUMAN: Don't take another step, you hear me?

(Oscar takes another step. Shuman rushes in, picks up Oscar and starts carrying him out. Oscar is flailing.)

OSCAR: No! NO! GET OFF ME!

(Oscar scratches Shuman's face. Shuman lets go of Oscar.)

SHUMAN: Ow! You — you — I — I — AH!!!!!

(Shuman starts to chase after Oscar.)

SAMANTHA: Stay away from him! STAY AWAY FROM OSCAR!!!!

(Samantha starts to chase after Shuman. For a moment Matilda can't quite decide whom to chase after. She then stops altogether.)

MATILDA: Oh my. OK. *(She does more of the Lamaze breathing.)* OK and roll up and down your spine. Oh fuck it. ALRIGHT MOTHERFUCKERS EVERYBODY STOP!!!!!!!

(Everybody stops.)

MATILDA: Good. OK. Now everybody find a seat.

(No one moves.)

MATILDA: FIND SEATS NOW!!!!

(Everyone finds seats.)

MATILDA: Good. OK. *(She walks over to Oscar.)* Hello I'm Matilda you must be Oscar.

OSCAR: Aren't you a genius?

MATILDA: I'm not quite sure what you just said but I have no doubt that it was sassy. You may be an alley cat but while you're indoors you will behave with a modicum of respect. Capiche? I've always wanted to say that . . . so, capiche?

OSCAR: Capiche.

MATILDA: I think you just agreed, otherwise you said, fructose. Now. Clearly words aren't working for us. So I'm going to insist that we communicate for a while using physical gestures.

ALL THREE: Physical gestures?

MATILDA: Yes, something physical that tells how you feel. My therapist uses it all the time with me in my therapy. It's much simpler than words. Here, I'll demonstrate. I'm going to do a physical gesture and I want you all to tell me what I'm trying to say.

(Matilda stands up and does a bizarre and complex series of movements. She then turns to Shuman, Oscar, and Samantha.)

MATILDA: Well?

ALL THREE: Uh . . .

MATILDA: Think about it. It's really simple.

SHUMAN: You were trying to tell us that you were sad.

MATILDA: No. Samantha?

SAMANTHA: That you were hungry?

MATILDA: I didn't understand what you said but I'm certain it wasn't right. No. Oscar?

OSCAR: That you like orange groves?

MATILDA: No, I do not watch adult movies on Showtime!

OSCAR: That's not what I said! That's not what I —

MATILDA: Oh forget it! I was simply saying that I feel sometimes like a lonely hunter . . . looking for another meal . . . in a forest dense and dangerous . . . in a foreign country . . . that I've never been to before . . . in the heat of the summer solstice . . . Well, perhaps that wasn't so simple. But you get the gist, simply convey through a gesture, how you feel. I'm going to ask you all questions and I need you to answer them. OK?

(No answer.)

MATILDA: OK??

ALL: Yes.

MATILDA: Show me with physical gestures!

(They all find various ways of saying "yes.")

MATILDA: Good. Now Samantha do you love Oscar?

SAMANTHA: Yes.

MATILDA: With a physical gesture. Again. Do you love Oscar?

(Samantha hugs herself tightly.)

MATILDA: OK. Yes. OK, it's obvious that Oscar loves Samantha, his breaking through the ceiling counting as his physical gesture. Now, Samantha do you love Shuman?

SAMANTHA: I don't know.

MATILDA: Physical gesture!

(Samantha does something to say, "I don't know.")

MATILDA: OK, Samantha doesn't know if she loves you Shuman.

SHUMAN: Well I don't know if I love her either.

MATILDA: Are you sure or are you just saying that because she said it first.

SHUMAN: I don't know.

MATILDA: That's what I thought. *(Beat.)* OK, so let's discuss compromises. Samantha if you could go outside, would you be willing to wear a leash and collar so Shuman could stay connected to you?

(Samantha indicates the sensation of choking and dying.)

MATILDA: I'll take that for no. Shuman are you willing to let Oscar live inside with you?

(Both Oscar and Shuman do gestures to indicate "Absolutely not.")

MATILDA: OK. Shuman are you willing to live outside with Oscar and Samantha?

SHUMAN: No!

MATILDA: Hmmm. Seems we've hit a sort of stumbling block. Give me a minute to strategize here.

OSCAR: *(Doing physical gestures while speaking.)* I just gotta say . . . And I don't care who does or doesn't understand me. I don't want to compromise. I love Samantha and I want to be with her. I don't want to share her. I want her completely. And I'm willing to do anything for that. Anything.

(Beat. They all look at Oscar. Everyone has understood him. Then, Shuman gets up.)

SHUMAN: Samantha, if you want to go. Go. I can't keep you.

MATILDA: No.

(Matilda rushes to the door.)

SHUMAN: Matilda, there's nothing left to do. She wants to go. I can't keep her.

MATILDA: But — no, I know if we fight through this, on the other side
there's —

SHUMAN: But I don't want to fight through anything anymore.

SAMANTHA: Why should we have to fight? Shouldn't it be easy?

MATILDA: No, not all the time. It's not easy all the time.

SHUMAN: Matilda, move out of the way.

MATILDA: But —

SHUMAN: Matilda. Please.

(Matilda steps aside.)

(Samantha and Shuman stare at each other.)

SHUMAN: I, I just wish I were enough for you. But if I can't be, then I can't.
Maybe I just held on to you too tightly . . .

(Shuman opens the door.)

SAMANTHA: I just need to know.

SHUMAN: I know.

*(Beat. Then, Samantha and Oscar without looking back, run right out the
door. Matilda lingers in the doorway.)*

MATILDA: I — I feel so silly.

(Matilda exits. The door shuts.)

*(Quite suddenly we're outside. Everything changes. Light, sound, color, all are
brighter, more vivid, more . . . wild.)*

(Samantha and Oscar come running on.)

SAMANTHA: We did it! You did it!

OSCAR: I did it! You did it!

BOTH: WE did it!

SAMANTHA: Wow! Will you look at it out here?

OSCAR: Yeah. Home sweet home!

SAMANTHA: It's so . . . wild!

OSCAR: So let me give you a quick tour . . . This is fresh air.

SAMANTHA: *(Breathing in.)* Hello air.

OSCAR: This is grass.

SAMANTHA: Hello grass.

OSCAR: And these are trees.

SAMANTHA: Hello trees.

OSCAR: And up there are clouds.

SAMANTHA: HELLO CLOUDS!!!!!!

OSCAR: And past the clouds is the sun.

SAMANTHA: HELLO SUN!!!!!

OSCAR: And down that way is a river.

SAMANTHA: Hello, river!

OSCAR: And I'm Oscar.

SAMANTHA: Hello Oscar.

OSCAR: Hello Samantha . . . And this is Oscar feeling shy.

SAMANTHA: Hi shy Oscar.

(The stare at each other a moment, awkwardly . . . and then . . . finally the two kiss.)

SAMANTHA: I love you.

OSCAR: I love you too.

(He starts to lead her off.)

OSCAR: Come on.

SAMANTHA: Where are you taking me?

OSCAR: To the beach.

SAMANTHA: To the beach!!!!

(Oscar heads off in front of Samantha. She starts to go and right before she's gone, turns to the audience.)

SAMANTHA: So that's what we did. We headed to the beach. And along the way we stopped all over — in the big cities, deserts, mountains, you name it, Oscar and I saw it. And loved it. Every minute of it. Every detail.

Think the Discovery Channel in 3-D.

And then finally we made it to the beach. During the day there were tons of people around but at night, just like Oscar had promised, it was all ours.

(Samantha sits on the sand looking out. Oscar enters.)

SAMANTHA: Where were you?

OSCAR: I couldn't decide where to dump! There's so much sand!

(Beat. The two stare out.)

OSCAR: Isn't this heaven?

SAMANTHA: Yeah.

(Beat.)

OSCAR: So I'm thinking that in a few days we should head out for Alaska. I hear it's almost all snow there. Sound good?

SAMANTHA: Oh. Well I —

OSCAR: You what?

SAMANTHA: Nothing. I just thought — never mind.

OSCAR: No. Tell me. What?

SAMANTHA: I just thought we were going to stay here.

OSCAR: At the beach?

SAMANTHA: Yeah. I thought we were going to make this our home.

OSCAR: What do you mean?

SAMANTHA: I mean, I thought we'd make a house here.

OSCAR: Like with walls?

SAMANTHA: Yeah wouldn't that be fantastic?

OSCAR: It sounds kind of . . . small to me.

SAMANTHA: It wouldn't have to be . . . We could make it as big as we want.

OSCAR: But the whole world is our home. What's bigger than that?

SAMANTHA: Well I don't mean as big as the world, I just mean some place that's just ours. Our own place in the world.

OSCAR: I don't think I want a house. Look, Samantha, I'm an alley cat, I roam, that's all I've ever done.

SAMANTHA: We could try.

OSCAR: I don't think I could settle. I'm not sure it's in my nature.

SAMANTHA: We don't have to stay there all the time but wouldn't it be nice to have a place to go to . . . to know it's there?

OSCAR: I don't want that. I want to be free. I want to live on the sun and the sky and ground and our love.

SAMANTHA: I want our love to make a home.

OSCAR: Our love is home enough for me.

SAMANTHA: I don't think it's enough for me.

(Beat.)

OSCAR: So.

SAMANTHA: So.

OSCAR: Where does that leave you and me?

SAMANTHA: Go to Alaska. Love Alaska!

OSCAR: But where will you be?

SAMANTHA: I don't know.

OSCAR: But how will I find you?

SAMANTHA: When you're ready, you just will. Oscar, I love you.

OSCAR: I love you too Samantha.

(The two kiss.)

OSCAR: See you soon sweetheart.

(Oscar exits.)

SAMANTHA: *(To audience.)* And then I was alone. For the first time in my life. I was alone. And for a while I didn't know what I was going to do. I knew I wanted a home. But I didn't know how to get one again.

And then one afternoon while passing through a city, I bumped into someone I never thought I'd see again.

(Mom enters. She looks fabulous. Very metropolitan. The two bump into each other.)

MOM: Oh excuse me.

SAMANTHA: It was my fault.

MOM: You look . . . familiar.

SAMANTHA: I think you're my mom!

MOM: I think I am!

SAMANTHA: But what are you doing here? When I left, you were trapped in that house with those people?

MOM: Oh it's a tragic story. Really terrible. One afternoon, while everyone was out of town, the faux wood paneling mysteriously caught on fire and the house burned to the ground. Some say it was arson . . .

After that I made my way to the big city and started fresh.

SAMANTHA: That's great!

MOM: It is! And I'm now living with the most fabulous family who not only loves me immensely but also has impeccable taste. Think . . . Diane Keaton's house in *Something's Gotta Give*. Do you live here too?

SAMANTHA: Oh . . . no, I was just passing through — I don't really — I'm a little lost I guess.

MOM: This is a very confusing part of the city. Are you going east or west?

SAMANTHA: No I mean, I'm lost. In my life. I don't know what I'm doing anymore.

(Beat.)

MOM: You know, I was just going to get a soy milk, would you want to join me?

SAMANTHA: I think I would really like that. *(To audience.)* And so I did. I spent the afternoon with my mom drinking milk and talking about everything I'd been through. A few hours later, Mom turned to me and said —

MOM: I'm so proud of you Samantha.

SAMANTHA: For what? For messing everything up?

MOM: For living your life. For being you! For being Samantha. Samantha. That's a fabulous name by the way, did you name yourself?

SAMANTHA: No Shuman did. When he found me at the shelter he named me.

MOM: You didn't tell me that before.

SAMANTHA: I — I guess I forgot.

MOM: That's a pretty big thing to forget.

Would you look at the time? I should be getting back. Every night the family does yoga together and it'd be strange if I wasn't there.

SAMANTHA: I understand.

MOM: This has been . . . fabulous.

> (*The two hug.*)

MOM: Good-bye Samantha.

> (*Mom exits.*)

SAMANTHA: After Mom left all I could think about was Shuman and how much I wanted to see him. Just to see how he was.

> And so I made my way back to Shuman's house.

> And when I got there, I realized, I'd never really seen his house from the outside before. It's yellow. Isn't that funny! Shuman lives in a yellow house. And it looked so small, with the trees and mountains around it. So small and safe. And I couldn't help but go up to the window and peek in. Like so.

> (*She peeks in.*)

SAMANTHA: And this is what I saw.

> (*Shuman sits on the couch. He's crying.*)

> I'd seen Shuman crying before. But somehow from the outside, looking in, he just seemed so vulnerable and beautiful and important to me. And every day after that, I'd sneak up to Shuman's house and look through his windows and watch him.

> I saw him cooking and singing and dancing and crying and sleeping and watching TV. And I saw him apologize to Matilda.

> (*Matilda and Shuman stand in the doorway.*)

SHUMAN: I'm sorry.

MATILDA: For what?

SHUMAN: For — Hey, do you want to, uh —

MATILDA: Sure.

> (*Shuman lets Matilda in.*)

SAMANTHA: (*To audience.*) And from then on, Matilda always seemed to be around. And then one night, while the two sat on the couch, watching a sappy movie, Shuman turned to Matilda and said —

SHUMAN: Matilda, I,

MATILDA: Yes?

SHUMAN: I —

MATILDA: Yes?

SHUMAN: I . . . was thinking of ordering pizza for dinner. Do you want some?

MATILDA: Oh. Oh yes. Yes.

> (*The two stare at each other awkwardly.*)

SAMANTHA: (*To audience.*) And of course from the outside, it was so obvious that they were in love with each other. And as much as I wanted to be upset or hurt, all I could be was happy. Look at them. Look at the way they're looking at each other. Matilda loves Shuman unconditionally. And he loves her, unconditionally. And I realized in that moment that by letting me come outside, Shuman had told me that he loved me unconditionally too.

And I knew then that this was my home. I'd had it and I'd lost it and I wanted it back. And I didn't know if Shuman would let me back in but I decided that I had to try.

So that's what I did.

One evening, I just walked back to the house. When I got there, the door was shut. So I sat down and let out the loudest cry possible. Like so. OPEN THE DOOR!!!!!!!!

(Shuman and Matilda hear Samantha and run to the door and open it.)

SHUMAN: Samantha?

MATILDA: Oh my!

SAMANTHA: *(To audience.)* And I looked Shuman right in the eyes and I said *(To Shuman.)* Shuman, if you let me in, this is what I can promise you . . .

That I'll love you. Unconditionally.

I promise you I won't always understand you but I'll love you.

And sometimes I'll be confused by you but I'll love you.

And sometimes you won't get me and sometimes I won't get you but I'll love you.

And sometimes I may not know how to show it and sometimes I may not want to show it but I'll love you. And sometimes I may want to show it too much and you won't want to hear any of it and sometimes you'll want to show me and I won't want to see it but I'll love you.

And every once in a while, we'll be able to look into each other's eyes and for a moment, even if that's all it is, a moment, for that moment we'll understand each other and I'll love you then too.

And together we'll be free.

So . . . will you let me in?

(Beat. Shuman looks at Samantha. Then turns and looks at Matilda. Then, finally, steps out of the way and lets Samantha in.)

(Samantha immediately runs to the couch, curling herself into a ball. Shuman holds her.)

SAMANTHA: *(Continued.)* And then I walked into my house, jumped onto the couch, curled myself into a ball and started to purr.

SHUMAN: She's purring.

MATILDA: It means she's happy.

SHUMAN: I know.

SAMANTHA: *(To audience.)* And I was finally home again. Home. And it was enough. And it has been. For all these years since then.

    Seventeen years to be precise. In this house. But Shuman and I haven't been alone. You see, right after I curled up on the couch, Matilda felt as though she should leave. So that's what she tried to do.

(Matilda starts to leave.)

SHUMAN: Where are you going?

MATILDA: Oh my, well I thought I should go home and —

SHUMAN: Oh, well, uh, OK. I — OK.

MATILDA: OK. Then. OK.

SAMANTHA: *(To audience.)* And I thought to myself that this is the most ridiculous thing I'd ever seen and that if after all they've done for me, I can't help them a little bit, well what's the point, so I did. I helped them. Like so.

(Samantha quickly jumps off the couch and into Matilda's arms.)

MATILDA: Oh my.

SHUMAN: I guess she wanted to say good night.

MATILDA: I guess. OK. Good night Samantha.

(She tries to get Samantha off of her but can't.)

MATILDA: Oh my.

SAMANTHA: *(To audience.)* I didn't let go.

MATILDA: She's dug her claws into my dress.

SHUMAN: Samantha. Let go.

SAMANTHA: No.

SHUMAN: SAMANTHA!

(Shuman tries to get Samantha off of Matilda. He is attempting to pull her off and is pulling with much force.)

SHUMAN: SAMANTHA! LET GO!!!!!!

SAMANTHA: OK. If you say so.

(Samantha lets go and then grabs onto Shuman who falls onto the floor. Matilda falls on top of them.)

MATILDA: Oh my.

SAMANTHA: *(To audience.)* Worked like a charm. And then I just wriggled out of the way and let nature take its course.

MATILDA: Oh my. I already said that I think.

(Beat. The two look at each other. Then, finally —)

SHUMAN: So, uh, I feel like I would like to kiss you now.

MATILDA: Oh, well, I feel like that would be a wonderful physical gesture.

SHUMAN: OK. OK. OK. Here goes. I'm going to kiss you now.

MATILDA: Oh my. OK . . . I think I should tell you that —

SHUMAN: Yes?

MATILDA: Well . . . I'm not simple Shuman.

SHUMAN: Me neither.

(And with that Shuman grabs Matilda and kisses her like a man kisses a woman in all your favorite romantic movies since the invention of film.)

SAMANTHA: *(To audience.)* And soon after that Shuman installed a new front door that had a flap in it, so I could come and go as I pleased. And I did. Like so.

(Samantha goes through the door.)

SAMANTHA: Yeah, I'm outside!

(Samantha goes back through the door.)

SAMANTHA: Yeah, I'm inside! *(To audience.)* And then soon after that Shuman built a Web site for Matilda's Cat Therapy Business and turned his extra bedroom into her office and soon she had more clients than she could ever have imagined.

(Matilda on the phone with a client.)

MATILDA: Oh my. Well if Beverly wants to drink out of a wine glass let her. She's a grown cat, she knows what she wants. OK, let me know.

SAMANTHA: And soon after that, they got married. And then three years later, they had a baby boy. Named Abbott.

And as Abbott got older he liked to chase me down the halls and try to pull my tail. Like so.

(Abbott chases Samantha.)

ABBOTT: TAIL!!!!! LONG!!!!!

SAMANTHA: And I would bite him hard on the hand. Like so.

(Samantha bites Abbott on the hand.)

ABBOTT: OW!!!!!! MOMMY!!!!!!!

SAMANTHA: But as we both got older, we found in each other a new friend. Like so.

ABBOTT: Sammy, you're so lucky you're a cat because you don't have to deal with stupid things like parents and school and girls. Is it possible to love a girl when you're only nine?

SAMANTHA: *(To audience.)* And one night while I was roaming in the backyard, an old friend found me.

(Oscar appears.)

OSCAR: Hey . . . sup sweetheart?

SAMANTHA: OSCAR!!!

(The two run to each other and hug.)

SAMANTHA: *(To audience.)* And after that, whenever he was passing through, I'd spend the night outside with him.

(Oscar and Samantha lying outside together, looking at the stars.)

OSCAR: And then I met up with a pack of mountain cats and we climbed the Himalayas. Here, I brought you some soil from up there. Feels pretty much the same to me though.

SAMANTHA: *(To audience.)* And time passed and life went on and things were good. Though that's not to say there weren't problems. Because there were like the time Abbott got caught shoplifting.

MATILDA: Did you or didn't you pay for this?

ABBOTT: I don't know.

SHUMAN: Abbott! Answer your mother!

ABBOTT: I didn't! I HATE YOU BOTH!

(Abbott runs offstage.)

SAMANTHA: *(To audience.)* Or the time Matilda and Shuman had such a bad fight, Abbott and I hid under his blankets out of fear.

(We see Abbott and Samantha huddled together under a blanket. Offstage we hear —)

SHUMAN: If I said we can't afford it, we can't afford it.

MATILDA: It doesn't seem like we can ever afford anything.

SHUMAN: Well if you could be a little more financially responsible Matilda, we could afford things.

MATILDA: Oh so it's my fault.

SHUMAN: It sure as hell isn't mine.

MATILDA: Don't talk to me like that. And don't you dare walk away from me.

SAMANTHA: *(To audience.)* But whenever things got to be too much, Shuman would say —

SHUMAN: Everybody dance!

SAMANTHA: And we would. Like so.

(They all dance to Dexy Midnight Runner's "Come on Eileen" together.)

SAMANTHA: *(To audience.)* And I got older. And older. And Oscar stopped coming. And I figured he'd probably died. And I hoped he was happy when he had and I let him go.

And then about three days ago, I started to feel really . . . sick. Not like sick to my stomach but tired sick. Like my bones were tired and . . . I just knew.

And so I've been waiting. And talking to you. Telling you about my life. For the first time, every detail.

(Shuman enters.)

SHUMAN: There you are. I've been looking all over for you. Are you OK?

SAMANTHA: No.

SHUMAN: Oh my sweet little baby. Oh, oh, oh, oh, oh . . .

(He picks Samantha up.)

SHUMAN: I think we're going to have to take you to the vet. I'm so sorry I didn't find you earlier. I'm so sorry.

SAMANTHA: No. No vet. I'll be OK. I'll be fine.

SHUMAN: Shhh . . . They'll take care of you.

(Samantha turns to Shuman and looks him in the eyes.)

SAMANTHA: Please Shuman, no vet. I don't want to die in the vet.

SHUMAN: OK Sammy, no vet. Oh, I, Oh, I. Then where do you want to be Samantha?

SAMANTHA: Right here. With my family.

SHUMAN: OK. Oh Sammy.

SAMANTHA: It's OK.

SHUMAN: Matilda! Abbott! Come here!

(Matilda and Abbott appear.)

SHUMAN: I found Sam. She's — she doesn't want to go to the vet. She —

SAMANTHA: It's OK, you can say it.

SHUMAN: She wants to be here. In the house. With us.

MATILDA: Oh my.

ABBOTT: Oh Sam.

SAMANTHA: It's OK.

MATILDA: Samantha, you beautiful girl, you. OK.

(Shuman rests her gently back on the floor and they all surround her. Beat —)

ABBOTT: She's purring.

SHUMAN: Yes she is.

MATILDA: It means she's happy.

ABBOTT: Are you happy Samantha?

SAMANTHA: Yes. *(To audience.)* I don't mean to be dramatic right now. Well, yes I do. But this would be a great time for some music. A great love song please.

("Silly Love Song" plays.)

SAMANTHA: Thanks. That'll do. Here's exactly what I feel. I feel the rug under me. And under that I can feel the floor. And as I spread out further I can feel the ground, the soil, the earth, the world underneath me. And through the roof, I can feel the sun, hitting my coat like the warmest hands petting me. And I feel the faces of my family. Their eyes. And their hands on my body. And their love. Letting me go.

Maybe life is just this. Just this. This brief moment we have together where we're inside each other and outside ourselves and we can all just let go.

SHUMAN: Oh Samantha. I love you.

SAMANTHA: I love you.

MATILDA: I love you.

ABBOTT: I love you.

(Lights fade.)

END OF PLAY

COWBOY VERSUS SAMURAI

Michael Golamco

dedicated to the memory of Morgan Jones

PLAYWRIGHT'S BIOGRAPHY

Michael Golamco's work has been performed at theaters and universities across the United States; he is a member of the L.A. theater company known as Propergander and a founding member of UCLA's Asian American theater company, LCC. His plays include *Achievers, Cowboy Vs. Samurai,* and *The Shadow on the Moon.* He lives and works in Los Angeles. For more information, access his Web site (www.michaelgolamco.com) where reviews of productions of this play may be found.

ORIGINAL PRODUCTION

Cowboy Versus Samurai's world premiere was produced at the Rattlestick Theater by NAATCO (The National Asian American Theater Company) in New York City from November 4th–27th, 2005. It was directed by Lloyd Suh with the following cast:

DEL	Timothy Davis
CHESTER	C. S. Lee
TRAVIS	Joel de la Fuente
VERONICA	Hana Moon

It also had a regional premiere in Minneapolis, Minnesota with Theater Mu from February 17th–March 5th, 2006. It was directed by Raul Aranas with the following cast:

DEL	John Catron
CHESTER	Sherwin F. Resurreccion
TRAVIS	Kurt Kwan
VERONICA	Jeany Park

In addition, a production is slated for Fall, 2006, in Seattle with SIS Productions.

CHARACTERS
DEL
CHESTER
TRAVIS
VERONICA

SETTING
Breakneck, Wyoming, population 1,000. Present day.

COWBOY VERSUS SAMURAI

ACT I
SCENE ONE

Breakneck, Wyoming. Population: One thousand. Present day. Outdoors.
Sound of the wind. Del, late twenties to early thirties, Caucasian, on the left.
He is ruggedly handsome, an All-American Cowboy. He addresses the audi-
ence directly:

LETTER #1:

DEL: Things in nature always hide. Lizards change the color of their skins. Moths live or die based on the color of their wings. They do these things because when you stand out in the world you invite danger. You will be caught by unseen teeth. You will be eaten alive by something that was waiting for you to show yourself.

And that's how I felt, standing like a shadow on your outskirts, invisible.

But with this letter, I throw away my fear. For you I am a bright green frog blazing on a lily pad. I am a million tropical birds roaring into the sky. I am a bee dancing across honeycombs; I am a baboon's blossoming ass.

And I suppose that's love. It wants to be heard. It needs to be heard. So please: Hear me out.

SCENE TWO

A small-town high school classroom. Travis Park, late twenties to early
thirties, Korean American, sits alone in one of the student desk chairs. He's
doodling on a piece of paper. Chester, twenties to thirties, Asian American of
unknown origin, stands at a teacher's desk. He is possibly dressed in black
military fatigues, Che Guevarran. He bangs a gavel —

CHESTER: Order! As president of the Breakneck Asian American Alliance, I call this meeting to order! Will the secretary rise and read the minutes from our last meeting?
(Travis stands, flips the piece of paper over and reads off of it —)

TRAVIS: Last week we discussed the fact that Shelby's Grocery Store doesn't carry tofu. Then we discussed boycotting Shelby's Grocery Store. Then our president attempted to find a method for ordering tofu through the Internet . . . And then the secretary called the president a moron.

CHESTER: Moving on —

TRAVIS: And then we voted on whether the president actually is a moron, which ended in a tie —

CHESTER: Yes, MOVING ON. Our first order of business is —

(Travis raises his hand —)

CHESTER: Yes.

TRAVIS: I move that we change our regular meeting place to Heck's Tavern.

CHESTER: Anyone second that motion?

(Travis sighs and raises his hand again.)

CHESTER: All right, let's bring it to a vote. All in favor, say "AYE."

TRAVIS: Aye.

CHESTER: All opposed say "NAY." Nay. All right, we have a tie. In which case, the bylaws of BAAA state that the president must make a final decision . . . And his decision is: NO.

TRAVIS: Oh come on, Chester! If I have to come to these stupid meetings I want to be able to drink a beer.

CHESTER: In order to preserve BAAA's integrity, BAAA must maintain meeting locations that do not serve alcohol.

TRAVIS: Would you quit saying "BAAA"? You sound like a militant sheep.

CHESTER: I am anything but sheep-like, my Brother. The Asian Man must stand for dignity and righteousness — not getting red-in-the-face while he falls off a bar stool.

TRAVIS: These meetings are a joke. You and I are the only Asian people in town.

CHESTER: Which is why we must maintain Solidarity, my Korean Brother. Solidarity in the face of constant and deliberate oppression. Shelby's Grocery Store: an openly racist seller of Occidental-only foodstuffs.

TRAVIS: Mr. Shelby has said, repeatedly, that he won't carry anything that only two people are going to buy.

CHESTER: Solidarity. Heck's Tavern: Center of Foreign and Domestic Imperialism, what with its so-called selection of "Import Beer." Where's my Tsing-Tao? My Kirin Ichiban? Can I get a fuckin' Hite?

TRAVIS: I thought you weren't into getting red-faced and falling off bar stools.

CHESTER: Well I might be if I could get a glass of something from the

Motherland. See, Travis, one voice alone accomplishes nothing. And that's why BAAA exists — to give us more than one voice.

TRAVIS: Two voices.

CHESTER: That's right: two strong Asian American voices. And if you and I stick together, we can affect some change in this shitty little town.

TRAVIS: But you see Chester, I like this shitty little town. I like the fact that Heck hasn't changed his tavern since 1973. I like —

CHESTER: Well —

TRAVIS: Shut up. I like bowling in a two-lane alley that's connected to an Episcopal Church. I like flipping through the library's *National Geographics* with all the aboriginal titties snipped out. I like all of these things because I enjoy certain charms. The charms, if you will, of small-town life. And I know you grew up here, but these things are still new to me.

CHESTER: If I had a car and some money, I'd be sipping iced green tea on a beach. But that's OK. Don't lift a finger, remain seated in your little Caucasian corner. I will handle this week's business by myself: the BAAA membership drive.

TRAVIS: Membership drive?

CHESTER: Yes. There's a potential new member moving into town. Last name Lee.

TRAVIS: There are plenty of Lees that aren't Asian. Christopher Lee. Tommy Lee Jones. Lee Majors.

CHESTER: From New York.

TRAVIS: Spike Lee.

CHESTER: From Flushing Queens.

TRAVIS: Flushing what?

CHESTER: You're from California, so you wouldn't understand. Flushing Queens is the Korean capital of New York City. And it gets better: last name Lee, first name Veronica. *(Deliciously.)* Korean Veronica Lee.

TRAVIS: Leave her alone, Chester. Keep your crazy militant shit to yourself.

CHESTER: No way fella. It's bad enough living in this two-donkey town. I'm an island of yellow in a sea of white.

TRAVIS: It's like someone took a piss in the snow.

CHESTER: We are going to embrace this hopefully lovely Korean Sister with open arms and show her that Asian America thrives in Breakneck, Wyoming. You actually have another thing in common with her: She's also a teacher.

TRAVIS: Wonderful. Now we know you won't be able to hypnotize her into drinking your Kool-Aid.

CHESTER: You always belittle my ideas, Travis. Why is that?

TRAVIS: It's because your ideas are stupid, Chester. If you tell her your conspiracy theory that American rice contains penis-shrinking chemicals, I'm walking out.

CHESTER: I am upholding our identity, my brother. For within that identity lies our dignity.

TRAVIS: Fine. But give it a rest sometime, OK? Support some other causes. Save the Whales. Stop deforestation. Become a Nazi or something.

(As he exits —)

TRAVIS: And one more thing — next time I'm going to be at Heck's Tavern, with or without you. I might even start my own club. The Breakneck Travis American Alliance. That's B-TAAH to you. B-TAAH! Anyone who wants to drink beer with me is in. Make it the Breakneck Beer American Alliance. Buh-buh-Ahh! Buh-buh-Ahh!

(Travis exits.)

(Chester in prayer:)

CHESTER: O Bruce, please show Travis the error of his ways. He's a good guy, even if he is a race traitor. Oh, and by the way, please make sure that Veronica Lee is hot. Hot-and-buttered. Shie-shie, O Great One.

(He bows.)

SCENE THREE

The classroom, a few days later. Veronica Lee, late twenties to early thirties, Korean American, sits at the teachers' desk. She's beautiful, glasses-wearing. She riffles through a cardboard box as Chester paces around, lecturing —

CHESTER: SD-3. Remember that name.

VERONICA: SD-3. Right.

CHESTER: Yes. It was created by scientists under the Truman administration. And it's been proven — PROVEN — that SD-3 can be found in all commercially available rice in America. How does it get there? Hmm? Do you know?

VERONICA: You're going to tell me, aren't you?

CHESTER: The GOVERNMENT sprays it onto every single grain of —

(Travis enters, surprised to see them.)

TRAVIS: Hello.

CHESTER: Hello, Travis. Have you met Veronica Lee?

TRAVIS: *(Handshake.)* Hi, I'm Travis Park.

VERONICA: Hello Travis Park.

CHESTER: I was just telling Veronica here all about SD-3.

TRAVIS: Right, SD-3 . . . Chester, aren't you late for your shift?

CHESTER: What? *(Checks his watch.)* Oh damn, you're correct. *(To Veronica.)* I'm the assistant manager of the only ethnic restaurant in town.

TRAVIS: Taco Tuesday.

CHESTER: *(Grumbles.)* Yes, Taco Tuesday.

VERONICA: I used to live right next to a Taco Tuesday. I'm a fan.

CHESTER: What a marvelous coincidence. You know, before I met you, I was drowning in the snide irony of being an Asian Man working in a Mexican fast-food restaurant. But now —

VERONICA: You're late.

CHESTER: I'm late.

(Chester hands her a flyer.)

CHESTER: We have a meeting this Wednesday at 8 P.M., right here in Travis' — I mean, yours and Travis' — classroom.

VERONICA: I'll see if I can make it.

CHESTER: That's all I ask. Stay strong.

(As Chester walks out —)

CHESTER: Thank you Bruce!

(Chester exits.)

(Veronica shows the flyer to Travis with a puzzled smile.)

TRAVIS: It's not his fault. He doesn't know what he is.

VERONICA: Somebody should let him know that he's kind of a creep.

TRAVIS: No, I mean he literally doesn't know what he is. He was adopted. And when his parents picked him up from the airport, they forgot to ask the adoption people which country he came from.

VERONICA: You're kidding.

TRAVIS: No, I'm not. And the organization that brought him here went out of business so . . . He never found out what kind of Asian he is. Don't worry — he's harmless. He's just a little confused.

(She starts to unpack a cardboard box.)

TRAVIS: So you're Veronica Lee from New York City.

VERONICA: That's right, Hoss.

TRAVIS: You've got the cowboy slang down. That's good.

VERONICA: That's my backup in case this teaching gig doesn't work out.

TRAVIS: So what are you doing in Wyoming?

VERONICA: I'm in this program that puts teachers where they're desperately needed.

TRAVIS: Well that's us, I guess. Desperate. We have graduating seniors who still like to eat paste.

VERONICA: They give you your choice of places, so I'm just here for a couple of semesters to try it out.

TRAVIS: Just to try it out?

VERONICA: Yeah. I've always wanted to live in a place that has a band that sounds like the Country Bear Jamboree.

TRAVIS: There's this bar in town that has a band that plays Beatles songs with a washboard and a jug.

VERONICA: That sounds perfect.

TRAVIS: So what are you teaching?

VERONICA: Biology. I cut open dead animals and show the insides to kids.

TRAVIS: That's great. Do you do that at parties?

VERONICA: You're an English teacher, aren't you?

TRAVIS: How'd you figure that out?

VERONICA: You don't have many weird quirks, so science is out. You are clearly not a math teacher. You look too sober to teach art, and history . . . Not history. So you must be an English teacher.

TRAVIS: That's amazing.

VERONICA: Plus I was looking through your desk and I found all these essays on Huckleberry Finn.

TRAVIS: Please help yourself to anything else you find in there.

VERONICA: Thanks. So what are the kids like?

TRAVIS: Well, all of the county filters into this school so we get a lot ranchers' kids. They're great for the most part. Except for Bobby Sorenson. He keeps making chinky-eyes at me.

VERONICA: You're kidding. I met Bobby Sorenson. He's a sweetheart.

TRAVIS: You have the advantage of being a beautiful woman. I'm just another jerk in a tie. He keeps asking me if I put pee-pee in his coke. And one of these days, I swear — I'm gonna do it.

(She picks up the empty box —)

VERONICA: It was good to meet you, Travis. Now if you'll excuse me, I've got to go home and tend to a sick cat with no tail.

TRAVIS: Sure.

Hey, so I know you've gotten a lot of offers — "If you need any-things" . . . But if you do need anything —

VERONICA: Like what?

TRAVIS: *Staples*, or glue . . . They're in the desk —

VERONICA: Uh-huh.

TRAVIS: Or if you're a bulgogi[1] fan, I think it's safe to say that I make the best bulgogi in the entire state of Wyoming.

VERONICA: Not anymore. Now that I'm here.

TRAVIS: You wanna bet?

VERONICA: You know Dr. Peters and his wife? They have the ranch with all the —

TRAVIS AND VERONICA TOGETHER: White horses —

VERONICA: Yeah. I'm renting the cottage at the end of their road. So if you've got a free evening, I suggest you bring over your bulgogi and we'll see what's up.

TRAVIS: I will.

VERONICA: See you soon, Mr. Park. And get ready to be number two.
(She exits. Lights dim on the classroom as Travis crosses over to Chester, who stands on the side, disappointed. He's wearing a billowy yellow robe.)

CHESTER: You didn't come to the meeting.

TRAVIS: I'm sorry, Chester. I was busy fixing my roof.

CHESTER: Neither did Veronica Lee.

TRAVIS: She's probably still settling in. When you move into a town full of strangers there are a lot of things you need to take care of.
(Chester looks away, defeated —)

CHESTER: I'll tell you what, Travis: She's yours. You have my blessing. I give her to you.

TRAVIS: What the hell are you talking about?

CHESTER: No, I insist. I've been a monk this long, I can keep on going.

TRAVIS: Don't do me any favors, Chester. Maybe she's looking for an anarchist-militant psychopath like yourself.

CHESTER: No, I give up. You two were meant to be together. You're both teachers, you're both Korean.

TRAVIS: Sure, we'll be right next to the kangaroos on Noah's Ark. Look — there's no guarantee that I'm going to be attracted to her just because she's Asian.

CHESTER: I don't see you mackin' on the Mackenzie twins.

TRAVIS: That's because I'm not attracted to the Mackenzie twins.

---

[1] A traditional Korean beef dish

CHESTER: Me either. Though they are gorgeous, they're still Caucasian she-devils. But Veronica Lee — her Ying smooths neatly together with our Yang.

TRAVIS: Listen to me carefully: Race has nothing to do with being attracted to someone.

CHESTER: Of course it does, my Brother! How are you, an Asian Man, supposed to replicate yourself without the assistance of an Asian Woman? Bruce sent you this Angel on a cloud, and you don't even want to give her a chance.

TRAVIS: OK, what's up with the Bruce Lee-as-God thing? I was letting everything else slide, but the action-hero-religification is beginning to worry me.

CHESTER: The Asian Man worships who he chooses. So logic dictates that he worship the Supreme Asian Man. And besides, I'm pretty sure I'm Chinese.

TRAVIS: You're not Chinese.

CHESTER: Yes I am.

TRAVIS: What makes you so sure?

CHESTER: I've been studying Mandarin and the words just roll off my tongue. Plus it explains why I'm so darned stingy with my money.

TRAVIS: Fine. "*Gong Xi Fa Cai.*"

CHESTER: What does that mean?

TRAVIS: "I'm glad you're Chinese."

CHESTER: Oh. Thanks! I'd continue chatting with you some more, but I have another meeting to attend.

TRAVIS: *(Re., Chester's yellow robe.)* You got choir practice or something?
(Chester pulls on a hood, completing his costume: the robes of a Knight of the Ku Klux Klan.)

TRAVIS: What the hell are you doing in that?

CHESTER: Undercover research. I'm learning a lot of organizational things. And if you replace the words *white* with "yellow," and *Aryan* with "Asian," they pretty much say the same things I do at our BAAA meetings. Plus these guys can fry a turkey like you wouldn't believe.

TRAVIS: You're crazy.

CHESTER: And dangerous. But that's how a true revolutionary has to live. Besides, it's not that tough. All I have to do is eat and drink through these little eye-holes.

And now before I depart, here's a pearl of wisdom, my Brother: Give Veronica Lee a chance. Who knows? You may end up banging her.
(Chester raises a fist.)

SCENE FOUR

Del stands at center wearing a baseball glove. He kneads the palm of his glove, then addresses the audience directly:

LETTER #2:

DEL: My Uncle Pinky had three ears. Two normal ears and a tiny little ear behind his left one. It was about the size of a nickel. He used to cover up his regular ears to see if he could hear out of it — and he could, just a little bit.

The only thing that Uncle Pinky ever wanted to be was a ball player. But three things kept him out of the game: One, he couldn't hit, Two, he couldn't catch, and Three, he was kind of an idiot. And then his hearing slowly went out. First the left ear, then the right ear . . . And eventually, all he had left was that tiny little third ear. Said it was like sucking the whole world through a straw.

Him and my dad once went to see Wrigley Field. Uncle Pinky had a friend there who was a custodian, and he let 'em out onto the field so they could see it from the right angle. And my dad walked up onto the pitcher's mound, and my Uncle Pinky picked up a bat, and they threw it around. And then, on the fifteenth pitch — wouldn't you know it — Uncle Pinky hit a moonshot that sailed out into the bleachers, just like Ernie Banks . . . You should'a seen it — pow . . . And he said he could hear the crowd roaring in his tiny little ear, even though no one was there.

He never swung at another ball again. 'Cause that one shot, that one homer, was enough. And my darling, that is love — when you feel something in your heart for the longest time, and one moment fulfills it. And it rings in one little ear for a lifetime.

SCENE FIVE

Veronica's living room, a week later. A futon surrounded by still-packed boxes. Around are a few skeletons of animals, models of dinosaurs, molecules. Travis and Veronica edge through the front door, both of them carrying bags of groceries. They're in mid-conversation —

VERONICA: — And I spent the rest of that summer taking apart owl poops and making little dioramas of mouse skeletons attacking each other. So welcome to my cottage.

TRAVIS: I like what you've done with the place. Jars of dead animals are supposed to be good feng shui.

VERONICA: You're dumb.

(She places a smaller grocery bag on the coffee table.)

TRAVIS: *(Re., his bag of groceries.)* Where do you want this?

VERONICA: I got it.

(She takes the bags offstage into the kitchen.)

(Travis explores the room. He picks up a jar of paper cranes.)

TRAVIS: You have a jar of paper cranes.

(She re-enters.)

VERONICA: Yeah, when I quit smoking I folded them to keep my hands busy. It's fun.

TRAVIS: How many did you make?

VERONICA: Two thousand three hundred and sixteen. So, I promised that you were in for a treat —

(She hands him a package of tofu.)

TRAVIS: This is impossible. Where did you get this?

VERONICA: Shelby's grocery store.

TRAVIS: No, see, this is tofu. Shelby's grocery store doesn't carry tofu.

VERONICA: I know. I asked Frank to order it for me and he had it in a couple of days later.

TRAVIS: "Frank"? . . . Chester's been trying to get "Frank" to carry tofu for years.

VERONICA: He should try asking nicely.

(Heading into the kitchen.)

Hey, you want some root beer? I brew it myself.

TRAVIS: Sure.

(She exits taking the tofu with her. Travis digs through the smaller grocery bag —)

TRAVIS: What else did you get Frank to carry?

VERONICA: *(Offstage.)* What?

(He comes up with a pair of Scratcher lottery tickets.)

TRAVIS: Scratcher tickets? You hoping for an early retirement?

(Hearing about the tickets, Veronica dashes back into the room —)

VERONICA: No, I —

TRAVIS: Hold on, I've got a coin.

(He's about to scratch them off, but she stops him —)

VERONICA: Don't. Stop — please.

TRAVIS: Don't you want to see if you've won?

VERONICA: Give 'em to me.

TRAVIS: You don't trust me with your scratcher tickets?

VERONICA: No — I mean, yes, I trust you with my scratcher tickets. BUT —

TRAVIS: I've never won anything in my life, so statistically, I'm about due —

VERONICA: No, see, Travis . . . It's dumb, but . . . I collect them.

(She hands him a shoe box. Inside are neatly organized stacks of scratcher tickets.)

VERONICA: I've been collecting them for a while now.

(Travis looks through the tickets —)

TRAVIS: "Lucky Dog" . . . "Cash Cow" . . . "High on the Hog" . . . And here you have the leprechaun section.

(She looks at the tickets fondly —)

VERONICA: Yeah.

TRAVIS: All very neatly organized and categorized —

VERONICA: Yeah. It's neat to see what images people associate with their dreams coming true. Animals, avalanches of gold coins, genies . . . These are the last things people see before they find out if they're rich or disappointed.

TRAVIS: You don't want to scratch any of them off?

VERONICA: I don't need to be rich or disappointed.

(He takes out a single ticket.)

TRAVIS: "Rainbow's End."

VERONICA: Yes. My dad gave me that one when I was ten . . . I looked at it and thought, if I scratch this off, the moment vanishes. Each of these tickets is like a little moment of truth. It's fun to save them instead of spending them.

And my dad owned a grocery, so I used to get paid in these for hauling gallons of milk.

TRAVIS: That's funny — most kids would've wanted an allowance.

VERONICA: I guess. Did you get an allowance?

TRAVIS: Yeah. In exchange for doing chores my parents would continue to feed me.

VERONICA: I heard from Maggie Reed that you're not from around these parts.

TRAVIS: Yeah. I moved down from L.A. a couple of years ago.

VERONICA: So what are you doing in Wyoming?

TRAVIS: Well, in L.A. I had this problem where I couldn't really sleep.

VERONICA: What do you mean?

TRAVIS: Every night I'd hear ambulances screaming in the distance. And I figured that eventually, one of them was going to come for me.

Anyway, it doesn't matter where we teach these days. The kids all look the same, talk the same. Same gang signs.

VERONICA: It's good to have someone to talk to. My greatest fear was that I'd come out here and I'd be forced to adopt more cats. —

TRAVIS: It takes a lot of guts to come out here by yourself —

VERONICA: Aren't you modest —

TRAVIS: I'm not . . . I'm just saying that it shows a great deal of courage on your part.

VERONICA: It's a pretty amazing thing though, you and me meeting here in the middle of nowhere.

TRAVIS: I was just thinking that.

(A short pause.)

VERONICA: But I've decided that I'm going to use this year to clear my head. Live in a wide-open space and get good at being single.

TRAVIS: Oh, yeah . . . Well this is the place to do it.

VERONICA: Yeah, the Right Man keeps coming along and screwing up my life.

TRAVIS: The same guy?

VERONICA: Oh, no. Different guys. Right Men, I should say.

TRAVIS: I thought there was only supposed to be one Right Man.

VERONICA: Nah, they keep on coming. They show up like puppies on my rainy doorstep. And every time I think, "Hmm, he seems like the right one. Better let him in." Then a few months later there's an igloo of poo on my living room floor.

TRAVIS: Maybe you haven't met the right Right Man yet.

VERONICA: My boyfriends start out all neat and cool but eventually they de-evolve into Neanderthal ape men. Like Donald Dabbraccio. [pron. "*dah-brac-ki-oh*"]

TRAVIS: That sounds like a disease.

VERONICA: Yes it does. And he was my first boyfriend. Donald Dabbraccio. The name says it all. There was something wrong with his saliva ducts. He had to put a sponge in his mouth before we could French kiss.

TRAVIS: *(Laughing.)* That's so sad.

VERONICA: Without the sponge it would be like making out with a bowl of soup.

TRAVIS: I had the same sort of situation with my first girlfriend. Hunter Kim. She was the only senior at our high school that still wore a retainer. But we made it romantic. She'd take it out at night and I'd clean it for her.

VERONICA: That's sweet.

TRAVIS: Nothing in the world smells worse than a kid's retainer. I only did it because I loved her.

VERONICA: So what happened?

TRAVIS: Eventually she began a career that consisted of being photographed while lying on the hoods of Japanese cars.

VERONICA: That's hot. But beat this: college. Ryan Perkins. Major stoner. He dealt to most of NYU. He could play a bong as a musical instrument.

TRAVIS: That's a highly sought-after skill.

VERONICA: Yeah. He could belt out any Grateful Dead song with bubbling noises. But eventually I found out that he was accepting sex for ounces.

TRAVIS: That sucks.

VERONICA: Yeah. The worst part was that he was still charging me.

TRAVIS: Well, my college girlfriend was this classic Korean bad girl. Karen Hong. She was on a full-ride scholarship from Crown Royal . . . Eventually we broke up and she became a born-again virgin.

VERONICA: Wonderful. But that's nowhere as bad as my last boyfriend. Todd O'Reilly. I-Banker. Mr. Big-Time-Big-Shot-Big-Boy.

TRAVIS: What happened?

VERONICA: He grew a white powdery moustache . . . One of the reasons why I decided to get out of the city.

TRAVIS: Good reason.

VERONICA: So when was your last relationship?

TRAVIS: A while ago.

VERONICA: Tell me.

TRAVIS: It was before I left L.A. Her name was Grace.

VERONICA: Can't stay away from those Korean girls —

TRAVIS: She was the doctor of the family.

VERONICA: She was the doctor, the next kid was the lawyer —

TRAVIS: *(Overlapping with "lawyer.")* Her brother was the lawyer, her sister was the accountant. So she and I were pretty serious but her parents decided that . . . She should be with someone of equal standing. So one afternoon I walk up to my car and there's a letter on the windshield.

VERONICA: Just like that?

TRAVIS: Yeah. And when you find a breakup note on your car, it's time to get the hell out of L.A.

VERONICA: That's terrible. I'm sorry.

TRAVIS: It's OK. We move on, right?

VERONICA: Yup.

TRAVIS: *(Recalls.)* Donald Dabbraccio, Ryan Perkins, Todd O'Reilly. I see a pattern here.

VERONICA: Yes. You only go out with Asian women.

TRAVIS: I was going to say that you only go out with —

VERONICA: Don't start.

TRAVIS: Don't start what?

VERONICA: The lecture you're about to give me.

TRAVIS: I was just going to point out a particular taste in men that you have.

VERONICA: And what is that?

TRAVIS: Oh, I don't know —

VERONICA: I just get along better with, and I've always only been attracted to —

TRAVIS AND VERONICA TOGETHER: White guys —

VERONICA: Yes, and that's my business.

TRAVIS: Yeah, but why is that?

VERONICA: I don't know.

TRAVIS: You've never dated an Asian guy?

VERONICA: I have. Once.

TRAVIS: Well I tried broccoli once, and I was sorta disappointed but I gave it a second chance.

VERONICA: Travis, does this bother you? You're acting as if this bothers you.

TRAVIS: Of course it bothers me. It's like when four out of five dentists recommend a brand of toothpaste. I'm like the crappy brand that the fifth guy recommends.

VERONICA: Look — it's what I'm used to and what I'm attracted to. And it's nobody's business —

TRAVIS: Fine.

VERONICA: So is that all right with you?

TRAVIS: Yeah.

VERONICA: Travis —

TRAVIS: No, it's fine with me.

VERONICA: Good. Because I don't want to find out that you're going to judge me just because of my likes and dislikes.

TRAVIS: All right. But for your information, I want you to know that I don't just date Asian women. I'm all over the color spectrum.

VERONICA: Oh yeah?

TRAVIS: Yeah. I once had this long, amazing relationship with this incredible Puerto Rican girl. A gymnast. Though I had to break it off with her when I found out that she had a fetish for Asian men.

VERONICA: Really?

TRAVIS: Yeah. She used to clip pictures out of *Martial Artist* magazine.

VERONICA: Come on — we'd better get started on dinner. Let's see you work your magic.

TRAVIS: All right.

(As she exits —)

VERONICA: You make me feel good, Travis. I move out here to the middle of nowhere, and I still find someone to eat tofu with.

(He lags behind, staring at the scratcher tickets with a slight frown.)

SCENE SIX

At center, Del addresses the audience directly:

LETTER #3:

DEL: Bruce Lee, aka The Dragon, created the martial art form known as Jeet Kune Do by studying all of the martial arts and combining the best bits and pieces. I don't know if you've heard this story, but once, he discovered this Shaolin Master who could channel his energy, his CHI, into any part of his body and become invincible. So Bruce went to check out his technique.

The master brought out his students to demonstrate. He said to one of them, "YOU — kick me in the stomach as hard as you can." And the master concentrated, channeled all of his Chi to his stomach — and the student KICKED him with all of his might . . . And nothing happened. The guy didn't even flinch. The master says to another student, "YOU — kick me in the face as hard as you can." Once again, the master concentrates all of his Chi, the student KICKS him in the face, and nothing. Not even a bruise. Bruce was impressed.

So the master says to Bruce, "All right, now you may punch me in the face as hard as you can." Bruce nods, the master concentrates all of his Chi, Bruce winds up . . . And KICKS HIM IN THE NUTS. And the master goes down clutching his crotch, gasping . . . And he says to Bruce, "Goddammit, I told you to punch me in the face!"

And Bruce says, "I know, but at that particular moment, I really felt like kicking you in the nuts . . . Your technique is useless."

And that is love. It gets you when you least expect it. And no matter how much you prepare to take it on the chin, you never know when it's going to kick you in the nuts.

SCENE SEVEN

Outdoors. Dusk. Sound of crickets chirping, a light wind, the hum of a faraway freeway. Del stands at the side, kneading his glove. Travis is on the opposite side, also wearing a baseball glove. Travis pitches an invisible ball at Del, who catches it.

DEL: *(Reciting from memory and often messing up.)* Ladies and gentlemen, welcome to Cheyenne Pete's Wild West Show and Indoor Rodeo —

TRAVIS: *(Coaching him through.)* Yee-haw. Don't forget the yee-haw, it's important —

(They pitch the ball back and forth, playing catch —)

DEL: Right. Yee-haw. I am Cheyenne Pete, your head honcho for this evening's . . .

TRAVIS: Entertainment —

DEL: Entertainment; you are about to witness the most earth-shaking —

TRAVIS: Earthshaking-est —

DEL: Earthshaking-est, most breathtaking buffalo —

TRAVIS: Breathtaking-est —

DEL: Goddamn — Breathtaking-est buffalo and bronco blowout . . . Uh . . .

TRAVIS: *(Finishing it.)* This side of the Mississippi. We got Figure-Eight trick ropers, we got Ornery Owen the Horn-Ed steer — but don't you worry 'cause the arena you see before you is TRIPLE RE-INFORCED — and if you'd like an autograph from a real live Indian, please ask your server. Now, get ready to cheer for your section's cowboy, 'cause Cheyenne Pete's Wild West Show has just begun. Yee-haw . . .

You were supposed to have that memorized.

DEL: Hold on.

(He produces a half-smoked joint, lights it, takes a long drag —)

DEL: OK. From the top.

TRAVIS: Is that a joint?

DEL: It helps me remember things. Gets me relaxed. I get a little stoned, go over what I need to know, and when it comes time to repeat the information, I get stoned again and it comes right back to me.

TRAVIS: So you were stoned when you were memorizing your lines?

DEL: No. But I am now relaxed.

TRAVIS: You shouldn't be smoking weed, Del. You're a teacher for christ's sake.

DEL: I'm a P.E. teacher. And this isn't even my weed. It's Bill's weed. So if I ever get caught smoking it, I'll just say, "Dad, sir, this is not my weed. It's Bill's. I found it in his room — see, he buys it from a quarter-Indian dealer named Mystery Dream. So as you can see, Sir, Bill is just as much of a hucklefuck as your other son. Me."

TRAVIS: That's good, that'll show him. You want to work on your audition now?

DEL: I don't wanna audition for Cheyenne Pete's anymore, Travis. That speech was probably written by a Texan.

TRAVIS: You can't move off of your dad's ranch on a part-time P.E. teacher's salary.

DEL: I know.

TRAVIS: So what are you going to do?

DEL: Man, I dunno.

(He pinches out the joint and sticks it in his mouth. He puts his glove back on.)

DEL: Toss me the ball.

(The game of catch resumes.)

DEL: You met the new teacher?

TRAVIS: Veronica? Yeah.

DEL: She's from New York City, Travis. New York City.

TRAVIS: You've talked to her?

DEL: Aww . . . Naw, man. I wouldn't know what to say. She's different.

TRAVIS: What do you mean, different?

DEL: She's not like the girls around here, not like the girls on TV . . . She's Ko-rean, right? Hooo — I didn't expect a Ko-rean girl to look like that.

TRAVIS: What did you think they looked like?

DEL: I dunno. Like you in a wig?

(Travis pitches a fastball that slams, hard, into Del's mitt. Del notices the extra heat on it —)

DEL: Ow . . . What?

TRAVIS: It's funny how a beautiful woman transcends all racial boundaries.

DEL: What's that?

TRAVIS: A beautiful Asian woman moves into town and you're biting your fist at how fine she is. But when I moved in? "Hey Jap! Go back to China!"

DEL: So you're still holding that over my head.

TRAVIS: I just think it's funny, that's all.

DEL: I didn't know you back then. I thought you were a tourist. I didn't even know you could speak English.

TRAVIS: I'm touched.

DEL: Yeap, I'm in-the-know now. I'm sensitive to things.

(Del begins to quietly chant her name as he winds up and pitches —)

DEL: Verrr-onica . . . Lee-lee-lee-lee . . .

TRAVIS: You really like her.

DEL: Why'dya say that?

TRAVIS: You're doing that lee-lee-lee-lee thing.

DEL: She's pretty.

TRAVIS: Why don't you introduce yourself?

DEL: I sorta already tried.

TRAVIS: And?

DEL: I saw her in your classroom at the beginning of lunch. And I dunno, I just kind of stood in the doorway for a little while trying to think of something to say. But she just looked so damn professional, y'know? And before I could speak up, she said, "Hey — you gotta mop up a bit more around the door 'cause one of the kids threw up during first period. And also please empty the trash on your way out 'cause you forgot to do it last night. Thanks." And when I got back from emptying out the trash, she was gone. Which is good, I guess, 'cause on the way to the dumpster I was rackin' my brain for something to say and I couldn't think of nothin'.

TRAVIS: What's the problem? You don't have any trouble talking to other women.

DEL: I know the girls around here. We got a common thing going. But not Veronica. She's got that big city get-the-hell-outta-my-way thing going on . . . And she's Ko-rean.

TRAVIS: So what if she's Ko-rean? She's just like everybody else. The only difference between us and her is that she's fine as hell.

DEL: I know. It messes up my train of thought.

So I was gonna ask you if maybe you could help me out.

TRAVIS: What am I supposed to do?

DEL: You lived in a big city. And, you're Ko-rean too — you don't know what it's like living here all your life. You've been other places, seen things.

TRAVIS: So what?

DEL: My whole life it's been the same stuff. The same people. And I want something different.

TRAVIS: Why don't you write her a note or something?

DEL: Yeah! What?

TRAVIS: A note: A nonverbal communication written on a piece of paper —

DEL: I know what a note is, Travis. I've written 'em many times to myself.

TRAVIS: So go. Activate.

DEL: But what's it supposed to say?

TRAVIS: Everything you just said to me right now sounds pretty good.

DEL: No it doesn't. It don't sound good, Travis. You gotta make it sound good, see? And you — you're good with words — I always see you readin' some book or other —

TRAVIS: Sure.

DEL: You're good at communicating with people, Travis. You're an English teacher — your job is to put words together —

TRAVIS: No. My job is to give kids books so they can draw penises in the margins.

DEL: All I need is a little cheat-sheet or something. Write something for me.

TRAVIS: Get off me.

DEL: Come on Travis. Please.

TRAVIS: I don't even know if it'll do any good. She says that she's intent on being single.

DEL: But why not give it a shot? "Stories are powerful" — that's what you say. So maybe write me a little story.

(A pause as Travis considers this.)

TRAVIS: All right.

DEL: *(Elated.)* Thanks Travis. I owe you, man.

TRAVIS: No more weed. That's my asking price.

DEL: Done.

(He makes a grand ceremonial gesture of tossing the joint away.)

DEL: By the way, I'm sorry I called you a Jap before.

TRAVIS: It's OK. I get it all the time.

(They continue to play catch.)

SCENE EIGHT

The classroom, the next day. Some of the animal skeletons and dinosaur models from Veronica's living room are now present. Travis sits in one of the student chairs writing on a piece of paper with a great deal of concentration. Chester stands behind the teacher's desk. He bangs a gavel.

CHESTER: Order! I call this BAAA Meeting to order. Will the secretary please read the last week's minutes?

TRAVIS: *(Without looking up.)* Screw you.

CHESTER: Fine. But please note that if the secretary continues to behave in a surly manner, he may find himself in poor standing with this organization. Furthermore, a member in poor standing may be removed from the —

(Lights fade on Chester as his voice drowns out. Travis reads what he has just written back to himself.)

TRAVIS: "Dear Veronica, things in nature always hide . . . Lizards change the color of their skins . . . Moths live or die based on the color of their wings . . . To stand out in the world is to invite danger. You will be swallowed alive by something that was waiting for you to show yourself.

But now I throw away my fear — "

(He writes something in, then . . .)

Signed . . .

(Travis signs the letter.)

(Suddenly, lights up on Chester —)

CHESTER: Travis, are you listening to me?

TRAVIS: Yeah. I've been kicked out of your gang.

CHESTER: That was five minutes ago. Now we're onto the railroad thing.

TRAVIS: What railroad thing?

CHESTER: Hello?! The Central Pacific Railroad celebration? The mayor has been planning it for weeks. A jolly top-hatted crew of Deathmongers are riding a train along the original route of the railroad. And of course, their literature totally omits the thankless roles suffered by our people: China men dynamited off mountains, their bones picked clean at the bottom of forgotten valleys. So when they stop in town to hoo-hah and pat themselves on their fat little backs, we'll be waiting for them.

(He holds up various hastily crafted picket signs that say things like "RIDE BACK OUT ON YOUR RAIL," "INDENTURE THIS" and "FUCK YOU.")

TRAVIS: All right, Chester. I'm with you.

CHESTER: *(Surprised and elated.)* You are? . . . Finally!

TRAVIS: I'll talk to the organizers and see if our school can put something together about the Chinese railroad workers.

CHESTER: Yellow Power in Action, Yellow People in Action!

TRAVIS: But personally, I think the picket signs are a bad idea.

On second thought, give me that one.

(He indicates the sign that says "FUCK YOU.")
(Chester gives him the sign.)

TRAVIS: This might come in handy sometime.

CHESTER: The railroad celebration will be in a few weeks. So you might want to jot that down in your notes —
(He snatches the letter from Travis' hands.)

TRAVIS: Hey!

CHESTER: *(Reads.)* "Things in nature . . . Roaring, dancing . . . I am a frog. I am birds . . . So here I am. Signed . . . DEL?"
(Furious.)
What are you doing, man?

TRAVIS: I'm helping out a friend.

CHESTER: You mean you're helping The Man to OUR woman —

TRAVIS: Our . . . ? Our woman? As in "Including You" — OUR woman?

CHESTER: You're like a Chinese waiter giving him a fork! You know what, Travis? I never wanted to say this to your face, but I've got to now: You're a Twinkie.

TRAVIS: I am not a Twinkie.

CHESTER: *(Shakes the note.)* Then what's this? Not only are you in love with The Man, you're writing love letters on his behalf. Hasn't the Asian Man suffered enough?

TRAVIS: It doesn't matter. I don't have a shot with her.

CHESTER: My Brother, you gotta lift that fist and raise up that self-esteem.

TRAVIS: No, see, Veronica . . . She only goes out with —

CHESTER: Goes out with what?

TRAVIS: White men.
(A pause as this sinks in.)

CHESTER: Ooooooo. Oooooooo . . . I'm gonna . . . I'm gonna go over to her house and . . . Gimme back my sign!

TRAVIS: Relax, Chester.

CHESTER: I knew she was the type that tongued for snowflakes! Playing a piano with no sharps or flats, is she? I guess that's the way it goes for the Asian Man, isn't it? Not only is she not — down with us, but she's trying to jump from the field into the motherfuckin' house!

TRAVIS: Veronica has a right to have her own preferences.

CHESTER: I thought I had to make up the balance for only one Twinkie in this town — but now I gotta deal with a whole snack-pack of you traitors. And you're helping Del? DEL?! A man whose social and cultural center is the parking lot at Safeway? . . . Whose Brother are you supposed to be?

TRAVIS: I'm nobody's brother. I'm just a guy helping out a friend. If she's not going to go for me, I might as well help him out. I'm not —

CHESTER: Asian —

TRAVIS: I wasn't gonna say Asian –

CHESTER: But you want to.

TRAVIS: Yes. I mean — no. Look, don't try to politicize this.

CHESTER: EVERYTHING is political. Don't you see that? You and I are the Fortress of Asian America in this town — and it will die without us. If you were a true Korean Brother, you'd see that. *Han gook mal arra?*
(Travis pauses, bewildered —)

TRAVIS: Oh God, no.

CHESTER: I don't know why I couldn't put my finger on it earlier.
(Points to his face.)
Just look at these cheekbones.

TRAVIS: Don't you dare —

CHESTER: And now that I've embraced my Korean heritage, I'm seeing you in a whole new light.

TRAVIS: If you do turn out to be Korean, I'm definitely switching to something else.
(Chester crumples up the note and tosses it at Travis.)

CHESTER: Do whatever you want. Write your little letters for Whitey McWhiteman. See what I care. I know I've always been on my own, a Ronin, masterless. And BAAA has always been an army of one. I just never wanted to believe it.

TRAVIS: When are you going to see that it's not about white, black, Asian, or whatever? We are all just people, Chester. Confused people, and it doesn't matter what the color of the wrapping paper is.

CHESTER: Tell that to your purely platonic friend with the preferences.
(Chester exits. Travis picks up the crumpled piece of paper, straightens it, and puts it into his pocket.)

SCENE NINE

The classroom, a couple of weeks later. Travis sits at the desk typing as Del watches over his shoulder.

TRAVIS: *(As he continues to type throughout —)* Almost done.

DEL: Thanks for writing these for me, Travis. She can't stop talking about them.

TRAVIS: So they've been working for you?

DEL: Yeah. Ever since I put the first one in her mailbox. The next day she comes right up to me, invites me over for dinner. And I seen her every night this week.

TRAVIS: Every night, huh?

DEL: Yeap. All thanks to you.

TRAVIS: So what have you two been doing together?

DEL: Oh, man, Travis — everything. Watch movies, eat cheeseburgers, play basketball, take pictures. We dance . . . Did you know she has a trampoline, Travis?

TRAVIS: No.

DEL: She has a trampoline, Travis! And we read your letters together . . .

Goddamn, they bring me back. Your stories, my stories, all mixed up together. I didn't know you and me combined could be so interesting.

TRAVIS: Me either.

DEL: Don't think that I don't appreciate this. You're going above and beyond the call of what you gotta do — you're giving me more than I even need. And I thank you for that.

(Travis hits a last key with a satisfying CLICK and whips the page out of the typewriter.)

DEL: What's this one about?

TRAVIS: My uncle. He had three ears.

DEL: Thanks.

(Del signs the letter and pockets it.)

DEL: So I got a question for you.

TRAVIS: Yeah?

DEL: Why don't you ever try to get anyone yourself?

TRAVIS: What are you talking about?

DEL: You've been single ever since I've known you. Why's that?

TRAVIS: There's no one in this town that I'm attracted to.

DEL: No one.

TRAVIS: Nope.

DEL: Come on . . . Daisy Sherwood — not attractive?

TRAVIS: No. Her head's too small. She wears those big hoop earrings to make her head look normal-sized, but it doesn't work.

DEL: Clarissa Jones?

TRAVIS: No. She's got that fe-mullet going on. Very unattractive.

DEL: Harriet Mackenzie?

TRAVIS: No. She looks too much like her sister.

DEL: Janie Mackenzie?

TRAVIS: No. She looks too much like her sister.

DEL: Big Roy? Little Roy? Heck?

TRAVIS: Now, Heck is very handsome for an eighty-year-old man, but he's got crazy-eyes from that long-ago bout with Syphilis.

DEL: I don't get you, Travis. You live your life in right field, and it ain't right. A man can't go forever without affection. We're supposed to cuddle.

TRAVIS: I moved here because I wanted to live in a small town. Get away from complications.

DEL: Complications are good. Before I met Veronica the only complex thing in my life was numbering the school's basketballs. But complications, attractions n' shit — these are good things! I mean, not to sound fruity or nothin', 'cause you know I'm All Man.

TRAVIS: Right.

DEL: And look at you — you're very handsome for a Ko-rean fella.

TRAVIS: Thanks. Most of us have large humps on our backs and monobrows.

DEL: You know what I mean. You're a good guy, and you have a good old soul. And with charm like this you could get any girl in this town . . .

But you're still hiding from her.

TRAVIS: From who?

DEL: Come on. Never mind all the hoo-hah about small towns and complications. You're still hiding from Grace.

TRAVIS: Grace was a long time ago.

DEL: I know. So —

(Travis turns away, inserts a new page into the typewriter.)

DEL: I'm just lookin' out, Travis. After all, winter's coming. It's a bad time to find yourself alone.

(Del exits.)

(Travis stares at the blank page. And he begins to type.)

SCENE TEN

At center, Del addresses the audience directly:

LETTER #4:

DEL: Just like you, my dad loved movies. Specifically, spaghetti westerns.

"American Made in Italy," he'd call them. But he would never go see a movie alone. "What kind of loser sees a movie by himself?" he'd say. He'd rather sit at home on a Friday night than bear the public humiliation of going to a movie theater by himself.

But when he met my mom, everything changed. From then on, he loved seeing movies by himself.

He'd get the extra-large tub of popcorn and put his feet up on the seat, make a grand show of being there by himself. He said it was because he knew that he had someone in his life — that he truly wasn't alone. People could think whatever they wanted, but they would be wrong.

He felt like a king sitting up there, sneaking in beers. And when the lights came up at the end, he'd always find his way back to her.

And when things got bad at home, that's where he'd be. At the Royale watching *The Good, The Bad, and The Ugly*, just him and Clint Eastwood.

And when she finally left him, that was still where he went.

(Short pause.)

What a fragile thing it is.

When you have it you might not know it, and when it's gone, it's as if it never mattered.

Because what the old man never realized was that he was always alone.

He was alone the entire time, with or without her.

SCENE ELEVEN

The classroom, a few days later. Veronica sits in a student chair reading a letter. Travis is at the teacher's desk, grading papers.

TRAVIS: What does that one say?

VERONICA: It's about spiders. Spiders that his cousin put on a twig to make them fight.

(She holds up another letter —)

VERONICA: This one's about atomic cold fusion.

(Reads.)

"We are fusion reactors reacting to each other, feeding off of this energy that comes out of nowhere — "

(Beat.)

It's dumb.

TRAVIS: Spiders and reactors, huh?

VERONICA: Spiders, reactors, baseball, Bruce Lee. Bruce Lee! I detect the influence of your friendship.

TRAVIS: Hmm.

VERONICA: Sometimes they're silly, sometimes they're serious . . . And they all fit together like a conversation. It's amazing. When I first saw him I noticed that sweet little cowboy smile of his. But I never saw . . . I never guessed that these kind of thoughts could be behind it.

TRAVIS: I guess some things are easier to say on paper.

VERONICA: I'm falling, Travis. I've fallen.

TRAVIS: What happened to getting good at being single?

VERONICA: That policy has been dismantled. It lies dead and buried next to my anger at the male species.

TRAVIS: It's nice to see you smiling like that.

VERONICA: Yeah. Because he's also a gorgeous specimen of manhood.

TRAVIS: So it's moving pretty quickly between the two of you?

VERONICA: Yeah. I've even tried looking for speed bumps and roadkill, but I just can't find any. And I'm positive that he's not one of those slimy guys with an Asian Fetish.

TRAVIS: How's that?

VERONICA: I located his porn stash.

(She produces a small, heavy cardboard box. It lands on the desk with a THUMP.)

TRAVIS: And you brought it to school to show me?

VERONICA: Travis, if this is the first time you've ever seen pornography and you feel uncomfortable, it's OK to let me know.

(She starts going through it.)

VERONICA: The truth in a man's heart can be found in his porn stash. I found it in the default hiding spot — the sock drawer.

TRAVIS: Brilliant.

VERONICA: I am the master of locating porn stashes.

(She shows the contents to Travis [videotapes, magazines] —)

VERONICA: It's your standard red-blooded American pornographic bric-a-brac. *Up-and-Cummers #23. Dirty Debutantes* . . . No *East Meats West* with *meats* spelled M-E-A-T-S. No *Eastern Anal Odysseys.* Nothing titled *Oriental Rug-Munchers* or *Dragon FIST-ing.* Do you know what this means?

TRAVIS: I think so.

VERONICA: He's into me for me.

TRAVIS: Is that supposed to be surprising?

VERONICA: It's surprising when there are so few obstacles. The only ones are his dad and his asshole-brother Bill. He makes chinky-eyes at me.

TRAVIS: Ah, don't worry about Bill. He's just bitter because he failed to break into the sport of Monster Trucking.

(She puts the box away.)

VERONICA: So. After next semester I think I'm going to stay.

TRAVIS: Hey — that's great.

VERONICA: Yeah. I called my dad and I told him that I'm staying. But I don't think he understands why.

TRAVIS: He probably misses you.

VERONICA: No. He can't understand why I don't just stay back east and have kids already and be done with it. And I don't know how to explain that . . . You know. His English isn't so good and my Korean is pretty much crap.

TRAVIS: Yeah. My parents never really got fluent in English. For instance, they're Catholic, right, and you know the concept of transubstantiation? Where the bread turns into Jesus' flesh?

VERONICA: Yeah.

TRAVIS: My dad explained it to me like this: He said: "It looks like bread, it tastes like bread, but it's not bread anymore. It's Jesus."

VERONICA: That's hilarious.

Well, I wish my dad would make an attempt to improve his English. Even after years of dealing with the customers in his store, he can't even understand when they're mocking him.

TRAVIS: Or maybe he doesn't care.

VERONICA: He could at least learn to speak better English for his kids.

TRAVIS: But he's old and he's probably set in his ways, and I think that's OK.

VERONICA: He stays cooped up in his little apartment and watches TV all night. And my sister's in Seattle and my brother doesn't give a shit, so it was up to me to check in on him. And now they're mad because I won't be able to do that anymore. But he barely says anything to me anyway.

Listen, I'm sorry to lay this out on you.

TRAVIS: It's fine.

VERONICA: Of all the new people in my life, you're the only one that can understand.

(She picks up the box —)

VERONICA: I'd better put this porn stash back in its sock drawer.

TRAVIS: Oh, hey — I discovered a certain Chinese restaurant in Chugwater.

They go through this distributor that can do small orders, and . . . This Friday, for the first time since I left California, I will have in my possession a jar of kimchee. So I was thinking that night we could get together and —

VERONICA: I'd like that.

TRAVIS: Yeah?

VERONICA: But maybe next week. Del and I are going up to the mountains this weekend.

TRAVIS: Oh. Well, it'll still be around when you get back.

VERONICA: But you don't have to wait around for me. You should enjoy it yourself.

TRAVIS: I'll bring you an extra jar. My treat.

VERONICA: Thanks. I'll see you tomorrow.

TRAVIS: See you tomorrow.

(She exits.)

SCENE TWELVE

Later. The classroom. Travis sits at a student desk reading over a letter. Del peeks his head in, knocks on the door.

DEL: I was sitting at the counter eatin' a piece of pie at Scullard's and a certain mutual friend of ours was parked right there next to me. Guess who it was.

(Del enters.)

TRAVIS: Daisy —

DEL: *(Overlapping.)* Daisy Sherwood. And we got to talking about traveling, and she asked if I'd ever been out of the country before and I said "No, but you know who has?"

TRAVIS: Travis —

DEL: Mr. Travis Park has. He's been all over the goddamned place. Well, I didn't say goddamn 'cause she bowls at the church, but you know what I mean.

TRAVIS: Thanks Del, but Daisy Sherwood and I have nothing in common.

DEL: Yes you do! You both love to . . . Uh . . . You're both ambitious. She's doing that art school through the Internet and you've already got a degree and everything. And you both play sports. You both bowl —

TRAVIS: If I make a move on Daisy, I'll let you know. Here.

(Travis hands the letter to Del.)

DEL: What's this one about?

TRAVIS: It's about how you spent years trying to teach your dog how to drink through a straw.

DEL: Oh yeah. Thanks Travis.

So if you say you don't have anything in common with Daisy Sherwood, who do you have something in common with?

TRAVIS: Why do you keep pestering me about this? I'm genuinely touched by your concern, but I'm doing all right. I got my deck built around my house, I've almost finished my barbecue made out of beer bottles and my soap carved chess set and I am this close to bowling a perfect game —

DEL: You come here at six in the morning, you teach these kids, you have dinner on Mondays, Wednesdays, and Fridays at Scullard's by yourself, and every other day you eat at home, alone.

TRAVIS: Yeah —

DEL: You read alone at the library, you drive an hour and a half just to rent videos to watch alone. And that ain't right, Travis. That's somebody else's life.

TRAVIS: Maybe I like living this way. Maybe it beats the hell out of L.A. traffic and smog and —

DEL: But lemme ask you somethin' — don't you want anything more?
(Short pause.) 'Cause I read your letters.

TRAVIS: Where's this coming from?

DEL: Last night I decided that . . . I have to tell you that I don't think you should write the letters to her anymore.

TRAVIS: Why?

DEL: 'Cause I'm moving in with her. And she doesn't need them anymore.

It'll be good to not have to wake up to oily pancakes with my dad and the guests. It'll be good to have a place to be. To be with her. *(A short pause.)* She asks me questions that I can't answer. There are details I can't fill in. And you were right to begin with — I should be tellin' her things about my life. So you don't have to write the letters anymore, OK Travis? 'Cause I don't think it's right. For you either.

TRAVIS: What do you mean, "for me either"?

DEL: Nothin'.

TRAVIS: 'Cause all this is for you, Del.

DEL: No. You . . . You need to stop writing them. OK, Travis?

TRAVIS: Is she happy, Del?

DEL: Yeah. She is.

I want you to pay Daisy Sherwood some mind, all right? And let's throw the ball around sometime, OK? It's been a while.

(Del exits.)

(Travis takes a deep breath, surveys the room. He sits at the teacher's desk, aimless.)

SCENE THIRTEEN

At center, Del addresses the audience directly:

LETTER #5:

DEL: My grandfather kept over two hundred horses. There was a sea of them, rolling over our land. You would have loved to see that sight. Me, I can barely remember it. See, over time their numbers were decimated as we went from keeping horses to keeping tourists from New Jersey.

As a boy, it was my job to feed and water the horses we had left. And like a person, every horse is a mix of clever and crazy, courageous, calm, and cunning.

I had a horse named Blue — blue because his gray coat had a tinge of it — and in the mix of that horse there was more crazy than anything else.

I loved that horse. He took to no one else but me. He was the first thing that was ever mine.

And he was mine until I was seventeen. There was the night when I woke up and saw an orange glint on my window. I looked out and saw the glow from across the circle — the stables were burning. They were disintegrating, being eaten alive by smoke.

I tried to wake my brother but he wouldn't budge. I pushed my dad out of bed, and we all rushed out with buckets, blew open the doors to let out the horses. And they came streaming out, panicked. And then I saw him.

He dragged himself out into the air like a crippled old man. His flesh was charred black, and there were tears in his skin through which you could see red. He was silent.

And there I was. And I didn't know how to save him.

And that is love, I think. Because maybe love isn't, by itself, a feeling. But the absence of love — of losing it — is. It eats us alive. It murders us.

ACT II
SCENE ONE

The classroom, a few weeks later. There's a muffled groan from behind the door. A few more, getting louder, then Travis enters dragging in Chester, who staggers in drunk.

CHESTER: Victory! Victory! Yellow people, yellow power! Yellow power, yellow people!
(Chester carries several papier-mâché severed limbs and a busted protest sign [from earlier]. He is covered in what appears to be blood. He groans as Travis helps him into a student desk chair.)
CHESTER: I got the bastards.
(Travis takes a roll of paper towels out his desk and cleans Chester's face up.)
TRAVIS: Sit still.
CHESTER: Did you hear that fat Animal Farm pig of an engineer yell, "Get that chink bastard off the tracks?" Little did Ignorant know that I'm Japanese.
TRAVIS: How much did you drink?
CHESTER: Not much. Jack Daniels. Just a little. Quart.
TRAVIS: You've really outdone yourself this time.
CHESTER: I was only exercising my right to free assembly and speech.
TRAVIS: Little Roy bursts into my kitchen yelling for me to get down to the tracks. When I get there everybody's in mob formation, and there you are, lying in front of the celebration train, covered in fake blood and surrounded by body parts —
CHESTER: *(Re., the severed limbs.)* These represent the pieces of our fallen ancestors.
TRAVIS: Why do you insist on making a fool out of yourself?
CHESTER: Are you afraid that my behavior casts a yellow stain on your lily-white reputation?
TRAVIS: Yes, I am. Because half the people in town can't tell us apart.
CHESTER: Some of us refuse to cooperate with the establishment. We are non-cooperational, and we have to take matters into our own hands. Because we aren't going to take things lying down. Even though, we sometimes have to lie down in order to stand up for ourselves.
TRAVIS: You know Hallsey's looking for you, right? If we hadn't gotten out of there, you'd be in a cell right now.
CHESTER: Let him come. There's no way he's gonna get me.

TRAVIS: And how's that?

CHESTER: 'Cause I'm a fucking Samurai, is why.

> And even though I'm lost in the wilderness of America, I don't care. And I don't care that I don't have a Brother anymore.
>
> *(He tries to get up but Travis eases him back into his seat.)*

TRAVIS: You're going to stay here until you've sobered up and quieted down. Then I'm taking you home.

CHESTER: I'm not going back to Randall and Betty's basement. There are fifteen taxidermied deer heads that stare at me while I sleep. And it stinks.

TRAVIS: Quiet down or I'll take you home right now.

> *(Chester leaps to his feet —)*

CHESTER: I'M NOT GOING BACK!

> *(Something heavy and wrapped in black cloth falls out of Chester's pocket and hits the ground with a THUD. Chester makes a swipe for it, but Travis beats him to it. Travis unwraps the object: a five-and-a-half-inch golden railroad spike.)*

CHESTER: You were not supposed to see that.

TRAVIS: What is this?

CHESTER: It's the Last Spike.

TRAVIS: The real —

CHESTER: The real Last Spike. Hammered into the ground in 1869 by Leland Stanford at Promontory, Utah. To celebrate the joining of the two halves of this chunky country.

TRAVIS: It's heavy.

CHESTER: Seventy-five percent of it is gold.

TRAVIS: My God.

CHESTER: Look at it, so shiny and innocent-seeming. And yet, this object is the pinnacle of a mountain of blown-up Chinamen. Its home was once a velvet cushion in the halls of Stanford University. But then the Railroad Tour brought it here. *(Beat.)* Look at it, Travis. It's caused us so much pain. But now it's come home to its rightful owner: the Asian Man.

> *(A pause as this sinks in.)*

TRAVIS: You're not keeping it.

CHESTER: You're right. I'm not.

> *(Recites.)*
>
> "Dear Stanford University, we have your artifact of atrocious history. If you want it back, prepare a hundred thousand dollars in unmarked bills. P.S. — fuck you."

TRAVIS: You can't hold this thing for ransom!

CHESTER: I'm going to do good with the money, Travis. I'm going to water the seeds of Asian America from east to west. I'm gonna bring the gospel of Bruce. That spike is my ticket out of this goddamned town. It's my escape pod.

TRAVIS: You're nuts.

CHESTER: I am sick of having to avert my eyes when they call me by their list of slurs. I wanna be set off like a firecracker. I wanna see an ocean.

Do you see, Travis? That spike was our past, beaten into the ground in the middle of nowhere. It kept us hammered down. But now it will set us free. That spike is me.

TRAVIS: No, it's not. It's going back.

(Travis wraps up the spike.)

CHESTER: No —

TRAVIS: I'm going to keep it safe until the heat's off. Hallsey can turn your parents' place upside down and he won't be able to find it —

CHESTER: No —

TRAVIS: And then I'm going to send it back to Stanford with a note that says that it was all a stupid prank —

CHESTER: NO!

(Chester makes a grab for the spike but Travis edges out of the way.)

TRAVIS: You're not going to get it.

CHESTER: I will use force, Travis.

TRAVIS: Let's see you try.

CHESTER: Is this what your Twinkification has brought you to? Asian-on-Asian violence?

(Chester pulls a pair of nunchucks out of his pocket.)

CHESTER: Maybe I shouldn't mind so much. After all, you are standing in the path of The Revolution.

(They circle each other slowly, Chester swinging the nunchucks, Travis feinting and dodging. Suddenly, Chester screams, whirls the nunchucks around and WHACKS Travis in the arm —)

TRAVIS: OW! You hit me in the arm!

CHESTER: Oh, sorry, I —

(Travis whips around and puts Chester in a full nelson. Chester struggles and drops the nunchucks. They twist and buckle as Travis' grip tightens —)

TRAVIS: I will not let you burn yourself down. Not for some stupid —

CHESTER: It's not stupid!

TRAVIS: You call yourself Asian, but you don't know a thing about it. You read magazines and books, you wear costumes and you call that your identity —

CHESTER: IT'S ALL I'VE GOT.

(Travis slowly lets him go. Chester is sobbing and blubbering now —)

TRAVIS: Chester . . . Please . . . Get up.

CHESTER: I wanna show her who I am, Travis.

TRAVIS: Who are you talking about?

CHESTER: I love her. I love Veronica Lee.

TRAVIS: No, you don't.

CHESTER: Yes, I do. I wanna curl up against the nape of her neck, let her hair drape over my eyes and hide them forever.

TRAVIS: You've just never seen an Asian woman before.

CHESTER: Don't protect me. I am not harmless. I am harmful — I am full of harm. So let me go. I wanna find my own Veronica Lee.

TRAVIS: C'mon. On your feet.

(Travis helps Chester to his feet.)

CHESTER: Why don't you let her see the truth? Why do you lie to her? At least you know who you are.

TRAVIS: I'm just a person.

CHESTER: You hide yourself. Even though you have everything to show.

TRAVIS: Go home. Go home and go to sleep, and don't make eye contact with anyone on the way there. Lay low until I can figure out what to do.

(Chester nods and slogs toward the door. He turns around —)

CHESTER: Can I have my spike back?

TRAVIS: No. Go home.

CHESTER: She gives her love to the wrong man. You throw it away.

(He exits. Travis locks the spike up in his desk. He paces around, blowing off steam. He gathers the pieces of garbage on the stage. He picks up the nunchucks. He puts them in his pocket.)

SCENE TWO

Late. Veronica's living room. There's a knock at the front door. Veronica answers it. It's Travis.

TRAVIS: I ran out of my house as soon as I got your message. What happened?

VERONICA: Bad stuff, Travis.

TRAVIS: What's going on?

VERONICA: I left my garage door open and the fence was open and one of Dr.

Peters' horses wandered into my garage and I came out and she was licking a puddle of antifreeze —

TRAVIS: My God.

VERONICA: So I called Dr. Peters and he called the vet and they took her away and now she's gonna die.

TRAVIS: No, she's not. They'll pump her stomach or something —

VERONICA: No. The antifreeze is going to destroy her kidneys and she's going to die.

TRAVIS: Her kidneys are going to be fine —

VERONICA: And Dr. Peters is being so goddamned nice but I just want him to get mad at me, y'know?

TRAVIS: The horse is going to be fine —

VERONICA: I want him to tell me that I that I'm a horse killer, that I fucked up —

TRAVIS: OK, listen: When I was three years old I drank antifreeze.

VERONICA: What?

TRAVIS: I drank antifreeze when I was three years old. We were visiting my uncle in Canada. I found this bottle of antifreeze with the lid off and drank it. I remember that it tasted like punch.

VERONICA: You're lying.

TRAVIS: My mom found me, she freaked out, they took me to the hospital. Pumped my stomach. Then on the way home, in a fit of rage, my dad threw my uncle out of a moving car.

VERONICA: Get out —

TRAVIS: They didn't speak to each other for two years. And my kidneys are OK, and I'm fine. So Dr. Peters' horse is gonna be all right. You aren't a horse killer, OK?

VERONICA: Yes I am.

TRAVIS: No, you're not. Animals are tough. When I was a kid I had a dog that used to eat glass.

VERONICA: Shut up.

TRAVIS: His name was Reggie. Eating glass was like his hobby or something. They had to operate on him twice to take things out of him. And one day, he broke into this packet of razor blades —

VERONICA: OK, you're just messing with me now.

TRAVIS: Yes, I am.

VERONICA: So stop.

TRAVIS: OK.

(A short pause.)

VERONICA: I watch them from my window. The horses. I used to watch TV, but now I watch horses. Let other people have a view of the ocean — I've got a postcard for a window.

When I watch them I wonder what they're thinking. What would you think of if your entire world was reduced to just grass and a blue sky?

TRAVIS: I don't know.

VERONICA: I think that if it was just that, and you didn't know what was coming next, then the only thing you could possibly be is happy.

What am I doing here? What am I doing?

TRAVIS: You are a great teacher in a school that is desperate for great teachers.

VERONICA: It's cold and windy and I've got to drive everywhere. People stare at me like I have Spock ears. And I hate country music.

TRAVIS: You'll get used to it.

VERONICA: I don't belong here.

TRAVIS: Everyone loves you.

When I first moved here someone threw a yellow-painted brick through my window. I think it was Heck. But all of these people love you because you're this amazing person.

VERONICA: But I'm not. People need to get that straight —

TRAVIS: I think that they've got you figured out.

VERONICA: No. If they're nice to me it's because you came here first and stuck it out.

TRAVIS: I didn't do anything.

VERONICA: You turned these people from being ignorant bigots into . . . Well, they're still ignorant, but at least they aren't throwing bricks through our windows.

TRAVIS: If they can't get rid of you then they eventually get used to you.

VERONICA: Did you know that's kind of courageous, Travis?

TRAVIS: I just can't tell when I'm not wanted.

VERONICA: I'm glad that you're here. God, I sound so wack right now.

TRAVIS: Wack?

VERONICA: Bobby Sorenson kept making blow-job hand motions at Elisha Nelson so I sent him to the principal, and on the way out he very loudly told the class that I was wack —

TRAVIS: You are so not-wack.

VERONICA: I'm glad that I'm not alone.

TRAVIS: Never in your life would you have to worry about something like that.

VERONICA: I don't know how you handled it. Being out here by yourself.

TRAVIS: It doesn't matter where we are. It's just —

(She moves closer.)

VERONICA: It's who's there with us.

TRAVIS: Yeah.

(He kisses her. She yields, but pushes him away.)

VERONICA: We can't, Travis. I'm involved with your friend.

(A short pause.)

TRAVIS: Is it because of my friend or because of something else?

VERONICA: What?

TRAVIS: Where is my friend?

(She backs off. No response.)

TRAVIS: All right, I should . . . I'll go.

(He exits. She straightens the pillows on her couch, and she lies down and closes her eyes.)

SCENE THREE

The classroom. Del sits in one of the student chairs turning a piece of paper around in his hands. Travis enters with his briefcase.

DEL: Hi Travis. Um —

TRAVIS: I've got a class starting. What's up.

(He hands Travis the piece of paper.)

DEL: Read it.

TRAVIS: *(Reads.)* "Something isn't being said. You're keeping something from me . . . I want you to know that I don't care what it is. What I do care about is that you are keeping secrets from me even though you said that you wouldn't hide . . . So I want you to tell me . . . What changed. Because I don't see you much anymore. And I miss you. Love, Veronica."

(Beat.)

What does this mean? Does she know?

DEL: I don't know.

TRAVIS: Have you been spending less time with her?

DEL: There's a difference between me just coming by at night and me being there all the time.

TRAVIS: Of course there is. You're supposed to be there for her.

DEL: I can't be there all the time. Not the way she wants me.

TRAVIS: You do care about her, don't you?

DEL: Yeah. Course I do. But, I don't know — it's just not the same, me livin'
there . . . I guess . . . I —

TRAVIS: I understand Del, but it's not that hard if you want to be with her.

DEL: Being there all the time, so close all the time . . . If she's smiling then
everything's all right, but if she's not . . . Or if it's quiet then . . . Somebody's gotta say something, right?

TRAVIS: So . . . What?

DEL: I don't know what to say. What do I say to this?

TRAVIS: I don't know.

DEL: What am I supposed to say when she expects all of these things —

TRAVIS: I don't know —

DEL: That I don't know anything about —

TRAVIS: Well you're the one that's with her.

(A short pause.)

DEL: Please, write her a letter —

TRAVIS: No.

DEL: Just one last time —

TRAVIS: You told me to stop —

DEL: I know I asked you to, but I shouldn't have. I just need you to get me
back on track and everything'll be fine —

TRAVIS: If you care about her, then write the letters yourself.

DEL: Travis, please —

TRAVIS: *(Furious.)* You're the one she wants, you write the letters.

DEL: I can't do it, OK? I'm stupid and I need your help. OK? Is that what you
want to hear me say? 'Cause I don't want to lose her, Travis. You don't
know what that's like.

(A bell rings.)

TRAVIS: Go.

(Del stands there.)

TRAVIS: GO. Please.

(Del looks back at him, then exits.)

*(Travis opens his briefcase, stares at it, then takes out a book and shuts it. He
takes his seat at the desk.)*

SCENE FOUR

*The classroom, later that night. A flashlight in the darkness. Chester rum-
mages through the teacher's desk, sliding drawers open and shut, searching for*

something. He's dressed as a ninja. There's the click of a lighter. The cherry of a cigarette ignites. Chester swings the flashlight around to find Veronica sitting in a student chair, smoking a cigarette.

VERONICA: Get the lights.
   (Chester flicks on the classroom lights.)
VERONICA: What are you doing in my classroom?
CHESTER: Travis sent me to retrieve his old quizzes for freshman English. Because he's writing a new quiz, you see, and he wants to use the old ones for reference.
VERONICA: What's with the sneaking around?
CHESTER: I'm not sneaking around.
VERONICA: You're dressed like a ninja.
CHESTER: This is what I sleep in.
   (There's a hook sticking out of Chester's pants.)
VERONICA: Is that a grappling hook?
CHESTER: Yes. Why are you smoking a cigarette in your classroom?
VERONICA: I like to do secret things in secret places.
CHESTER: I should go.
VERONICA: You just broke in. Sit.
   (He sits.)
VERONICA: So . . . I know you hate my guts.
CHESTER: No, I — what makes you say that?
   (She hands him a letter.)
VERONICA: Read it. Aloud.
CHESTER: *(Hesitates, then reads:)* "Did I ever tell you that your physical attributes are what get me off the most?"
VERONICA: Keep going.
CHESTER: *(Reads.)* "Your silky-straight black hair, your, um, almond-shaped eyes . . . One of these nights before we get it on, do you think you could serve me some tea? Let us sexualize your traditions, my little dragon — "
VERONICA: That's a little out-of-character for Del, wouldn't you say? . . . Does it sound familiar?
CHESTER: No.
VERONICA: Come on, you little Malcolm lower-case x — I saw you slip that into my mailbox!
CHESTER: What do you want me to say? That I forged that letter? That I'm guilty of information warfare? Fine. Guilty.
VERONICA: Be straight with me. Tell me what you really think: Veronica, you

are a yellow cab sucking down white semen in an attempt to remove the jaundice from your complexion.

I've heard it before. And I don't care if you hate my guts.

CHESTER: I don't hate your guts. I hate the guts of your choices. You choose Del — DEL? He uses the word *dumb* as a noun — "you DUMB!" . . . And he used to beat me up in junior high because my parents made me get a crew cut.

VERONICA: You forgot the fact that he's white.

CHESTER: I was just getting to that.

VERONICA: You think that I'm ashamed to be Asian, don't you? How do you think I grew up? Nestled in pink sheets combing the blonde hair of my Barbie dolls? . . . I'm from New York City, pal. So don't think I'm immune to hate. It seeks me out just as much as it does you.

CHESTER: Then what purpose does it serve to slink into The Man's ivory embrace?

VERONICA: Because despite all that, I think that people shouldn't be separated into colors.

CHESTER: Hmmm.

VERONICA: There are only assholes and non-assholes. I choose who I love. And no one will choose for me.

CHESTER: Right. But some colors are better than others, aren't they?

VERONICA: Don't confuse my pride with being ashamed. I'm not ashamed.

CHESTER: So why only white men?

VERONICA: Because that's my choice.

CHESTER: Well, you may have your preferences, and I shall have mine.

VERONICA: And I suppose that your preference is that she be Asian.

CHESTER: Yes.

VERONICA: Why?

CHESTER: Because I have chosen to perpetuate my people. To maintain a strong culture in this outpost of barbarians. But don't think for a second that I want a kow-towing, subservient jade circlet of a wife.

VERONICA: You don't?

CHESTER: No. I want a strong, dynamic Asian Sister. With the rustic beauty of a pony-tailed farm girl off a Maoist propaganda poster. Because I want to find someone that understands me. That shares my skin.

But to encounter a Sister like yourself — one that rejects the Asian in the Asian Man . . . Why, it appalls and bewilders me.

VERONICA: So just because I'm Asian I'm automatically supposed to hook up with an Asian guy? There are only two of you in this town. Doesn't that kind of limit my options?

CHESTER: You haven't even given this little horsie a ride.

VERONICA: You? No way. But keep in mind that I'm not rejecting you based on race.

CHESTER: Well when you look at me, what do you see?

VERONICA: What?

CHESTER: Do you think that I'm harmless? . . . Do you think that I'm a weak, snivelling pussy that would rather cross the street and push up his glasses instead of confronting trouble?

VERONICA: No.

CHESTER: Then do you think I'm a nerd? A fuckin' FOB-style nerd studying for the GREs in the corner?

VERONICA: You're dressed like a ninja —

CHESTER: Ninjas are fucking cool, lady —

VERONICA: No, I don't think of you as a nerd. Do you think that *I think* that I'm superior to you —

CHESTER: Yes —

VERONICA: Because of who I choose to be with?

CHESTER: Yes — do you think that I'm a misogynist?

VERONICA: Yes.

CHESTER: Do you think I'm effeminate?

VERONICA: No. Do you think I'm a sucky-sucky love-you-long-time leg spreader?

CHESTER: No. Do you think that I'm a racist?

VERONICA: Absolutely — do you think that I would allow myself to be submissive —

CHESTER: Yes —

VERONICA: I'm not finished — that I would stay in a relationship even if I was being mistreated?

CHESTER: . . . No. So do you think that I'm cold, unemotional —

VERONICA: No; do you think that I'm ashamed of myself?

CHESTER: Why, do you think that I'm ashamed of myself?

VERONICA: I think you are.

CHESTER: Then I think you are. Let's get to the meat: Do you think that I have a small penis?

VERONICA: Yes. Do you think that I want to be white?

CHESTER: Yes.

VERONICA: Do you think that I hate myself?

CHESTER: Yes.

   (Beat.)

   Do you think that I hate myself?

VERONICA: Yes.

   (A long pause.)

CHESTER: And what about Travis?

VERONICA: What about Travis?

CHESTER: I don't care what you think about me. But do you think the same things about him?

VERONICA: I don't know.

CHESTER: What would you do if he made a move on you?

VERONICA: We're friends.

CHESTER: Right. Travis is the friend and Del is the personal rodeo system. Gotcha.

   You know, you're amazing, lady. You think you're flapping around the heavens on your white winged steed, but . . .

VERONICA: But what?

CHESTER: I'm just saying, you might not like egg yolks, you avoid 'em as much as possible, but sometimes you just can't help biting into them.

VERONICA: You're weird.

CHESTER: I've been called worse. Especially by your cow-boyfriend.

VERONICA: If you're trying to allude to some problems Del and I are having, it's none of your business.

CHESTER: Sure.

VERONICA: But if you know something that you're not telling me —

CHESTER: I know what I know what I know.

VERONICA: And you knowing something that I don't truly sickens me. So spill it.

CHESTER: I have nothing to spill.

VERONICA: How about now?

   (She produces the Last Spike, holding it before him like a dagger. His eyes seize upon it, hypnotized —)

VERONICA: I found it locked up in the desk. And I've heard the back story of how it turned up missing at the railroad celebration. "Stolen" is the exact word used. So if someone wants it, all he has to do is spill his guts.

CHESTER: This is a bribe?

VERONICA: I'm either giving it to you or the cops.

CHESTER: And that's all you're offering?

VERONICA: What more do you want?

CHESTER: The spike and a thirty minute make-out session.

VERONICA: You only get the spike.

CHESTER: Lady, do you think that I'd snitch out a Brother? And for what . . . For a measly spike-shaped piece of gold? These aren't my secrets. They're not mine to give. And that's something you don't know about the Asian Man — something you'll never know. He's Upright. And he doesn't need your gold or anybody else's.

(As he's out the door —) So you do what you will with that. And if you ever want to see if you're right, call me up. I'll come over and whip it out. (He exits.)

SCENE FIVE

Outside Travis' house, that night. Sound of traffic on a nearby country road. Del is smoking the roach-remains of a joint. Travis enters with a bag of groceries, approaches.

TRAVIS: Put that out.

DEL: It's almost gone anyway.

TRAVIS: I don't want people seeing some guy smoking weed in front of my house —

DEL: You care what they think. I ain't got that problem.

(Travis fumbles for his keys, makes a failed attempt to open his front door —)

DEL: I moved back to my dad's ranch. Or at least I tried, 'cause . . . When I woke up this mornin' . . . You know that plan I had to put the blame on Bill if my dad caught me smoking weed? Bill thought of it first.

TRAVIS: Are you all right?

DEL: You know my old man. He doesn't like to raise his voice, so all my stuff had already been put in my truck. Secured. No good-byes. Just nowhere to go. *(Re., the joint.)* Though I managed to steal a consolation prize from Bill.

(He produces a small .38 revolver from his back pocket.)

DEL: And a parting gift from dear old Dad.

TRAVIS: Give me that —

(Travis tries to snatch it, but Del pulls it away.)

DEL: No way, son. If I give it to you now, I won't be able to use it later.

TRAVIS: Goddamn it Del, you give me that gun —

DEL: If you ask nice sometime, I may let you borrow it.

TRAVIS: Where's Veronica?

DEL: Back at her place. She sat me down, told me to write her a letter, right then and there. So I took your advice. I did.

TRAVIS: What did you tell her? . . . You didn't —

DEL: Where did all of it come from, Travis?

TRAVIS: I don't know.

DEL: Man, I am such a *dumb* . . . I'm such a stupid *dumb.* My balls are cold and empty, and I wanna die.

    The person you've made us out to be is a lie. He's fiction. And I can't live up to that. What she and I had didn't even match. *(A short pause.)* Do you love her?

TRAVIS: I never had a chance with her.

DEL: Fuck that. You love her, you do something about it. If you've got the skills to love her, you use them. Why did you let me take your place?

TRAVIS: Because I never had a chance. She has preferences.

DEL: Whaddaya mean "preferences"?

TRAVIS: You don't get it, do you? She doesn't like men of my persuasion.

DEL: What?

TRAVIS: She doesn't date Asian men.

    (A moment as Del tries to comprehend this —)

DEL: Why the hell not?

TRAVIS: I don't know.

DEL: That's crazy. You're Ko-rean, she's Ko-rean —

TRAVIS: She's only attracted to white men.

    (Del tries to comprehend this as well —)

DEL: Aw, that's horse shit! She loves your letters — it wouldn't matter if you were a chimpanzee. You were just afraid to give 'em to her on your own —

TRAVIS: No. It's because you are my friend. And if you've got a chance and I've got none, I have to give you what I've got.

DEL: But that's not the American Way, Travis. That's, like — I don't even know what that is — but it ain't right.

TRAVIS: Look, you're the one she wanted.

DEL: Why me? Look at me, Travis! I've been wearing these same pants for three years. I won this hat in a contest. My dad keeps a collection of priceless gold coins and I steal his cheap motherfuckin' gun? . . .

TRAVIS: Yeah, look at you. You're all rippled and blonde, and everyone wants a piece of apple pie —

DEL: Without you I wouldn't have had a chance with Veronica.

TRAVIS: But the ladies sure do love the cowboys.

DEL: I'm not a real cowboy, Travis. Let's get that straight right now. The real cowboys are dead. All that's left is dude ranches and souvenir belt buckles. This ain't about cowboys. This is about you feeling sorry and scared for yourself. And I don't like having cowards as friends.

TRAVIS: I'm a coward? Look, you had me write the letters for you because you couldn't get up the nerve —

DEL: I haven't spent the last few years hiding in a little shithole town where I don't belong! For what? 'Cause you can't own up to yourself —

TRAVIS: It was my choice to come here. I decided to start over —

DEL: Starting over means beginning a brand-new life. But you won't do that — you refuse to take any chance that comes to you —

TRAVIS: What do you want me to do?

DEL: Speak for yourself. But you won't. Because you ran away from your own life. You came here to die.

(A short pause.)

TRAVIS: Does she know who really writes the letters?

DEL: Do what you shoulda done and ask her yourself.

(Del re-lights the joint, takes a drag.)

TRAVIS: What are you going to do with the gun?

DEL: Drive back to my dad's ranch and kill everyone I see. *(Beat.)* I'm just kidding, man. I'll probably sell it at a pawn shop. I wasn't gonna do nothing with it. It ain't even loaded —

(The gun goes off in Del's hand — he drops it, and both of them leap out of their skins —)

TRAVIS AND DEL: JESUS CHRIST!

(A pause as they check themselves for bullet holes — they're intact.)

DEL: You shot?

TRAVIS: No, are you?

DEL: I'm all right, I think. Ow . . . What'd I tell you, Travis? I ain't no cowboy.

(Del offers the joint to Travis, who declines. Travis gingerly picks up the gun.)

TRAVIS: Come inside. You can stay with me.

DEL: I was hoping you'd say that.

TRAVIS: You think she'll be mad?

DEL: Yeah. But she probably won't stay that way forever. After all, she didn't want another cowboy, Travis. She wanted you.

(They stare at each other as the sound of traffic slowly fades to silence.)

SCENE SIX

The classroom, the next day. Veronica hastily packs her things into a cardboard box. Travis watches her from the doorway —

TRAVIS: Grady says that he wants to give you your own classroom. So I take it you're moving your things there?

VERONICA: *(Cold.)* No, Travis, I'm not.

(An awkward pause.)

TRAVIS: So you know who really writes you the letters.

VERONICA: Your scumbag friend ratted you out.

TRAVIS: Chester?

VERONICA: No. Del.

    See, that's courage, Travis. You could learn a lot from him. He popped his head out of his little rat hole even though a lawn mower was about to run right over it —

TRAVIS: Veronica —

VERONICA: You lied to me —

TRAVIS: I meant everything that I said to you in those letters —

VERONICA: With the exception of Del's signature at the bottom. You scared me into thinking that he couldn't fully open up to me. He had to write me letters to communicate? . . .

TRAVIS: Oh God —

VERONICA: You made me question myself and our relationship, and in the end the whole thing turned out to be a gigantic lie.

TRAVIS: What was I supposed to do?

VERONICA: You were supposed to sign the letters, "Love, Travis."

TRAVIS: Yeah, well, you have preferences.

VERONICA: What the hell is that supposed to mean?

TRAVIS: Oh come on, Ms. When-The-Right-Man-Comes-Along — let me rephrase that — Ms. When-The-White-Man-Comes-Along!

VERONICA: Fuck you, Travis — you know I'm not like that —

TRAVIS: Sure. You're all set on being alone but shazam — along comes Del with his Ford F-150 —

VERONICA: You're ridiculous, you know that?

TRAVIS: Yeah, you think you've got a Genuine Cowboy, but oops, out pops a guy with chopsticks.

VERONICA: Yes, it's all my fault for thinking I was in a relationship with one great guy when, in reality, I was in a relationship with two dumbs —

TRAVIS: You wanted it all — all the poetry and romance combined with Mister steak-eating America —

VERONICA: And you were full of shit when you said that you didn't care. When you found out that I was attracted to white men it cut your dick off. And you decided to punish me —

TRAVIS: Hah —

VERONICA: Because of who I am —

TRAVIS: Then tell me what it means when a woman who is so afraid of being fetishized by the American porno industry declares that you are only attracted to — I mean, you only fetishize — white men. Isn't that just slightly hypocritical?

VERONICA: What?

TRAVIS: You heard me.

VERONICA: If I were you I wouldn't bring up Asian fetish porn.

TRAVIS: Why is that?

VERONICA: Because I've been to your house. And your underwear drawer isn't something that I'd show to your mother.

TRAVIS: Why, you . . .

VERONICA: That's right, I located it: *Oriental Lesbo Sluts #3? Spankable Japanese Panty-Nurses? FAR EAST FUCK FEST?!*

TRAVIS: It's not like porno companies produce non-Asian-Fetish porn! If I wanna see naked Asian women, I don't have a choice!

VERONICA: So do you think that you're being a racist when you buy that garbage?

TRAVIS: No. When I buy that garbage I'm being horny.

VERONICA: So you have aesthetic tastes and needs. And so did I. Del is sweet and simple, but that by itself isn't enough. By reading his letters he was showing me who he was. But when I found out that they weren't from him, my love for him fell apart. I let him down. And the love he was giving me was all fiction. You let me down.

TRAVIS: I didn't mean to.

VERONICA: And neither did he. But the two of you never figured it out. It wasn't about his skin. It was about how you made me feel. Because for a moment . . . For quite a few moments, you made me feel good. Was it real?

TRAVIS: You let me know from the start that you have preferences —

VERONICA: Then fuck the preferences.

But even then, you're still ashamed of who you are.

TRAVIS: No, I'm not.

VERONICA: Then what about Grace?

TRAVIS: What about her?

VERONICA: You let me think that she was Asian, but she wasn't. Grace Thompson. There is a shoe box in your closet full of pictures, wedding invitations. And Del told me the rest —

TRAVIS: That —

VERONICA: Her father said that if she went ahead and married you, her family would not be present at the ceremony. And so it never happened. And so here you are.

TRAVIS: That wasn't her fault.

VERONICA: But do you think that it was yours? . . . And when are you planning on letting that go?

(Travis is silent now.)

VERONICA: By the way, this belongs to your friend.

(She puts the Last Spike on the desk.)

VERONICA: I tried to bribe him with it, but the little creep wouldn't take it. That's courage.

(She heads toward the door.)

TRAVIS: Veronica, I'm —

VERONICA: I know you are. But it doesn't matter much anymore.

(She exits. Travis watches her go. He walks over to his desk, unlocks a drawer. He is about to put the spike in, but stops. He sits at the desk, holding the spike in his hands.)

SCENE SEVEN

Outdoors. A slow, warm spotlight comes up on Del wearing a baseball glove. He pitches out an invisible ball. Another slow, warm spotlight comes up on Travis on the opposite side, also wearing a baseball glove. He catches the ball. The game of catch continues.

DEL: Have you met TJ?

TRAVIS: He's your replacement, right?

DEL: Yeah. He's from Great Falls. Man, he's a professional. He brought a uniform to teach in and everything.

TRAVIS: The kids are going to miss you.

DEL: Me? Naw. They'll be all right. Though I am going to miss throwin' dodgeballs at 'em. That was a perk.

TRAVIS: Are you sure you want to move to L.A.?

DEL: It's Hollywood, Travis. I'm going to Hollywood.

TRAVIS: Hollywood is pretty much in L.A.

DEL: It is? Goddamn. They should let people know that.

Man, I wanna see palm trees and cars with hydraulic bumping action. I'm gonna learn to surf. I wanna get lost.

And I know it's an easy out with Veronica, but I figure it's for the best . . . Hey — remember that letter you wrote to her about Blue?

TRAVIS: Your horse?

DEL: Oh man, you got that all wrong. I hated that fucking horse.

TRAVIS: What?

DEL: He was a mean son of a bitch. We had this theory that he started the fire in stable.

TRAVIS: Horses don't start fires.

DEL: This one did! He'd do anything to escape. He was straight-loco. The night of the fire we let out the horses, and yeah — Blue burst out burning. But instead of lying down to die, he took off like a bolt. A fireball, man. And we never found his body.

TRAVIS: Really?

DEL: Yeah. He got away clean, one way or the other. And I always thought, "Good for him."

(A short pause.)

TRAVIS: It's gonna be hard starting over by yourself.

DEL: Don't worry about me, Travis. I got a roommate.

(Chester enters carrying a box filled with various Asian goods —)

CHESTER: Can we stop by my parents' place? I need to pick up my zither.

TRAVIS: Now this I can't believe. You're moving in with Captain Rice over here?

DEL: It'll be nice to know someone from my home town, even if he does have controversial beliefs. And if he gets to worryin' me I'll give him a poke in the eye.

CHESTER: And I'll do anything to escape from Randall and Betty's basement. I will miss Betty's apple turnovers, but she is willing to FedEx them.

TRAVIS: Where'd you find the money to leave?

CHESTER: I sold everything I own, including a few stolen cases of Fire Sauce culled from Taco Tuesday. Survivalists, Travis. They'll buy anything in bulk. And it's all worth it — I'm gonna inject myself into an enormous Asian female population.

TRAVIS: If you do, try to keep the hard-core militancy down to a low rumble.

CHESTER: Of course. I plan to bring the honey when I tempt the baby bees.

TRAVIS: *(Amused.)* It sounds like Chester A. Arthur is finally growing up.

CHESTER: PLEASE: Don't call me by my full name.

DEL: He doesn't like that.

CHESTER: Oh, and by the way — about —

TRAVIS: The Last Spike?

CHESTER: Yeah — did you —

TRAVIS: Well, Hallsey's been sniffing around but he hasn't been able to connect it to us.

CHESTER: Great. So can I have my spike back —

TRAVIS: NO. I got rid of it.

CHESTER: What?

TRAVIS: I walked along the railroad tracks until I forgot where I was. Then I dug a hole and buried it. I don't think that even I could find it again if I tried.

CHESTER: I see.

TRAVIS: I'm glad that you do.

CHESTER: Travis, before I depart, I wanted to say that . . . I never knew what brotherhood was until I met you. Before you arrived, I was an only child.

TRAVIS: That's probably the most touching, least-offensive thing I've ever heard you say.

CHESTER: Well, we Vietnamese know the importance of family.

(Travis and Chester shake hands.)

DEL: Come with us.

TRAVIS: I can't.

DEL: Come on, Travis. You got nothing left for you here. Heck's gonna close up the bar and become a greeter at Wal-Mart. And Shelby's going under because of the Albertson's in Cheyenne. Everyone's taking off.

TRAVIS: Well, I'm staying. I like it. I can finally sleep.

DEL: All right, Travis. *(Nods to Chester.)* You wanna get on?

CHESTER: Yeah. I wanna see an ocean.

(To Travis.)

Stay strong, my Brother.

DEL: So long, cowboy.

(Del and Chester exit.)

(Travis squeezes his baseball glove, handles the invisible ball in its palm. He tosses it way up into the air and catches it. He repeats, playing catch by himself in slow, lonely turns.)

SCENE EIGHT

The classroom, the next day. Veronica sits at the teacher's desk. Across its surface are piles of scratcher tickets. She scratches them off one by one. Travis enters, surprised to see her. She quickly begins to gather up the tickets.

VERONICA: I know all of my things are supposed to be out of your room, but — I'll be gone in a second —

TRAVIS: No, it's OK. *(Re., the scratcher tickets.)* I thought you just collect them.

VERONICA: Yeah, well . . . I thought I could stand to open myself up to a little disappointment.

TRAVIS: Did you win anything?

VERONICA: Seven years ago I won fifty thousand dollars.

TRAVIS: You're kidding.

(She hands him a scratcher ticket.)

TRAVIS: *(Reads.)* "Happiness."

VERONICA: Do you think I should be upset?

TRAVIS: It depends on whether you think fifty thousand dollars is a lot of money.

VERONICA: I could've used it seven years ago.

TRAVIS: And now?

VERONICA: There are more important things, don't you think?

(A short pause. She gathers up the scratcher tickets.)

TRAVIS: You know, I walked to school today along the highway. I hadn't done that since I first got here. I walked past Dr. Peters' place —

VERONICA: Travis —

TRAVIS: Looking for you. I looked through the window of your cottage, saw that the place was empty — nothing left, not even a jar with a dead animal floating in it —

VERONICA: Travis, please . . .

TRAVIS: I was looking for you because —

VERONICA: Maggie's driving me to Jackson. I've got a flight to catch.

TRAVIS: I wanted to give you this.

(He produces a sealed envelope.)

VERONICA: So what does it say?

(He holds it up, still sealed —)

TRAVIS: It says that . . . It's strange how we can become whatever we want on paper.

It says that it's a powerful thing, the closest thing we have in the world to real magic.

That when you write something down, you become words, you shed everything that you really are. And I was ready to become whatever you wanted in order to earn your love. Because you collect scratcher tickets. Because you came two thousand miles to just try it out. Because you're funny, and you're beautiful, and you're a nerd.

And it says that I'm sorry that I was afraid to love you, and that I'm not afraid anymore.

Because all these things that you are, Veronica: They are greater than the sum of my fears.

And then it says my signature at the bottom.

(He offers it to her.)

VERONICA: I can't.

TRAVIS: Why not?

VERONICA: Being loved on paper is not enough. I need to learn how to love someone in person. And so do you.

TRAVIS: Maybe we can learn to do that together.

VERONICA: I'll tell you what, Travis: I'll make you a deal. Give me some time. Take some time for yourself. And then you come find me.

TRAVIS: Veronica —

VERONICA: When you're ready, you come find me. I won't hide.

(She produces a stack of letters bound by a string. She places it on the desk.)

TRAVIS: No — I want you to keep them.

VERONICA: But they're yours. Hold on to them. Look them over, see who you really are.

(After a pause, he accepts the letters. She takes her things and exits. Travis stares at the closed door, paces. He looks at the stack of letters in his hand. He tears off the string, quickly scans the first letter and throws it on the ground. He looks over another letter, throws it away, he tosses all of the letters into the air. They float downward in a cloud, and Travis looks up at them as if lost in a storm. And he rushes over to the door, opens it to go after her — But Veronica is standing there behind it, her back turned, apparently trying to convince herself to walk away. They are surprised to see each other. He smiles. And she does as well. She holds the door open for him. And he exits with her, closing the door behind him.)

END OF PLAY

IN THE CONTINUUM

Danai Gurira and Nikkole Salter

To the memory of my phenomenal, fearless grandmother
Miriam Mutambara Chiza.
Let me become just half the woman she was . . .
—— DANAI GURIRA

PLAYWRIGHTS' BIOGRAPHIES

Danai Gurira was born in the United States to Zimbabwean parents. She was raised in Zimbabwe and earned her MFA at NYU. Her theater career includes *The Story,* Philadelphia Theater Company; *Forbidden City,* Lincoln Center Workshop; *God Botherers,* NYSF New Yorks Now; *King Baabu,* Edinburgh Theater Festival. Her film career includes *Trial of Charumathi* (short); *Patience"*(UNESCO). Her television career includes *Law and Order CI.* She just filmed *The Visitor,* Tom McCarthy's (*The Station Agent*) second film, opposite Richard Jenkins. She has received the following awards: Laura Pels Acting Award (NYU), Global Tolerance Award from Friends of the UN for *In the Continuum.* Thanks to family and friends for unshakeable support and to the Lord, my God: my muse, my light. And to the women of Africa, my beautiful Africa: I live and strive to give you voice.

Nikkole Salter's regional theater career includes The Story, Kesselring Project; Stop Kiss, Studio Tisch; Jitney, Studio Theater, Washington D.C. At NYU she performed in such plays as *King Hedley, We Won't Pay,* and *Gum.* Her film and television career includes *The Architect, Pride and Glory, Whispers* (UCLA short film), and *Moesha.* She has received the following awards: Howard University Hilltop Scholar; NYU Graduate Acting Fellow; Global Tolerance Award from the Friends of the United Nations for *In the Continuum.* Nikkole is a graduate of Howard University's College of Fine Arts and NYU's Graduate Acting Program.

ORIGINAL PRODUCTION

In the Continuum had its World Premiere at Primary Stages, New York, September 11, 2005. It was directed by Robert O'Hara with the following cast:

ABIGAIL .... Danai Gurira
NIA .... Nikkole Salter

CHARACTERS
ABIGAIL
NIA

SETTING
South Central Los Angeles and Harare, Zimbabwe.

NOTE

This piece was born of two actors deeply concerned about the experience of black women in the present fight against HIV/AIDS. Presently, with black women being the population with the highest rate of new infections both in the United States and Africa — the co-creators of this piece (one African and one African American) felt the need to have a story told from the black woman's perspective: for her to be more than a statistic on a news report. This piece is designed for two actors to dramatize separate, yet parallel stories of an African and African American woman, and for both worlds to parallel and sometimes collide. Each character is real and is performed as such, not a commentary on a stereotype, but an illustration of three-dimensional human experiences in these societies. The piece as presently designed allows each actor to create their environments, both with sound and movement and minimal props. It is a minimalist piece, performed with no set, and only two stools on stage. Lighting and sound elements can enhance the creation of each world but are used supportively and only when necessary — the actors create the environment with their bodies and voices. Though the piece is performed with mainly one character onstage at a time, there are moments where the worlds are shuffled in such a way that both the performers and worlds flow, overlap, juxtapose, and cohabitate the stage throughout the performance. The stage directions are meant to clarify the way the piece is presently performed, but they are by no means meant to restrict future incarnations of this piece.

In the Continuum employs overlapping dialogue using this symbol: //. It will appear inside a particular character's line. It simply means that the next character to speak should begin his or her line where the // appears in the speech of the character who is currently speaking.

The symbol * means that the characters speak almost simultaneously, closely trailing each other.

IN THE CONTINUUM

PROLOGUE: BACK IN THE DAY

*Children playing together — Child #1 in South Central, Los Angeles, California; Child #2 in Harare, Zimbabwe. (The symbol * means Child #1 and Child #2 speak simultaneously, with Child #2 slightly trailing Child #1.*

*CHILD #1: Come on! Com' on! I wanna play . . . I wanna play hopscotch! Come on! Hopscotch! Get some chalk. Oh. Just get a brick. Bang it out. Then you draw a circle. *(Draws circle on the ground with a "brick".)* I'ma show you how to play hopscotch with a circle! Alright, I go first cuz I drew the circle? Ready? OK . . .

*CHILD #2: OK saka, totamba chi? Totamba nodo? Ya, saka mune chalk? Auna? Oh, ndaona, mirai, Mira ini ndotanga — necircle- mirai, totamba necircle, rakadai, rakadai *(Draws circle on ground with chalk.)* OK, ininidotanga, mirai, mirai.

BOTH: One! Two! THREE! *(Child #1 throws her marker into the circle. Child #2 throws stone in the air, tries to catch it, and it flies behind her.)*

CHILD #2: Oh, shiiit.

CHILD #1: No!

*CHILD #2: Aiwa, it's still my turn, aiwa, no man, ahh, saka apanaairkutamba, apanaarikutamba! *(She rubs out the chalk with her feet.)*

*CHILD #1: No, it don't have to land in the middle! No it don't! It can land anywhere in the circle! You stupid! Fine! Fine! *(She rubs out the chalk with her feet.)* Then nobody's playin' then! Nobody playin'!

BOTH CHILDREN: *(Singing and dancing together.)* Tomato sauce, sauce,
    Sauce, sauce, sauce, sauce (2x)
    Elizabeth, abeth,
    Abe, be, be, beth (2x)
    Chipikinringo, go
    Go, go, go, go (2x)
    Cousin's on the corner in the welfare line
    Brother's in the slammer, he committed a crime
    Preacher's in the club on the down low creep
    And yo' mama's in the gutter screamin' HIV
    (The children no longer play together.)

*CHILD #1: What you say about my mama?

*CHILD #2: Mati mama wangu ane HIV?

*CHILD #1: *Yo' mama got HIV.*

*CHILD #2: Mama wako ane HIV.

*CHILD #1: Yo' mama, yo' daddy, yo' whole generation got HIV!

*CHILD #2: Amai wako, nebaba, nemhuri wako futi.

*CHILD #1 You stupid! And you got HIV! And yo' mama got a cauliflower in her pussy!

*CHILD #2: Iwe maka pusa, unane HIV neamai wako ane masores panapa. *(Child points to her crotch.)*

BOTH CHILDREN: Uuuggh!

ONE: IN THE BEGINNING

The two actresses enter their separate worlds as Abigail and Nia. Abigail walks in looking over a news report. She takes a seat. Nia is in a stall of a bathroom in a hip-hop night club, hovering over the toilet.

ABIGAIL: Good evening and welcome to the eight o'clock main news bulletin. I am Abigail Murambe.

Harare: The minister of agriculture comrade Nixton Chibanda warned against any reports by the biased and slandering Western Media which assert that Zimbabwe is facing a famine. He further commented that these irresponsible journalists and their evil cohorts have been the source of Zimbabwe's expulsion from the Commonwealth as well as the crippling sanctions imposed by the United Nations. He asserted that contrary to such reports, Zimbabwe will in fact produce a surplus of agricultural crops in the coming harvest. He admonished against nastyers who . . .

Ahh, ahh, what is nastyers? Naysayers? Whooa, ah, but it says nastyers ka. And what's a naysayer, someone who says nay? Ah, hey, are we in Shakespeare or what. OK, why can't they just say liars or something?

Ahh, ahh, look at all these typos man!! And since when was the vice president's name Janet Mujuru? It's Joyce Mujuru, you want to get me killed?

NIA: *(She vomits.)* It feel like I'm dying.

No, I'll be OK. Just give me a second.

I haven't had nothin' to eat — I keep throwin' everything up, nasty cafeteria food. All I had was that Long Island Iced tea. I should eat something.

No, don't go. Give me a minute. I'll get it myself.

It coulda been in the weed, I don't know — I ain't the weed expert.

They was passin' it, it was free, I took some. I think it's somethin' else.
Nothin' taste the same, don't nothin' smell the same —

I ain't old! Just cuz you popped outta yo' mama coochie yesterday
don't make me *(Starts to throw up.)* — . Trina, just pass me some tissue.

ABIGAIL: Ewe, wait, is there any shine here? OK *(Drops tissue to the floor, Nia
picks it up.)* And, can I have the rest of the report please?!

Hey, it's getting harder and harder to say this stuff.

Huh? No I wasn't saying anything. But, Evermore, have you gotten
your pay check? Ah, NO I haven't, it's been six weeks now, how am I supposed to pay school fees with air? Right now I am near penniless. This is
what we get for working for the government, ini I want to move into the
private sector, South Africa man! SABC! Real money, shamwari! Ah, I am
just as good as them, probably better! Then from there, who knows?
CNN!!! Why not, I bet I am just as good as them, probably better. *(Nia
flushes the toilet and exits the stall.)* Where is my tea by the way, Evermore,
can you please, please bring me my tea BEFORE we start, I need to calm
my nerves. Four sugars *(Sits down, goes over report.)*

NIA: My breath smell like raw fish and old tacos.

No, I don't wanna go. *(Looking in the mirror.)* I got all dressed up to
celebrate with Darnell, so that's what I'ma do. I don't see him every day
no more, so when he get here I gotta look good.

(Fixing her hair.) No, he always out doin' his college thang, but in
two more days, all this scholarship stuff will be done. We been together
ten months and three weeks, I can wait two more days. *(Searching for lip
gloss.)*

Yep, it's almost been a year. He practically my husband. *(Applying lip
gloss.)* We been through so much. Last summer, he got jumped by some
Piru niggas; girl, I was so scared! But I was the first one to visit when he
got home. And when everything went down at my mom's *(Searching for
mascara.)* I would run away from the foster homes and Darnell let me
sneak and stay with him till I got a spot at Good Shepard. And if that
ain't love, — He even came to see me when I won that poetry contest.

Girl, yes! They had a big banquet; I got $500 and a plaque. *(Apply-
ing mascara.)* The judges said I was — what they call it? — "full of potential." I know I didn't have no potential before, but now that I can talk
they poetry language, I'm full of potential. It ain't hard, you just follow a
pattern, OK like:

Bright ass sun-ny day — 5 syllables
Burn-in' the shit out-ta me — 7

I wish it was cold — 5

No, I think about them all the time. It just come to me like that.
You try. It's just like flowin', you can flow. Look, I'll start you:

Dir-ty ass, skank . . . hoe —

Wit yo' crun-chy hair — (To Trina.) wit yo' fake weave? — no, no,
wit yo' crun-chy ba-by hair —

Leave Dar-nell a-lone —

(Continuing to apply mascara.)

ABIGAIL: By the way, before I forget, I want to be dressed by Truworths next
time, Edgars keeps bringing these clothes that make me look like I have
grandchildren. Thank you for that Evermore, I know I am a married
woman, that doesn't mean I have to look like I am selling vegetables
paroadside. Next time they bring such things I am just going to say no,
they must know I am their model, saka they better make me look good.

NIA: Shut up, Trina! I always look good. *(Putting mascara away.)*

Please! I look better than those groupies — so.

So what! Darnell looked at them, so what! Girls walking around
with they titties hangin' out tryin'ta get looked at. *(Fixing her clothes.)*
Tonight, I'ma let him celebrate. But then, Saturday night, after his scholarship ceremony, *(Doing a sexy dance.)* I'ma give him somethin' to look at.
(She laughs.)

What?

My new purse?

Yeah, it was a gift — courtesy of Nordstrom.

Girl, please. A playa like me don't pay fo' nothin'. *(Pretending to steal
the purse.)* Everything I got on was a five finger discount. Cuz, the way I
see it, it only cost fifty cents for these companies to make; they only pay
Javier and them ten cent to put it together; they pay me five wack ass dollars an hour, then they go sell it for a hundred and fifty? Do I look like
a dummy? Please, me takin' this purse is part of my community service.
I wish I would pay a hundred and fifty!

ABIGAIL: Mmm, mmm, Evermore, forget about that tea. I am not feeling well.
Ahh, we better do this thing quickly guys. Where's the cameraman? Oh,
oh, oh, is Gibson not here yet? Finish. But shame — he told me he has
no transport, hanzi he has to wake up at 3 A.M. to reach here by 7!
Ahh, times are hard suwa — munomuZimbabwe sha. Oh, is he still feeling sick? He wasn't looking very well. Shame . . . but you, Evermore,
you are looking plumper these days, where are you finding

sadza munomuZimbabwe? Please can you direct us? No, no tea please, I'm not feeling well . . .

NIA: I never get sick.

Never.

I don't be sick for real at school.

No! I be fakin'! Yeah.

I guess I'ma good actress — liar, actress, whatever. Like you ain't never lied about havin' cramps to get outta sex ed. Shoot, when I realized that worked, I would be havin' my period two, three times a month. It's not like they gon' check — What they gon' do? Look? Oooh! Oooh! Shh, shhh! Be quiet. You hear that?

ABIGAIL: Ahh, I think I hear Gibson out there.

NIA: That's my jam. Me and Darnell always dance to that. They would play our song when I'm on the toilet.

ABIGAIL: Yes Gibson, muri right? / Are you feeling better — good good. / Evermore checkai for lint! / Let's go. / Yes I am ready! / Wait where is my special ballpoint?! / Oh, it's OK, it's here. / Totanga ka! / Let's go!

NIA: Trina . . . ? / Trina, why you so quiet? / You takin' a dump? / You don't take a dump in a public bathroom! / You nasty! / *(Looking in the mirror.)* Yeah, I guess I feel a little better. / Do me a favor: go get me a breath mint or somethin. / Then hurry up!

(Gunshots. Nia runs out.)

(Blackout in Both Worlds.)

ABIGAIL: Oh, no tell me your joking, another powercut!! This is the third one today! We won't be finished till night time! Twenty minutes? OK please, ndapota. AND can we get some sort of lights here please!

Better be twenty minutes, last time it was over an hour. Ha, it's bad enough having to work so late all last week, you know ma in-laws they start to say marara — "Hey, hey that is why she only has one child" — imagine! "We want more children here, Simbi is getting lonely! You mustn't work so much!" This coming from in-laws who have never even given me a bubble gum or a fork at my wedding. But, *(Looks around.)* they can shut up now Evermore, baby number two is on the way!! Ya! Pururudza! Tofara tese! No, I just found out on Monday! Stamford doesn't even know yet, I am going to tell him and that family of his at Simbi's birthday party on Sunday. Ya, he's turning seven, he's a big boy now — time for another, one that looks like it's mother. Simbi looks just like Stamford with that big nose — shame. Stamford? He's fine. But he keeps doing too much of those late nights I told you about — I don't like it.

These men, they want to play away and have us at home at the same time — he's got to stop that. But I think another baby will make him act better; Auntie always said showing the husband you are a good and fertile wife will keep him indoors. Saka you chased your man out when you caught him with another woman Evermore? Ah no that's not the answer man — no it's not, because then that other woman, hure that she is, will get everything you have been working for! Ah, no, me, I realized the solution: Men are like bulls searching for pastureland, you show them greener grass and they stay put, and this baby is greener grass. He's going to stay put now. Hey, Stamford, he wants to forget how hard he had to work for me! I was known as the Ice Queen! Hmmmhmm! No one could get near me — I was very picky. I used to go to those house parties and I was the best dancer . . . EH HE, suwa, *(Gets up, begins to dance.)* ha, I've still got it! Do you remember this one Evermore? It was big around '92, '93 — I hated it but it was so popular I had to know how to do it — WELL. Do you remember what it was called — ABORTION!! Imagine! So nasty hey! And the men wanted to come from behind! Ha, no me I would say, "Just look hey, don't touch!" But then along came Stamford Murambe — to him I said, "You can touch, please touch!" Ya, ya he won me over, fair and square, but he had to persevere! With maletters, flowers what what! He wants to forget all of that!

He'll come around, he just needs another boy, that will help. A girl?! What am I going to do with a girl in this world? No, two boys that's perfect. And they're going to grow up in Chisipiti or Glen Lorne, — we are not going to stay in Hatfield anymore, ahh, it's too filled with strong rural types, too many muboi! No more people with chickens and goats in their backyard, I want to be around the poshy!! Those who know how to eat with a knife and fork. And our new house will have a swimming pool, DSTV, maybe a tennis court. Stamford will drive a Pajero, me — I'll drive the benz. And the boys will go to St. John's prep or Hartman house and learn the best these whites can teach, I have a good feeling about this baby he will become the next Kofi Annan, or Bill Gates — why not! Stamford will love this one so much, he will take one look at him and never forget where home is again.*(Phone rings.)* Oh, it's me! I didn't turn it off! Oh, its the clinic, let me take this Evermore . . . Hello . . . yes . . . this is Mrs. Abigail Murambe . . . *(Exiting.)*

NIA: *(Looking behind emergency room curtains.)* Trina . . . ?

Trina . . . oh, sorry! My bad.

Trina? Hey. How you doin'?

Did you do what I told you?

(Trying to remove her hospital bracelet to exchange.)

Lemme see your wrist then.

Why not?

You gave them your real information?!?

You did give them your real name! You such a scaredy cat. What they gon' do, spank you?

Cuz! Now they gonna call Good Shepherd and then everybody gon' be all up in our business. Has the doctor even come in here yet? Be right back? Please, if we was dyin' we'd already be dead. Lemme see it. *(She looks at Trina's wound.)*

It don't look like it bleedin' no more. *(Sitting.)* I think I got to get a couple stitches. The doctor asked me how I got glass stuck in my side. I was like, "*Duh! They was shootin', people was goin' crazy! You get knocked over and stomped on you while you lyin' on a floor full-a shot-up glass and see what happen to you!*" Yeah, you laughin' now, but you looked fucked up then. I ain't gon' lie — all I saw was blood, you know, and I got scared. I was like, *(Like an exaggerated mother crying over a child's coffin.)* "*Please don't let Trina die! Pleeeease don't let Trina, DIE! Not my baby Trina!*"

(Laughing.) Shhh! *You* silly!

Lemme see it again.

At least it's gonna make a cute scar.

I'm just glad *you* OK.

Trina, if I tell you somethin', you promise not to tell nobody? OK. The doctor wanted to give me a X-ray to see if I broke a rib or somethin', but she made me pee in a cup to see if I was pregnant first, and . . . I am.

I know.

I don't know — she gave me all these pamphlets, she did all these tests, now I'm supposed to —

Of course, I'm gonna tell Darnell!

Yes, I am! I'ma go right up to his practice, and I'm gonna take his hand and put it on my stomach, look up at him and say, "*Darnell, I'm pregnant.*" And he gon' look down at me and say, "*For real?*" and I'ma say,

"*ummm, humm.*" *(To Trina.)* I'm serious. Then, he gon' get on his knees and put his ear against my belly and listen. Then he gon' look up at me and say, "*My son in there?*" and I'ma say, "*umm-humm.*" *(She laughs.)* Then, we're gonna get married . . . move into a big ass house, cuz he's gon' play . . . He'll play for the Lakers and I'll, . . . I'll be rich doin' somethin'. Just like that, watch. *(Getting her cell phone out of her purse.)* I'ma call him right now. I will tell him. Just watch and learn. *(She dials.)* Voicemail? "*Hey, Darnell, it's Nia. Where are you? I was at the club waitin' for you. You will not believe what happened. I'll tell you when you come pick us up — me and Trina at the hospital.*
(To Trina.) I am!
(To phone.) And, uh . . . I . . . I got somethin' to tell you. Call me back. Why haven't you called me . . . ?"

THREE: THE DIAGNOSIS

NURSE MUGOBO: *(Banging her clipboard.)* Please, this is a clinic.

NIA: *(As if the nurse has told her that there is no cell phone usage in the hospital.)* Oh, I'm sorry. My bad.

NURSE: Can you control your children, they can't run around like monkeys.

NIA: I'm comin' back! Dag! *(Putting away her cell phone; applying lip gloss.)*

NURSE: *(Looks through folder, pulls out piece of paper.)* Right, Mrs. Choto? You are not Mrs. Choto. Mrs. Choto, Mrs. Choto!!!!

NIA: That is my real name.

NURSE: Ha, and vanhu vatema vanonetsa. *(Pulls out another piece of paper.)* Mrs. Murindi, Murambe, sorry, Abigail? Right. *(Looks through chart.)* I have your chart here . . .

NIA: My chart . . .

NURSE: Everything looks fi — oh.

NIA: What?

NURSE: You have tested HIV positive.

NIA: I'm sorry . . . what?

NURSE: This means you have the virus that causes the Acquired Immune Deficiency syndrome . . .

NIA: What?

NURSE: there is no cure for Aids, it is generally transmitted through unprotected penetrative sex //, with a person infected with HIV. Unprotected sex means sex without a condom, male or female, to protect the sexual organs. In Africa that is generally through heterosexual contact.

NIA: // You trying say I'ma hoe? Do I look like a junkie? Do it look like I'm gay? Do I look like I'm from Africa? No! Every time we come in here ya'll try to make us feel like we're dirty or stupid or something. *(Pulling out her cell phone.)* You don't know what the fuck you're talkin' about — s'cuse you — no, S'CUSE YOU! *(She exits.)*

NURSE: We therefore recommend that from now on *(Eyes wander.)* Ewe what are you doing? Yes I can see that — those are contaminated can't you see they are dripping on the floor? Take them to the back, barance. We therefore strongly recommend you practice abstinence from now on but if you must, please protect others, there are three condoms, sorry we have run out. If you want we can show you how to use them on a banana in the next room. *(Eyes wander.)* But then you will only have two. Excuse me. Eh, Mai Getty, are you going to the shops? Please sisi, can you buy me a sweet bun ne a coke, help me sha I am so hungry, thanks, aiwa, I have the money, mirai.

(Looks over at Abigail.) Ah Miss, Miss — *(Looks at chart.)* Miss Abigail, why are you crying? No, aiwa, you must think clearly mange. I see here you have a son? We can test him also. *(Finds no money in bra.)* Ahh, oh, thanks Mai Getty, you are a lifesaver. *(Back to Abigail.)* Right. And we must see your husband in the next few days — he must be formally informed and tested. Ah, Ah, Amai, Miss Abigail — there are no exceptions for that — I know it can be dangerous to tell him, many women are scared he will beat them and take the children — what, what, even though usually it's coming from him, but, sorry you tested first so you must tell him and bring him for testing. Even with the risky business of it. We must see him as soon as possible, nhasi riri Friday saka on Monday, latest; we can make the appointment right now.

(Looks down at chart.) Ah, *(Stops, puts down pen.)* you are pregnant? Ah . . . you women. You go and get this HIV then you want to get a baby or two? It's not good, munoziwa, its not good.

(Goes back to chart.) Drugs? Ah we don't have them here, if you have money you can try to find them, they are very, very expensive. Otherwise, change your diet — eat greens, negrains, nemeat. And don't breastfeed. We will test the baby soon after it is born.

So we will see you and Mr. Stamford Mirindi, sorry Murambe, on Monday, ten A.M. Please amai, if you don't come I will be forced to call him. Right. *(Flips to next chart.)*

Mrs. Choto, Mrs. Cho — there you are, you are late, sit down. Ha, and vanhu vatema vanonetsa.

FOUR: NIA'S DENIAL

NIA: Trina, get your stuff. We gotta go.

These doctors is crazy. I seen this shit on Sally Jesse —

Nothin's wrong — c'mon. Get your stuff. I called Patti. She's comin' to give us a ride.

Yes, I called probation Patti —

To get us a ride. Who else was I gonna call?

My mama? What for? She don't care about me. Why don't you call yo' mama? Darnell . . . forget Darnell —

Whatchu yellin' at me for? How is any of this my fault?

You the one said you could hang. You the one begged me to come — If you didn't go and get yourself shot we wouldn't have this problem.

Did I stutter? You the only idiot walkin' around when they shootin'. Ain't you ever heard gunshots before? You supposta get down. Duck, stupid! You messed everything up! We was supposed to sneak out, go to the Club, have fun, sneak back in — nobody would know. Now I gotta listen to Patti's bougie mouth all for what? — a bullet scratch and a couple-a stitches that you won't even see after two months with some cocoa butter? I'm the one made sure you got here and got taken care of. I coulda left yo' stank ass there. And just went back by myself. Then I wouldn't even be here — I shouldn't even be here —

Nothin's wrong!

I'm pregnant stupid! Whatchu think?

I don't know what you so worried about. All they gon' tell you is not to sneak out no more. I'm the one who can't go back to Good Shepard. I wasn't even supposed to be livin' there in the first place. If anybody should be mad, it should be me. I figured Patti was gon' find out anyway cuz you used your real name.

So if we gon' get caught, we might as well have a ride!

Just get your stuff. Let's go.

FIVE: HAVE MERCY

Abigail on the street, trying to flag down a ride.

ABIGAIL: *(To street kids.)* Fotsek! You kids get away. NO I don't have any money. Don't touch me! I'll beat you like your mother should have. *(Pause.).* Just go away. *(Phone rings.)*

Hello Stamfo-. Simbi. *(Laughs/cries — relieved.)* Hello big boy. How are you — no Mummy is just happy to hear from you that's all — ah but what did Mama say to you about calling her cell phone from the land-line? NO, I said its very expensive so you mustn't. What's wrong my beby, why are you calling me? Is Daddy home? No don't put him on. Simbi don't put him on. Don't. OK. *(Trying to flag down omnibus taxi.)* No, I am catching a commuter omnibus, so let Mummy go so that I can catch one OK. *(To street kids.)* Ewe fotsek, I said I don't have any money. No, no not you baby. What? What did you put in my handbag? On the left — Simbi, I don't have time for thi — OK, OK, OK what is this Simbi? This is beautiful, did you draw it yourself? So you are a big boy now. OK, so who is the first person? Quickly, quickly. That's Deddy, OK. And who is the one in the middle? That's Mummy?! OK! And who is the last one? That's you? Simbi you are funny! Why are you bigger than everyone else Simbi? But Simbi this is beautiful, we will to put it on the fridge when I get home. But Simbi, next time you draw Mummy don't draw her with hair that's going all over the place like that! Mummy's hair doesn't do that beby. Just draw me with simple hair, one, two, three neat strokes that's all. But this is beautiful. *(To pestering street kids.)* Go away, you kids, where are your parents . . . FOTSEK!!!!! Simbi, Mummy has to go now, OK, now you go to eat beby, see I just stopped one beby, I have to go. Mummy's coming. *(Rushing to catch ride. Stuffs drawing in bag.)*

SIX: CHATTER HEADS

PATTI: Nia!

PETRONELLA: Abigail!

PATTI: Not you Trina, you wait inside.

PETRONELLA: Abigail Moyo!

PATTI: Nia, you get in.

PETRONELLA: Get in, get in! It's me, Petronella Siyanyarambazinyika!

PATTI: *(To driver.)* Beach Avenue and Centinela, please.

PETRONELLA: How are you my dear??? I haven't seen you since, is it high school? Oh, my gosh its been too long! AH, but you're looking well, kept that figure. Just tell Lovemore where you want to go. The city center? *(To Driver.)* Is that safe Lovemore? OK. Good.

PATTI: I am not angry, Nia. Did you think I was angry? 'Cause I'm not. I'm worried, I'm dumbfounded, I'm completely devastated! We've been through Independent Living Classes, Life Skills Assessments, Job Readiness Training — we were getting somewhere, Nia! What was so important at this club that it was worth jeopardizing everything we've worked for? And I tell you, if I miss my flight to Milwaukee for the second part of the Journey toward Self Discovery Conference I'll —

PETRONELLA: And did I hear correctly that you married Stamford Murambe? HAA well done my dear, he was gorgeous!! What a bloody catch! Oh, you still have him right? Whew! But good work my dear, everyone wanted a piece of him!!! I too have officially joined the married club! Mmmhmm, just two years ago, do you remember Farai Mungoshi, Prince Edward, head boy, captain of the rugby team, a real feast for the eyes? No, I married his younger brother Richard.

PATTI: . . . you tell the universe exactly what you want to experience by the choices you make every moment. And we don't always make the best choices . . . even me. Like yesterday, I was having lunch in the cafeteria and I had not one, but two helpings of macaroni and cheese. Not the best choice, no, but it's not going to drastically change my life.

But you — you take the good job I found you at Nordstrom and chose to get fired by stealing — again. I've given you the easiest course curriculum developed for continuing education and you choose to throw away your chance at a diploma by ditching. You take the free housing in Westwood I gave you, and you were asked to leave because you wouldn't keep curfew. I've even violated the state's abstinence-only policy and given you condoms! Now you're telling me that one night of "hangin' wit the homies," "rockin' your phat gear" and "sportin'" your big chain with the medallion of the motherland and shakin' your booty with some boy at some club is worth getting shot at? *(Beat.)* No. Good answer. So with my choices . . . *I'm* telling the universe that I want to be fat. So what. Big deal. But *you're* telling the universe you want to be an uneducated, unemployed, homeless, kleptomaniac, soul train dancer. Is that what you want? If you were in my shoes, what would you do?

PETRONELLA: . . . oh you got those here? They look just look just like my Stella

McCartney pumps. I know her personally actually, she gave me a pair — she couldn't give them to her stepmum — she only has one leg! Did you say you worked ZBC? Oh, *(Laughs.)* no, I am sorry, I just got back home so I am still adjusting to all the lingo, and someone the other day called it Dead BC. Good for you though hey! You were always a great public speaker! Me, oh, well . . . I went abroad soon after high school, to study at London School of Economics, I was there for both my undergrad and my masters, International Relations with a focus on Human Rights and Gender Development, and I am still there mostly, I work as a consultant for big organizations, the UN, OXFAM, stuff like that. Right now, I have been really focused on HIV and Southern African women and of course all the big organizations abroad are going to hire me right? Perfect poster child — but I can't complain, I've been working with DATA — that's Debt, AIDS, Trade, Africa — Bono — he's a rock star — has an organization. *(Car swerves.)* Careful Lovemore!

PATTI: Ah, pardon, sir —

PETRONELLA: God, the way people drive in this country!

PATTI: Yes, but it clearly says, "no left turn" —

PETRONELLA: In England he would have been arrested on the spot!

PATTI: But it's illegal — well, I would hate to have to write down your number and report — it's just that it's a very risky turn and we have precious cargo.

Thanks.

(To Nia.) Perfect example: There are many ways to get to Inglewood, but making an illegal shortcut turn here is not one of them. There are no shortcuts, Nia! The laws are designed to keep us safe. And I hate to burst your bubble, but, no matter where you go there will be rules. On this road there are rules, gangs have rules, even in the wilderness there are rules. And there are consequences in choosing to violate the ru — are you listening to me? Nia, NIA!

PETRONELLA: . . . there's not even any bloody petrol! This is not the country we grew up in. How do you survive . . . anyway, concerning the whole AIDS issue — I'm actually trying to get some statistics — that's why I was at the clinic — naturally the head nurse was on a two-hour lunch or something! Zimboes! And of course you have to get the highest statistics possible in order to get them to do anything. That's when they get all aghast and say, "Oh those poor Africans who can't help themselves — let's bring them our great answers" — which are WHAT? OK — they are manufacturing some drugs here, but they aren't the best kind and how is anyone supposed to pay for them long term in this economy? It's a bloody mess! And you want to know why? You want to know why? I'll tell you why. It's because we've been programmed. We look to them as our source of hope and redemption. Meanwhile we have the answers and we don't know it. I have been thinking a lot about our own traditional AFRICAN healing. I am not saying they have the cures or whatever, but there is something to it, you can't argue that. Remember Sisi Thembi?

PATTI: . . . the value is not in material things. Nia, I don't know what I can give you that's more important than the opportunity to lift yourself up. That's what I did. Yeah. It may not look like it, but I'm from the 'hood — well, Ladera Heights — but I drove down Crenshaw every day — and it doesn't matter your race or gender or where you're from, it's where you're going. I think you want to stay in the ghetto because no matter what I show you, no matter where I put you, you carry it with you in your mind.

Now, you can either call that Emergency Services number and stay in a shelter for the night or you can go in there and try to patch things up with your mother. A girl needs her mother. My mother and I never got along either — it's 'cause she never really cultivated my garden of talents, it was either her way or no way, and I know you and your mother are experiencing a rift that is very similar, that's why I feel so close to — OK, OK, I know, I'm all in the Kool-Aid —

PETRONELLA: . . . remember when we caught her talking to trees?

PATTI: — my bad . . .

PETRONELLA: And she roasted grasshoppers?

PATTI: . . . I learned that yesterday.

BOTH: hahahahahhahahahahahaha . . . hheee . . . heee . . .

PATTI: Nia?

PETRONELLA: Abi?

PATTI: Are you alright? OK. Wait. I was surfing the Web yesterday and saw that the city is looking for poetry to display on the MTA trains . . . and I think your work is perfect. Go online, download an application and submit some of your work. If you win, it's more scholarship money that you can use if you decide to go to college. Your poems won at the Success is Our Future Ceremony, that's something. Believe you me there are plenty of opportunities out there for a girl like you. You can still be anything you want to be. Change the course of history. Don't let yesterday's bad choices keep you from making good choices today. But I know you.

I can tell, you're gonna do the right thing. There's no place for you to go but up — well, you could spiral down . . . OK!

PETRONELLA: . . . she was such a mad mad, MAD, woman Sisi Thembi, I can't believe she is in the church — like what, every day now? Oh what a shame — remember how she swore by witchdoctors? Remember how her daughter had some sickness no one could figure out — she said her witchdoctor — sorry — traditional healer — fixed it! She had to do some strange things but it worked and nothing else did. There is something to it I tell you. Oh, wooah, you want to get out here? What are you doing the car is still moving. Stop the car Lovemore! *(Getting out of car, yelling.)*

PATTI: Bye, Nia!

PETRONELLA: Abigail, wait!!!!

PATTI: *(Getting out of car, yelling.)* Nia, wait!

PETRONELLA: You work for ZBC — do you host that show Breaking New Ground?

PATTI: Tell you mother I said hello!

PETRONELLA: I really want to be on it, I think I have a lot to say that the country needs to hear, I am breaking new bloody ground . . .

PATTI: I'm an Audi.

PETRONELLA: How do you say "bye" again Lovemore? Oh — CHISARAI!!!

PATTI: I mean, I'm Audi.

PETRONELLA: NO, what's the other one — TICHAMBOONA!!! Bye . . .

PATTI: Five hundred! Nevermind . . . just . . . bye, Nia.

SEVEN: MAMA

Friday morning. Mama's porch. (* = Imani, a six-month old baby, crying.)

MAMA: *Hey! Hey!! Get offa my grass! Get offa my grass and take your Funyion bag with you. *(To herself.)* Bad ass kids. *(Beat.)* * I knew you'd come back. Lemme guess: They didn't believe your lies at Good Shepard either? You thought it was gon' be easy as that. Well, life is not easy, guess you have to learn the hard way. And now you wanna come back. I'm still goin' to family court cuz of the shit you pulled; anger management, freakin' parenting classes like I don't know what the hell I'm doin', and you wanna come back just like that? No apology, no nothin'? And then you got the nerve to ask me for $400. How you gon' pay me back, you got a job? You look like a damn prostitute. What are you wearin'? It's nine o'clock in the morning, walkin' round like you been walkin' the streets.

(Seriously.) You walkin' the streets, Nia?

Don't get smart with me!

Then what you need $400 for, huh? Probably some Guess jeans or something. What happened to that money from the poetry contest? Ain't nobody payin' you to put'ch'a little rhymes together no more? Ain't got no place to live, no job, but spend all yo' time writin' poetry and shoppin' for $400 Guess jeans. Are they self-cleaning? Do they pay rent? If anybody's getting $400 'round here, "*guess*" who it's gonna be — ME. I'm tired of comin' second to ya'll. I can't remember the last time I had me some lotion or some new panties. Besides, you grown, remember? And us grown folk, we pay for our own shit. You old enough. Hell, when I was nineteen I was * — And don't think you slick goin' behind my back askin' Marvin for the money. I thought you didn't like him. He ain't yo' daddy, so stop askin' him fo' shit. *(To Imani.)* He's yo' daddy, huh? Yo' daddy! *(To Nia.)* You should ask that lil' boyfriend of yours, Darnell, for $400. He'll buy them pants for you . . . since he the one like to get in 'em so often. Don't think I didn't usta hear your little narrow behind climbin' outta the window to go oochie coochie with that boy. Like you the first one discovered how to sneak outta the house. I invented that shit. I already been everywhere you been, Nia. And I was just tryin' to keep your fast ass from goin' to half of them places. But you grown. Well, I'ma tell you this: I know you like him, and he look like he goin' places,* but don't end up pregnant, Nia. Cuz once you turn this switch on, you can't turn it off, and I'ma be damned if I end up raisin' your kids cuz you couldn't use a condom. Oh, oh! *(To Imani.)* She woman enough to do the do, but she can't talk the talk. *(To Nia.)* What would you rather I say, strap on the jimmy? Pull the balloon over the sausage? I wish somebody had told me about this shit, half-a ya'll wouldn't be here. And now days, you can catch all kinda stuff. Stuff you can't get rid of cuz it gets in your blood. Trust me: Three minutes of slappin' bellies ain't worth death. And that's what it is, death. It's a government experiment. They've done it before and will do it again. You think it's consequential that we the ones got it the most out of everybody. They been tryin' to get rid of us since the Emancipation Proclamation. First they lynched us, then they got us high so they could send us to prison. Then they got the ones that ain't incarcerated to shoot each other and now they brought this hopin' we'd fuck ourselves to death. And you know they got a cure. What you think the whole civilian rights was about? That's why they assassinated Martin: to distract us from the monkey fuckers that brought it back from Africa to kill us. And they killed Malcolm cuz, on his pilgrimage, he found out who the monkey fuckers were. You got to know your history. It's outta control —

I know, I know, you love Darnell. Darnell love you. Ya'll invincible in love. Yes, I know. I was in love too. Five times. Remember that. All I had to worry about was getting pregnant, but you got a whole slew of other stuff to think about. Real love lasts forever, but so do real mistakes.

(To Imani.) Huh? And I'ma tell you, just like I tol' them, yes I am, yes I am, you only got me 'til you're eighteen. That's it! *(To Nia.)* That's it. Now you can go on in the back and get sixty dollars outta my purse so that you can get you a room to stay for the night, cuz you can't stay here. I ain't gonna let ya'll run my world forever. And I ain't gonna let you scare this man away. Uh, uh. One down four to go.

Hey! Look at them. HEY! Stop sprayin' paint on them walls, that shit ain't art.* *(She exits.)*

EIGHT: THE CHURCH

"Akuna wakaita saJesu" is being sung by the congregation, Abigail rushes in, trying to look normal, greets people and sing and dances along as she searches for Sisi Thembi.

ABIGAIL: *(Singing along.)* Hallo auntie! Muri right? Ya, Stamford is fine thanks!
Hi Pastor Manyika! How are you? No, we have had trouble with transport, no petrol ka! Otherwise twice a week I would come to worship!!
Shit!
(Sees Sisi Thembi.)
Sisi Thembi — Sisi Thembi wuya! Ahh!
(Makes her way through the pews.)
Excuse me, sorry, pamsoroi! Sorry baby, don't cry. Excuse me please . . .
(Reaches Sisi Thembi tries to sing, and look natural.)
Sisi Thembi, I need the address of the, eh, remember that man you said helped you when your sister or your cousin, ahh, when your relative was sick?

You know, the man with the eh, eh — herbs —
Come on the — *(Imitates a witchdoctor possessed.)*
THE WITCHDOCTOR MAN!!!!
(Everyone stops, music stops.)
He is the devil! Praise GOD!!!
(Raises arms in the air dancing, after awkward pause, music resumes.)
Come on Sisi — please!
(Gets address.)
121? Oh I know it.
Thanks Sisi — Thank you.
(Makes her way back through the pews.)
Excuse me, sorry, pamsoroi, sorry baby, pamsoroi . . .

(To congregation member.) Ha? Oh I am fine, I just felt the spirit telling me to go see a friend in need — but praise God, He is from where all blessings flow! *(Rushes out.)*

NINE: KEYSHA (SHORT FOR KEYSHAWN)

KEYSHA: Should you have his baby? Should you have his baby? Should a dope fiend in a crack house run from the police? Hell yeah, you should have his baby. *(To the waiter.)* Waiter! *(To Nia.)* No, I don't, Nia. I really don't see what the dilemma is. It's not like you got pregnant by some ole, dirty, jerry curl juicy, gold-tooth pimp. We talkin' Darnell Smith. Dar-nell Smith. The crem de la crem. Do you know how many girls pokin' nee-dles in condoms tryin'ta have his baby. And here you sit, on the come-up like Mary pregnant with Jesus, talkin' 'bout should have his baby. Have Miss Keysha taught you nothin'? What else you gonna do? That's Dar-nell Smith's baby and everybody know Darnell Smith. And these re-cruiters is lickin' his anus tryin' to get him to go to they school. I'm talking UCLA, Notre Dame. Indiana-A, all of 'em. And you know what's gonna happen when he get outta school. He goin' straight to the NBA. Do you know what that mean? Do you know what that mean? That mean we about to be set for life. For LIFE. I'm talkin' Malibu mansion, Mercedes Benz SL class on the Sprewells, Louis Vetton luggage, VIP par-ties, backstage passes . . . hold on. *(He has an orgasm.)* Ooooo! I can't be-lieve I gave him to you. Yes, I did! He was right on the line, girl, he coulda went either way, either way. I was the one introduced ya'll when you was eight cuz I was tired of you followin' me around. Those were my dark days of hiding — before I became the beautiful specimen you see before you; we was all stayin' wit Auntie Gina — all of us up in that one room, but it was clean though; her makin' me take you with me when I went out, knowin' you'd tell if I did somethin' wrong. Why you think I'd have you to go play with Darnell? To get yo' nosey ass out my business. Who knew Darnell would end up a damn star? He about to be so rich. I shoulda went ahead and did him then, with his little eight-year-old pee pee. Speakin' of pee-pee. I gotta go tinkle. Order for me! *(He exits.)*

WITCHDOCTOR: *(Sings and dances complete with fly whisk and headdress.)* Mhondoro dzinomwa muna Save. Mhondoro dzinomwa muna Zambezi (x2) *(Sits.)*

Don't mind all this *(Indicating traditional attire.)* I had some whites, matourist, they wanted to see the witchdoctor like the one they see on TV. I didn't know I could do those dances, hey! *(Dances from a seated position a bit.)* It was good, I give them a show, they give me some money, everyone is happy!

But, we are happy to see you here my daughter. The spirits are glad for your return. Your ancestors were angry going to other cultures for your answers; but now you have returned to your roots they are happy. You know that this is from where all answers flow. These are your roots. So what's the problem here, eh, don't tell me, the ancestors will speak it. *(Throws bones.)*

Mmmm, you are a professional woman, very well dressed what, what. I see you are married, ya. Not enough children, not enough children from you yah. But you're hips are looking like you want to have some more. Don't tell me you are pregnant — I knew that, I was going to say it. Don't anger the ancestors. *(Beats his shoulders with flywhisk.)* Mmmmm, saka, what wrong here. *(Throws bones, sniffs the air, rubs nose.)* I'm smelling fear, fear of the husband, fear of the husband, fear of the husband — but why? *(Silences her with his hand, throws bones again, looks at them, then at her, then at them.)* Why are you so sad, you are pregnant, but you are sad, scared, and sad, scared and sad — but you are pregnant — he doesn't know eh? But what are you scared of . . . Why are you telling me? You are going to bring on the wrath of the ancestors!!

So you are sick . . . its The Sickness hmm?

Picking up bones. OK, OK, OK, OK, we don't cure that.

No one can heal that. There was a time, we thought it was a joke, we would call it American Ideas for Discouraging Sex. But now, now ahh, what we have seen, we know better.

But you can come back to me when the illnesses start, I can help you with those symptoms.

You can bring your husband to me too, if you tell him, I have a couples' discount.

(Claps his hands.) Hey! Stop crying! Musachema mwanawangu!

You think you are the only one dealing with this problem?

If you go outside you can count, one, two, three — he has it.

One, two, three — she has it.

You are not special, there are many people who have this thing and still live their lives!

As for the other problems I've seen here *(Indicating bones.)*, I can help you with those today.

For the fear of your husband beating you or leaving you, here is a love potion, a muti, it is very popular these days. I am running low.

Rub it on his penis thrice a day. He will never leave you or forsake you.

Don't ask the great ones how to do it!

That is your concern.

But, you women know how to get it when you want it, he he hehehehe.

(Points with flywhisk.) That one will allow the baby to die before it is born.

That way it won't have to suffer.

But don't confuse the two or your husband's penis will surely look like a piece of tree bark by morning. *(Winces continually at the thought. Beating his shoulders with flywhisk.)*

(Starts singing again.)

That is all. Don't worry my daughter, you are not alone.

(Holds out hand while singing, gets $ looks, holds out hand again, looks satisfied.) *(Keysha re-enters.)* Sharp. Be gone. *(Keeps singing.)*.

KEYSHA: *(To the waiter.)* Merci.

Uh, is this fresh brewed, cuz it smells like Sanka?

I'm allergic to generic.

Ya'll got hot chocolate?

Hot chocolate then.

(To Nia.) Stop lookin' so sad. You not dyin', the world ain't over. You ain't the first one to end up pregnant. You should be happy, you in the game with the big dogs now, but let me warn you: This ain't high school — these girls are after Darnell and these bitches is ruthless. Don't

trust none of 'em. They would fuck yo' man and yo' daddy in the same day. I've seen it happen a million times: Sports can make these men act a fool, but it'll turn women into Halle Berry in *Jungle Fever*. "Can I suck yo' dick? Uh, can I suck *yo'* dick? Anybody's disk? Everybody's dick?" Just wait 'til he get a little money, a little more fame — I already see that nigga every weekend with his hand indiscriminately placed between somebody's legs. And them girls love it. Well, they may come, but they will go cuz they ain't shit to him. You got his baby. You stayin'. But it won't be easy. He'll be out with two, three of 'em at the same time every night and won't think nothin' of it. Then he'll bring you back some nastiness, his PR person will get involved and the next thing you know, you readin' about how you gave it to him to bribe him outta some money. Hell yeah, we want to be paid and pampered, but not enough to be catchin' no STD. You remember my roommate Monica?

You know, *(He imitates Monica.)* yeah her.

(With discretion.) She had Chlamydia. Girl, yes! Walkin' around with it, thought it was a damn yeast infection. By the time she asked me to help her to the clinic, she couldn't even walk. When she got there they said she had waited so long it turned into P-I-D — Pussy in Distress, yes. She got that shit from Jerry — that muthafucka didn't even know he had it. He coulda been walkin' around with AIDS and never know it. She was afraid to tell him, so I confronted his punk ass and he said, "I don't know whatchu talkin' 'bout. That's on her," like she gave it to herself. That nigga was on the DL, had Chlamydia and he was still tryin' to make it seem like — the point is this: These men don't give a fuck about you. All you are to them is a piece of ass. And I'ma be damned if I'ma let my cousin get used up and then end up with nothin'. If you're givin' it up, then you best believe he givin' it up too. And you sho' ain't havin' no babies for free. That is not prostitution, that's takin' care-a you. I mean, look-atcha Mama! And she dated some first-class negroes, had they baby, and still couldn't pay her rent. The last thing you wanna be is some hood rat, baby mama, walkin' around with cold sores and house shoes; buyin' government cheese with food stamps when yo' baby daddy in the NB fuckin' A, and playin' husband to some other bitch and her kids. Then who the one lookin' stupid? At least if you his wife, you get half, even if he divorce your ass; even if you do get Chlamydia. Then, whatever way it go, you won't never have to worry about money, and can do whatever the fuck you wanna do. Write your poetry, be Maya Angelou. Whatever.

Don't let that boy out your sight. Remind him that you was the one at his games before anybody knew his name. Tell his mama you carrying his baby. Aw, yeah, make it a family affair. Didn't you say you met her at they family picnic?

See! She probably already like you! Once you have her, then it don't matter what he say. Don't stop 'til you get the keys to the crib and a ring on that finger. Should you have his baby . . . how else you gon' pay me back for all the shit I did for you? Nia, havin' a baby is a blessing. I mean, I look better than all ya'll heifers put together, but I cannot have a baby out my ding-a-ling. Whatever you do, I'ma always be your cousin, but remember, we already live in hell. Don't make it so you have to spend eternity there too. God gave you that baby. That baby is yo' ticket out. *(He exits.)*

TEN: SEX WORKER

SEX WORKER: *(Enters smoking.)* Dahling, dahling, dahling. How the bloody hell am I supposed to know how to make a man fall asleep so you can put a n'yanga's potion on his penis? Don't believe those stories about us sex workers stealing the penises of men who don't pay. It's bullshit! Wish it wasn't. *(Starts to sit, gets back up.)* Just give me a second my dahling, *(Takes cloth that is tucked at her waist, wipes between her legs.)* What a messy bastard.

(Sits.) Ahh that's better. Right, shit, you've got yourself into a pot of poo my girl!

Who would have thought Miss Priss Abigail would get herself in such a bind!

Let me help you out my sister, since you have come to your old high school chum for advice.

You have to face the truth.

Your marriage is ova

You think you can make him stay?

You know how these men are!

He will blame you for everything, even though you got it from him

And the in-laws!! Do you remember Elizabeth Chidzero?

It happened to her! Sent back to her village, penniless, the kids taken by the bastard and his family, even though she got it from him! Now she is waking up to the cockerels singing "kokoriko" — dancing at those fucking village pungwes for those old farts and washing in the river, while she's as sick as a bloody dog! You think it won't happen to you? You'll find yourself back in your village, grinding corn singing dum dum duri, dum dum duri.

Ha, and you were always the one who was going to go to America or something and become rich and famous.

What did you say your man's name was again? AHHHH *(Deep in thought, then looks back at Abigail.)* All I'll say is I am not surprised.

Shame.

The best thing I can offer you

My sister

Is a new lifestyle.

Leave the bastard.

Because he gave you AIDS! I can hook you up with a nice beneficiary

Who will take such good care of you

My love,

You will never need that man of your again.

He will give you enough cash

Get the medicine, save your baby!

It's nicer to feel a beautiful piece of life pushing out of you

Than a dead piece of flesh coming inside you

You can take your son

Stay in your own place.

Take care of the man every now and then.

Get the doughs, buy the drugs.

And you will live so much longer futi.

And no bullshit in-law stress.

What have you got to lose my dahling?

You think this lifestyle is planned?

The economy is shit, my dear.

I was a secretary, couldn't pay for my rent,

Couldn't pay for my electric, couldn't pay for my DSTV!

And I was NOT going back to watching Dead BC.

No offense.

So I did it once, did it twice, next thing you know I had a business.

Listen, there is NOTHING wrong with being a kept woman, it's the least these bastards can do for us.

It's a fair trade, almost like going back to the barter system.

And these African men, they love to flex their dollars, makes their dicks hard.

So, its there for the taking.

You have to decide what's more important to you

Remain Miss Priss Abigail, or become a survivor

Because, you can't save both your marriage and that baby.

You can keep quiet about it, act as if nothing is wrong and die horribly — watching your kid die too, all because you

Wanted to remain the perfect little shona wife.

Which many have done.

Or you can take care of yourself and your child.

Personally, I want to be a mother.

I have this one guy, he's a client, a really nice guy hey! He wants me to have his baby.

He says, no condoms.

Saka, me, I say, why not!

It's important to be a mother, it's the one thing we can do that these bastards can't!

This is just a hope for me, but you, you have children, so be a mother.

And forget about that potion girlie

Those n'yangas are mad.

If they had anything that worked

Africa wouldn't even have AIDS. *(Looks outside.)*

Shit! Sorry beby, a new customer —

This one needs a little bit more time.

One of those old government chef bastards.

The machinery takes a little longer to oil.

Abi, Abigail — you have to do something, you can't keep running around like Speedy Gonzales! It's the best offer you are going to get!

(Puts out cigarette, straightens out wig and shirt, looks over at client approaching.)

Hi, howzit!?

(Ad-libs and overlaps with Gail: " . . . I'm fine," "Just don't be rough today, Chef!")

ELEVEN: GAIL

GAIL: Just be quiet, please!

Damn it, Darnell! Take your medication. Use a condom. Use a condom. I told him to —

You children don't think! You don't think beyond your own little circle of existence. You think this is a video game? This is life. You don't get to start over!

You kids — ! He's a boy, he's just a baby, how is he supposed to — when you all just keep tossin' yourselves at him and tossin' yourself at him.

Don't give me that look. I see the way you look at him. Salavatin' with dollar signs in your eyes. You probably thought that if you latched onto him you could ride him all the way to the top. You think you the first one to try to lock him down? Ask his agent: He's already had two paternity claims.

Sit down. Sit back down! Why should I have told you? This is a private family matter. You should have kept your legs closed. I warned Darnell about ya'll. I said, "Darnell, baby, watch out. Stay focused. Don't get caught up." I made sure he played in all the right districts, with all the right coaches, was seen by those recruiters — look at all these trophies. Look at them! Does this look like AIDS to you? Do you think he would have been recruited if anybody knew? Do you think he would be getting a scholarship? A scholarship for outstanding athletic achievement — to my son. No, nobody knows. It's none of they damn business.

Nobody knows, Nia. Look at me. Nobody can know. Consider what people will think about you if they knew. You think they gon' treat you the same? You mention it and even the people you thought loved you will make you eat from paper plates. Them tears won't mean nothing. Everybody will turn on you; little kids will say nasty things to you. Even the folks at church — they'll whisper behind your back and point at you in the pew and say, "That's what happens to people who sin with the devil."

I'm trying to help you, Nia, but you have got to promise me —

Is this about money? Huh? I can get you money. Just give me a couple of hours. I'll get you $5,000. *(Maid enters singing.)* How's that sound? That'll be enough to get you set up, get you a place for you and the baby, have some money left over to do what you got to do. That's what we'll do: I'll get you $5,000 for now, and we can worry about later, later.

TWELVE: MAID

Maid, on hands and knees, cleaning the floor, singing 'Tauya naye nemagumbezi.'

MAID: Oh . . . Miss Abigail, Masikati, maskwera sei? Ndaskwera. I have put out the chicken and samoosas for Simbi's party, and the man is outside with the jumping castles, but he wants to know if you want the jumping castle, kana the jumping giraffe. And that crazy little friend of Simbi's Fungai Mparaza he had to come early — and he has already broken two plates Miss Abi! And Bhudi Gilbert is on his way with the braaai stand — are you OK Miss Abi? My husband? I don't have a husband Miss Abigail. No, ya, of course, my family wants me to have one but I don't want. Anyway my family now it's just my brother and aunts and uncles. My mother and father — they died kuma 1998 and 1999, then my sister kuma 2001. They had a long illness. Anyway, me I said, it's better to be alone, love between a man and a woman seems to end in death around here. And people say stupid things to me, but I don't care. Oh they say things like, "Eh, she thinks she is too good to get married, maybe she thinks she's a man. Eh, you don't want us — you are ugly anyway." *(Talks to imaginary men.)* I would like to say to them, *No, I don't want you, YOU are ugly anyway and you probably have something then you will beat me and leave me to suffer when I get it from YOU!!! No thanks.* *(Collects herself.)* But I just keep quiet. Saka, me I am alone. I work here and go to night classes — I want to get a degree. Like you Miss Abi, you work, you went to school, and you are a mother and a wife futi — I don't want that part but I admire that — then I know I can do it too zvangu. People say, you can't do anything without a husband in Zimbabwe — but I will try anyway. At least like this I can say, Ini I know who I am, where I am going — I know what I am working for. And I am moving forward, forward, forward, not like this or like that *(Indicates with hand.)* but forward. Maybe I stand alone, but I know who I am — Mary Chigwada — not Mrs. So and so with in-laws, lobola — bride-price, going to his village to cook at funerals, chi chi — no! Just me, Mary Chigwada.

AHH, Miss Abi, — your mother and father are coming through the gate — ah, your mother looks so pretty! Ah, I am so glad you are back Miss Abi, there is so much to do, I haven't even put out the drinks yet and . . . Miss Abi — Miss Abi? *(Rushes out.)*

NIA: *(Drunk.)* It smell like booty
> I wish I could fly away
> Dirty ass motel.

> Guess what, baby. Guess what? *(Dumping her purse.)* Today your mommy opened her purse to see how much money she had and she had a five dollar bill and a $5,000 check. $5,000. *(Folding up the check and putting it aside.)* No, baby, we don't need his money. No, we don't! Mommy will go tomorrow and see if they still want her at Nordstrom. What was they payin'? Five dollars. No, baby, no, we can do it. We just have to budget.

> *(Tearing a piece of the five dollar bill with each item.)*

> This, this right here is for my retirement fund. Cuz Oprah says you should pay yourself first.

> This, this is for your college fund, cuz you going to college.

> This is for rent . . . on our mansion in Beverly Hills.

> And my Mercedes.

> What else? What else you want, baby?

> Oh yeah. Gas, water, and lights.

> That's it. That's the life right there, baby. You got, retirement, college, mansion, Mercedes, gas, water, lights. Yeah!

> Ooooo! Mommy forgot to put food in the budget! How mommy forget about the food? But there's no more money.

> $5,000.

> *(She breaks down in tears.)* He knew! He knew! And he knows you're his baby cuz he the one made me pregnant. And she thinks she can throw $5,000 at me and I'ma just be quiet?

> $5,000 dollars. I sold myself for $5,000. That's how much I cost. No, baby, that's how much you cost.

> *(Balling up the check and throwing it down.)* No, no, we don't need his money. This is what we gonna do, baby. *(Picking up the pieces of the five dollar bill.)* We'll make the light money the food money. Cuz we gotta eat, but we don't need no lights.

> We don't need no lights let the muthafuckas burn!

> *(She b-boxes and makes a beat on the furniture.)*

> Come on, baby. Cuz we got, what we got? What we got?!? Huh? We got, we got

> Sunlight

Insight
Out of sight — out of mind.
Full-time
Lifetime
Out-of-time
I'm outta my mind.

I should
Re-define
Discipline
Undermine this bottom line *(Applying lip gloss.)*
Drench myself in Vaseline
to make myself look feminine
Dressed and caped in Calvin Klein
He comes home at dinnertime
My womb is free of guilt and grime
Before this change, before this crime
Before the fall, before the climb *(She begins to pray.)*
Please keep me from this constant grind
Help me see, although I'm blind
Help me breathe despite the slime
Help me live if you're inclined
Please don't decline my prayer.
I know it's nobody's fault but mine
I won't bitch, complain or whine
If you help me out, one more time
I won't let you down.
I'll give up sex, weed, and wine
Plant my feet on solid ground.

Yeah, baby, tomorrow. *(Picks up the check.)* Tomorrow we're going to go up to that scholarship ceremony. I'm going to make Darnell look me in the face and tell me I'm only worth $5,000. Then, I'm going to stand there in front of all those recruiters, in front of the whole world and say it. And then all the women he been with will know. And all the women he was thinking about doin' will know. And everybody will know. *(Balling the check up and throwing it down again.)* I'm worth more than this money. *(She begins to exit. She doubles back for the check.)* Tomorrow.

FOURTEEN: ABIGAIL'S PRAYER

ABIGAIL: *(Enters, reading an old, framed certificate.)* Huh, I won that thing, I won that thing! *(Reading.)* This is to award Abigail Moyo of Malbereign Girls High as the winner of the National Interschools Public Speaking Championship, 1994, Harare, Zimbabwe.

I won that thing. What was my speech again? Oh, oh! *(Jumps up on bed.)*

"The New African Woman — Modernizing and Post Colonizing.

I was once number three of four wives — yet I chose to rise.

I was once denied usage of the same toilet as you," — I always had to look for a white — "yet I chose to rise.

In me is the blood of the great Mbuya Nehanda — the spiritual medium who fought and died for this land.

In me is the pride of Winnie Mandela who marched the streets of Soweto singing 'Free Nelson Mandela' until they did.

In me is the ferocity of the woman freedom fighter who let go of the milk of human kindness to fight for a free Zimbabwe!

I am no longer the third of four wives, but the first of the first.

I can become whatever I please.

My dreams can be a reality . . . "

He knew, he knew, that bastard.

That bastard . . . was he bringing his hures into my house?

Doing his business in my Truworths Sheets from Joburg? That BASTARD!

But I knew it all along, with the late nights and the way he was smelling.

But what could I do Baba?

You are the one who said two become one, two flesh become one — and that's what I did baba

So how did you allow one flesh to rot into the other when I lived according to your word? How can this be your plan for my life?

You want me to die like a prostitute?

That's your plan?

That's what you have been building me up to?

And don't give me that trial and tribulation bullshit!

I have come too far,

I have done everything the right way

What more did you want from me?

You have to help me Baba!

(Goes silent for a moment, drops to her knees.)

OK, OK, I will tell them.

But this is what I ask:

DON'T you let them blame me.

You make them stand by me.

And support me.

And you make Stamford stay put.

You make him still love me and take care of me.

He's still mine, I am not giving up everything I worked for.

And I want my baby, so don't you let it have this illness.

You have to fight this baby with whatever you have.

And if I must die — don't let me die like Sisi Stella who was convulsing in so much pain they had to strap her to a bed. And don't let me die like Sekuru Lovemore who was covered in so many sores they couldn't even show him at the funeral. And if I must die let my chil — *(Knock on the door — Abigail starts, sits on chair and composes herself.)*

Come in. *(Enter Simbi.)*

Hello my big boy. Are you enjoying your party? You look so smart, is this the outfit daddy bought you? They want to sing Happy Birthday already. OK, tell them I am coming — Tell them Mummy spilt something on her dress and I need to change it. You go ahead.

Simbi, dzoka mwana, dzoka. *(Calls him back.)* Munoziwa kuti mummy loves you? OK, taura, taura kuti mummy loves me. Taura futi, mummy loves me. Good, OK, go ahead, mummy's coming.

FIFTEEN: THE END

ABIGAIL: *(Enters — singing Watinti bafadzi.)* "Pamsoroi, hello, Baba naAmai, ne babamukuru, naBhudiGilgert, navatete. Tafara, we are happy you have come to celebrate Simbi's birthday with us.

In our culture I know the family shares everything, and takes good, good care of one another. So I know I can share this with you and get your support. Stamford, I am telling you this here so we can find a harmony OK. Stamford, we have to go to the clinic tomorrow morning because I . . . you . . . uh, you and therefore we have acquired the acquired immune deficiency syndrome virus HIV and I am pregnant."

NIA: "Good evening ladies and gentlemen. My name is Nia James, and I'm here to say that Darnell Smith gave me AIDS!" // Then I'ma rip up the check. No, I can't say that . . .

ABIGAIL: // No — that acquired acquired thing is stupid . . . no, no this is good, he can't beat me or throw me out with my mother and bhudi Gilbert there at his son's birthday futi . . .

NIA: . . . no, it's the right thing. Everybody should know . . .

ABIGAIL: He will have to beg my forgiveness. "OK, OK, yes I still love you — but you can't cheat anymore" —

NIA: "He could be giving it to everybody. If I had know, I would have never — "

ABIGAIL: "Now we must plan ahead for us and the children."

NIA: "I'm not a hoe. Everybody has sex."

ABIGAIL: "Yes I forgive you — no don't hit him Bhudi Gilbert."

NIA: "I didn't make this disease. I didn't give this to myself."

ABIGAIL: "I choose to stay with you but you must find the money for treatments,"

NIA: "I should have protected myself, but he — "

ABIGAIL: "Because you got us into this trouble. OK!"

NIA: "I just wanted . . . "

(Abigail and Nia face each other in a mirror, but remain in opposite worlds.)

ABIGAIL: "And you must now look at me and see me, Abigail Moyo Murambe."

NIA: "There's no amount you can pay me to take this away."

ABIGAIL: "You must treat me like a wife you respect" —

NIA: "Naw, I don't want yo' apology!"

ABIGAIL: "Because I know who I am!"

NIA: "I'm changing the course of history!"

ABIGAIL: "And I am moving forward, forward, forward — not this way or that. OK!"

NIA: That's fine.

ABIGAIL: That's good.

ABIGAIL/NIA: So help me God. Let's go.

ABIGAIL: OK kids, go play on the jumping castle! *(Ushers kids out.)*

NIA: *(To herself.)* Damn, it's a lot of people . . .

ABIGAIL: Pamsoroi Baba, naAmai ne babamukuru, neBhudiGilbert, navatete.

NIA: *(To herself.)* There he is . . .

ABIGAIL: Tafara, we are happy you have come to celebrate Simbi's birthday with us . . . eh . . .

NIA: *(To herself.)* Just say it.

ABIGAIL: In our culture, we . . . move forward, forward, forward . . .

NIA: *(To the crowd.)* Hey! I have — uh . . . something to say.

ABIGAIL: I mean . . . with a family . . . eh . . .

NIA: *(To the crowd.)* My name is Nia James . . .

ABIGAIL: we share everything . . .

NIA: *(To the crowd.)* I just came to say . . .

ABIGAIL: so, I want to say what has happened with Stamford . . . and me . . . here . . .

ABIGAIL/NIA: eh . . . eh . . .

*ABIGAIL: Stamford and I are having another baby!!! Eh, suwa, tofara tese! Thank you! Congrats to us all! Eh? That was the news! That was it! A boy ya! That's what I said, ya. Tofara tese . . . hehe.

*NIA: Congratulations! No, no that's what I wanted to say. Congratulations. Ooa, Ooa!! I'm sure your mother is proud. Can I get some tickets to the game? OK, OK, just one ticket? Not one?? Aw, man! Heeee . . . .

(Both characters laugh into a blackout.)

END OF PLAY

SHONA/ZIMBABWE GLOSSARY

Aiwa: no

Amai: mother (also used as a sign of respect to a woman)

Beby: baby

Baba: father (also used to substitute as Lord, God)

Babamukuru: older father (usually refers to an older uncle)

Bhudi: brother

Babasimbi: another term for talking to the father of a child, 'father of Simbi'

Barance: idiot

Chef: a term used to describe men of power and influence in Zimbabwe

Chi chi: etcetera etcetera

Chisipiti: an affluent suburb of Harare

Commuter omnibus: A van used as a form of public transport.

Dahling: darling

DSTV: equivalent of digital cable

Deddy: daddy

Dum dum duri: a song traditionally sung while grinding corn into flour with a large pestle and mortar

Dzoka mwana: come back child, come back

Fotsek: An expletive originally used to address dogs.

Futi: again

Glen Lorne: An affluent suburb of Harare

Guyana ramwari munobvisa, matadzo epasi tinzireiwo tsitsi, ndipeyeiwo rugare: lamb of God you take away the sins of the world, have mercy on us, grant us peace

Hartman House: one of the most affluent boys prep schools in Harare

Howzit: how is it going?

Ini: me

Iwe mune AIDS nemhuri wako futi: you have AIDS and so does your family

Kana: or

Kokoriko: Sound used to depict cockerels crowing

Kuma: in

Kumusha: a person's rural homeland

Kwete: no

Lobola: bride-price

Makadei: How are you?

Maskwera sei: A respectful greeting

Marara: bullshit/garbage

mati amai vangu vane AIDS: did you say my mother has AIDS

mira: wait

Mhondoro dzinomwa muna Save, Mhondoro dzinomwa munaZambezi: a
    song describing a lion drinking from the Save and Zambezi rivers.

Musachema mwanawangu: don't cry my child

munoziwa kuti: do you know that

ndaskwera: I am fine

ndibatsirewo: help me out

ne: and

nhasi ririFriday: today is Friday

n'yanga: witchdoctor/traditional healer

Pamsoroi: excuse me

Pajero: prestigious Mitsubishi SUV in Zimbabwe

Pururudza: A celebrative expression.

Saka: so

SABC: South African Broadcasting Corporation

Sha: exclamation substituted for "man"; *for example* "Come on *man*," "Come
    on *sha*." Also short for *Shamwari*

Shamwari: friend. Also used as an exclamation.

Sekuru: grandfather/older uncle

Sisi: sister

Suwa: sure

Tafara: we are happy

Tofara tese: we can all be happy

Tomato sauce: children's play song

Vanhu vatema vanonetsa: black people are a pain

Village pungwe: traditional village meetings conducted in the rural areas

Wuya: come here

ZBC: Zimbabwe Broadcasting Corporation ("Z" is pronounced "Zed")

Zvangu: myself, used as an emphasis

SIX YEARS

❧

Sharr White

PLAYWRIGHT'S BIOGRAPHY

Sharr White's *Six Years* was produced as part of Actor's Theatre of Louisville's 30th Anniversary Humana Festival of New American Plays. Other plays include *The Dream Canvas* (downtown New York at Todo Con Nada); *The Last Orange Dying* (Off-Broadway at the Ohio); *Safe from the Future* (Off-Broadway at Raw Space); *(Heaven) and All Things Lovely* (far above Broadway in the Mariott Marquis, room 3806); *Iris Fields* (Lincoln Center Theatre Directors Lab, Key West Theatre Festival), *Satellites of the Sun* and *The Escape Velocity of Savages* (Dr. Henry and Lillian Nesburn Award as part of the Julie Harris Award in Playwriting). Sharr is a member of the Ensemble Studio Theatre's Playwrighting Unit in New York, and a company member of Apartment A Productions in Los Angeles. He is a recipient of a 2006 New York Foundation for the Arts fellowship.

ORIGINAL PRODUCTION

Six Years premiered at Actors Theatre of Louisville's Humana Festival of New American Plays, March 2006. It was directed by Hal Brooks with the following cast:

PHIL GRANGER	Michael J. Reilly
MEREDITH GRANGER	Kelly Mares
TOM WHEATON	Harry Bouvy
JACK MUNCIE	Frank Deal
PEG MUNCIE	Marni Penning
DOROTHY	Stephanie Thompson
MICHAEL GRANGER	Isaac Gardner

INTRODUCTORY STATEMENT

It was 1997 and things were not going particularly well. I was a waiter and I was living in Hell's Kitchen and I couldn't get a manuscript read to save my life. I had self-produced once before and thought, Well, I'll do it again. Fine, except that I didn't have any money and I didn't know anybody except for a few friends — who had talent, but also didn't have money or know anybody — but everyone was enthusiastic. So we started this series of very small theatrical events that never ran more than four performances and we tried to take advantage of what we didn't have — money — by designing these events (which took the form of short plays) to take place anywhere. We called the effort *Absolute Scratch,* and we created these evenings three times, the last of which was set in a hotel suite on the thirty-eighth floor of the Mariott Marquis overlooking Times Square; that was my favorite. It was intimate and intense in a way that stays with you.

It stayed with our producer, Matt Olin, too, because four years later he found a job with Charlotte Repertory Theatre in North Carolina and in-between seasons was producing his own projects, and he wanted to do another hotel piece. I had a scene I'd written for *Naked Angels Tuesdays at Nine*, a weekly development series in New York, about a lost World War II veteran who finally comes home to his wife. It was sticking with me, so when Matt told me about *The Hotel Project,* as they titled the event in Charlotte, I worked to expand that scene into a one-act play. With minor alterations that one-act remains as the beginning of what is now *Six Years*.

I like to think that the intimacy we achieved through the two hotel projects — with audiences silently huddled over, almost on top of the actors' laps, surrounding the bed around which most of the action took place — made an indelible mark on *Six Years*, as well as me as a writer. I can trace what I'm interested in now back to the site-specific work we all did in New York. So to all involved in the two hotel projects I owe a tremendous thanks: Matt Olin throughout both projects, and in New York, director Ron Bashford, playwright David Simpatico and actors Liz Sherman and Ross Minichiello. In Charlotte, Director Lon Bumgardner, co-producer Anne Lambert and actors Beth Pierce and Brian Lafontaine.

After *The Hotel Project, Six Years* truly began to take shape. The primary person to thank for much of what it is now is my agent, Peregrine Whittlesey, who took me to lunch after reading the one-act and gave me the sort of talking-to that makes her so terrific.

In the early stages of writing I continued trying scenes out at *Naked Angels Tuesdays at Nine* and owe many actors there thanks, including Jeff Pucillo and Melinda Wade, and particularly the fine Chris Stack, who was instrumental in later readings of the play.

I finished the play while participating in HB Studios Playwright's Unit, and I owe former Artistic Director Billy Carden thanks for the two crucial readings *Six Years* received there. I owe Nela Wagman a debt of gratitude for taking me into the "small unit" at HB; for her tremendous ear, advocacy, acceptance, and — along with playwrights Frank Basloe and Susan Bernfield — good, critical conversation.

The play's most crucial development occurred when it was produced as part of Actor's Theatre of Louisville's 30th Anniversary Season of the Humana Festival of New American Plays. A tremendous thank you to the entire generous, supportive staff at Actor's Theatre, especially Merv Antonio and dramaturg Julie Dubiner in the tremendous Lit Department. Thanks to Zan Sawyer-Dailey for her presence and many kindly delivered insights. Great thanks to Artistic Director Marc Masterson, whose quiet advocacy, tough structural eye and frank words all pale before his fairly staggering sense of trust.

Within the Humana production itself, I owe a deep thanks to our exceptional, collaborative cast: Michael J. Riley, Frank Deal, Marni Penning, Stephanie Thompson, Isaac Gardner and especially Kelly Mares and original *Absolute Scratch* actor Harry Bouvy for their friendship and continued insight into what remains a living manuscript. A deep thanks to director Hal Brooks, seasoned friend and fellow A.C.T. alum, for his frankly enormous talent and relentless pursuit of perfection.

Additional thanks to Adam Forgash for his constant, driving inspiration, Paul Bravmann for his honesty, Matt Dawson for his enthusiasm and insight, Jen Albano for her excitement, hilarity, and general sense of scheming, brother-in-arms Guiesseppe Jones for, among countless other acts of friendship, propping me up again and again, and most crucially, thanks to you, Evelyn — for everything, of course — but in regards to this and things written, for listening so carefully to what is unready to be heard.

NOTE

Each scene of this play occurs six years beyond the scene proceeding, beginning in 1949, and ending in 1973. The ages and dispositions of the actors should be such that they can be aged convincingly throughout the course of the play; Phil and Meredith span from twenty-seven to fifty-one years old. For reasons of efficiency, the same actress may play the roles of Peg Muncie and Dorothy. The sets are intended to be minimal.

CHARACTERS

PHIL GRANGER

MEREDITH GRANGER

TOM WHEATON

JACK MUNCIE

PEG MUNCIE

DOROTHY

MICHAEL GRANGER

SETTINGS

ACT I:

A motel room in a small town outside St Louis, Missouri, 1949.

Phil and Meredith's small home in St. Louis, Missouri, 1955.

Split stage: a Chicago cocktail lounge/Phil and Meredith's St. Louis
bedroom, 1961.

ACT II:

Phil and Meredith's modern St. Louis home, 1967.

A motel room in Vacaville, California, 1973.

Six Years

ACT I
SCENE ONE

Night. Heavy rain. A motel room on the outskirts of St. Ann, Missouri. It is 1949, and everything in the room exudes the hopeful newness of postwar construction: taut, optimistic bedspread; smart drapes; dim, stylish lamps; thin, new carpeting. As if in direct contrast with the surroundings, a suitcase so ragged that it is close to useless lies open on the bed. Its owner is in the bathroom. Water runs in the sink.

There is a nervous knock on the door. After a few moments, another. We hear a key in the lock and Meredith Granger, twenty-seven, enters. She is completely soaked through: pinned-up hair, careful dress, a stylish but now-ruined coat, a soaked handbag. She shuts the door and stands in silence, shivering and dripping as she listens to the water run in the bathroom.

The water shuts off and we're left only with the sound of the rain. The bathroom door opens and Phil Granger enters in trousers and undershirt. A towel is slung over his shoulder and bits of shaving cream adhere to his face. He is a worn and weary twenty-seven with the bearing and looks of one much older. They stare at one another.

MEREDITH: I'm . . . I'm . . .

(Meredith quickly turns and makes for the door. Phil's voice stops her.)

PHIL: *(Hollow.)* — Something — uh . . . happened? To the car? There was a *car*, wasn't there?

(Meredith turns back, utterly unsure of what to do.)

MEREDITH: *(Nervous torrent.)* I uh . . . I just never . . . there was rationing and all and I just . . . there was this . . . bedroom set that was so pretty and I thought we'd never really begun furnishing our . . . and so I sold it and now we have this bedroom set and no car which is fine because I'm in town now I'm not at your mother's — at *your* — out at the farm . . . I've taken a room and it just made sense because we didn't have any. — Furniture. *(Miniscule beat.)* June — June Whitley — ran in and announced you were back, just like that, and the whole shop turned and looked at me and I . . . I didn't want to be in a car with any of them, not with news like that, so I . . . uh . . . ran. *(Miniscule beat.)* The whole *world's* buzzing.

PHIL: Hank and Snow saw me. At the bus station.

MEREDITH: June Whitley sure made a big deal over . . . wondering why it
looked like you were . . . headed to the *Starlight.*

PHIL: I . . . I just wasn't really ready to —

MEREDITH: — The . . . manager . . . gave me a key. I told him . . . uh . . . that
I was . . . that I'm your . . .

(Slight pause.)

PHIL: You're . . . you're wet.

MEREDITH: *(Quickly.)* — I knocked! And when you didn't answer, I —

PHIL: — Do you . . . want . . . to take off your —

MEREDITH: — I don't know. I don't know if I'm staying. I mean . . . long
enough . . . I mean for very . . . *(Taking him in.)* I just . . . can't believe . . .

PHIL: *(Trying desperately to sound normal.)* — I saw the funeral notice. In a
newspaper somebody'd dropped. *The Dispatch,* of all things. In the . . .
the Kansas City bus station.

MEREDITH: *(Disbelief.)* Kansas City? This whole time?

PHIL: — Just for the last few weeks. I was uh . . . I had a . . . *(Staring at the water
dripping from her.)* — Do you want a . . . I . . . I have clean towels . . .

MEREDITH: — No . . . No, I . . .

PHIL: *(Straightforward.)* — They come free with the room here.

(Pause. Meredith takes a small step toward him.)

MEREDITH: I'm *sorry.*

PHIL: What for.

MEREDITH: About your *mother.*

(Phil moves to the bed. He sits and digs into his bag for a flask. He drinks.)

PHIL: *(Struggling.)* I'm a bit of a wreck, Meredith.

MEREDITH: *(Approaching him.)* What are you doing here? Why haven't you
just —

PHIL: — I didn't know she was —

MEREDITH: — Your mother was so . . . worried.

PHIL: Meredith, I . . .

MEREDITH: — Where've you *been,* Phil?

(Phil considers this for a small beat, then shakes his head.)

MEREDITH: The room I'm letting, it's at the Fulton's, you remember George
Fulton, he was two grades behind us, well he —

PHIL: — Meredith —

MEREDITH: — joined up a year after you did —

PHIL: *(Short.)* — I remember George Fulton.

(Slight pause. Phil is unable to look at her.)

MEREDITH: And I have a job that everyone finally approves of. You remember

Mrs. Sampson's dress shop, well . . . well it's a nice little boutique now and . . . and I'm measuring the ladies and bringing them tea . . . I . . . I just couldn't stay out there with your mother after everyone started . . .

PHIL: — Of course.

MEREDITH: *(Struggling against defeat.)* Do you . . . do you want me to go?

(Pause. Phil struggles to give some response.)

MEREDITH: *(With finality.)* I only thought that . . . if I could just *see* you, then you could tell me *yourself*, that's all. I'm sorry.

(Meredith turns and makes for the door again.)

PHIL: *(Quickly.)* — Tell you what.

MEREDITH: *(Stopping.)* — Whatever you haven't been able to. Uh . . . for the last . . . six years.

(Phil stares at the trail of water that leads to Meredith's coat.)

PHIL: — It's dripping . . . your . . . your coat is dripping.

(Meredith stares at him. She decides to take off her coat. It is a quietly daring act that will leave her looking somehow unprotected. Phil stands and goes to her, as if small social mores are all he has left. An awkward exchange occurs, Phil trying to take her coat, Meredith trying to do it herself while holding her handbag, etc.)

MEREDITH: No, you don't have to —

PHIL: — I'll —

MEREDITH: — If you just —

PHIL: — Here, *I'll* take it —

MEREDITH: No, I *have* it, I just . . .

PHIL: — No, the *other* arm —

MEREDITH: — It's soaking *wet!*

(Slight pause. They stand awkwardly. He holds her coat.)

PHIL: Well let me hang it up at least. That's what people do, right? They hang up coats?

(She gives a small nod. He goes to a closet and hangs it.)

MEREDITH: *(Bravely.)* I wanted to bring a couple of your suits.

PHIL: *(As if he's never heard the word before.)* Suits?

MEREDITH: *(Struggling not to lose control of her emotions.)* I don't know why I figured you might . . . need that . . . black one . . .

(Phil at last understand what she means. As if by rote, he turns to comfort her.)

MEREDITH: — No, don't. — DON'T!

(He reacts almost childishly to her tone, dropping his arms and turning from her.)

MEREDITH: *(Surprised at herself.)* — I'm sorry, I uh . . .

PHIL: No. No, it's OK.

MEREDITH: I just don't really know what this means. You *do* understand . . .

PHIL: . . . Yes.

MEREDITH: Are you . . .

PHIL: I don't know.

MEREDITH: Were you planning on . . .

PHIL: I don't know.

MEREDITH: Well . . . can you at least . . . tell me . . . how long . . .

PHIL: No.

MEREDITH: Can you . . . can you tell me . . . anything at all?

PHIL: Meredith, I . . .

MEREDITH: You what.

PHIL: I don't know.

MEREDITH: *(Briefly letting a deep anger slip out.)* Well how do you expect to just show up here and not at least have some idea HOW LONG YOU'RE STAYING . . . for people, Phil. Because we're going to want to know that. — And don't say you don't know again! *(Long pause, then, almost softly.)* Mrs. Fulton, she's kept all the things in George's room; the trophy from that freshman game . . . all sorts of things. She . . . she asked me to ask you if . . .

PHIL: *(Tersely.)* I never saw him.

MEREDITH: Everyone came home, Phil.

PHIL: — I know.

MEREDITH: And those *cards* the . . . hospital sent said you weren't . . . so we didn't know . . . *why* . . . you would be . . . there. You . . . you don't have any . . . ?

PHIL: *(Almost resentfully.)* — No, Meredith.

MEREDITH: You stopped writing to us in '44. We thought you were *dead.* The same thing happened to Mrs. Fulton except there was a *reason* for it because George Fulton actually *is* missing, but you . . . Can't you just tell me where you've *been?*

(Slight pause. Phil searches for some explanation.)

PHIL: *(Almost childish.)* A lot of places.

MEREDITH: That's *it?*

(Slight pause. Phil thinks, then nods. Meredith gathers herself, attempting as best she can to become businesslike. She brings her handbag to a small desk.)

MEREDITH: So. I had some papers drawn up. But there was no way to finalize everything . . . I ran to Mrs. Fulton's and . . . Look. I thought that if this was going to be the only time I would ever . . . I uh . . . they're divorce papers.

PHIL: *(Again, as if not immediately recognizing the meaning of the words.)* Divorce papers.

MEREDITH: Your mother . . . thought that . . .

PHIL: *(Not quite alarmed.)* My mother?

MEREDITH: Yes, that . . . well, it's just . . . I mean — *I* thought too. That if . . . if something . . . if someone else were to — for me — and something were to happen, you know . . . if I were ever to have . . .

Well I would never be able to . . . remarry.

PHIL: *(Fear and a long-forgotten taste of jealousy rising through him.)* Do you . . . have . . . is there . . . anyone . . .

MEREDITH: *(Quickly.)* No! Gosh no, Phil, I . . . *no,* I've been . . .

PHIL: — You've been what.

MEREDITH: *(Almost to herself.)* — Nothing, never mind, I . . . I don't think I should tell you certain things. It's too much.

PHIL: *(Intently.)* Certain things like *what?*

MEREDITH: Things that might make me seem . . . *desperate.*

(Meredith opens her handbag and takes some folded papers out. She turns to Phil as she opens them. Water gushes out of the sodden mass.)

MEREDITH: *(Meekly.)* Oh.

(Slight pause.)

PHIL: I don't suppose you'd like a drink.

MEREDITH: I'd like a drink very much.

(Phil turns and disappears into the bathroom. Meredith calls after him.)

MEREDITH: Because I'm . . . I'm *not.*

PHIL: *(Offstage.)* Not what.

MEREDITH: — Not desperate!

PHIL: Over *what.*

(Phil re-emerges with two motel glasses.)

MEREDITH: *(Carefully.)* Over *you.* I don't want you to think that I've rushed right over to claw at you or something. I've only come so quickly because . . . well who knew if you were just going to turn around and . . .

PHIL: *(Knowing.)* Yes.

MEREDITH: *(Softly.)* I . . . I feel like I just . . . want to look at you. Can I look at you?

PHIL: *(Miniscule pause, then quietly.)* Yes.

(Meredith takes him in. She almost raises her left hand as if to touch his face, but then thinks better of it. She still wears her wedding ring.)

MEREDITH: *(Plainly, quickly.)* There was that movie starring that fellow who had his hands shot off, you know the one that won the award, and there was this article in *Life* about him, how they made him new hands out of hooks and they showed him playing with his wife and his daughter and they all had these terrible smiles on their faces and I kept thinking what if you had something shot off like that, I supposed maybe that's what made you stay away but that didn't make sense because everything they sent . . . said just . . . exhaustion . . .

(Pause. Meredith gulps her drink without flinching.)

PHIL: Do you want another?

MEREDITH: No thank you.

(Slight pause.)

PHIL: *(At last truly focusing on her.)* What things?

MEREDITH: What?

PHIL: What things do you not want to tell me?

MEREDITH: *(Almost shyly.)* Oh well I'm sure I'm supposed to bluff or be a tease with you or something make you think all the guys are chasing me home every night that's probably what the girls would tell me to do but I . . . the truth is . . . I'm not making plans. In any way to be with . . . anyone else. That's what I don't want to tell you. *(The dark truth.)* That I never want to be with anyone else.

(Phil goes to pour himself another drink, but his flask is empty.)

MEREDITH: Here . . .

(Meredith efficiently reaches into her purse and comes out with her own, much larger flask. She pops the top, pours one for both Phil and herself, then sticks it back in her purse. She whirls back to Phil. Phil stares. She catches herself.)

MEREDITH: We all just do what we can, right?

PHIL: Sure.

(They actually each smile a little.)

MEREDITH: *(A little more confidently.)* You don't think it makes me seem . . . desperate? What I told you, I mean.

PHIL: No, Meredith.

MEREDITH: You don't . . . think that I'm clawing at you?

PHIL: No, Meredith.

MEREDITH: Poor Mrs. Fulton . . . *She* drinks. She drinks *plenty.* Some nights

I help her out of her chair and upstairs and in the mornings we both pretend not to remember.

(The following exchange is almost, though not quite, a shy seduction; we see the demure push and pull of a couple who once shared many things.)

PHIL: And what do *you* do?

MEREDITH: About . . .

PHIL: You said we all do what we can.

MEREDITH: Oh. Well I . . . I just work in the dress shop.

PHIL: And then what?

MEREDITH: I . . . I stay late. I . . . Most nights I'll close up. And even then sometimes I'll stay. It's nice when things . . . empty out, I guess.

PHIL: And then what?

MEREDITH: And then I go home.

PHIL: Every day?

MEREDITH: I listen to the radio with Mrs. Fulton, but it's not much fun since Fred Allen went off. In fact it's not terribly fun at *all*, Mrs. Fulton, she . . . she's so . . . *(Slight pause.)* George . . . George was in the 29th.

PHIL: *(Not unkindly.)* Someone sent me a letter.

MEREDITH: *(Desperately relieved.)* So you . . . you did at least *read?* Your *letters?*

PHIL: *(Intently.)* Every one.

MEREDITH: When I told Mrs. Fulton it appeared you'd come back, she . . . she wanted to go to the bus station right away. She thought *George* might've . . . that some . . . *miraculous* . . .

(Phil reaches out and moves a lock of Meredith's wet hair away from her face. It is the first time she has felt him touch her in six years.)

MEREDITH: You look . . . older.

PHIL: *(Quietly.)* You don't. Not a day.

MEREDITH: *(Admitting a terrible, long-held fear.)* Phil? You're not already . . . ? You haven't . . . ? Has there been . . . anyone?

PHIL: No, Meredith.

(She nods in relief. She begins crying. Phil looks surprised, like he's forgotten that people actually do that. He puts his arms around her with a tentative, wooden awkwardness.)

MEREDITH: Why were you in the hospital?

PHIL: You sure do look beautiful, Meredith.

MEREDITH: *(Fighting to regain control of herself.)* What's . . . *exhaustion.* We thought after you'd had a good rest . . . And we couldn't travel of course because . . . And then we got the *release* notice and we just . . .

PHIL: You look more beautiful than I can remember.

MEREDITH: Why didn't you come *home?*

(Pause. Phil struggles to answer.)

PHIL: It's . . . *hard* . . . for some fellows to . . . *(Slight pause.)* . . . and . . . and so they . . .

(Pause. Phil shakes his head, unable to articulate. He takes his towel and sets it into Meredith's hands. She wraps it around herself. Sensing an opening, she gently, insistently, presses him.)

MEREDITH: Hard for some fellows *what.* So they *what.*

(Pause. Phil shakes his head.)

MEREDITH: *(Hopefully.)* There are people who care about you, Phil. There are people, friends, people you know who don't want anything other than to know you're safe. It's . . . it's like a miracle. That you're even here. Don't you know that? We'll . . . give you whatever you need. We'll give you plenty of room to . . . to figure things out. You can go out there to the farm and . . . and . . .

PHIL: *(Almost fierce.)* — It's not that, Meredith!

MEREDITH: *(Long-suppressed anger, building to a devastated crescendo.)* Well what is it, then? You have to tell me what it is! I've been alone in this . . . *goddamned town* too long to let you go again without knowing what it is! The war comes and we lose everybody, and we suddenly have to be . . . ! And we are! All of us! Even June Whitley and Mrs. Fulton, and me, little Meredith! And the girls in town used to be so . . . but now that their husbands have come back they've all turned into cats again and I'm the one they talk about because *my* husband isn't dead or wounded or missing, he just hasn't come *home* yet, and I just . . . haven't known what to do with this *goddamned . . . !*

(Meredith sobs, desperately tugging at her ring as if attempting to commit to some grand, dramatic gesture, but the ring foils her and refuses to come off. Finally, she stops trying. Her sobs subside.)

PHIL: *(Haltingly.)* This . . . this fellow on a bus not long ago. He was talking at me. He was saying had I noticed how hard it was to know where the good places to eat were along the road. And I . . . said that I had. And he said he was going to open a whole bunch of restaurants and put them along the highway. And all these restaurants would be exactly the same, so no matter where you were, you would get the same great food.

MEREDITH: *(Quietly.)* Is that so?

PHIL: He . . . he told me the word of the future is *big.*

MEREDITH: *(Almost resentfully.)* There are a *lot* of words for the future.

PHIL: He said now is the time to move on big ideas or see the world move on without you.

MEREDITH: — It's just talk, like anything else!

PHIL: *(A deep admission of failure.)* I . . . I don't have any big ideas, Meredith.

MEREDITH: *(Softening, insistent.)* I don't *care* if you do.

PHIL: I feel . . . like . . . some sort of a . . . I just feel so behind that no amount of . . . running will catch me up to it.

MEREDITH: Maybe you need to just stay in one place for a little while.

PHIL: I was . . . Meredith . . . I was . . . uh . . . I . . . I . . .

(Phil attempts desperately to articulate his greatest shame. Sensing the importance of what he is about to say, Meredith moves closer to him.)

MEREDITH: *(Quiet.)* What are you trying to . . .

PHIL: *That's* why I was in the hospital. Because I . . .

(Pause. Phil is unable to say it. Meredith reaches over and takes a corner of Phil's towel. She gingerly wipes a bit of remaining shaving cream from his neck, then from his cheek. It is a gesture of the most profound acceptance. She lowers her hands.)

PHIL: Everything seems so *wrong*.

MEREDITH: I don't *care* what you've done.

PHIL: I can't explain it.

MEREDITH: You don't *have* to.

PHIL: The world just . . . keeps . . . moving on, doesn't it.

MEREDITH: Yes it does. Whether you're ready or not.

PHIL: *(Building to a quiet emotional crescendo.)* I thought between being over there and coming back I could . . . have a minute. To take a breath somehow. I thought maybe everybody could have a minute to . . . to let . . . what we've been through . . . sink in. I don't even know what that means. I guess that's what I've been trying to do. Let it all sink in. But everything just moves so fast. The clothes keep changing. The cars keep rolling off the production lines. The houses keep going up. And . . . you let yourself be taken away from it all for long enough, you find when you come back that you . . . just . . . don't fit there anymore. You find that there's another puzzle piece that's been made in your shape and it's been stuck in the picture without you.

MEREDITH: *(Quietly.)* It's OK Phil.

(Pause. Phil sits on the bed.)

PHIL: You . . . you don't think maybe you wouldn't . . . want me to leave so you could maybe find someone who wasn't . . .

MEREDITH: Who wasn't what, Phil?

PHIL: Who wasn't . . . uh . . . so . . . uh . . . so goddamned broken?

(Long pause.)

MEREDITH: Can I . . . Can I put my . . . my arms . . . around you?

(Phil adjusts himself just enough to signal yes. Meredith sits on the bed next to him. She puts her arms around him, tentatively at first, and then tightly.)

PHIL: It's just that you're so young.

MEREDITH: I don't feel it.

PHIL: You're so full and pretty. You're not used up yet, like that Mrs. Fulton.

MEREDITH: I haven't had quite enough heartbreak yet.

PHIL: *(Pulling away from her for a moment.)* That's what I'm saying. Don't you see?

MEREDITH: I just think that . . . that I might have enough if you go away again.

PHIL: I . . . I can't promise you that.

MEREDITH: I'll take a maybe. I'll take just a night and a day so long as it's a night and day of maybe.

(Pause. Meredith reaches up and lets her hair down. Pause. Phil reaches up and feels it.)

MEREDITH: So . . . a night and a day?

PHIL: Maybe.

MEREDITH: And maybe then . . . another?

PHIL: Meredith.

MEREDITH: And one day . . . maybe even yes. *(Quickly, hopefully.)* Yes, Phil. Just say yes. It's easy.

(She puts her arms around him again. She rocks him.)

PHIL: Meredith . . .

MEREDITH: — Yes! Shhh. Yes. Shhh. It's me, remember? Remember me? It's me, Phil. Say yes to me. Say yes to me.

(She rocks him for a long time. The lights fade.)

SCENE TWO

In the dark, we hear the frantic sounds of a rare 1940's big-band Samba. The lights rise to reveal the living room of Phil and Meredith's cozy St. Louis house containing a not terribly ill-matching couch, chairs, and coffee table. A well-stocked bar unit occupies a special place, like a small shrine. Even more revered in its placement onstage is a credenza unit with its top open revealing a state-of-the-art hi-fidelity record player. Sleeves of records are neatly cataloged in matching storage units to either side of the credenza. Dessert plates and half-full cocktail glasses fill most of the available surfaces.

Meredith's older brother, Jack, dances his wife, Peg, onstage with a drunken sense of abandon. At thirty-six, Jack is a habitual and breathtakingly unsuccessful salesman; jovial and loud-talking even as he moves from scheme to scheme. Peg, thirty-two, is prim and groomed, and her loyalty to Jack is inexplicable, and often total. They work their way across the stage and exit, only to dance back on a few moments later. Their dancing is light-hearted and joyful, and they are very good — reveling in show-off, almost comical maneuvers.

Following them onstage with a valise and rolled map is Tom Wheaton, thirty-two, good-looking, slightly uneasy in his association with Jack; admiring Jack's bluster, but uncomfortable with the lack of modesty associated with Jack's personality and profession.

All are dressed well, almost too well for an informal supper. It is a warm summer night in 1955.

JACK: *(Derisively to Tom, voice raised over the music.)* In the *water?*

TOM: *(Rhetorically.)* From a seventeen *thousand* acre plant?

JACK: They shut it down in '44!

TOM: Things leak! I don't know, munitions chemicals, *TNT*, whatever they —

JACK: — now that's just the most —

TOM: — My wife's skin is *yellow*, Jack. OK? Almost orange.

JACK: Well heck it's probably *jaundice!*

TOM: *(Almost furious.)* — *Jaundice!* It's . . . it's not . . . ! My wife doesn't have —

PEG: *(To Tom, mollifying.)* — He's only saying it would be nice if she were *here*, Tom, that's all! *(Quickly, insisting.)* — Aren't you sweetie, *aren't* you saying that —

TOM: *(Almost to himself.)* — Well she doesn't have jaundice —

JACK: It ruins the symmetry of the *pitch*, that's all!

TOM: *(Present again, derisive.)* Symmetry!

JACK: — Three couples! Three gals and three fellas! *You* show up alone like a sore *thumb* and now everyone's *tense!*

TOM: *(Incredulous.)* Because my *wife* is sick?

(Meredith enters. A very well-dressed thirty-three, she exudes a hopeful confidence, at times genuine, at times strained, as if willing the world around her to become a place her husband can more easily move through.)

MEREDITH: Jack, let up on him for crying out loud!

JACK: Well here we've got the idea of a lifetime and he's thrown off the symmetry!

MEREDITH: Just *relax*, Jack, you'll have your *say*, I *swear* you drive into people like some mad bulldog — *(Calling offstage.)* — Hon, what are you doing?

PHIL: *(Calling back, almost a reprimand.)* Nothing! What do you think! Listening!

MEREDITH: *(Cheerfully overcompensating.)* We're out here again, Phil, so why don't you come and join us?

PHIL: *(Enthusiastic, vulnerable, as if explaining a deep, newfound love.)* . . . but just *listen* . . . ! Just stop and . . . and *listen* to it will you!

(Phil enters with a small stack of records in his hands. Also now thirty-three, his plain trousers, open-collar white shirt, and workman's boots act in stark contrast to the clothing of everyone around him. He moves to a chair by the credenza and begins flipping through the other albums. Jack, Tom, and Peg give each other looks, trying to decide how to move forward.)

MEREDITH: *(Chatty attempt at defusing tension.)* So Phil bursts in with this new crate of records and announces . . . *I just want you to appreciate . . .* how'd you say it, Phil? *(Imitating Phil.)* . . . *this is the moment. Right now. That Brazilian Jazz came to America.*

PEG: *(Following Meredith's lead.)* Well! Well . . . So many . . . things . . . to appreciate tonight!

MEREDITH: — Turns out there's this guy! Charles Cloud, Phil? Who introduces him to some . . . *Brazilian* at Ford . . .

PHIL: *(Listening.)* . . . Ricard.

MEREDITH: *Whoever*, turns out he's a fanatic like Phil and shipped these records all the way up just to trade for American jazz and he heard Phil had some —

PHIL: *(Proud.)* — reel-to-reel of Monk and Bird at Monroe's! Offered the entire crate! —

MEREDITH: — and I'm saying oh gosh, because Phil's promised — you've *promised* to stop — and he says *Look Em! Jazz is over for me! American Jazz at least. From now on it's all Brazilian!*

PHIL: *(As if everyone knows what he's talking about.)* Because Charlie Parker's *dead*, that's what I'm saying, and his sidemen are taking heroin or whatever and the whole scene is circling the drain now! Just *listen* to this . . . one and two ba da da da da! —

(Phil obsessively observes the rhythm through the next exchange. Peg, thinking she's found the way in, urges the men into action.)

PEG: *(Pandering.)* — Gosh, but it . . . it sure *is* great, Phil. Why . . . let's everyone get a little more dancing in while we have the chance! Tom, get up and —

TOM: — No, I —

MEREDITH: *(Joining in.)* — oh, come on, Tom —

(Meredith pulls Tom up as Peg and Jack dance again. Tom half-heartedly goes through the motions with Meredith. As the others swirl around him, Phil makes a vain attempt at waving them to a halt.)

MEREDITH: — besides I'm going to hear this a hundred times by tomorrow morning, I may as well dance while I still like it —

JACK: *(Barely hiding his contempt.)* — See Tom? You *see?* What's *next?* Toy trains? Bird-watching? Farm team *baseball's* out, we already went through that at *dinner* —

(Phil rips the needle off the record player and slams the lid of the hi-fi down. He turns to them, aching with fury.)

PHIL: — YOU KNOW WHAT? FORGET IT. FORGET THE WHOLE FUCKING THING. IF NOBODY'S GOING TO LISTEN TO THE FUCKING THING, THEN I'M NOT GOING TO PLAY IT!

(Silence. Everyone freezes at Phil's outburst. Phil angrily takes the record off the turntable and replaces it in its sleeve. He begins flipping through the pile of records, concentrating on them as he talks.)

PHIL: *(Quietly, quickly.)* This is what's the matter with people, Meredith, they can't just stop for a fucking minute, one fucking minute, to fucking appreciate something. Somebody pours their fucking heart into something and people just jabber away until it's over and then it's all gone and that's it! They've missed it! It's like people aren't comfortable unless there're sound waves coming out of their fucking necks! All I was saying was to listen to the goddamned thing, but can anybody do that? Can they just do that one simple thing?

PEG: *(Quiet offense.)* Oh *my.*

(Pause. Everyone stares at Phil, who continues flipping through the records. From another room, a small boy begins crying.)

MEREDITH: *(Disappointment.)* Oh, Phil. *(Rushing offstage.)* . . . Mikey . . . Michael . . . I'm *coming* . . .

(Uncomfortable pause. Jack and Tom see this as their opening. They circle Phil.)

PEG: *(To the room.)* Maybe . . . those drinks just need freshening up, fellas, and we'll all just . . .

JACK: *(Quieting her.)* Peg.

TOM: *(Sharing a glance with Jack.)* Phil, we didn't mean to —

PHIL: *(Tersely, quietly.)* — Forget it.

TOM: We just liked it that's all and so —

PHIL: — I said forget it so let's forget it.

TOM: Look. Just tell us what we can do, Phil. You know? To get you to . . . I mean you bring out your . . . baseball cards at dinner, OK, and then there was the fuel-efficient carburetor issue and . . . well I guess we didn't appreciate that correctly either, but we . . . we . . . *tried* to listen to you. And now with the *music,* we —

JACK: — We just think we have a good *idea,* Phil, and —

PEG: — Oh Phil, they've been talking about it for days! —

PHIL: *(Quietly.)* Has he told you? Tom? About the guy? Convincing him the government was researching avocado oil as a substitute for gasoline?

JACK: *(Angrily.)* Oh for cryin' out loud!

PHIL: *That* was a good idea too —

JACK: *(Pleading.)* — that's just a —

PHIL: — He wanted . . . I don't know how much. To buy a whole orchard of trees that didn't produce anything in California. Cash, of course. Personally I've . . . I've —

JACK: *(Going for the throat.)* — and what, I suppose you're providing for my sister? Are you? On the assembly line at Ford when you have a thousand acres —

PHIL: *(Squaring off with him.)* — I guess that's between me and your *sister,* isn't it!

TOM: OK guys, I think we're all just getting a little hot under the collars here . . .

JACK: *(Turning on Tom, meanly.)* Yeah? You think that Tom? Really?

TOM: *(Privately.)* Fuck you, Jack.

JACK: *(In Tom's face.)* Fuck you too!

PEG: *(Halting them.)* — Boys, please, everybody's handsome.

JACK: *(Breaking from Tom, dropping all pretense.)* You know what, Tom? Forget him. Forget the whole — *(Suddenly.)* — I told you he's got no sense! This is all just the biggest . . .

PEG: — Well! Well look at the time! Jack, let's go, you can talk about this in the morning.

JACK: No I think I want to stay a little while! Have another drink of Phil's liquor! Here in my sister's house!

(Meredith appears in the doorway.)

MEREDITH: *(Coolly.)* It's his house, Jack, I just own all the furniture. *(To Phil.)* I can't find his space book.

(Phil stands. He glances at everyone in the room. He exits quietly. Meredith stands in the doorway.)

JACK: *(Homing in on her.)* Come on, Meredith, what are you doing? You who see potential in everything. You're just gonna let him pass on this? What else is he gonna do with his life, huh? Get himself drunk at night —

MEREDITH: — oh *that's* the pot calling the kettle black —

JACK: *(Picks up a record, tosses it aside.)* — get all wrapped up in . . . whatever weirdo obsessed —

MEREDITH: — The thing that kills *me?* Is that as soon as you get one of your *schemes* together —

JACK: — this isn't about any scheme —

PEG: — Meredith, no, it's up-and-up, honestly it is!

MEREDITH: — I'm sorry, Peg, I wish I could say otherwise, but it's always been something or other with him, and what am I supposed to think?

TOM: *(Jumping in.)* — it's just that it's a uh . . . it's a solid plan, Meredith. It really is.

MEREDITH: That's beside the point, Tom. Look. Phil's . . . found something. That works. OK? You take the ten thousand directions he's running in and you put it together and somehow, it . . . it works. He's . . . he's . . . holding himself together! So how dare you . . . come here and . . . and . . . *(Phil reappears in the doorway. Almost as if he wishes he were invisible, he goes to the record player, picks up a new record from the stack and examines the sleeve. He takes the record out of the sleeve and swaps it with the one on the turn table. Soft music plays. Everyone stares. Embarrassed silence.)*

MEREDITH: *(Re., their son; returning to a delicate social pretense.)* How is he?

PHIL: *(Quietly, still examining the sleeve.)* The book was under the bed.

MEREDITH: *(To the others.)* There's this space book . . .

PHIL: *(Quietly.)* . . . *Young Adventurer's Pocket Book of Space Travel.* Not up to par with the other space books out there, you know, it's . . . it's . . . pulpy, but he . . . he uh . . .

(Long pause. Phil is drawn into an intensely emotional reverie.)

TOM: *(Carefully.)* Phil? Meredith? I just want to . . . I want to pick up where we left off at dinner. Can I . . . can I . . . change gears here? *(To everyone.)* Does anyone object if I . . . ? I brought a map along, Phil. Uh. If that's OK.

(Pause.)

MEREDITH: Phil?

PHIL: *(Quietly, snapping out of it.)* Look, I . . . I'm sorry. About everything. I don't know what . . . I uh . . . OK? But I am. Uh. Sorry about it.

MEREDITH: *(To Tom.)* Sure, Tom. Sure. You . . . you show him what you . . . you go ahead.

(Relieved, Tom, Jack, and Peg eagerly leap into action. Peg clears glasses and plates from the coffee table, Tom unfurls his map on it, Jack takes off his sport coat and they all rendezvous at the couch as Meredith leads Phil to a solitary chair facing the three of them. She stands nearby, as if on guard. Jack takes a breath and jumps directly into salesman mode.)

JACK: It's like this, Phil. People're wanting things right now —

TOM: *(Quickly, quietly, with a nice smile.)* — Jack, would you shut up? Just for a minute?

(Jack opens his mouth like he's going to protest, then claps it shut. He sits. Tom leans over the map.)

TOM: OK, here it is. St. Louis. The river. Your land. Now, the route of the highway is —

(Tom takes out a pen and draws a line down the map.)

JACK: *(Can't help himself.)* — The first interstate highway to be installed in the U.S. of A, Phil. You think about that.

TOM: — Right past with a quarter mile buffer, OK? At forty-five miles per with no stoplights, you'll be able to hit downtown in twenty minutes.

(Everyone stares at Phil.)

PHIL: Go ahead.

TOM: *(Gaining steam.)* Now like we said during dinner, we don't have capital. So what we want is you to come in with us on this thing as a . . . Well look. We take a loan out against your land. With that financing, we use Levittown as a model like everyone else is doing —

JACK: — How many men on that line over at Ford got a house they can call their own?

TOM: Almost none, Phil. Say we price these just within reach at eleven thousand dollars —

JACK: — Eleven thousand! But where we really make our money? We set up a private loan company, see, which bundles loans and delivers them to the bank, who charges us an administrative fee, but essentially we're the *lenders*. So not only do we get the cash up-front from the house, we're loaning the buyer the money they're giving us! That same house'll pay off for —

TOM: — With that first two million in the bank we can build about five hundred houses. We gross five point five million dollars —

JACK: — A 120 percent profit per house and all we need is the land, that's what we've been telling you. We'll do everything. Everything, Phil. All you have to do is show up at the bank with us. Put your Hancock on some papers.

TOM: St. Louis is changing, Phil. People do want things. A yard. Convenience. Safety. That's what we're talking. It's happening everywhere else and people want it here, too.

(Pause. Everyone stares at Phil.)

PHIL: *(A careful edge to his voice.)* That's it?

TOM: I mean that's just the beginning, but there's . . . there's paperwork. But uh . . .

PHIL: *(Almost friendly.)* So . . . It's going to be what. House house house house house? Spread out? Over the entire thing?

PEG: Oh well there's a cute little area for shops and stores they've been talking about, Phil, and —

(Jack grabs Peg's leg tensely. Peg self-consciously claps her mouth shut. Tom smoothly attempts to keep everything on track.)

TOM: That's right, Phil. And a clubhouse. Maybe a few of them. With swimming pools. Like little . . . country clubs. If you will. Right around the corner from people.

PHIL: OK. So . . . house house house swimming pool house?

(Miniscule pause. Jack and Tom glance at each other. An air of panic begins to dominate the sales pitch.)

JACK: *(Condescending, to Phil.)* It's far more complicated than that —

PHIL: *(Rising, approaching the coffee table.)* Well right Jack, OK? I would . . . uh . . . assume. That a two square mile development would be —

TOM: *(Trying in vain to keep everything afloat.)* — The figures are great, Phil. If we can get anywhere close to the figures, we'll —

PHIL: *(Picking up the map, examining it.)* — I'm not talking figures, I'm talking about you building an entire city from —

JACK: — Exactly! A brand new city! Everything clean, everything safe! —

PHIL: *(Intently.)* — Could you stop with the sales routine for a minute? Could you?

TOM: What can . . . what can we do? To . . . to convince you of our good intentions here.

PHIL: I believe in your good intentions fellas, but you know what they say about that.

JACK: All we're really asking is that you come on board for the . . . the concept, Phil —

PHIL: — Really! Wanting to build some houses! Gee, you want to — ! *(Tossing the map back down, angrily.)* — because that's . . . that's not a

concept! That's barely even an idea! Do you have *anything?* Beyond your
good intentions? Studies? Sketches?

MEREDITH: Go easy, Phil . . .

PHIL: *(Resentfully.)* No! These guys walk in here like a couple of hack brush
salesmen and try every line in the — *How many guys at Ford have houses,
Phil, People're wanting things, Phil,* but they don't have the slightest . . . I
suppose you're just "idea men"? Is that it?

JACK: That's . . . that's right! We're . . . !

PHIL: — So I'd like to see some *ideas!* Sketches! Houses! Clusters! Streets!
Stages! Parks! The way you talk, you'd think I have . . . drool coming out
of my mouth! I worked construction all over for four years fellas, so I
think I know which way is up, and I think I know when some guys are
feeding me a line of bull, so I'd like to see some studies! And I'd like to
see — what do you call it, Meredith?

MEREDITH: *(Sweetly.)* A business plan.

PHIL: — I'd like to see one of those! And I'd like to see if you really mean what
you say about selling houses to my friends on the line at Ford because I
bet you don't realize half of 'em are negro. And I happen to want to look
my friends in the eyes when I talk to them about this!

JACK: *(To Peg.)* What kind of Communist bullshit is this?

*(Phil turns on Jack, trembling, as the house explodes into a cacophony of over-
lapping voices. Through the next sequence, Phil and Jack will press violently
toward each other. Tom will hold Jack back, Meredith with cling desperately
to Phil.)*

PHIL: — How . . . *dare* you! Not in *my* house! Not in *my* —

JACK: *(To Meredith.)* — I mean don't you get tired of this routine!? This inces-
sant crackpot —

PHIL: — JUST BECAUSE I —

MEREDITH: — Phil! —

PHIL: — I AM NOT SOME —

MEREDITH: — Phil, calm down! —

PHIL: — THIS IS A . . . ! I'M NOT NUTS! I'M NOT NUTS! JUST BE-
CAUSE I HAVE QUESTIONS! —

(Michael calls from offstage.)

MICHAEL: — Daddy . . . !

(Long pause. The men stop, quietly panting. Pause.)

MICHAEL: Daddy . . . !

MEREDITH: *(Fiercely, to Jack.)* This is why you've made a shambles of your life,

Jack, you've got to push everybody past the edge. *(To Phil.)* Phil, you go put your son to bed again.

(Phil seems to sink back into himself once more. He exits.)

JACK: *(Turning on Meredith.)* But this is what I'm talking about!

MEREDITH: — I don't want to hear it anymore! —

JACK: — But I mean really! *I* was over there, Meredith! You know? Look at *me!* I'm *fine!* I was on *Utah beach!*

TOM: *(Quiet disgust.)* Bullshit, Jack.

JACK: I *was!* Even got a little jar of sand I've been saving!

TOM: You landed two days after D-Day!

JACK: Day after, day of, I don't really see the difference!

PEG: — She's right, Jack, that's about enough —

JACK: *(Turning meanly on Peg.)* — Won't you shut the hell up when I'm talking for the last time!

PEG: *(Shocked.)* What did you say?

(Slight pause. Jack realizes he's overdone it and quickly switches tactics to one of honeyed kindness.)

JACK: Look Meredith, I know I've been involved in a few things, but . . . but I'm just the kind of guy who —

(Peg gets up and gathers her hat and purse.)

JACK: — Wait a minute, where're *you* going?

PEG: *(Quietly, firmly, to Jack.)* I suppose you think you think you can speak to me like that anytime it's convenient.

JACK: Peg, it was just a —

PEG: — Save it, will you. I can't pretend anymore tonight. You're drunk and obnoxious and I'm taking the car.

JACK: *I'm* drunk?

PEG: *(Fishing in Jack's sport coat for keys.)* Oh, I *wish* I were drunk! And you'd better pray I can get the sitter to stay or we'll be dealing with an eight-year-old at six A.M. *(To Jack.)* I'm talking about Jackie *Jr.*, if you're wondering. *(To everyone.)* I'll be thrilled if I never have to hear about construction or houses or loans again, I've heard nothing but for two months. This is almost as bad as the canned hamburger idea.

JACK: *(To everyone.)* It was a hamburger. Already cooked and in the can, even had the grill marks on it. You just pull the lid back and pop it in the oven. It was going to work. It was going to be big —

PEG: Good night, Meredith, thank you for . . . oh gosh.

(Slight pause. Peg looks pained. She exits.)

JACK: Wait a minute! Peg — I'll be right back, don't anybody — Peg . . . !

(Jack follows her out. Phil appears in the doorway. Long pause. He goes to the hi-fi and calmly flips the record. Quiet guitar music begins again. Phil sits in his spot near the hi-fi and concentrates on a plain brown record sleeve. Tom clears his throat and stands awkwardly.)

TOM: Well that went up like a lead balloon.

MEREDITH: *(Bustling after him.)* Oh sit, Tom, it wasn't so bad.

TOM: *(Small laugh.)* That was . . . terrible. Really. Just. Terrible.

MEREDITH: *(Cheerfully.)* But it *wasn't.* Was it, Phil. Truly.

PHIL: *(Regarding the album.)* . . . I can't figure out who this is.
(Distracted, Phil rises and exits again.)

MEREDITH: *(Following him for a few steps.)* Can't you find some way to figure it out in the morning? Tom's still here.

PHIL: *(Offstage.)* I'm calling Ricard.

MEREDITH: Who?

PHIL: The guy!

MEREDITH: You'll see him *tomorrow.*

PHIL: *(Offstage.)* For *fuck's sake!* Can I call him? Can I do that?

MEREDITH: *(Reprimanding him through the doorway.)* Don't you for fuck's sake me, I just don't want to be up until three in the morning listening to you . . . catalogue . . . every single record!

TOM: . . . But really, thanks for a swell dinner, I'm just . . . sorry we botched it so badly —

MEREDITH: — Absolutely not Tom, just . . . will you sit? It's just a little downturn, you can't go throwing in the towel at the first sign of trouble or this thing will never get off the ground, will it.

TOM: Well maybe it doesn't . . . deserve to. I don't know, I'm . . . *(Honest, almost good-hearted admission.)* . . . I'm just not cut out for this sort of thing.

MEREDITH: *(Soothing him.)* You're doing *fine*, Tom. I just . . . think you should ask . . . my opinion, I've been here the whole time, haven't I?
(Meredith pours an indiscriminate glassful of something into a seemingly random glass, presses it into Tom's hands and leads him to the couch. Tom doesn't sit.)

TOM: You mean . . . you're saying you . . . what . . . want to be . . . ?

MEREDITH: Yes, Tom. Involved. I do. I mean I don't think there's any other way to move forward . . . do *you?*
(Tom almost laughs again and then shakes his head.)

MEREDITH: What.

TOM: Just . . . forget it. Jack's right, we should drop the whole thing. I mean . . . it's . . . it's a construction project.

MEREDITH: So? I own a successful business, don't I?

TOM: Sure, but no bank would . . . I mean no offense. I mean hell, you're . . . a . . . well you own a *dress* shop, Meredith.

MEREDITH: Oh *relax,* I'm not going to make you fellows walk in front of a bank president with *me,* I'm not an *idiot,* but . . . but . . . I think I can . . . guarantee Phil's consent. I mean . . . so long as there's some sort of agreement. Beforehand. Between you and . . . and Jack and me.

TOM: What . . . what sort of . . .

MEREDITH: *(Competently, swiftly, as if she's planned it all out.)* Well Phil would obviously require a majority share, he's assuming absolutely all of the risk, I think that's not even negotiable. That is if you were to forgo forming a limited partnership I guess you'd call it and go right on to . . . setting up a . . . a proper company. I mean. With . . . with voting stock. And . . . *(Suddenly modest.)* . . . and everything.

(Tom looks strangely at Meredith.)

TOM: Uh. *(Sounding her out.)* OK, but say we do. And . . . there is. All of that. Don't you think that if we went to the bank right now as individuals, me, your brother and Phil . . . well . . .

MEREDITH: — Well what?

TOM: I mean we've got to face facts here. Jack and Phil . . . they'd . . . get laughed out of the place.

MEREDITH: *(Telling herself as much as him.)* There's nothing wrong with Phil, Tom.

TOM: Come on, Meredith, you . . . *(Realizing she's serious.)* . . . Sure. . . . I mean *I* know Phil's fine . . .

MEREDITH: . . . It's just that he's . . . better than he's ever . . . he's not . . . He's being very . . . *careful.* With us.

TOM: I'm only saying that with a project this large, you . . . I mean there are *approvals,* there are . . . you know, city *agency* stuff, it really helps if the principals are . . . upstanding.

MEREDITH: *(Keeping herself from becoming offended.)* Phil's upstanding, Tom.

TOM: *(Approaching Meredith earnestly, sitting.)* Look. I like Phil. We used to be friends. I was . . . over there. I . . . think I . . . know. The sorts of things. He must have been through.

(Long pause. Meredith stares hard at Tom. Her coded answer is couched in a measured, false cheerfulness that almost fails to cover a deep, irrepressible sadness.)

MEREDITH: I sure . . . I sure do hope Mary starts feeling better, Tom. We . . . we sure were sorry she couldn't come.

(Long pause. Tom stares back at Meredith, realizing that he's breached a forbidden topic.)

TOM: *(Quietly.)* Sure. *(Politely backing off.)* — Sure, Meredith. She's . . . on the mend. We hope. *(Understanding that he should get back to business.)* Uh. So I'm sorry. Perhaps then I'll just —

MEREDITH: *(Bravely keeping her cheerful facade in place.)* — Yes, Tom. Why don't you —

(Tom opens his valise and takes out a typed sheet of paper and a pen. In the middle of this, Phil will step quietly onstage, limply holding the brown record sleeve. It is obvious he has heard the majority of this conversation.)

TOM: — scratch out a few things and I'll just write your name in here under Phil's, how's that? It's a simple statement of intent, really, about future partnership, so we can . . . well . . . put that business plan in shape. In . . . in good faith.

(Tom holds the sheet out to Meredith.)

MEREDITH: *(Lost in thought.)* I'll have Fred Maples look it over in the morning.

TOM: Actually a . . . a signature might be — from both of you — Just to signal . . .

PHIL: *(Surprising them both a little.)* Baden Powell. *(Off their looks.)* His name is uh . . . Baden Powell. He's uh . . . he's a songwriter. Plays guitar. A guitar player. Uh. With . . . uh . . .

MEREDITH: *(Kindly, sadly.)* Phil?

PHIL: *(Quiet.)* Yeah.

MEREDITH: *(As if to a child.)* Do you . . . do you want to put the record down for a minute? Do you? Please?

(Phil unquestionably obeys her. Tom stands, awkwardly. Slight pause.)

TOM: On second thought. Well. Well look. Phil. I know you both . . . have some . . .

MEREDITH: *(Ushering Tom to the door.)* We do, Tom. Don't you worry. And I'll get the paperwork to . . .

TOM: *(Twisting to make any last contact with Phil over the deal.)* — Sure. Yes. I mean as soon as you . . . but . . . but uh . . . Well.

(Tom exits. Silence. Phil marches restlessly about the stage, from chair to hi-fi to bar, as if he can't quite figure out how to put things in order.)

MEREDITH: You're . . . Phil? You're . . . how are you . . . doing?

PHIL: *(Stopping.)* I know.

MEREDITH: You know what.

PHIL: *(Angrily.)* I know people think I'm . . . *sick*, Meredith.

MEREDITH: Are you? Would you even . . . be able? To tell me?

PHIL: I'd be sick if I . . . *didn't* have questions, wouldn't I? I'd be sick if I . . . *didn't* feel the way I feel. I'd be *sick*. But look. Here I am, Meredith. I . . . I . . . get up. In the morning. Don't I. I put my own shirt on. Comb my own hair. I know the way to go when I leave the house. I bring my own money home and it's just the same color as anyone else's. I . . . don't see terrible things when my eyes are open anymore. I'm . . . here. And you're here. And Michael's here. And I'm good to you. What more am I supposed to do but that?

(Meredith sits Phil down in his chair.)

MEREDITH: *(A deal.)* You just . . . just hold it in, then, sweetheart. You feel these things come up and you just . . . for me. For Michael. If you can just concentrate. A little more. I'll take care of everything so long as you do that.

PHIL: *(Hollow, almost bewildered.)* I'm not sick, Meredith.

(Meredith takes him in her arms. She rocks him.)

MEREDITH: Shhh shhhh, I know, sweetheart. Shhhh shhh shhh. I know. *(Breaking from him, taking his head in her hands.)* Look at me. Look at me. *(Slight beat. Phil does look at her.)*

MEREDITH: I love you, Phil Granger.

PHIL: I know.

MEREDITH: I always have.

(Phil reaches out with both hands and brings Meredith's face to his. He stares at her.)

PHIL: Meredith?

MEREDITH: *(Hopeful.)* Yes, sweetheart.

(Meredith watches as Phil fights for something to say. At last, he realizes he cannot find the words. She catches her breath and sadly, kindly, rises.)

MEREDITH: I'm going to go check on him.

(Phil nods. She moves offstage. Stops. Turns to him.)

MEREDITH: Turn . . . turn out the light? If you're up late?

(Phil nods again. Meredith turns and flips out the lights. Phil remains in the spot of a single lamp. She exits. The light fades.)

SCENE THREE

In the dark, we hear a track from John Coltrane's "Blue Train." As the lights rise, we see a split stage.

    Stage right is a bedroom, well-designed with recognizable modernist

pieces; bed, side tables, vanity, a small selection of liquor bottles and glasses.
A man's suit jacket, shirt, and undershirt are draped, neatly folded, over the
back of a chair. Meredith reclines nervously on the still-made bed in modest
lingerie.

Stage left is the suggestion of a modern bar/lounge circa early sixties with
Sputnik-style lighting. Phil, extremely well-dressed, sits next to Dorothy, early
thirties, who exudes a cool and cynical sexuality. In his every aspect, Phil ex-
udes a profound, infectious excitement, one that is at once charismatic, exhil-
arating, childlike and needful. It is a joy driven by a deep sense of emotional
release. It is late January, 1961.

PHIL: *Ask not what your country can do for you?* You know? I mean . . . I mean.
About time. Right? About time. But not in this fall-in-line-with-every-
damned-fool-headed-witch-hunt-your-country-forces-you-to-embark-
on kind of . . . of . . . *zealotry* that we've had for the last . . . what. Eight?
Ten? *Years?* You know? With that Dick Nixon attack dog barking down
everybody's door? *Ask what you can do for your country* and what was it?
Together what we can do for the freedom of man? I mean look, if that's not
a call to *service!* You know, finally these . . . mean little men have been
beaten and this country's ready to be *worthy* of service again. And I can
say that, see? I'm *allowed* to say that. Because I've — Look. A nation . . .
a nation has to *earn* service, that's all I'm saying, you can't . . . stand up
with a bullhorn and a club and demand that the believers rip the non-
believers limb from limb like we've been doing. Neighbor turning neigh-
bors in! And if you so much as have a wayward thought? You know? But
we've said enough is enough, haven't we, and here we are! And all of a
sudden? Today? Tonight? I want . . . I want to buy it! I want to bite into
it and chew it and swallow it, like everybody else! By God it's like he said,
the torch has been passed! It has! Born in this century. Tempered by war.
Disciplined by a . . . a hard and bitter peace? Boy wouldn't it be great
to . . . to . . . to be . . . someone. Who can believe in that again.
DOROTHY: *(Coolly charmed.)* Yeah? Believe in what, fella?
PHIL: Something! Anything! Tonight! This minute!
DOROTHY: *(An admission.)* Well I *suppose* it's exciting.
PHIL: — Is that what you think?
DOROTHY: *(As if no one's ever asked her before.)* Well I . . .
PHIL: *(Earnest.)* I really want to know.
DOROTHY: I mean like it or not there *is* a glamorous feeling to it all —

PHIL: — Right! That's what I'm saying! Look. First thing I did when I got in was buy a copy of *Life* —

DOROTHY: *(Almost catching his enthusiasm.)* — I mean of course they're in *Life* magazine, they're just so . . . *Life* —

PHIL: — plus a whole stack of things. *The Times, the Tribune, The New Yorker,* you name it, I brought 'em to my room and I . . . You know how long it's been since I've read anything but the sports pages? Here, close your eyes.

DOROTHY: *(Truly amused.)* Close my . . .

(Phil pulls a square of newspaper from his pocket.)

PHIL: Listen, I just want you to listen.

(Dorothy actually closes her eyes. Phil speaks as if he's committed the passage to memory.)

PHIL: *Together let us explore the stars, conquer the deserts, eradicate disease, tap the ocean depths, encourage the arts and commerce. Let both sides unite to heed in all corners of the earth the command of Isaiah — to "undo the heavy burdens and let the oppressed go free."*

(Dorothy opens her eyes, inexplicably moved.)

PHIL: Right. You see?

DOROTHY: *(Laughs, in spite of herself.)* What are you, some sort of a preacher?

PHIL: You know who I am? I'm a guy who's been sitting in his office all day. Biggest office you've ever seen. A little . . . lounge area, bar setup, little patch of green carpet for putting — all mine, and what've I been doing? Where've I *been?* Where've any of us *been?* Do you ever feel that way?

DOROTHY: What way?

PHIL: Like you've been . . . sleepwalking! *(Beginning a proclamation.)* — Deirdre!

DOROTHY: — Dorothy —

PHIL: — *Dorothy!* It's a brave new world, I'm telling you! — Ulp!

(Phil suddenly slips halfway off his chair.)

DOROTHY: Hey, you OK? That martini going to your head already?

PHIL: *(Almost bewildered, getting himself straightened out.)* I just . . . can't explain what's happening to me, it must have been the flight.

DOROTHY: Oh, so you're a *New York* fella.

PHIL: — St. Louis.

DOROTHY: Little *fancy* flying from St. Louis, ain't it?

PHIL: — That's my wife all over for you, I schedule a train ride, after she talks to the secretary, it's first-class with a car and driver at the other end.

DOROTHY: Must be rough.

PHIL: It's like living in the future. *(Fighting to regain his exuberance.)* Hey! Here's a question for ya'. You like *architecture?*

DOROTHY: *(Laughing at him.)* Gee I . . . I don't rightly know.

PHIL: Tell you what! We'll run a cab along Lakeshore, I just read about some buildings going up, real space-age stuff! And then we'll have a night on the town! Tell me where you want to eat! Wherever you want, I'll take you!

DOROTHY: Gee, that sounds awfully swell fella, but I'm — well I'm meeting some friends here soon, that's all, a few girls I know —

PHIL: — Bring 'em! Bring everyone! I . . . I feel . . . I feel like being around *people* tonight.

DOROTHY: You mean *girls.* You feel like being around girls.

PHIL: It's not *like* that. *Honestly* it's not I . . . I'm *married.*

DOROTHY: *(Knowing.)* Sure fella, you keep telling me that, I've heard it before. *(Business.)* Tell you what, if you're serious about dinner I'll phone Nancy just to give her a warning that there's a night on the town in store, how's that?

PHIL: That's . . . well that's fine.

DOROTHY: *(Getting up.)* But if she's against the idea, then you find your own way tonight, alright?

PHIL: Alright, but look. I . . . I don't want you to think I've got some . . . *idea.* I don't have *any* idea.

DOROTHY: *(Dry.)* Yuk yuk.
(Dorothy picks up her bag and takes a few steps upstage. She stops, turns around, comes back, and kisses Phil on the cheek.)

PHIL: What's that for?

DOROTHY: It's because the fella I had a steak with *last* night made me go Dutch. Don't go anywhere, OK?
(The lights rise slightly on the other side of the stage. Meredith rises nervously and quickly checks her hair and complexion in the vanity mirror. Tom Wheaton enters in just a robe. Meredith whirls nervously to face him. Pause.)

TOM: *(Nervous anticipation.)* Are you OK?

MEREDITH: I could . . . I could use a drink.
(Pause.)

TOM: Sure.

MEREDITH: The uh. The scotch? No ice.
(Pause.)

TOM: Sure.
(Tom pours two stiff drinks. He turns to Meredith. Pause.)

TOM: Look. We could *still* just —

MEREDITH: — No.

(*Tom approaches Meredith and sets one of the glasses in her hand. He touches her cheek. He kisses her lightly. She kisses him back, lightly, then suddenly with a surprising ferocity. He takes the drink out of her hand and turns to set it on the side table.*)

MEREDITH: No! — Sorry. I uh . . .

TOM: — Of course. Sorry. Sure.

(*Tom hands the drink back. Meredith gulps it and hands the glass back, jiggling it to signify more. He turns to refill it. She goes to the bed and nervously pulls the covers back. Tom turns to her with the fresh drink. She whirls to meet him. They stare at one another.*)

MEREDITH: Can I have a cigarette first?

TOM: Uh . . . of course.

(*Tom shakes his head before gamely moving to a side table, opening a cigarette box and holding it out to her.*)

MEREDITH: (*Taking one.*) What.

TOM: . . . Nothing.

MEREDITH: Tell me.

(*Tom lights a bed-stand lighter and holds the flame out at arm's length for her.*)

TOM: . . . It's not an execution, Meredith.

MEREDITH: (*Quickly, lighting cigarette.*) I *want* to. I *told* you I wanted to and I *meant* it. OK?

TOM: Sure.

(*Meredith smokes. Beat.*)

MEREDITH: So I . . . guess . . . you wouldn't be able to . . . stay.

TOM: (*Proud of thinking ahead.*) I sent the kids to their grandmother's.

MEREDITH: (*Officially cheerful.*) . . . I see. Good. Uh. (*Business.*) And I should let you know that I have to get myself together on the early side because I'm . . . well I'm having Michael picked up at the bus station, he's returning from his first big class trip, a . . . well a whole inaugural week in Washington.

TOM: — That's . . . that's fine.

MEREDITH: (*Conflicted pride.*) He's Accelerated Learning, Tom.

TOM: . . . You've mentioned.

MEREDITH: Very . . . highly principled. Christ, I don't know how he got so principled. Or hell, I suppose it's entirely obvious. An upstanding . . .

Accelerated Learning . . . chip off the old block. *(Realizing she's off-track.)* Sorry! I'm sorry, here . . . *(Putting out her cigarette.)* OK?

TOM: *(All is forgiven — it's the moment he's been waiting for.)* Yeah. OK. *(With an almost adolescent eagerness, Meredith climbs into bed and Tom takes off his robe and slings it over the back of a chair. He whirls to her, stares, and then halts himself.)*

TOM: So . . . you *haven't* ever . . . ?

MEREDITH: *(Definitive.)* Let's just do this, Tom. I want to do this.

(Pause. Tom approaches her, eager again.)

MEREDITH: *(Quickly.)* Well I mean . . . do you *really* want to know? If I've . . .

TOM: *(Stopping.)* I don't know. Uh. I guess.

MEREDITH: Well. . . . I have, then. I have. Once. Um. Just so you know. But it was only once. OK?

(Slight pause.)

TOM: *(Quietly, disappointed.)* OK.

MEREDITH: Why? Did you?

(Slight pause.)

TOM: Yeah. Once. When Mary was . . . was sick. I did. She was sick for so long, I uh . . .

MEREDITH: *(Confessional, introspectively needful.)* — I had this . . . It was . . . It was . . . random. Almost. I never thought I could *be* someone who . . . I don't know. Phil was at the office. And I uh . . . took myself to lunch. A *nice* lunch. And there was this *fellow*. At the table next to mine. And he talked. *I* talked. We *talked* to each other. It was so . . . he was so . . . *attentive*, Tom.

TOM: Does Phil know?

MEREDITH: *(Quickly.)* Look, it was *more* than once, OK? With this fellow. OK? It went on for while. But it *was* . . . just one fellow.

(Pause. Tom gulps his drink.)

MEREDITH: And one evening . . . late afternoon, rather. He was driving me back to my car. And by God if we didn't . . . Phil was — I don't know what I was thinking, I knew he'd be picking Michael up from — well they — Christ, there they were, coming the other way. And uh. And I know Phil saw me. Michael I'm not so sure about, but uh . . . but . . . lately he's certainly been . . . *(Pause.)* Are you . . . does that make you . . .

TOM: I don't know. No. I guess.

MEREDITH: Gosh, did you ever . . . ? Did you ever just feel like . . . you'd gone so far you . . . might as well . . . just go all the way?

TOM: *(Quietly.)* Sure.

MEREDITH: Phil was home when I got in. Puttering around, trying to . . . have something. *Interesting.* To say to Michael, which doesn't matter because the boy *idolizes* him, and I went upstairs and showered and our help, Sally, had dinner on and . . . not a *word!* Not a word. But that's Phil all over, isn't it. Anyway, it's over. Partly because it was the best thing to do, partly because I . . . I don't know. How do you let something like that go unpunished?

TOM: When.

MEREDITH: *(Consoling.)* It doesn't matter.

TOM: Tell me when.

MEREDITH: Uh. Almost three . . . *(Pause.)* Well three weeks ago.

TOM: *(Struggling for something to say.)* Fuck.

MEREDITH: *Tom.*

TOM: I mean really. Fuck. Just . . . Fuck.

MEREDITH: So what? What does it matter?

TOM: *(Standing, putting on the robe.)* I don't know.

MEREDITH: What, you have some image of me as being . . . pure as the driven *snow?* I'm here with *you,* aren't I? And what do you think I'm *doing* here?

TOM: I just thought that . . . That you were . . .

MEREDITH: — That I was *what.*

TOM: . . . at the end of things.

MEREDITH: — It's complicated. You should know how complicated it is.

TOM: What's that supposed to mean, are you or aren't you?

MEREDITH: It means *maybe* I am. What do you want me to tell you? Yes Tom, I've been growing fond of you? For years? That I . . . think you're a good person? That I admire the way you raise your children? That Michael likes you and . . . Is that what you want to hear? That after tonight I'll visit Fred Maples and have papers drawn up so Phil can have something waiting for him when he gets back, and . . . and suddenly you'll have three children instead of two! Are you ready for that? Are you telling me you've been waiting for me? To be finished with him, is that what you're saying?

TOM: I don't . . . I don't . . . need. To be *ridiculed,* Meredith.

MEREDITH: I'm not ridiculing you!

TOM: Well I can tell at least that you think that idea . . . is ridiculous.

MEREDITH: — Wait, so it's *true?*

(Pause. Tom turns and exits.)

MEREDITH: Tom!

(Meredith sinks slowly down in front of the vanity. The focus shifts to stage left as Dorothy re-enters.)

PHIL: *(Excited anticipation.)* So?

DOROTHY: Oh, she'll be here.

PHIL: *(Like it's the best news he's ever heard.)* Good! Good! We'll go out and have a great time!

(Dorothy smiles and shakes her head.)

PHIL: What.

DOROTHY: Are you for real? Are you?

PHIL: *(Innocently.)* What do you mean?

DOROTHY: I dunno, look, I'm sorry, but I guess I've seen one lounge too many because I see a married guy like you and all I can think of is getting pawed at all night. So . . . sorry if I've been a little rough with you, that's all.

PHIL: *(Happily.)* Rough? You weren't being rough!

DOROTHY: — Wasn't being rough, my kind of fella, you sure you're married?

PHIL: *(Enthusiastically.)* Of *course* I'm sure, I've got a *kid* even! A *boy!* Twelve years old . . . Look, I admit I'm in a funny mood, but I'm . . . I feel . . . I don't know — I feel *excited* tonight!

(Dorothy laughs.)

PHIL: What.

DOROTHY: You know what fella? There's something about you? I'll tell you what you come across as. To a girl like me. — Of course, I know you're from out of town and you have to take into account the lounge atmosphere and everything . . .

PHIL: What.

DOROTHY: To me? Right now? You're coming across like you're maybe the loneliest guy in the world?

PHIL: *(Laughing, though unable to fully cover the truth of it.)* What? What makes you say that? Because well I've got . . . I've got plenty to do.

DOROTHY: *(Immediately sorry she's said anything.)* — I didn't mean it like you *don't.*

PHIL: — I've got . . . well my *son* for instance! Which can be a *lot*, you know —

DOROTHY: — I didn't mean to get you all excited, fella, I was just *talking* that's all —

PHIL: — I mean, well. . . . I mean he's *Accelerated Learning!* In school, so I . . . I try to keep up! So I'm . . . well I'm taking *classes!* There's this new community college and . . . well I sneak off during the day and . . . I mean I have to find *something* to talk to the kid about, don't I, so I'm taking . . .

well, trigonometry and engineering and . . . and . . . Medieval history. Uh. This . . . *this* semester.

DOROTHY: *(Amused.)* Yeah? How're your grades?

PHIL: Uh. Straight A's.

DOROTHY: I rest my case.

PHIL: *(Momentarily deflated.)* Yeah, shit, it sounds pretty bad, doesn't it?

DOROTHY: Sorry.

PHIL: *(Devastated admission.)* I mean *I* know I bore the kid! I bore him to *tears!* But he's . . . he's really *good* about it! I mean he *wants* to like me. You know? He wants to *know* things about me . . . he's just so full of these . . . *questions! (Suddenly.)* — You know what he did? He's gone and written to all these damned *military* academies.

DOROTHY: — Well that's all about girls, take it from me, they really go for that, God knows I did a lot.

PHIL: — Yeah, but *military* academies! If his mother ever finds out . . . ! — She should never have kept that *picture*, there's this picture he found, I took it after basic training — *(Suddenly desperately hopeful.)* — but you know what I'm gonna *do?* I'm gonna talk to him about this *Peace* Corps idea, you heard about this? *Ask what you can do for your country*, right? Right?

DOROTHY: *(Gently.)* Hey. It's OK, fella. It's OK. You OK?

(Pause. Phil isn't, and he struggles to hide it.)

PHIL: Sure. Well . . . well sure. Fine! I'm fine. Let's have another round, huh?

DOROTHY: Hey. I lost my . . . my brother. Bill. In Italy. If that's what this is all about.

PHIL: Oh I'm . . . I'm . . .

DOROTHY: And I just want to say that . . . well that . . . well you're not alone. Even if you might be . . . lonely.

(Pause.)

PHIL: I was in the lounge. At the airport today. And I see a guy. A guy I used to know. Robert Kilner. By God if that's not Bobbie Kilner. And . . . and I go over to him. And I call out . . . Bobby. And he doesn't look at me. And I get closer, and I get this big dumb grin on my face and I spread my arms out and I shout Bobbie. Bobbie Kilner! And this fellow . . . he looks at me. Like I'm some crazy man. Right? And he says to me that he thinks I have the wrong guy, but I won't let it go. I say no. You're Bobby Kilner, First Division, 16th Infantry regiment, etc. etc. you old so-and-so, you can't pretend you don't know me and . . . and . . . the guy . . . the guy who I thought was Bobby. He gets this look in his eyes. His eyes sort of soften up on me. And he says real softly. Well. Sure. OK, Mac. I'm Bobby. And he gets up and he . . . shakes my hand and we . . . catch up. He tells me where he's been and what he's been doing, and I sort of tell him the same. And there's this announcement made and he . . . he shakes my hand again and says . . . says . . . real genuine . . . says it's . . . it's really good to see you again, Phil. Real good. I'm real glad you said hello. And I turn around and I'm walking back to the lounge and . . . and damned if I don't stop dead in my tracks. Because this guy . . . he can't be Robert Kilner. Because Bobby Kilner . . . His face. His face . . . came off. Of his head. At Aachen. He looked around a corner and there was a boom and he . . . looked back at me. Before he dropped. And there wasn't anything under his helmet. The damndest thing. And so this guy . . . he couldn't have been Bobby Kilner, could he, because they can't do things like that. And I . . . Dorothy, I . . . I went into the men's room and I . . . well I . . . I wept. For a bit. I locked myself in and I . . . wept. I'm not afraid to say it. I did. And when I get out of the bathroom. There's this . . . shine. To the lights. And everything seems to be in this . . . focus. Like I've put on eyeglasses. And I . . . well I decide against having another drink. And I . . . I walk out on the tarmac and get on the plane. And we take off and climb up past the cloud layer. And I . . . and we outrun the clouds so that I can see the fields down below and the roads, and . . . and this voice. Comes to me. And it sounds like my voice. And I realize that I'm talking to myself. I can hear myself saying. I am Phil Granger. It's 1961. I live in a large house outside of St. Louis. I have a beautiful wife and a son who both love me. And uh . . . and I'm alive. I'm alive. I'm alive and I'm here and I . . . I lived. *(Long Pause.)*

DOROTHY: Oh. There she is. My friend. Over there. *(Waves.)* Well she's not waving back, but . . . *(Waves again.)* Nancy! Nancy! No, she's . . . well look let me just —

PHIL: — That's . . . that's not your friend, is it.

DOROTHY: Well . . . well of *course* it is. That's her right over *there*, she's . . . with the . . .

PHIL: — You didn't even go call her, did you.

DOROTHY: Well I called her. Of course I called her.

PHIL: But that's not her.

DOROTHY: *(Not unkindly.)* Look. Sometimes a girl just . . . likes to go out and have a nice time, that's all. A little laughing. A little eating. Like you said it would be. Things are hard for people. Yours truly included. I'm sorry. I just thought this was gonna be . . .

PHIL: Sure.

(Dorothy rises, picking up both her coat and purse.)

DOROTHY: You . . . you OK fella?

PHIL: Sure. Yeah, yeah. Yeah, I'm OK.

DOROTHY: I'll just . . . Um . . . Well. Pretend like I'm coming right back, OK? People don't stare too much if you do that.

(Dorothy exits. The focus shifts to stage right. Tom comes out of the bathroom and starts dressing.)

MEREDITH: You understand this makes you exactly like everyone else around here, Tom. You're shocked, *shocked,* to discover I've had an affair as you stand there drinking my husband's scotch, I mean really. And after admitting you yourself had an affair on your dying wife.

TOM: That's a low blow.

MEREDITH: The truth is never low, it's just the truth.

TOM: Look. It does sound . . . completely absurd. But I just thought. Meredith, of all people. If I were to . . . Well she's the type who only has room for . . . one . . . person. In her life. And I thought . . . if you were willing to . . . with *me.* Then that person would be —

MEREDITH: Oh Tom . . .

TOM: — I don't need that. I don't need a tone of pity from you, Meredith.

(Tom continues dressing. He stops.)

TOM: Why don't you divorce him?

MEREDITH: You'd think that would be better than the way I've been treating him, wouldn't you.

TOM: This . . . this *fellow.* Did you . . . did you *want* to stop seeing him?

MEREDITH: It's just that . . . it seemed like a good arrangement.

TOM: Well I'm not really too good at arrangements.

(Meredith stands up. She drains her drink.)

MEREDITH: *(Sharply.)* Well that's that then, isn't it.

TOM: Well now. Now wait a minute —

MEREDITH: — Button your shirt, Tom.

TOM: Well *look.* Look, I'm . . . I'm . . .

MEREDITH: Go on, it's just like un-buttoning except in reverse. And then we'll shake hands and see each other around the office, how's that?

TOM: *(Quietly.)* Jesus Christ, Meredith, I'm not some *general contractor,* you don't have to talk to me like that.

MEREDITH: . . . Sorry. Sorry about that. I just . . . I . . . I . . . gosh I just . . . life is uh . . . a real balancing act around here, that's all. You'll forgive me I hope.

TOM: Look. Maybe if I had a little more time to get used to the idea, I could . . .

MEREDITH: You're very kind, Tom. But it's OK. *(To herself.)* We're all going to be . . . OK.

(Tom exits as the lights fade to a pool of light around Meredith. The phone on Meredith's vanity begins to ring. She turns to it.)

MEREDITH: Yes hello? . . . I'm sorry I can barely . . . Yes. Yes, of course I'll accept.

(A phone booth appears in a pool of light on the apron of the bar side of the stage. Phil stands at the phone, shivering, his sport coat collar turned up.)

PHIL: It's . . . it's *me.*

MEREDITH: *(Sadly amused.)* Hi, Me.

PHIL: I'm calling you. From *Chicago.*

MEREDITH: I *know* sweetheart, I *sent* you there, remember?

PHIL: — Are you *lonely*, Meredith? Is *that* what it is?

MEREDITH: *(Beat, then almost lightly.)* That's a can of worms, don't you think?

PHIL: Is it because it's lonely being with *me?*

MEREDITH: *(Not wanting to be drawn in.)* It's more than a call from Chicago will take care of, Phil.

PHIL: — I want to come home.

MEREDITH: *(Miniscule beat.)* When.

PHIL: — Now. I'm going to catch the overnight.

MEREDITH: *(Reluctant.)* I'm having Michael picked up tomorrow and I want to be here waiting —

PHIL: — Why don't you go yourself for once? You can pick me up beforehand, the train comes in early. I don't want to be at any furniture convention, I don't want to shake hands or take business cards —

MEREDITH: — I don't know, Phil.

PHIL: *(Dropping the bomb.)* Have you stopped seeing him?

MEREDITH: *(Miniscule, dreadful, pause.)* Look. OK? I —

PHIL: — I'm not so dead inside that the idea doesn't . . . *kill* me, Meredith.

MEREDITH: I've . . . I've —

PHIL: — Are you going to leave me?

MEREDITH: *(Miniscule pause, still avoiding the conversation.)* Yes why don't you come home.

PHIL: If you left me, I don't know what I would . . .

MEREDITH: — I know, Phil.

PHIL: I . . . Meredith. No matter what . . . I've always . . . I will always . . . I'll always . . .

(Long pause.)

MEREDITH: I'll . . . I'll arrange to have you picked up at the station.

PHIL: Sure. Arrange for that.

MEREDITH: Or . . . sure. I suppose I could. Meet you myself.

PHIL: And then we'll meet Michael. That'll be good. The three of us? All together? Don't you think? *(Pause.)* Don't you think? *(Pause.)* Meredith?
(Pause.) Don't you think?

*(Meredith quietly sets the receiver into its cradle. Phil slowly lowers the phone
from his ear. They both look up from their pools of light on opposite ends of
the stage, their eyes meeting across a thousand miles of darkness. The lights
fade.)*

ACT II
SCENE ONE

Dusk. A late-July Sunday in 1967. We are in the suggestion of Phil and Meredith's large modernist home. A television set in a corner shows images of rioting in Detroit: towering flames, looters being sprayed with fire-hoses, burning police cars, crowds in the streets.

As the lights rise, we see a tall, breathtakingly young soldier in dress greens standing in the middle of the room, breathing hard, as if he's been running, although now he is deeply arrested by the images. This is Michael Granger, seventeen.

Outside, we hear the searching shouts of Meredith and Peg.

PEG: Michaaaaaaal?

MEREDITH: Michaaaaaaal!

PEG: Michaaaaaaal?

MEREDITH: Michaaaaaaal!

(Jack marches in and comes to a halt when he sees Michael. Jack is now in his late forties and grayer and far heavier than when we last saw him. Though he tries to project the contrary, he can't help but give the impression of a man who has slowly, over the years, become broken.)

JACK: Hey!

(Michael turns. He and Jack regard each other for a moment. Michael runs quickly out.)

JACK: HEY!

(We hear a bedroom door slam closed. Jack wheels around and dashes to a doorway that leads outside.)

JACK: *(Calling out.)* WELL HE'S COME BACK INSIDE FOR CRYIN' OUT LOUD! PEG? MER! *(Exiting as he calls through a different doorway.)* Phil! He's back inside now! Will you at least talk to him?

(Meredith enters, followed closely by Peg, both groomed for a summer occasion. Now forty-five, Meredith has kept her figure even as her hair has taken on substantial gray streaks, which she has elected to keep, and which she works into her hairstyle with elegant effect. Peg is a more humbled version of her former self, having endured years of changing fortunes.)

PEG: Stop, Meredith! Mer, *stop!* *(Catching her, an authoritarian voice of reason.)* You *listen* now, I won't have you going after that boy any *more*, it's not his *fault* —

MEREDITH: *(Controlled fury.)* — *HE* forged the signature, Peg! *HE* snuck off

to basic training! *HE'S* the one who treats his mother like some . . .
STRANGER —

PEG: — and we agreed that you would leave him *be* tonight! Didn't we! —

MEREDITH: *(Avoiding Peg, calling offstage toward Michael's room.)* — and HE'S
the one who will come back to the dinner table and *apologize*, and let my
guests finish what they've come to *propose!*

PEG: *(Calmly, reprimanding.)* — Honestly, Meredith, you ought to be
ashamed —

MEREDITH: — ME! —

PEG: — You can't bear to face Phil so you go after the *boy*, it's just so . . . *animal! (Off Meredith's protest.)* — It *is!* You've got to get *Phil* to talk to him,
he's the only one Michael will listen to!

MEREDITH: — I KNOW! I know. But every time I open my mouth and try
to . . . Well you saw him! Just . . . sitting deaf and dumb with a FORK
in his hand through the whole conversation! *(Staring in disbelief at the
TV.)* I mean my . . . Gosh . . . it's like the whole world is . . .

PEG: *(Softly.)* Meredith? Meredith.
(Peg approaches Meredith.)

MEREDITH: *(Still at the TV.)* I won't let him, Peg. I won't.
*(Peg puts her arms around Meredith, but Meredith, barely able to contain
her iron-clad composure, pushes Peg away.)*

MEREDITH: I'm . . . I'm . . . well I've got to get my face together . . .
(Meredith dashes offstage with Peg on her heels.)

PEG: — Mer? Oh! —

MEREDITH: — No! I'm fine! —

PEG: — Oh, hold on, sweetheart . . . Meredith? —
(Phil enters, futilely concentrating on his tie. Jack follows.)

PHIL: Every time, without fail! The two of you come to dinner and there's a
fucking ambush!

JACK: It was *Meredith's* idea, Phil!
(Phil wheels darkly to face Jack.)

JACK: I mean it was *my* idea too. And *Peg's*. We all —

PHIL: — Can't a guy just have a nice farewell dinner? With his son? Can't he?
Without there being some —

JACK: *(Almost pleading.)* — Yeah, but this time is different! I wish I could
just . . . peel it all back and show you what's in my . . . my *heart*, Phil,
we're not putting together some . . . *scheme* this time! — there isn't anything in it for us, not at all! I know I always say that, but . . . We just
want you to *talk* to him! Just . . . *talk!*

PHIL: — Yeah, but you had to do this during his last dinner? Jack? You couldn't've screwed everything up for us *yesterday?*

JACK: Well we would have been glad to, but my sister invited us here *tonight,* Phil.

PHIL: *(To Meredith, offstage.)* MER! TIME CHECK! THAT PLANE'S NOT GOING TO WAIT!

MEREDITH: *(Sobbing.)* HOW WOULD I KNOW, PHIL! HOW THE HELL WOULD I KNOW ANYTHING, WHY DON'T YOU LOOK AT YOUR DAMNED WATCH!

PHIL: I . . . ! *(Feeling his empty wrist.)* Oh. I've lost my watch. *(To himself.)* I need a drink. *(To Jack.)* Pour me something.

(Jack goes to a small bar setup. Phil starts searching the room for his watch.)

JACK: Don't do this. Don't pretend I'm some . . . half-wit! Like I've got nothing to *say!*

PHIL: — On the rocks!

JACK: *(Pouring.)* Look, Phil. Just listen. How many times have you bailed me out? How many?

PHIL: I wouldn't know anymore.

JACK: *(Setting a glass in Phil's hand.)* Right! Right, you see? And I've always tried to pay you back the best I can, but you know how things go.

PHIL: *(A stare and a gulp, then.)* Yes I do.

JACK: So . . . so I'm . . . I'm trying to pay you back *now.* That's what I'm saying. We're talking about your son.

PHIL: — Are you out of your . . . ! The kid just told you! At dinner! You drove him out of our *house* with that talk!

JACK: And *Meredith's* son. He's her son too, Phil.

PHIL: But what do you expect me to *do* about it!

JACK: We've found an honorable solution. That's all we're saying.

PHIL: — Honorable!

JACK: *(Emotional, letting years of ruined opportunity spill out.)* Look, I know what you think of me! I know what you think of my whole *family,* but Jackie Jr., he's *not* me. He's not just some . . . fuckwit dodger . . . running up to Canada to have fun! He's organizing people! Kids just like Michael!

PHIL: *(Breathing heavily.)* Look. My wife and me. We have to get our son to the airport. And there are a lot of things. That I'd like to concentrate on in the few minutes that we have left with him. If that's OK with you.

JACK: *(Intently.)* — So listen to what we're *saying.* Peg and me, we will *drive* him to Toronto. Jackie Jr., he's got a whole network of guys up there, ready to help him out.

PHIL: *(Quietly.)* — He enlisted. He *enlisted.* He went and forged my signature and he's taken basic training and he . . . I mean . . . HE'S GOING!

JACK: Yeah, but who for? You think he's doing it to impress his *country?* Do you? He's just a . . . a scared kid! And he's waiting for you to talk him out of it!

PHIL: MEREDITH? *(Pulling at tie.)* Jesus Christ — This damned . . . !

JACK: ARE YOU LISTENING TO ME?

PHIL: *(To Jack, furiously.)* Please, Jack! Please! Just . . . just . . . shut! Up! Please! Will you do that!
(Pause.)

JACK: *(Quietly, with a broken dignity.)* You don't have to talk to me like that. Like a . . . like some . . . some kind of dog. For *once* in my life, I . . . I got something to tell you that . . . that *matters.* Somethin' that . . . *(Slight pause.)* . . . aw, what's the use. I'm sorry for you, Phil.
(Jack exits. Phil looks helplessly around the room. All the life just seems to spill right out of him. He pours himself a tall scotch. He throws it back. He goes to pour himself another, but his hand starts shaking uncontrollably, then his arm, then his knees. He braces himself against the bar and then sinks to his knees, putting his hands up to his chin as if to pray.)

PHIL: God! God! You . . . you . . . *(Defiantly.)* . . . fucking . . . *cocksucker!* *(Pleading command.)* I don't even *believe* in you, but you'd better keep him safe! You keep my son safe! Keep him safe!
(Peg enters.)

PEG: *(Startled and embarrassed.)* . . . Oh.

PHIL: *(Covering, quickly drying his eyes.)* I . . . I'm looking for my watch. Watch fell off somewhere and I just can't find it.

PEG: Are you all *right,* Phil, you're —

PHIL: — Damned tie, it's . . . it's too tight for my throat! —

PEG: — Your *collar's* all wrong, you have it all *buttoned* wrong. Here . . .
(Peg goes to Phil, she helps him adjust his tie.)

PHIL: *(Helpless.)* I keep tying it and re-tying it and the damned thing looks good in the mirror and then by God a second later it's —
(Suddenly engrossed by the TV images.)

PEG: — It's OK, you're just nervous! *(Off Phil's stare.)* . . . What. What is it.
(Peg follows Phil's gaze. The television images have turned to fighting in Vietnam.)

PHIL: *(Lost in the glow.)* Damned . . . *Kennedy.* LBJ.

PEG: *(Quietly.)* — *Please,* Phil. *Please* think about it. *Please.*

PHIL: It was going to be . . . a new world. Don'tcha' remember? Doesn't anybody remember? *(Suddenly enraged, pulling at his tie.)* Goddamned tie's goddamned choking me to fucking death, Peg! *(Running offstage.)* What's the matter with this . . . goddamned . . . !

(Meredith enters quickly, but she too is immediately arrested by the images of fighting. Peg glances at the TV.)

PEG: Well *this* will never do.

(Peg moves to the TV and changes the channel. A banal commercial plays.)

MEREDITH: *(Mournfully.)* He . . . He won't open the door for me. He won't even talk to me.

PEG: *(Insistently.)* Mer.

MEREDITH: *(Quietly.)* I know.

PEG: *(Finality.)* So you go get Phil and you march him in there and you get him to speak to that boy for you.

MEREDITH: *(Quietly.)* I'm . . . I'm . . . *afraid.*

PEG: *(Comforting, moving her to a chair.)* I'll mix you another drink. A little something.

(They share a small, terribly sad laugh.)

MEREDITH: I've . . . I've ruined *everything.*

PEG: Nonsense! — Maybe just a little something. — A little gulp.

MEREDITH: From the day he came home from the . . . recruiter's office, I've been . . . by *both* of them! Well how am I *supposed* to take news like that? How am I supposed to . . . to . . . be *cheerful* about it! And now I'm living in this house, *my own* house, like . . . like . . . not *even* as if I were the enemy — if that were the case I would be relieved — but . . . almost like I don't even exist at *all!*

(Peg brings a drink to Meredith and kneels down next to her.)

PEG: Here. Here. You drink this up. Go on.

(Meredith takes the glass. She swallows the drink. Peg takes the glass back.)

PEG: Mer. We're . . . we're . . . Me and Jack. We're right here. We'll *be* right here. Right behind you. So you . . . you go ahead and be as afraid as you'd like. *(Finality.)* But you speak to him. You do that.

(Phil enters, pulling at his tie — a new one. He stands helplessly in front of Peg.)

PEG: *(Rising.)* What is it *now* Phil.

PHIL: Necktie again.

PEG: *(Helping him.)* Well what's the matter with *this* one?

PHIL: *(Obsessing.)* How should I know? Do I look like a maker of neckties? Do I know what particular stitch is out of place that would make a fucking necktie pull at my damned throat in such a way that —

PEG: — Phil, can you stop for a minute? Can you do that?

(The commercial on the television has been replaced with Walter Cronkite at his news desk followed by images of fighting in Vietnam again. Phil is suddenly engrossed, almost paralyzed by the images.)

(Peg glances at Phil and then stares at Meredith. Meredith stares nervously back at Peg. Then both Peg and Meredith turn their eyes toward Phil. Jack enters with car keys, defeated.)

JACK: It's no use. We'd better get on the road . . . we've got a long . . .

(Jack stops. Glances at Peg and Meredith, and suddenly understands. He too stares at Phil. Peg urges Meredith to speak.)

MEREDITH: Ph . . . Phil?

(Phil doesn't look at her.)

MEREDITH: *(Emphatically.)* Phil . . .

(Long pause. Meredith can't continue. Peg turns off the television. Phil glances up at everyone.)

PHIL: Why are you looking at me? Don't everyone look at me. What have I done that you should all look at me?

MEREDITH: *(Carefully.)* You . . . you haven't done anything, sweetheart. That's . . . *that's* why we're all looking at you.

PHIL: Well what do you suggest I be doing, Meredith? Huh?

MEREDITH: — *Don't,* sweetheart, *don't* do that.

PHIL: — Don't do *what?* What am I *doing?* Just what sorts of things am I *supposed* to be doing!

MEREDITH: I . . . Phil? I . . . I want you to . . . *(Glancing at Peg, who urges her on.)* . . . to go! Go in! There! To . . . to *Michael's* room. And . . . and I . . . I want you to . . . to *tell* him. For *me.* That you . . . *don't want him to go!*

PHIL: *(Almost bewildered.)* He doesn't want to go to *Canada,* Meredith.

MEREDITH: But maybe. Maybe he thinks . . . *you* want him to . . . go over there.

PHIL: Why would *I* want him to go over there?

(Jack and Peg leap to Meredith's side, desperately hopeful.)

MEREDITH: Then if you don't *want* him to! Ask him to go to *Canada!*

PHIL: But he wants to go over there, Meredith.

MEREDITH: But what if he really doesn't?

(Miniscule pause.)

PHIL: But he wants to go, Meredith.

MEREDITH: I JUST WANT YOU TO TALK TO HIM! TALK TO HIM! YOU GO IN THERE AND TALK TO HIM!

PHIL: I'VE TALKED TO MY SON! He doesn't want to go to Canada!

He wants to go find out what it's like to kill some Gooks! What do you want me to do, march in there and tell him everything he's about to go through is for . . . for . . . for nothing? Meredith? Is that the last thing you want him to hear from us?

MEREDITH: — Yes! *Yes!* Because it *is* for nothing! It's for *nothing!* And I'll be *damned* if my son's going to become YOU for nothing!

PHIL: IT'S NOT FOR NOTHING! IT'S NOT FOR NOTHING! BE-CAUSE LOOK AT MY LIFE! Because my friends died by the fucking . . . armful! Sc . . . sc . . . scared! K . . . k . . . k . . . k . . . k . . . KIDS! Just trying to keep their sh . . . sh . . . SHIT TOGETHER SO THEY CAN MAKE IT HOME OK AND GETTING MUTIL . . . MUTIL . . . MUTIL . . . CUT TO PIECES AND . . . AND . . . SHITTING THEIR PANTS WITH . . . WITH FEAR! AND IF WE DIDN'T BELIEVE ALL THAT WAS FOR SOMETHING . . . IF ALL OF THAT WASN'T FOR SOMETHING . . . ! IF MY SON'S NOT GOING TO VIETNAM FOR SOMETHING . . . Oh . . . Jesus! . . .

(Phil staggers back and clutches desperately at his chest. Peg and Jack rush to him and sit him down in a chair. Meredith, however throws up her arms in furious exasperation.)

MEREDITH: Oh hell, Phil!

(Peg and Jack loosen Phil's shirt as he grabs frantically at them.)

MEREDITH: *(To Phil.)* What. What are you doing *this* for, Phil? — He needs some water, Peg, could you run get him some water?

PHIL: *(To Jack and Peg, speaking simultaneously with Meredith.)* No. No. No. I'm OK. I'm fine. I'm OK. Just got to . . . got to sit. Jesus Christ, what's the matter with me.

PEG: *(Running offstage.)* I'll get some water!

JACK: *(Following.)* He doesn't need water, he needs a damned *doctor!* I'm call-ing a doctor!

(Meredith is left alone with Phil. Hiding an intense worry behind her anger, she storms to the chair and bends over him.)

MEREDITH: *(Stern.)* Goddamnit Phil, let's loosen the Goddamned shirt! Loosen it up! Now you take a deep Goddamned breath and you get it to-gether, Phil. *(Almost ritualistic.)* Get it together. You get it together and keep it together. OK. OK. OK.

PHIL: *(Struggling, speaking simultaneously with Meredith.)* Jesus Christ I think I . . . yeah, let's . . . loosen it up! Loosen it up! Jesus Christ, I . . . I got to . . . tryin' to! Tryin' to breathe! Take a deep breath and . . . *(Almost ritualistic.)* . . . get it together. Gonna do that. Gonna keep it together. OK? OK? OK?

(A pause. Panting, Meredith straightens as Phil straightens in his chair. The familiarity to each other of the final words have made us realize that this is something they've done many times before. They regard each other, recognizing in a terrible way the shared intimacy of the exchange that has just passed. Phil opens his arms and leans forward to her, in desperate need. Meredith is almost drawn in, but then jumps back, regaining her full fury.)

MEREDITH: I CAN'T!

(Meredith moves as far away from him as she can. She hugs herself. Phil stares helplessly. Their son Michael, concerned, appears in the doorway with a duffle.)

MICHAEL: Dad?

(Meredith turns and stares at Phil. This is the moment.)

MEREDITH: *(Pleading.)* Phil?

(Silence. Phil is frozen.)

MEREDITH: *(Emphatically.)* Phil.

(Phil looks at her, as if snapped out of a trance.)

MEREDITH: Phil . . .

(Phil understands. He half-rises out of his chair toward his son before looking at him. He stares at Michael, caught halfway between rising and sitting. A short, agonizing pause as he takes in the sight of his son. He sinks back down in his chair and covers his face with his hands in complete failure. Choking back sobs, Meredith dashes to Michael and throws herself into his arms. Blackout.)

SCENE TWO

Night. Heavy rain. A motel room in which the décor of two eras seems to collide, with aged mass-production 1950's prints and furnishings standing out among cheaper, newer additions. As if in direct contrast to the surroundings, an expensive set of luggage lies strewn across the bed and various surfaces. Their owner is in the bathroom. Water runs in the sink.

There is a light knock on the door. After a few moments, we hear a key in the lock. Phil opens the door. He hesitates in the doorway for a long moment, then finally steps in and closes the door behind him. He is a soaked, exhausted fifty-one years old, heavier again since the last time we've seen him. He stands helplessly in front of the closed door.

The water in the bathroom shuts off and we're left only with the sound of the rain. It is February 15, 1973. Pause.

PHIL: *(Hoarsely.)* Mer . . . *(Emotional, clearing his throat.)* M . . . Meredith?
(Meredith steps into the lighted doorway of the bathroom. She wears a long bathrobe. A towel wraps her wet hair. Long pause.)
MEREDITH: *(Unhappy surprise.)* What are you . . .
(Pause. Meredith glances quickly at the telephone. She lunges for it, but Phil anticipates her.)
MEREDITH: NO! NO PHIL! NO!
(They struggle. Phil wrests the phone out of Meredith's hands. He yanks the cord out of the wall.)
MEREDITH: HELP ME! SOMEBODY HELP Mmmmfff . . . !
(Phil puts his hand, hard, over Meredith's mouth. She struggles.)
PHIL: No! Enough! No more! No more! Stop it! Stop it! Stop!
(He presses his hand harder and talks almost soothingly to her the way one might to an animal. Meredith struggles intermittently through the next beat.)
PHIL: Right? OK? I'm gonna . . . OK? Let go? And . . . and I don't want any . . . raised voices, I don't want any screaming, I'm not here to . . . I just . . . I need everything to stop. For a second. Just for a second. — I'll stop too. We'll both just . . . OK? I'm going to lift the hand?
(Meredith nods. Phil gingerly lifts his hand.)
MEREDITH: *(Venomous.)* Get out of here! What are you even doing here, you . . . you . . . crazy . . .
PHIL: *(Reflexive anger, simultaneously with Meredith.)* It's you! It's you! . . . you've been . . . and you can't even . . . ! *(Instantly repentant.)* — Sorry. I'm sorry.
MEREDITH: — Don't tell me that!
PHIL: — *Sorry* —
MEREDITH: — I said *don't tell me that,* you don't tell me that *any* more. *(Commanding.)* Let go of me.
(Phil lets go. She pulls herself to her feet. So does he. Meredith takes stock of the room.)
MEREDITH: *(Regaining control.)* Put the phone back in the wall.
PHIL: *(Innocent.)* It's broken.
MEREDITH: Way to go Phil.
PHIL: Don't start with that chickenshit . . . *bullshit!*
MEREDITH: How did you get the key. Give it back.
PHIL: I told the office that —

MEREDITH: — They should have called —

PHIL: — I told them not to *bother* because I —

MEREDITH: Put it on the *desk* there, Phil. I mean it.

(Pause. Phil reaches over, hesitates, and drops a motel room key on the desk.)

MEREDITH: Now go. You go. Now. And we'll . . . we'll . . . forget about the whole thing.

(Pause. Phil turns. He opens the door. The sound of the rain overwhelms us. He steps into the night and shuts the door. Meredith turns and sits on the bed. She puts her face in her hands and cries. The door slowly opens and Phil steps back in, even more soaked than before. He slowly shuts the door and stands in front of it again.)

PHIL: *(Quietly defiant.)* No.

MEREDITH: What no. No what.

PHIL: No I'm not going to.

(In a fury, Meredith rises and pounds on Phil with her fists.)

MEREDITH: GET OUT OF HERE. YOU GET OUT OF HERE.

PHIL: No.

MEREDITH: I'LL TELL THE POLICE! AND THEY'LL TAKE YOU AWAY! I'LL SAY YOU'RE VIOLENT! I'LL PUT YOU IN PRISON!

PHIL: I don't care.

MEREDITH: I'LL KILL YOU, PHIL! I'LL STAB YOU IN THE HEART! DON'T THINK I WON'T DO IT!

PHIL: I don't care.

MEREDITH: I'LL KILL MYSELF THEN! I WILL, I SWEAR TO GOD, AND THEN WHAT'LL YOU HAVE? NOTHING! NO SON! NO ME! NOBODY! NOTHING!

PHIL: No.

(Long pause. Meredith breaks from him.)

MEREDITH: I thought you put the key on the desk.

PHIL: That was the key to *my* room.

MEREDITH: What do you *mean* the key to . . . *(Realizing.)* — *you're* not . . .

PHIL: — I'm three doors down.

MEREDITH: *(Flabbergasted.)* You . . . I don't . . . You're not going to start this up again!

PHIL: I'm *better*, Meredith.

MEREDITH: Then what are you . . . ! I can't believe you have the *nerve* to . . . !

PHIL: Listen! I'm . . . I'm uh. I . . . have a . . . a doctor. That I have appointments with. Every week. He's a . . . Back home. A psychiatrist.

MEREDITH: See? See? I knew it! You're . . .

PHIL: *(Righteous.)* CAN'T YOU JUST STOP? WHY DOES EVERY LITTLE INCH OF GROUND HAVE TO BE SOME . . . SOME . . . THAT DOESN'T MEAN I'M CRAZY! THAT MEANS I'M GETTING BETTER!

MEREDITH: AND YOU FOLLOWED ME ALL THE WAY OUT HERE TO TELL ME THAT!

(Slight pause.)

PHIL: *(Caving.)* OK, *yeah*, well that's . . . *that's* . . .

MEREDITH: Right. People don't *do* that. Don't you understand? People don't do *half* the things you do.

PHIL: *(Innocent.)* I mean I just . . . ! I drove! For . . . one day! And when I got to the place where you'd stayed that night, I . . . ! And then I drove another day, and then . . . ! I didn't mean to go all the . . . ! But then I thought you know, halfway through . . . Hell, it was actually kind of a nice vacation you were on, Meredith, and —

MEREDITH: — How did you —

PHIL: — That Bank *Americard*.

MEREDITH: *(Actually confounded.)* Are you kidding?

PHIL: No. It was easy. You should really use cash if you want to run away.

MEREDITH: *(Skeptical.)* Really!

PHIL: Every hotel. Every gas station. Every restaurant. I'm not lying, I stopped there.

MEREDITH: Bullshit!

PHIL: Bullshit!

MEREDITH: Tell me your favorite.

PHIL: Uh. Green River. In Utah. I don't know what you had, but I got the hamburger.

MEREDITH: The hamburger was your favorite?

PHIL: It was dry.

MEREDITH: Then why'd you like it.

PHIL: *(Dryly.)* I like a dry hamburger.

(Pause. Meredith stares, resenting the impulse to be charmed by him.)

MEREDITH: You kill me, you know that?

(She breaks from him and picks up the broken telephone. She wraps the cord around the phone.)

PHIL: Can I have a towel?

MEREDITH: *(Slamming the phone back onto the desk.)* Go to hell, why don't you.

(Pause. They gather themselves.)

PHIL: *Tom.* Let them . . . give me my membership back.

MEREDITH: He *shouldn't* have.

PHIL: The . . . that jackass *manager* kid —

MEREDITH: *(Like he's forgotten the name a thousand times.)* — Edward? —

PHIL: — picks up the phone when I go in and calls Tom. You ever hear of probation? At a country club? But guess what, I'm allowed to have lunch there again! My own club that was built in my name with my own . . . ! And I groveled! In order to have a dried out turkey sandwich and a cold cup of soup across the room from *sneak* who —

MEREDITH: *(Sharply.)* — we had our settlements, Phil.

PHIL: *(Regaining a false calm.)* Anyway, I uh . . . declined. Very nicely. To join him. Tom. I thought it was very polite of him to ask, though. And I was very nice in return, I didn't . . . I didn't . . .

MEREDITH: That's not a miracle, you know. Being civil.

PHIL: Sometimes it is. When your whole life disappears it is. You try it sometime.

MEREDITH: *(Almost childish.)* I *have. I* can do it.

PHIL: *Really!* You call that *civil!* So you're suggesting that I use *your* behavior as a model to follow. You know. To prove to everyone I'm not the way you *say* I am.

MEREDITH: People *do* things, Phil.

PHIL: Yeah? Why is that a reply I'm not allowed to use for *myself? (Miniscule pause.)* Just give me a towel, will you?

MEREDITH: *(Finality.)* I'm . . . I'm sorry, Phil, I . . .

(Pause.)

PHIL: *(Back on the trail.)* Tom. Told me. Uh. That you'd left him.

MEREDITH: That's none of your business.

PHIL: *(Childish.)* It is if *Tom* told me.

MEREDITH: Then it's just *information*, Phil, that's all, it's not your *business*, it doesn't give you the right —

PHIL: — what *denies* me the right —

MEREDITH: — you made an agreement —

PHIL: WELL YOU MADE AN AGREEMENT TO ME, MEREDITH! WHAT ABOUT THAT! WHAT ABOUT THAT AGREEMENT!

MEREDITH: *(Almost calmly.)* I'm not going to go into this.

(Long pause.)

PHIL: So uh . . . he's uh . . . he's devastated. Tom. I . . . uh . . . had a . . . pretty hard time. Uh. Feeling sorry for him, though, I'll tell you that.

MEREDITH: So what about this makes you better, Phil.

PHIL: Well nobody *else* was looking for you! What was I *supposed* to —

MEREDITH: — I left a note!

PHIL: — A note! You don't get a note like that and . . . ! I mean he was just sitting there! At the . . . at the . . . ! Crying into his soup! And you've packed your bags and . . . and . . . ! Well people . . . don't get to just . . . disappear! Without someone looking for them! They don't! Especially not . . . you! *You* disappear, you deserve to have someone looking for you! It's the least they can do! And he was just . . . ! Just . . . ! How dare he! *(Long pause. Meredith looks for a split second as if she could melt before bitterly fighting to regain herself.)*

MEREDITH: Well I'd be lying if I didn't admit I wasn't a little impressed.

PHIL: I didn't do it to impress you.

MEREDITH: *(As if she's caught him.)* Following me all the . . . Phil? You could have just called that credit card a month from now to see where I'd —

PHIL: — It wouldn't have mattered because by the time I got to Reno I figured it all out.

MEREDITH: Don't pretend to be so —

PHIL: — I'm not pretending anything! I'm *serious*, you don't think I — !

MEREDITH: — I think you have to believe that you know me! I think you have to believe you're still intimately connected with me with so you won't feel . . . as lonely as you really are! But I've —

PHIL: *(The trump card.)* — I've been in this motel since *yesterday*, Em. So in a way, actually, you followed me.

MEREDITH: *(Confused.)* How did you . . .

PHIL: I can put two and two together. I saw the headlines. The route you were on was heading right for it.

MEREDITH: *(Flatly.)* Right for what.

PHIL: *(Knowing he's caught her.)* Travis Air Force Base.
(Pause.)

MEREDITH: That's . . . well that's *ridiculous*, I wouldn't — !

PHIL: *(Bitter.)* Of *course* not! Because you're not the *crazy* one! You wouldn't drive all the way across the country to see . . .

MEREDITH: You're *sick*, Phil. You're . . .

PHIL: — So you were just taking a random . . . very *long* route —

MEREDITH: *(Desperate denial.)* — Yes! I was!

PHIL: — That just happened to take you past Travis Air Force Base the morning the first POWs were coming home? *(Pause.)* I was *there*, Em. *Today.* I saw you. You were standing over by the fence. Pretending to wave at someone so you'd blend in.

MEREDITH: *(Quickly.)* You're *obsessive*, Phil, you've been —

PHIL: *YOU'RE* THE OBSESSIVE . . . ! *YOU'RE* THE OBSESSIVE! *I* GET PEGGED AS THE SICK ONE ALL THE *TIME* WHICH IS MIGHTY *CONVENIENT* CONSIDERING YOU'RE THE ONE WHO CAN'T LET GO OF HIM! YOU DROVE ALL THE WAY OUT HERE! TO WATCH A BUNCH OF KIDS YOU DON'T EVEN KNOW COME HOME FROM VIETNAM WHEN OUR SON HAS BEEN DEAD FOR *SIX! YEARS!*

MEREDITH: *(Simultaneously with Phil.)* — You shut up! Shut up! You don't know anything! What do you know! You don't know why! You don't know anything!

(Meredith covers her ears and runs into the bathroom, sobbing. Phil follows her to the door and shouts through it.)

PHIL: AND I'LL TELL YOU! I AM SICK TO DEATH OF BEING HELD TO BLAME! I WAKE UP EVERY DAY AND I DON'T KNOW WHO TO MOURN THE LOSS OF! YOU OR HIM! *(Saddening.)* But I'll tell you it sure does put a little extra sting in the cuts knowing you've made every arrangement possible to see that I am somehow punished.

(Phil sits on the bed. Long pause. The sobbing eventually stops. Phil looks over into one of the open suitcases. He lifts out a framed picture. He stares at it. He rises and sets the picture on the dresser. Long pause. Meredith opens the bathroom door. She re-enters.)

MEREDITH: *(Sadly unapologetic.)* Someone's got to be held accountable, Phil.

PHIL: And I'm the logical choice?

MEREDITH: You're the only one I can find. So I'm sorry. I mean what am I gonna do, write to my senator?

PHIL: I have an idea. Why don't you divorce your husband and dismantle every sliver of his life you can possibly get your hands on. Oh, sorry, I forgot, you've already done that. Well in that case why don't you attempt to commit him as a severe obsessive because he's completely unable to accept being blamed for the death of his son. Oh my apologies, you've already tried that, too. But you know I think you're right about your ex-husband's mental state. Because a well-adjusted person would accept the accusations you've leveled against him! But not Phil! Phil's got to reject them! Because he's a nut case! And to cement it all, he makes a couple of very public scenes, one of which involves throwing an entire banquet table full of shrimp and cheese through his club's window and into the pool during his ex-wife's engagement party! So now he's a fucking pariah! And you know what? He deserves to be! Because you know what else? His son's death and mutilation in the central highlands of Southeast Asia is his! Fucking! Fault!

(Pause.)

MEREDITH: *(Bare.)* I'm . . . I'm . . .

PHIL: What! Sorry? Are you sorry? And why would you be sorry? Because our lives have been torn to bits? Or is it that after everything that's been done, you still don't feel any better?

MEREDITH: Why did you come here?

PHIL: Because this time you're wrong. And if you're going to live the rest of your life without me, I want you to know in no uncertain terms that you're doing it for the wrong reasons.

MEREDITH: *(Almost pleading.)* I left him, didn't I? Didn't I do that?

PHIL: Why.

MEREDITH: Because . . . because.

PHIL: Well you're setting records left and right. People talked enough about the first divorce. How bad is this one going to be?

MEREDITH: I don't know.

PHIL: What are you going to blame *him* for?

MEREDITH: Something, I'm sure.

PHIL: They'll hound you out of St. Louis for good. Forget going near the club again.

MEREDITH: Yeah. Well it doesn't really matter, does it? I could go anywhere and nothing would ever be . . .

(Realizing what she's about to say.)

PHIL: *(Emphatic. he's won.)* Yeah. That's right.

(Pause. Meredith sits on the bed. There is a tone change now, a hesitant, yet easy intimacy between them.)

MEREDITH: I . . . I had a long time to think on the way out.

PHIL: Yeah.

MEREDITH: I . . . It's funny, Phil. I . . . I did . . . think. Of you. Quite a lot.

PHIL: Yeah?

MEREDITH: I started wondering. About the years after the . . . well after the war. About . . . where you might have been.

PHIL: *(Quietly.)* Yes.

MEREDITH: I . . . liked . . . feeling a little . . . lost. I liked . . . how you start to wonder about all the places you pass through. What your life might be like if you stopped there for a while. How long you could last there before you catch up to yourself. And . . . if that would be . . . OK. In the end. If you did. Wherever there is. *(Slight pause.)* The West. Is a strange place, isn't it.

PHIL: Utah sure is beautiful.

MEREDITH: Too barren.

PHIL: I like Colorado.

MEREDITH: Except that I'm tired of being . . . cold. In the winter.

PHIL: The grapevines here . . .

MEREDITH: I've never seen grapevines.

PHIL: *(Plainly.)* They had them in Sicily.

MEREDITH: That doesn't . . . ? That wouldn't . . . ? It doesn't remind you of . . . ?

PHIL: It was a long time ago.

MEREDITH: Not really too long, Phil.

PHIL: Can I please have a towel? Please?

(Pause. Meredith stands and goes into the bathroom, returning with a towel. Phil stand and meets her in the middle of the room. She holds it out to him. He takes one end of it, delicately. She doesn't let go of her end.)

PHIL: *(Quietly.)* When you left me. You told me that I just didn't live for you the way you lived for me. But you never understood I think that you were the only . . . *(Miniscule pause.)* And thinking of us. Today. The both of us standing in the rain at the base. You over by the fence in the crowd. Me watching you, near the parking lot. The both of us waiting for the transport to land so that . . . we could watch . . . three hundred other people . . . get their children back. I realized that . . . dying, Meredith. Is not the ultimate sacrifice. Uh. *(Miniscule pause.)* We are.

MEREDITH: They all looked so . . .

PHIL: . . . Yeah.

MEREDITH: You looked like that, Phil.

PHIL: Yeah?

MEREDITH: And Michael would have . . . and then . . . and then I would've had two. And I would have taken you both of course . . . But somehow. When it turned out I just had the one again . . . it was just more than I could . . .

PHIL: I know.

MEREDITH: I'm only fifty-one, Phil. I might be . . .

PHIL: What.

MEREDITH: . . . Ready.

PHIL: For what.

MEREDITH: For . . . I don't know. One last . . . hoorah. Or maybe . . . my first hoorah ever.

PHIL: What am I supposed to do with that?

MEREDITH: I don't know.

> *(Phil sits on the bed again. Meredith slowly sits next to him. They don't touch. They both stare straight out.)*

MEREDITH: Phil, I'm —

PHIL: — I know. Me too.

MEREDITH: There's been so much —

PHIL: — So just forget about it.

MEREDITH: I want to.

PHIL: Then why don't we?

> *(Pause. Phil reaches over and takes Meredith's hand.)*

MEREDITH: Because it's not as easy as just saying "we" again.

PHIL: Why not?

MEREDITH: Well because it's . . . it's not. It would be . . . ridiculous.

PHIL: Maybe to people in St. Louis. But uh. Nobody knows us here, Em.

MEREDITH: You're not saying you would . . . I mean that really would be a little crazy, wouldn't it?

PHIL: Everybody thinks I'm crazy anyway, so it's no skin off my back. Besides, it's not like we just met each other or anything. I mean are you really that different?

MEREDITH: No.

PHIL: Neither am I.

MEREDITH: That's what I'm afraid of.

PHIL: We'd just be . . . a . . . couple. From the Midwest. Taking in the sunshine. Getting . . . drunk in the afternoons. Doing things we . . . we . . . we could have done. We could . . . Have someone . . . send some trucks! I don't know, arrange the packing! Change our addresses! My God, it would be simple!

MEREDITH: *(Falling for it.)* I'm not going to fall for this.

PHIL: Can't we just . . . give ourselves a night and a day?

> *(Slight pause. Meredith looks at Phil.)*

PHIL: You owe me a maybe.

> *(Pause. Meredith reaches over and lightly touches Phil's face.)*

PHIL: And then maybe . . . another. Remember?

MEREDITH: Phil . . .

> *(Phil embraces her.)*

PHIL: It's me, remember? Remember me, Meredith? Say yes to me. Say yes to me.

> *(The lights fade.)*

END OF PLAY

RIGHTS AND PERMISSIONS

Almost, Maine. © 2002 by John Cariani. Reprinted by permission of Bruce Ostler, Bret Adams Ltd., 448 West 44th Street, New York, N.Y. 10036. For performance rights, contact Dramatists Play Service, 440 Park Avenue S., New York, N.Y. 10016. www.dramatists.com

Bulrusher. © 2007 by Eisa Davis. Reprinted by permission of Val Day, William Morris Agency, Inc., 1325 Avenue of the Americas, New York, N.Y. 10019. For performance rights, contact Ms. Day. (E-mail: vday@wma.com)

Cowboy Versus Samurai. © 2007 by Michael Golamco. Reprinted by permission of the author. For performance rights, contact Smith and Kraus, Inc., 177 Lyme Road, Hanover, N.H. 03755. 603-643-6431. (E-mail: sandk@sover.net) www.smithandkraus.com. For further information about Michael Galamco, including reviews of this play, visit his website: www.michaelgalamco.com

Indoor/Outdoor. © 2004 by Kenny Finkle. Reprinted by permission of Mark Christian Subias, 331 West 57th Street, #462, New York, N.Y. 10019. For performance rights, contact Broadway Play Publishing, 56 E. 81st Street, New York, N.Y. 10028. 212-772-8334. www.broadwayplaypubl.com

In the Continuum. © 2005 by Danai Gurira and Nikkole Salter. Reprinted by permission of Ronald Gwiazda, Rosenstone/Wender, 38 East 29th Street, New York, N.Y. 10016. For performance rights, contact Ronald Gwiazda. (rgwiazda@rosenstonewender.com).

Six Years. © 2007 by Sharr White. Reprinted by permission of Peregrine Whittlesey, 279 Central Park West, New York, N.Y. 10024. For performance rights, contact Peregrine Whittlesey. (E-mail: PWWagy@aol.com)

War in Paramus. © 2003 by Barbara Dana. Reprinted by permission of the author. For performance rights, contact Sonia Pabley (spabley@rosenstonewender.com), Rosenstone/Wender, 38 East 29th Street, New York, N.Y. 10016.